São Tomé and Príncipe

the Bradt Travel Guide

Kathleen Becker

edition
2

www.bradtguides.com

Bradt Travel Guides Ltd, UK
The Globe Pequot Press Inc, USA

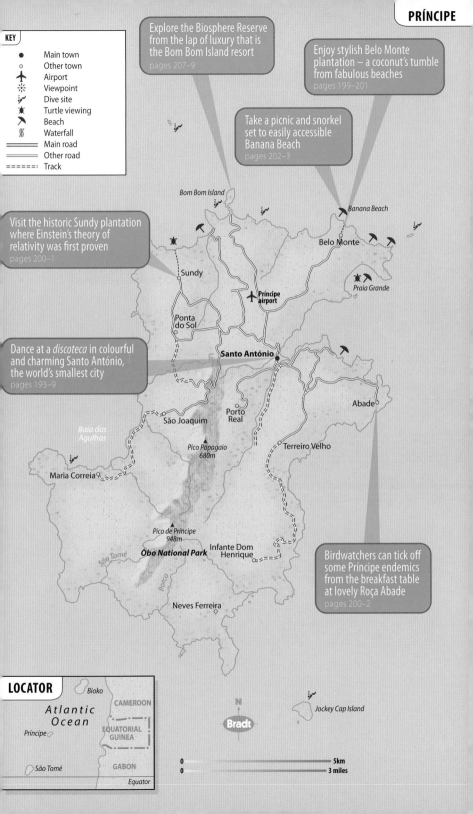

PRÍNCIPE

KEY

- ● Main town
- ○ Other town
- ✈ Airport
- ☀ Viewpoint
- Dive site
- Turtle viewing
- ⤢ Beach
- Waterfall
- Main road
- Other road
- ====== Track

Explore the Biosphere Reserve from the lap of luxury that is the Bom Bom Island resort
pages 207–9

Enjoy stylish Belo Monte plantation – a coconut's tumble from fabulous beaches
pages 199–201

Take a picnic and snorkel set to easily accessible Banana Beach
pages 202–3

Bom Bom Island

Banana Beach

Visit the historic Sundy plantation where Einstein's theory of relativity was first proven
pages 200–1

Belo Monte

Sundy

Praia Grande

Príncipe airport

Ponta do Sol

Santo António

Dance at a *discoteca* in colourful and charming Santo António, the world's smallest city
pages 193–9

Abade

São Joaquim

Porto Real

Baía das Agulhas

Terreiro Velho

Pico Papagaio 680m

Maria Correia

Birdwatchers can tick off some Príncipe endemics from the breakfast table at lovely Roça Abade
pages 200–2

São Tomé

Pico de Príncipe 948m

Ôbo National Park

Infante Dom Henrique

Porco

Neves Ferreira

LOCATOR

Bioko

CAMEROON

Atlantic Ocean

Príncipe

EQUATORIAL GUINEA

São Tomé

GABON

Equator

N

Bradt

Jockey Cap Island

| 0 | | 5km |
| 0 | | 3 miles |

São Tomé and Príncipe in colour

above   The fishing community of Ribeira Afonso on the east coast of São Tomé (MM) page 93

left   A girl carries a container of palm wine on her head (CW/AWL) page 84

below left   One of the oldest cathedrals in sub-Saharan Africa: the cathedral of São Tomé provides a fresh space on a dusty day (MM) pages 131–2

below right   These colourful wooden houses at Abade are typical of the islands (MM) pages 201–2

above   Belo Monte plantation, Príncipe (MM) page 201

right   Banana Beach on Príncipe was once the location of a
famous Bacardi ad (MM) pages 202–3

below   Straddling the Equator, Ilhéu das Rolas is a small island off
the southern coast of São Tomé (CW/AWL) pages 178–84

bottom   Built on the orders of a mystical king, São Sebastião Fort
in the capital now houses the national museum (CW/
AWL) pages 133–4

above The Príncipe golden weaver (*Ploceus princeps*) is endemic (FM) page 7

above left Cracking open a cocoa (*Theobroma cacao*) pod on Paciência plantation, Príncipe (MM) pages 20–1

left The porcelain rose (*Phoemeria magnifica*) grows wild but is also cultivated for export (MM) page 4

below left Flame trees (*Erythrina poeppigiana*) provide valuable shade to the islands' cocoa and coffee plants (MM) page 4

bottom The hawksbill turtle (*Eretmochelys imricata*) is critically endangered after centuries of hunting (RC/S) page 11

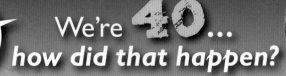

We're 40...
how did that happen?

How did it all happen? George (my then husband) and I wrote the first Bradt guide – about hiking in Peru and Bolivia – on an Amazon river barge, and typed it up on a borrowed typewriter. We had no money for the next two books so George went to work for a printer and was paid in books rather than money.

Forty years on, Bradt publishes over 200 titles that sell all over the world. I still suffer from Imposter Syndrome – how did it all happen? I hadn't even worked in an office before! Well, I've been extraordinarily lucky with the people around me. George provided the belief to get us started (and the mother to run our US office). Then, in 1977, I recruited a helper, Janet Mears, who is still working for us. She and the many dedicated staff who followed have been the foundations on which the company is built. But the bricks and mortar have been our authors and readers. Without them there would be no Bradt Travel Guides. Thank you all for making it happen.

Hilary Bradt

AUTHOR

Kathleen Becker is a German–Irish travel writer, guide and translator who over the past 20 years has reported from various European countries, the Americas and Africa. She has written travel guides to London and Lisbon and co-authored guides to the literary landscapes of Norfolk and British detective fiction, as well as guides to Portugal. Today, Kathleen leads guided walks around her adopted home town of Lisbon (contact kathleenlx@gmail.com) and hiking groups in the Azores, Cabo Verde and São Tomé and Príncipe.

AUTHOR'S STORY

These two African islands have so much more to offer than their tiny size would suggest, and this book is mainly for the adventurous traveller dabbling with the idea of exploring them. To write the first edition of this guide I spent months hiking through dense rainforests, lounging on empty beaches, visiting crumbling colonial plantation houses, climbing extinct volcanoes (sweating for Britain, or Bradt, rather), and tasting roasted cocoa beans – as well as some of the best chocolate in the world.

Today, São Tomé and Príncipe are still largely undiscovered but the buzz of change is unmistakable: ecotourism and investment are beginning to take root, on Príncipe in particular. One only hopes that the natural beauty of the islands will be preserved. What I can say for sure, though, is that São Tomé and Príncipe changed my life, transporting me to Portugal where I have lived since 2006.

Working on the new edition of this guide introduced me to more new experiences, not least to diving and the beautiful underwater world of the islands. And the sensation of dancing on the veranda of the Bombaim plantation at Christmas, with bats flying around us, will stay with me for a long time. As I said, research was a huge amount of fun, but if the shy ossobó bird could finally show its face next time I visit, rather than just its bright green behind, that would be nice, thanks …

The first Bradt travel guide was written in 1974 by George and Hilary Bradt on a river barge floating down a tributary of the Amazon. It was followed by *Backpacker's Africa*, published in 1979. In the 1980s and '90s the focus shifted away from hiking to broader-based guides to new destinations – usually the first to be published on those places. In the 21st century Bradt continues to publish these ground-breaking guides, along with guides to established holiday destinations, incorporating in-depth information on culture and natural history alongside the nuts and bolts of where to stay and what to see.

Bradt authors support responsible travel, with advice not only on minimum impact but also on how to give something back through local charities. Thus a true synergy is achieved between the traveller and local communities.

* * *

Bradt has always championed the 'little' places, pretty spots that tend to fly beneath the tourist radar – and are often all the more rewarding for it. São Tomé and Príncipe squarely fits the bill. Together the two islands form Africa's second-smallest country, but what they lack in size they make up for in charm. This is a destination that drips with colour, from its turquoise waters and deep green foliage to the bright clothes worn by the people themselves. Furthermore, Kathleen presents its attractions with a relish that makes this book a vivid portrait of a truly enticing country.

Second edition published August 2014   First published 2008
Bradt Travel Guides Ltd, IDC House, The Vale, Chalfont St Peter, Bucks SL9 9RZ, England
www.bradtguides.com
Print edition published in the USA by The Globe Pequot Press Inc,
PO Box 480, Guilford, Connecticut 06437-0480

Text copyright © 2014 Kathleen Becker; Extract (translation: KB) from Miguel Sousa Tavares *Equador* printed with kind permission by Bloomsbury, London, who published their translation (by Peter Bush) in 2008; recipe on page 81 courtesy of João Carlos Silva and Oficina do Livro (translation: KB)
Maps copyright © 2014 Bradt Travel Guides Ltd; special thanks to Marcelin Ouangraoa, Burkina Faso
Illustrations copyright © 2014 Individual photographers and artists
Editorial Project Manager: Claire Strange
Cover image research: Pepi Bluck, Perfect Picture

British Library Cataloguing in Publication Data
A catalogue record for this book is available from the British Library
ISBN-13: 978 1 84162 486 0
e-ISBN: 978 1 84162 782 3 (e-pub)
e-ISBN: 978 1 84162 683 3 (mobi)

Photographers: AWL: Camilla Watson (CW/AWL); Filippo Marolla (FM); Marco Muscarà www.marcomuscara.com (MM); Shutterstock: Rich Carey (RC/S)
Front cover: Children sit on a fishing boat in the village of Porto Alegre (CW/AWL)
Back cover: Pico Cão Grand monolith, São Tomé (MM)
Title page: On the way to Abade, Príncipe (MM); Parrot beak flower, São Tomé (MM); Woman carrying a bunch of bananas, Terreiro Velho, Príncipe (MM)
Illustrations William V Clarke
Maps David McCutcheon FBCart.S
Typeset from the author's disc by Ian Spick, Bradt Travel Guides Ltd
Production managed by Jellyfish Print Solutions and printed in India
Digital conversion by the Firsty Group

Acknowledgements

A big thank you to Luis Manuel Beirão from the Navetur agency in São Tomé for making things happen in the country, as well as to Susana and Miguel in the office, to Marie and John O'Donoghue in Ireland for love and support, Wolfgang Becker and Sabine Wölm back in Germany, and to Pedro Luis Bidarra in Lisbon, for taking so much interest in my stories and patiently hanging on to dodgy Skype connections. Thanks to Brice Monteiro from Monte Café, guide extraordinaire who took me up the Pico half-a-dozen times; Tiziano and Mari Pisoni, whose ecotourism concept at Mucumbli is the one I'd like to see grow; Nora Rizzo for being a dynamic friend; João Santos from Tropic Venture for introducing me to diving in São Tomé; Gerhard Seibert, who knows much more about the country than fits into the meticulously researched doorstopper he has written about it; Reto Scherraus for good ideas; Joachim and Kerstin Schulze for hospitality and good laughs; all my fun One World clients; linguist Tjerk Hagemeijer; Bastien Loloum of MARAPA; Bob Drewes of the Californian Academy of Sciences; naturalist Mike Unwin; readers Pablo Strubell and Itziar Martinez-Pantoja; and to all the travellers who shared tips, experiences and pictures with me, all the STP researchers and bloggers, as well as Claire Strange, and others in the Bradt office. And a special thanks to the countless Santomeans who gave me a warm welcome – in the hope of a brighter future for everyone.

In memoriam Sophie Warne, who first discovered São Tomé and Príncipe for Bradtpackers.

HOW TO USE THIS GUIDE

MAPS

Keys and symbols Maps include alphabetical keys covering the locations of those places to stay, eat or drink that are featured in the book. On occasion, hotels or restaurants that are not listed in the guide (but which might serve as alternative options if required or serve as useful landmarks to aid navigation) are also included on the maps; these are marked with accommodation (🏠) or restaurant (✕) symbols. Note that regional maps may not show all hotels and restaurants in the area: other establishments may be located in towns shown on the map.

Grids and grid references Several maps use gridlines to allow easy location of sites. Map grid references are listed in square brackets after listings in the text, with page number followed by grid number, eg: [108 C3].

Contents

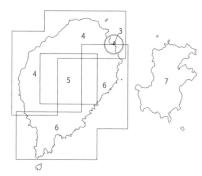

Introduction   vii

PART ONE   GENERAL INFORMATION   1

Chapter 1   **Background Information**   3
               Geography and climate 3, Natural history and
               conservation 4, History 16, Politics and society 22,
               Economy 26, People 30, Religion 32, Education 33,
               Culture 33

Chapter 2   **Practical Information**   47
               When to visit 47, Highlights and itineraries 47, Tour
               operators 49, Red tape 53, Embassies and consulates 54,
               Getting there and away 56, Health 62, Safety 74, What
               to take 75, Money 76, Budgeting 77, Getting around
               78, Accommodation 78, Eating and drinking 79, Public
               holidays and opening hours 85, Shopping and services 85,
               Activities 88, Arts and entertainment 94, Photography 94,
               Media and communications 95, Language 99, Business
               100, Buying property 100, Tourism 101, Cultural etiquette
               101, Travelling positively 102

PART TWO   SÃO TOMÉ   107

Chapter 3   **São Tomé: the Capital**   109
               Highlights 110, Getting there and away 110, Getting
               around 110, Tourist information and travel agencies
               112, Where to stay 114, Where to eat and drink 118,
               Entertainment and nightlife 121, Shopping 123, Other
               practicalities 126, What to see and do 131

Chapter 4   **The North and Northwest**   137
               Highlights 137, Getting around 137, Northern beaches
               137, Guadalupe town 140, From Guadalupe to Neves 142,
               Neves 143, Neves to the end of the road 144

Chapter 5	**The Interior**	**151**

Highlights 151, Getting around 151, Madre de Deus 151, West of Madre de Deus 153, Trindade 155, From Trindade to Bombaim 156, Towards Bom Sucesso, Monte Café and Nova Moca 158

Chapter 6	**The East and South**	**163**

Highlights 163, Getting around 163, From São Tomé to São João dos Angolares 163, São João dos Angolares and around 168, From São João dos Angolares to Porto Alegre 173, Porto Alegre 173, Ilhéu das Rolas 178, The Southwest 184

PART THREE	PRÍNCIPE	185

Chapter 7	**Príncipe**	**187**

Highlights 188, History 188, Culture and tradition 188, Getting there and away 189, Getting around 191, Other practicalities 192, Santo António: the capital 193, Exploring the rest of Príncipe 199, Activities 204, Bom Bom Island resort 207

Appendix 1	**Wildlife Glossary**	**210**
Appendix 2	**Language**	**219**
Appendix 3	**Further Information**	**233**
Index		**246**

LIST OF MAPS

East coast	162	Santana	165
Guadalupe	140	Santo António	194–5
Ilhéu das Rolas	180	São João dos Angolares	171
Interior, The	152–3	São Tomé	
Neves	143	& Príncipe	1st colour section
North, The	138	São Tomé town	108
Northwest, The	145	São Tomé town centre	113
Porto Alegre	177	South, The	169
Príncipe	186	Trindade	154

Introduction

'Amiiiiiiga!' Friend! 'Taxi?' These bright yellow taxis are everywhere – so many zoom around the central market square of São Tomé, they show up on Google Earth. But isn't life here supposed to be *leve-leve*, calm, easy-going, relaxed? Escaping from the clinch of yellow fenders into the maze of the market building leads you straight into the rich colours of São Tomé: neat piles of green limes, red chilli pepper, yellow turmeric, dark grey charcoal, herbs and plantains, and the metallic shimmer and glassy stare of a swordfish in a bucket. Further afield, you'll find more colours: the waxy pink of the porcelain rose, the turquoise of a coastal bay, the rainbow of clothes spread out to dry across the stones along one of the many rivers, and the luscious greens of the trees, plants and ferns of the rainforest that covers three quarters of the islands – nourished by rivers, waterfalls, and the tropical downpours of the rainy season. The forest creeps down to sandy beaches, white, golden, graphite-grey, where you are unlikely to meet a single tourist – but maybe a fisherman who'll sell you a fish from his catch. Freshly grilled fish 'belly', the sides of the Atlantic sailfish, is only one of the taste sensations of the archipelago; the delicious stickiness of the jackfruit, the acidity of a coffee cherry and the aromatic bitterness of a toasted cocoa bean are others.

A hundred years ago, this archipelago was one of the world's biggest producers of cocoa; today, the faded glory and tumbledown charm of the plantations tell the story of the decline of colonial rule and the monocrops that helped to sustain it. Rest your hiking feet on the creaking wraparound balcony of a restored plantation house, clutching a cold beer by candlelight, and you are in the middle of a living history lesson – on the story of West Africa, colonialism and the slave trade, and the crops that shaped these islands: sugarcane, coffee and, most of all, cocoa. Chocolate from 'the cocoa islands' is starting to appear on the shelves of supermarkets abroad, however, only one gourmet brand is actually produced here. Most Santomeans, working for a monthly wage many expats spend on a night out, certainly can't afford this luxury.

In Africa's second-smallest country, political power and business are concentrated around the capital and the northeast of main São Tomé island. In the poorer south, phallic phonolite outcrops, rising hundreds of metres above the surrounding oil and coconut palms, shrouded in mist, create a certain *Lord of the Rings* atmosphere. And really, this is Middle Earth: São Tomé and Príncipe is the closest land mass to the point in the Atlantic where the meridian, the line of zero longitude running through Greenwich in London, crosses the line of zero latitude, in other words, the Equator. The equatorial archipelago's diverse habitats include rocky reefs covered in sea fans, hiding places for colourful parrotfish and snappers, grumpy-looking moray eels and majestic barracudas – and five species of turtle. São Tomé and Príncipe is one of West Africa's most important nesting sites for marine turtles and each winter they come to lay their eggs on the small strips of sand separating the Atlantic from the dense rainforest. Two dozen endemic bird species are starting to attract birdwatchers from all over the world, tick-lists in hand.

Over the centuries, the arrival of slaves and 'contract workers' from the Congo basin, Angola, Cape Verde and Mozambique created a unique ethnic and cultural blend of musical and dramatic traditions, and a deliciously varied cuisine. Today, more than half the population continue to live on US\$1 a day, amid speculation about where exactly the millions of dollars that the government received for the oil discovered in Santomean territorial waters actually went. So far nobody has seen a drop of the black stuff, but if and when it starts flowing, *petróleo* is supposed to solve all the islands' problems …

Some people will breezily tell you that you can see all of Príncipe in a day. You can of course, if you zoom along the island's few kilometres of tarred road in a jeep. However, you can spend weeks here and not see every corner of this spectacular island. In the 'city' of Santo António, the rainforest keeps trying to impose its grip on the crumbling colonial houses; a handful are restored in pretty colours, of others, only their stark façades are left. Maybe because of the splendid isolation of the island, experiences stay in your mind even more clearly: wonderful meals on the deck at the Bom Bom Island four-star resort, frugal picnics of biscuits and corn rolls atop an unknown waterfall, the shadowy silhouettes of a guide's siblings dancing to *kizomba* tunes from a battery-powered stereo or an afternoon at the beautiful Banana Beach, perfectly curved around turquoise waters.

On Príncipe, the transition from beach paradise to rain-soaked misery can be quick. Retracing the steps of a scientist who had reported sand sharks feeding at the mouth of a particular river on an isolated beach in the southwest of the island involved a lot of walking, a lot of machete work to clear the path, a lot of aggressive mosquitoes, a lot of rain, more rain … so it was 18.00 and nearly dark when we finally stumbled down to the beach. We had barely finished wading through the river, water up to our hips, when we suddenly saw them: a pair of sand sharks, elegant fins slicing the water. The evening's entertainment consisted of flapping a sopping Gore-Tex jacket over the campfire in the rain, trying to dry-grill my legs at the same time. Minus my hammock, which got left behind, I snuggled up to the unconvincing fire, piling all the soaked wood within my reach on to it, too wet and cold to sleep. The next day, my walking socks had gone, quietly consumed by the fire in the night. *Caca–ôôô!* is, I think, the expression Santomeans use for this kind of thing.

A touch of mystery, farce even, also clung to my departure from the archipelago. Spending hours having my African braids rearranged, I managed to miss the plane from Príncipe back to São Tomé. But wait, the supply plane from São Tomé is due in, I can get that! But then no, a bird had wrecked the turbine, the plane couldn't take off, leaving me stuck on the island for two more days. Funnily enough, I heard the 'bird-in-turbine' story again, not long afterwards, when I was due to travel home. This time though, it turned out to be the sound of my airline folding. Over 100 people were left stranded, amidst the constantly changing rumours that are so typically Santomean. (I did get off the island, only four days late.) So, São Tomé and Príncipe is certainly not a tropical 'all-included' paradise, but you won't be short of good stories to tell!

Part One

GENERAL INFORMATION

Islands Two main islands: São Tomé and Príncipe; inhabited Ilhéu das Rolas (straddling the Equator), and several uninhabited islets: Ilhéu das Cabras, Ilhéu de Santana, Ilhas Tinhosas, Ilhéu de Caroço

Location Atlantic Ocean, approx 250km off the West African coast; the two main islands are about 150km apart

Size 1,001km^2 (São Tomé 854km^2, Príncipe 142km^2, Ilhéu das Rolas 3km^2, plus small uninhabited islets)

Status Independent republic

Government Multi-party democracy; semi-presidential system

Population 190,000 (estimated 2014): Creole, Cape Verdean/Angolan descent, Angolan, mixed-race

Life expectancy 65.3 years (2012)

Capital São Tomé, on São Tomé island (population c70,000)

Economy Cocoa, tourism, coconuts

Religion Roman Catholic (56%), other (20%), no religion (21%) (2012)

Currency Santomean dobra ($), euro (€) widely used, US dollar (US$)

Exchange rate US$1 = 18,450$, £1 = 28,500$, €1 = 24,500$ (2014)

International telephone code +239

Time GMT

Electricity supply 220V round, European two-pin sockets

Flag Two black stars on three horizontal bands of green–yellow–green and a red isosceles triangle on the left

Public holidays: 1 January, 3 February, 1 May, 12 July, 6 September, 30 September, 26 November, 21 December, 25 December. See also page 85.

1

Background Information

GEOGRAPHY AND CLIMATE

With thanks to Dr Bob Drewes, California Academy of Sciences, for the 2014 update

São Tomé and Príncipe lie in the Gulf of Guinea, some 250km east of Gabon on the African mainland. At 1,001km², the archipelago is the second smallest country in Africa after the Seychelles; it is roughly three-quarters the size of Greater London, or a third of Rhode Island state. Nicknamed the 'Centre of the World', it is the closest land mass to the point in the Atlantic where the imaginary line of the Equator crosses the zero meridian. The larger island, São Tomé, has a surface area of around 854km² and lies 250km off the Gabonese coast. At 142km², Príncipe, some 150km to the northeast and 225km off the coast of Equatorial Guinea, is about nine times smaller. Both islands are criss-crossed by rivers; on São Tomé most rivers have their source in the Obô National Park, around the Pico de São Tomé. The islands' soil is fertile, thanks to their geologic make-up. São Tomé and Príncipe form part of the 1,200km Main Cameroon Line volcanic chain, stretching southwest from the Nigerian Jos Plateau on the mainland and including Bioko (previously called Fernando Pô), Príncipe and São Tomé down to Anobón (previously called Pagalu). Both Bioko and Anobón now belong to Equatorial Guinea. Geologically, São Tomé and Príncipe consist mainly of hard undersaturated basalt lava – the Holocene shield volcano – that is reflected in the landscape of greatly eroded, precipitous mountains and dramatic **phonolitic rock towers** rising up vertically out of the rainforest of the south: the mighty Cão Grande, or *Pico Caué* (633m), and its smaller and slightly more drooping counterpart, Cão Pequeno. The latter, curiously, is only really visible from the Ilhéu das Rolas, unless you take to the southwest on foot. Phonolite is much more resistant to weathering and erosion than basalt; these volcanic plugs or dikes were created by the phonolite intruding into a basaltic volcano, and the softer surrounding basalt subsequently eroding away. Most of the time these phallic-looking towers are shrouded in mist, *leite de voador* ('flying fish milk'); getting a clear shot of Cão Grande has defeated more than one photographer. The oldest part of the archipelago is Príncipe, which has been reliably dated to 31 million years. Volcanic activity stopped earlier here than on São Tomé, some 15.7 million years ago; the island is much more deeply eroded, resulting in spectacular phonolitic rockscapes on a small surface area, seen particularly well along the southern coast. The oldest exposed rock on São Tomé is the Ilhéu das Cabras off the northern coast of São Tomé, at some 13 million years of age. The most recent dated volcanic rock, the basaltic cinder cones, mainly in the southeast of São Tomé, only formed around 100,000 years ago. The fact to remember to impress your friends is that São Tomé and Príncipe are respectively three and six times older than the oldest Hawaiian and Galapagos islands.

At each side, the islands' rocky flanks plummet down to a depth of 3,000m below sea level, with a large part of the continental shelf around Príncipe – the archipelago was never part of the African mainland. A look at Google Earth will show you the original outline of Príncipe, with the Tinhosa Islets, the original southern tip of the island, some 30 million years ago. This separate evolution and zoogeographical isolation accounts for the high level of **endemism**: many plant and bird species can only be found here, making the islands a paradise for wildlife lovers, birdwatchers and botanists. While the equatorial climate means maximum average daily temperatures of 27˚C to 29˚C, there is a massive **difference in rainfall** across these small islands. The dry savannah area in the rain-shadow to the northeast of São Tomé island, including the capital, only receives around 60cm of rain per year, whereas the mountainous southern and western parts of the island, in the path of the mainly southwesterly winds, receive about 6m. Of the two islands, Príncipe has the wetter climate, again with the south of the island receiving much more rain than the north. Most rain falls in March and April.

NATURAL HISTORY AND CONSERVATION

TREES AND PLANTS The dense rainforest of the islands is home to about 900 species of vascular **plants,** 130 of which are endemic: on São Tomé 14%, on Príncipe 11%. The most dominant plant family is the *Rubiaceae*, ie: flowering plants, containing over 10,000 species (coffee is one of them). The flower that is most associated with the country is the **porcelain rose** (*Etlingera elatior*, also known in English as torch ginger), a tropical pink flower with waxy stems and petals; it grows wild and is also cultivated at some plantations. In the interior of São Tomé island, discover bright red rod-like monkey flowers, whose stems are boiled up with red wine to help women after childbirth. **Bamboo** rods as thick as arms line the paths – planted in the colonial-era to shore up the ground for their narrow-gauge trains transporting cocoa. You will find both the world's largest and smallest **begonia** here, *Begonia baccata*, up to 5m high (on São Tomé), and *Begonia annobonensis* (on Príncipe) which reaches only 1cm. For number and diversity, **tree ferns** have no equal on the African continent: there are over 150 of them.

The archipelago's plant world still holds many mysteries for botanists in terms of geographic distribution – for instance, why is the *Grammitis nigrocincta* fern found only on Príncipe and Madagascar? And why do the nearest relatives of the tall *Afrocarpus mannii* tree, common above 1,000m, grow in East Africa? And every scientific expedition yields new species, species thought to be extinct and species under threat. The magnificent trees with massive trunks have a multitude of uses: in construction of the traditional Santomean plank houses on stilts, canoe-building and in traditional medicine (see box, opposite). **Forest** covers about 90% of the islands. With the right guide, any walk yields new discoveries and stories: hibiscus branches were once used as toothbrushes, with charcoal as toothpaste, and *selosonsumaiá* is a wonderful wild coriander/cilantro with serrated leaves and looking nothing like what we know.

Coconut palms reach right down to the fringes of the beaches, and **oil palms** are cultivated for the palm oil used abundantly in the local cuisine. In the towns, **almond trees** and **breadfruit** trees line the streets, and **banana** plantations and fields of **sugarcane** abound. The most conspicuous trees on the plantations are the imported fast-growing **flame trees**, with their bright orange flowers, giving shade to the cocoa and coffee plants (**shade forest**). In the dry plains of the northern part of São Tomé, that are burnt regularly in the dry season, **acacias**, **tamarinds** and **baobabs** are dotted around the grasslands and the fields of millet and sugarcane.

The rainforest is a natural pharmacy and herbalists use many of its plants and tree barks. For example, the roots of the wild ginger, *gengibre*, are used to treat various conditions, from colic to impotence and asthma. Papaya, *mamão*, contains papaine, aiding digesting, and carpaine, acting as a depressant on the nervous system. The bark of the wild quinine tree contains an anti-malarial agent, quinidine. *Folha d'amina* serves as a natural painkiller against headaches; the liquid is drawn out through little holes in the bark. A stomach-calming tea can be made from the bark of the wild cinnamon tree, *canela*. There is a huge body of local knowledge, and with new studies carried out, plants are beginning to be commercially exploited now too. An ethno-pharmacological project involving the University of Coimbra in Portugal and the Santomean Ministry of Health, as well as 40 local traditional healers, has been working for 20 years cataloguing local medicinal plants. This powerhouse of natural remedies also attracts wild and unproven claims though, such as that a plant syrup developed by the foremost traditional healer in the country can 'put the virus to sleep'. HIV activists fear such claims will result in a more relaxed attitude to prevention, amongst the still very contained incidence of HIV/AIDS.

The best contact on the islands for information on traditional remedies is the author of the authoritative study on traditional medicine, Maria do Céu (e mceu.madureira@gmail.com), though she is very busy and often researching on Príncipe or working on volunteering projects such as Projecto Pagué, bringing the knowledge and application of traditional plant medicine to a wider audience. One such recent initiative by young Portuguese volunteers has been Sota Kuyu – involving short stories, short films and creative workshops on traditional medicine (www.aguede-ale.com; also available in English).

Primary forest (*obô*) still covers about a quarter of the islands, and it is for the protection of this sensitive and species-rich area that the **Obô National Park** was established, covering some 300km² across both islands. Most of the **lowland rainforest** (0–400m) was cleared in the first half of the 20th century, to make way for cocoa cultivation. Containing populations of every endemic species, this type of forest is now restricted to small areas in southwestern and central São Tomé. **Upland primary rainforest** (400–800m) is confined to the centre of São Tomé island, around the source of the Xufe-Xufe and Ana Chaves rivers and south of Lagoa Amélia. For the lay person it is not that easy to distinguish between primary forest and mature **secondary forest** (*capoeira*), which represents about 30% of the islands' forest cover and is reclaiming crumbling plantations. At higher levels, between 800m and the top of the Pico de São Tomé at around 2,000m you find beautiful **montane** and **mist forest**, with mighty endemic trees, such as the *Afrocarpus mannii* yellow-wood stretching their branches towards the sky or smaller trees like *Cratispermum montanum*, whose bark is used in a fortifying drink for swordfish hunters and as an aphrodisiac – there are many of these around. These areas (Lagoa Amélia/Carvalho), receive very few hours of daily sunshine.

Orchids *With special thanks to Faustino Oliveira and Dr Tariq Stevart*

The queen of plants finds perfect conditions in the lush rainforest. To date, 129 species of orchid are known on the archipelago, of which 101 are on São Tomé and 64 on Príncipe and, of these, about a quarter are endemic. Both in numbers of species and in terms of frequency, orchids are the most important amongst the spontaneous plants on the islands. Tropical orchids are classified according to the supporting organism. Three-quarters of orchids on São Tomé and Príncipe are **epiphytes** (ie: they live on trees), the rest are **terrestrial,** planting their roots in or on the soil, and only a few are **lithophytic**, rooting themselves on rock; some orchids combine two modes.

On São Tomé, the botanical gardens at **Bom Sucesso** are the best base for orchid-themed walks (contact Navetur or Lucio, see page 112), as the arboretum houses nearly all species from the islands. To the untrained eye, out of season they don't seem much to look at, but in the flowering season (winter) they exhibit their full beauty. *Angraetum doratophyllum* has lovely delicate white flowers with a hooked spur, and *Cribbia confusa* has small, strongly scented greenish-orange flowers (both are available for cultivation over the internet). The prolongation of the Lagoa Amélia trail towards Morro Porvaz and Chamiço (not often undertaken) yields mountainous orchids, amongst them endemic epiphytes such as *Chamaeangis thomensis*, *Polystachya parivlora* and *Cribbia thomensis*. The most commonly found terrestrial orchid is *Cheirostylis lepida*. Climbing towards Pico de São Tomé from Bom Sucesso, the mountain crests display a rich variety. Escadas is a good spot for epiphytes such as *Liparis gracilenta* covering the tree bark. The Mesa Pico Pequeno, a 1½ hour's walk from the summit, on the way down towards Cascata and Manual Morais is another, and is easier to get to. Guides are needed as the paths can change and the information contained in Oliverira/Tariq's authoritative study (see page 238) should not be used as a hiking reference. Last, but not least, few people realise that the vanilla plant is also an orchid!

On Príncipe, it is the southeast (only accessible with a guide) which is of most interest to orchid lovers. One of the most commonly found species (also available in cultivation) is *Cyrtorchis acuminata*, with broad leaves and large waxy-white flowers.

MUSHROOMS The mycoflora on the islands is only starting to be properly catalogued. From 15 listed species on São Tomé only, their number has risen to over 225 on both islands, of which 30% have never before been described to science. From fiery-orange minuscule fungal spores via beautifully shelving tree sponges looking like curlicued wooden ornaments to big, smelly, impressive specimens with a white netted cloak around them, they make for great visual interest when on a demanding mountain slog. On the Pico de São Tomé, for instance, they can keep your mind off the fact that there is yet another fallen tree trunk to clamber over!

BIRDS *With thanks to Ricardo Lima, Faculty of Sciences, University of Lisbon*
The birdlife of the islands is exceptional, boasting the highest density of endemic birds worldwide, including the world's largest weaver bird, largest sunbird and smallest ibis. Of the over 75 species that regularly occur on São Tomé and Príncipe, the islands are home to 28 endemic species and 11 endemic subspecies. São Tomé holds 17 single-island endemic bird species, while Príncipe holds eight. They share three other endemic bird species, one of which can also be found in Annobón island (Equatorial Guinea). The first species you are likely to encounter is the **black kite**, circling above Ana Chaves Bay at São Tomé town, hovering over the harbour looking for scraps of fish. The locals called it *falcão* (plural *falcões*). You will see them on the national coat of arms too. For reasons of space, only the English name (and occasionally the local name) is given in this section – the local names, often onomatopoeic, are the ones you are most likely to hear. Birdwatchers should bring their own binoculars

The rarest bird on the islands is the endemic São Tomé grosbeak. First described in the late 19th century from specimens collected in the south of the island, the dark chestnut bird, with a strong, parakeet-style beak and bullish head, eluded ornithologists for more than a century, and had even been considered extinct by some. In 1991, it was spotted again, along a ridge above the Xufe-Xufe River in the southwest, by the British ornithologist David Sargeant. David was in the company of Tom Gullick, a British birder who in 2012 was to clock up the world record for listing 9,000 bird species. The only musem specimen of the grosbeak is in the Natural History Museum collection in Tring, Hertfordshire, UK. Two other specimens were in a museum in Lisbon, but were destroyed in a fire. The first ever photograph of this bird was taken in 2006, and it is now known also to occur near Lagoa Amélia

and bird book, as none are for sale on the islands. If you're lucky, some guides know the French names; consider photocopying our glossary (see pages 210–18) to take with you or better still, buy the photoguide published in 2009 (see page 238).

There are few cattle on the island, apart from meagre specimens from the southern Portuguese Alentejo region, but nevertheless the **cattle egret** (*garça*) is one of the easiest birds to spot in the lowlands of São Tomé, with its white plumage and yellow beak and crest. One of the best-loved and most easy to spot **endemics** is the small prinia, whose wing-clapping gave it its local name, *truqui-sum-Dessu*, referring to its greeting of 'God' early in the morning. More difficult to find is the endemic and threatened São Tomé oriole, commonly known as *papa-figo* (it is featured on the 5,000$ banknote), with its pronounced red beak and yellow-tipped tail. Living mostly in the forest, it responds to imitations of its distinctive call. Other birds to look out for are the São Tomé scops owl, São Tomé spinetail, starlings, drongo, seedeaters, São Tomé green pigeon and São Tomé bronze-naped pigeon. With a bright yellow belly, the emerald cuckoo, *ossobó*, has a prominent role in Santomean culture and appears on the 10,000$ banknote. On forest hikes or during stays on plantations, you are likely to hear its call, thought to announce rain, but the beautiful bird itself is very hard to see.

Príncipe has its own eight endemics: the Príncipe glossy starling, the Príncipe speirops, the Príncipe sunbird, the Príncipe thrush, the Príncipe white-eye, the Dohrn's thrush-babbler, the Príncipe drongo and the Príncipe weaver – a few amongst them easily seen along the roadside in the north or walking along the river from Santo António to Bela Vista.

Hunting is poorly regulated and constitutes a threat to some of the endemic birds. In rural areas it is common to find people carrying firearms, or kids chasing small birds with slingshots or stones. Land-use intensification is the biggest threat to the conservation of birds and biodiversity in general in São Tomé and Príncipe. These two factors largely contribute to the fact that 11 out of the 28 endemic bird species are currently considered as threatened. Four of them, the São Tomé grosbeak, the São Tomé fiscal, the Príncipe thrush and the dwarf olive ibis, have even been classified as critically endangered.

Top birdspots of São Tomé and Príncipe

North of São Tomé The savannah zone to the north of São Tomé, around the town of Guadalupe, and the coast road from Diogo Nunes to Praia das Conchas is home to many species thought to have been introduced, such as the red-winged bishop. The common waxbill is common there, and it is also the main habitat for the bronze mannikin. The blue waxbills are locally known as *suim-suim*, an onomatopoeic, suggesting their chant. They are easy to spot even in the shrubs and gardens of the capital of São Tomé, including the Parque Popular and even outside the Miguel Bernardino bakery. However, the main habitat of this small cream-blue bird is the savannah and it can be seen in the grass along the side of the western coast road down to Santa Catarina. Other birds common in the savannah are the swifts, the white-winged widow bird, the golden-backed bishop, the fire-crowned bishop and the Vitelline masked weaver. In the dry lowlands of the northwest, also look for the endemic São Tomé bronze-naped pigeon and for the endemic subspecies of arlequin quail.

Bom Sucesso and Lagoa Amélia (interior of São Tomé) The botanic gardens of Bom Sucesso and the dry crater lake of Lagoa Amélia are great sites for easy birdwatching. An easy-to-spot endemic is the São Tomé weaver, found at Nova Moca and Lagoa Amélia. The higher-altitude primary forest around Lagoa Amélia is also a good place to go looking for two threatened species: the elusive maroon pigeon and the São Tomé scops owl (common in the forests; it also responds to its call). The threatened São Tomé white-eye and giant sunbird are also relatively easy to find here.

South of São Tomé The rivers and streams of the east coast road are good places for birdwatching. The best place to spot the endemic dwarf olive ibis is around the ruins of Monte Carmo (Ribeira Peixe), an area where all the endemic birds occur. The ibis is dull olive-brown in colour, with flesh-coloured legs and short flesh-orange bill, which is usually first seen flying from the ground, where the birds feed silently. The ibis is quite tame and normally perches on a low branch, a behaviour that makes it vulnerable to hunters, who occasionally catch it for its meat. Hard-core birdwatchers might want to head for the Xufe-Xufe river area in the southwest, where all 20 endemics also occur, including the elusive São Tomé fiscal. This bird has a long tail, yellow underparts, glossy black plumage on the back and a white broken line across the wing. Forests in the south of São Tomé are considered the second-most important for threatened bird species in Africa. The giant weaver nests around Santo António de Mussacavú, while the beautifully coloured giant sunbird is most easily found in primary forest above the Xufe-Xufe River.

Southern forests of Príncipe Birders are usually able to tick off most of Príncipe's endemics and the charismatic African grey parrot – also represented on the nation's coat of arms – on a wander from the capital to Bela Vista or around the Bom Bom Island resort. While the terrain is very difficult, attracting only the most determined explorers, a night camping in the southern forests gives the advanced birder the chance to see some elusive species like the Príncipe thrush, the Príncipe white-eye or the endemic subspecies of Príncipe seedeater. There is also the unlikely possibility of finding the undescribed species of scops owl, thought to be endemic to the island, and the subspecies of olive ibis endemic to Príncipe, which some people fear might already be extinct.

At sea and along the coast Identifying **seabirds** can be tricky, as colour range is generally narrow, the plumage of juveniles is often drab and breeding species mix with migrants. The Sete Pedras rocks, in the south of São Tomé, have a nesting colony of bridled terns. The white-tailed tropicbird, with its long white double tail, is one of the most conspicuous sea birds; its white plumage is marked by a black V, and it has a yellow beak. It is easy to see in gracious flight around Jockey's Cap islet (Ilhéu Boné de Jóquei), off Príncipe, and can sometimes be spotted breeding on trees inland in both São Tomé and Príncipe. Brown and white-capped noddies, as well as brown boobies, nest and feed around the Pedra da Galé, off Príncipe. The Tinhosa Islets have large colonies of sooty terns and are a key area for breeding seabirds in West Africa. Amongst the **shore birds**, reef herons can be seen throughout the year and along most of the coast. The most common migrants are the whimbrel, with its curved beak, the wintering greenshank, with its distinctive 'barking' cry when taking off, and the common sandpiper. The rivers and mangroves are the haunts of the malachite kingfisher with its metallic plumage, the African cormorant and the shy green-backed heron.

REPTILES AND AMPHIBIANS There are two dozen species of reptiles, most of them endemic. The one everybody thinks about first, the *cobra preta* or **black cobra** (see pages 71–2), was most probably introduced. It is joined by four endemic Santomean snakes (two of them burrowers), including the light-green **grass snake** and the *sássua* – looking like a thin twig and difficult to spot, unless it turns up outside your bungalow – and three Príncipe endemics. The eight endemic amphibians include the legless caecilian, *cobra bôbô*, on Príncipe. Two endemic **frogs** span the range between Africa's largest tree frog and a tiny brown puddle frog, both from Príncipe. There are seven endemic **lizards** on the islands, each unique to its island: two geckos – the endemic *Lygodactylus thomensis* gecko identified by its yellow eye-band – two skinks, and a legless light-purple skink on Príncipe.

MARINE LIFE *With thanks to Peter Wirtz, Centre for Marine Science, University of Algarve*
The Gulf of Guinea is one of the world's hotspots of marine biodiversity. In terms of species present, this area of the Gulf is similar to the Caribbean, if with slightly less variety. Despite lying so close to the African continent, the **fish** fauna of the islands has its own particularities. Amongst the approximately 240 species recorded so far, many are endemic and the waters are still largely unexplored. Fish fauna are of particular interest because, at the latitude the islands are on, the easterly flowing equatorial currents link the western and eastern Atlantic. The high number of rivers result in low salinity in the waters around the island. It is not just invertebrates (sea slugs, etc) that present a mix of the two regions; many of the species found here are 'amphi-Atlantic'. The best-represented families are *Carangidae, Serranidae, Gobiidae* and *Scombridae*. The fish market can give you an idea of the most commonly seen fish: the horse-eye jack, various types of spear fish, as well as yellowfin tuna, with its greenish back, golden-yellow flanks and belly. Divers can look for snappers, sweetfish, stingrays, octopus, sea horses, turtles, fan coral, moray eels and giant sea slugs. Around the islands, the bottom of the sea shows high relief, as much so as the surface. This 'upswelling' brings in many smaller fish that in turn attract the big game fish. The littoral (surrounding fringe) is very narrow, and São Tomé island is separated from the neighbouring Gulf of Guinea islands and the mainland by depths of up to 2,000m. The fish fauna also shows some similarities with the western Indian Ocean.

The Gulf of Guinea has fewer species than the Caribbean and **coral** cover, at under 10%, is relatively low. The most abundant hard coral is great star coral (*Montastraea cavernosa*), in mid-depth to deeper areas in particular, followed by the golden cup coral (*Tubastraea aurea*), its orange-glowing polyps opening up at night. A recent expedition found that Ilhéu das Cabras/Kia had the highest fish density and species richness of the sites studied. As the underwater world around Príncipe is less disturbed by dragnets, the marine fauna here is even more amazing. It is a favourite habitat of **billfish**: predators include marlin, sailfish and swordfish. Blue marlins can weigh over 750kg, but take about 30 years to reach 450kg. Atlantic blue marlins travel thousands of kilometres for their food; the waters off Príncipe are said to have some of the best **marlin fishing** in the world. The best time to see them is July to September. The most common billfish, the Atlantic sailfish, *peixe andala*, has huge sail-like dorsal fins. The best time to see them is September to December. On the market or the beach in São Tomé you often see Atlantic swordfish, pulled by their long flat bill. Swordfish can reach weights of over 500kg and dive down to a depth of more than 600m.

Watching **flying fish** (popular in Santomean cuisine) propel themselves like rockets out of the water by their tail fins to whir across the waves for up to 400m is a fascinating sight. In the dry season the *peixe voador* or *peixe apanhá* is caught using straw matting. One of the most appreciated fish is the flying gurnard, *concón*, which gets its name from the sound it makes when taken out of the water.

The largely unexplored coastal waters bear many surprises and mysteries still. Every new National Geographic Society marine expedition has recorded new discoveries. An expedition in 2006, for example, found nearly 60 new fish, ten of these from a species never before described. One was a near-blind shrimp lobster living in symbiosis with a goby fish, the first goby–shrimp symbiosis to be found in the eastern Atlantic. Although the exact dynamics of the relationship are not clear, the goby guards the shrimp's nest against predators while living in the tunnel dug by the shrimp. In 2012, a new, large and very colourful species of parrotfish was discovered near Praia Francesa, and I have the feeling a couple of them live amongst the gorgonian soft corals at Mucumbli beach. One very strange type of fish to be found on São Tomé and Príncipe is the **mudskipper**. *Cucumbás* are the only fish on earth that can 'walk' – on their webbed fins – and stay out of water for hours, thanks to their ability to store water in their gills and to breathe through their skin. They can be seen near the Bom Bom Island resort on Príncipe, near the coastline at Ribeira Izé, and along the Papagaio River in the capital, Santo António, and generally at stagnant ponds of water near beaches, like at Praia Micoló. I've found them easier to spot on Príncipe.

Turtles
São Tomé and Príncipe has the most diverse range of **sea turtles** (*tartarugas*) in central Africa, with four of the five species nesting here. Sea turtles belong to the most ancient reptile family (*Chelonidiæ*), and have been around for some 200 million years. Marine turtles migrate several thousand kilometres from their foraging grounds to their nesting sites where they deposit several clutches of eggs between October and February, mainly at night. Today, they are all endangered.

Turtle species
The **green turtle**, *mão grande*, weighs up to 230kg. Its carapace, around 120cm long, is green-grey in colour, with occasional olive brown, yellow or dark streaks and spots. It is dome-shaped in front, flattening out towards the back. The upper parts of the green turtle's small rounded head are greenish or yellowish, its underside is yellowish-white, and it has a single visible claw on each flipper. It only eats plants such as seagrass and algae. Its preferred nesting beaches have dense vegetation and a gentle slope down to the water. Green turtles have a very developed sense of orientation; a female green turtle born on a Santomean beach can cross the Atlantic and return 20 years later to nest on the same beach!

The **olive ridley** (*tatô*, only nesting on São Tomé, not Príncipe) is the smallest turtle (weight 35–50kg) and has a wide heart-shaped carapace (around 75cm long), and is olive-green to brown in colour, with a hump. The olive ridley's toothless jaw resembles a beak; it feeds on shellfish, molluscs, jellyfish and algae. Olive ridleys lay their eggs on the top of sandbanks, preferring open beaches with a gentle slope. Unlike the other species which lay eggs only every two to three years, olive ridleys tend to reproduce every year.

The omnivorous **hawksbill**, *sada*, critically endangered because of the popularity of its shell for crafts and jewellery, has a serrated amber carapace of up to 90cm long, mottled with dark and light spots and streaks, and a small head with a hawk-like beak. When laying their eggs – up to 200 – hawksbills prefer small isolated beaches bordered by thick overhanging vegetation to shelter their nests.

The most impressive of them all is the **leatherback**, also critically endangered. Known locally as *ambulância*, 'ambulance', it is huge – up to 180cm long and weighing in at an average of 500kg. Leatherbacks' carapace is a thick layer of fat and tiny bones covered with a bluish-black skin with white spots; they also have no horny scales or claws. Feeding mainly on shellfish and jellyfish, they can dive as deep as 1,000m. On São Tomé and Príncipe, leatherbacks nest on beaches with a shallow slope to make it easier for the female to haul her bulk to the nesting site.

The **loggerhead turtle** has a brown-orangey carapace and is on average 70–90cm long. It has been seen in the waters around São Tomé, and seen mating, but has not yet been observed nesting.

Nesting The nesting season lasts for several months, and the nesting process itself has seven phases that can last between one and three hours: crawling up the beach, sweeping the chosen area clear, digging the nest, laying the eggs, filling in the nest, camouflaging it and returning to the sea. What seems like sea turtles' 'tears' during the nesting process is in fact a salty fluid secreted by a salt gland behind the eye to keep its eyes free of sand. It is during nesting that the turtles are most vulnerable.

The **turtle tracks** you see in the sand vary from symmetrical (green and leatherback turtle), where the fore and hind legs move together, to asymmetrical (olive ridley and hawksbill), where diagonally opposite limbs move together. The nests of olive ridleys are about 40cm deep, whilst leatherbacks' nests are on average 70cm deep. Depending on the species, the female drops 80–130 eggs into the incubation chamber of the flask-shaped nest; the eggs' soft shell membrane stops them from cracking. Luckily for turtle tourists, during egg laying the females are not sensitive to disturbance and may be observed from fairly close up. After laying their eggs, the turtles fill in the nest, shovelling sand and compacting it with their flippers, and camouflage the nest by sweeping sand across the area. When the turtles return to the sea, they orient themselves by the light; all artificial lights, including photo flash, need to be turned off so as not to confuse them. The sex of the hatchling is determined by the temperature during the middle period of incubation. If the temperature in the nest is above the 'pivotal' temperature (depending on the species, between 28–30°C), there will be more female hatchlings; if it is below this temperature, there will be more male hatchlings. After several weeks, the hatchlings leave the eggshell. Using their caruncle (temporary egg tooth), the hatchlings break open the egg membrane and wiggle out of the shell. They then take four to five days to dig their way up through the sand and emerge. The hatchlings race down the beach to the water and start swimming straight away.

Threats and conservation The turtle has a special place in Santomean **folklore**, as a heroic creature that by clever and astute actions manages to outfox its opponents;

the turtle is indeed seen as the equivalent to the fox in Western fairytales. Always hungry, *Senhor Tartaruga* (*Sum Tataluga*, in the national creole) is usually trying to work out new ways of finding food – if need be, behind the back of his family. In local culture, the turtle is, however, also a symbol of courage and resistance; accordingly, the forro expression *cloçon tataluga* (*coração* means 'heart') refers to a fearless person. That being said, turtles and their eggs are still cooked and eaten by many Santomeans – the meat of the olive ridley, in particular, is popular – while hawksbill turtle scales are turned into crafts items, such as bracelets, hair clips, combs or boxes. An adult turtle yields about 2kg of useable shell. São Tomé and Príncipe

ON TURTLE PATROL

Every night between September and April, Hipólito Lima patrols the 4km stretch of beach from Morro Peixe to Praia Micoló, protecting and marking egg-laying turtles, checking the hatchlings, disguising nests and carrying buckets of turtle eggs back to the incubator. Tonight, when Elísio Neto, the marine charity MARAPA's turtle patrol co-ordinator, and I get to Morro Peixe on his motorbike, the sea is too rough still for the turtles to venture on to the beaches, so we join Hipólito for a dinner of cooked bananas and fish, with cool beers from the village store. Just as well, because, as it turns out, turtle patrols take time. The strong moonlight makes it easier to see, but unfortunately more unlikely for turtles to risk coming out. At the top of Praia Governador, Hipólito digs a tiny grey olive ridley hatchling out of its nest, carefully disguised by the volunteers. The miniature turtle squirms between Hipólito's fingers, but it is still too early for this one; all its brothers and sisters are waiting below in the sand for the opportune moment to be released back into the sea, so Hipólito puts it back in. Elísio and Hipólito shine their torches across some tracks, showing that a turtle did come crawling out of the sea, but changed her mind and went back in. Making our way through the low shrubs bordering the beaches, Elísio and Hipólito tell me funny *tartaruga* stories. Goats mill around the broken pier of the Fernão Dias plantation. There, clearly, are tracks coming up from the sea, but then they suddenly stop. 'An element of the local population got to this one', says Hipólito, matter-of-factly. Sometimes the patrol apprehends the *tartarugeiras*, but as it is not illegal to hunt turtles in São Tomé, there is nothing they can do to stop them. We wade through the river and cross the endless shell-strewn stretch of Praia Micoló, finally resting for half an hour before the 4km walk back to Morro Peixe. I am walking on autopilot, with my eyes practically shut, and bitterly regretting not taking more water with me, when at last, at 03.30, back on Praia Governador, Hipólito and Elísio point out an olive ridley busily sweeping a space with her hind flippers, her head half hidden under a twig. The turtle is measured and marked and her scales are counted, as are her eggs: 128 in all. Hipólito digs them all out, arranging them in a bucket, to be taken to the incubator, where they will be safe from dogs, crabs – and humans. In the incubator patch, the eggs are put into an artificial nest of exactly the same depth as the natural one. In recent years, while Príncipe's new status as a UNESCO Biosphere Reserve has outlawed turtle hunting there, the situation has actually worsened on the main island. Beaches such as Fernão Dias are no longer patrolled, as armed turtle hunters will confront them. It is estimated that only 1% of turtles that reach the sea will survive to grow to maturity and reproduce.

is a signatory to both CITES (Convention on International Trade in Endangered Species of Wild Fauna and Flora) and CMS (Convention on the Conservation of Migratory Species of Wild Animals), but lacks the means and political will to enforce either. You don't see whole conserved turtles for sale anymore, as happened in the early 1990s, but turtle meat and eggs are openly on sale at São Tomé market. The only way to diminish this trade is to **refuse to buy turtle crafts** and be sure to tell the vendors why. Export is legal but most countries, including the EU, the US, Australia and New Zealand, prohibit the import of tortoiseshell goods. In 2000, the Tatô Project successfully re-trained tortoiseshell artisans to work in fishing, tourism or to use other materials – wood, coconuts, cowhorn – but, with few project funds available, it is difficult to make a living turtle worth more financially than a dead turtle. In São Tomé, the MARAPA conservation and fishing organisation looks after turtle projects and the burgeoning 'turtle tourism'. MARAPA discourages tourists from paying locals to liberate turtles if they see them being caught, as it encourages the practice even more. There is a good display on turtles and their protection in the museum in São Tomé town. The stretch of beach between Praia Micoló and Morro Peixe is probably the most famous for turtles on São Tomé; all four species come here to lay eggs. But in 2013, for instance, dozens of turtles were captured and killed on that stretch alone. In the south of the island, there is an incubation centre near Praia Jalé and there are various successful turtle projects on Príncipe – where the sale of turtle meat has been prohibited since the awarding of UNESCO Biosphere Reserve status. However, on a recent visit to Banana Beach, we came across parts of carapace, suggesting the trade still goes on.

Natural threats include water entering a nest built too close to the sea, erosion, wild dogs and pigs feeding on the eggs, and seabirds and crabs eating the hatchlings. Apart from being hunted for their meat, eggs and carapace, manmade threats include plastic bags thrown into the sea – leatherbacks confuse them with jellyfish and can asphyxiate. To protect the turtles, every year tens of thousands of eggs are taken out to be incubated in one of the incubation centres.

ENVIRONMENTAL THREATS AND CONSERVATION As there is hardly any industry, the waters around São Tomé and Príncipe are pristine, around Príncipe in particular. Yet, the Gulf of Guinea islands that the archipelago is part of, exceptionally rich in endemic species, were named in a 2002 conservation report as number two in a list of ten threatened coral reef hotspots. **Fishing stocks** are starting to suffer from foreign fleets trawling in Santomean waters. One of the aims of the new radar system set up by the US in the Gulf of Guinea is to stop this. The US Navy are also engaged in mapping the ocean floor around the islands.

In the face of the ongoing energy crisis and, according to local media, some of the highest energy prices in the world, **renewable energy** projects (wind and solar) are starting up, with German and Spanish co-operation. These will take Santomean electricity production from the current 10MW (mainly generated by the capital's thermic plant, dependent on imported diesel) up to 40MW. For the time being, visitors will continue to see the many small shops lining Santomean streets illuminated by (imported) candles.

It might not look like it, but **forest conservation** is a vital issue on the islands. In the past, large areas of lowland forest were cleared for cocoa plantations. Today, partial land privatisation has brought the division of farm plots and more tree clearance. Some exotic species are threatening to upset the ecological balance: in the case of the forest snail, for instance, the exotic species is putting pressure on the endemic one. **Illegal logging** of tropical hardwood continues despite technically being prohibited, especially

1

around the 'end of the road' in the north of the island, whilst Santomeans use the trees for cooking charcoal and to carve their dug-out canoes. Luckily, the primary forest, which has the highest number of endemic species, is difficult to access. The forest is as yet unprotected, but a new law on protected areas and the protection of threatened species is currently awaiting final ratification. At the moment, the only real demarcation of Obô National Park is a wooden entrance sign near Bom Sucesso on São Tomé. Because tourism is growing and the road network is being extended in the east and west of São Tomé, species will be pushed deeper into the forest. Deforestation, erosion and exhaustion of the soil are issues. Twenty-six tree species are considered vulnerable.

A few **birds,** such as the dwarf olive ibis, *galinhola de São Tomé* and the maroon pigeon are shot to be eaten. Currently, ten bird species are threatened, with the dwarf olive ibis, the São Tomé fiscal shrike and the São Tomé grosbeak 'critically endangered'

PALM TREES: DEGRADATION RISKS TO THE ECOSYSTEMS IN SÃO TOMÉ

Thanks to Signe Mikulane, geographer at the University of Heidelberg, and Bastien Loloum, MARAPA

São Tomé and Príncipe's large number of floral and faunal species and significant old-growth forest make it a remarkable hot spot of biodiversity, and the number of endemic plants and animals (found nowhere else in the world) makes these islands specifically valuable to science. New species are constantly being discovered. A major contribution in this area is provided by Dr Bob Drewes and his team from California Academy of Sciences, who have been leading expeditions to these islands since 1998 (http://islandbiodiversityrace.wildlifedirect.org/; http://www.calacademy.org/medialibrary/blogs/gulfofguinea/). Worldwide awareness of the current situation in São Tomé has grown since the 1992 Convention of Biodiversity in Rio de Janeiro.

An area of about 30% of both islands was designated as a conservation area in 1993 and as the Obô National Park in 2006. Still, illegal activities such as logging inside Obô National Park continue due to a lack of enforcement and reluctance to confront traditional practices.

There is a distinctive human impact caused by local land-use pressure: illegal logging; agricultural cultivation of steep slopes prone to degradation risks; charcoal production and the cutting down of selected economically valuable trees; coastal sand depletion for construction causing recession of the coastline; litter pollution, and so on. Add to that deforestation and interventions into ecosystems by international players (for instance oil palm plantations by Belgian Agripalma, see opposite) and consequences from global climate change (including longer periods of drought and more torrential rains). All these actions and incidents together are increasing natural risks of degradation and causing new conflicts and dangers for the environment and biodiversity of São Tomé. Previously resistant areas are becoming more vulnerable and the vulnerable ones are expanding even faster.

Monocultures like oil palm plantations are not only hostile to biodiversity but they also exhaust and degrade soils rapidly. While the volcanic soils of São Tomé are still rich in minerals, after years of monoculture cultivation they can become depleted, as has happened to soils in oil plantations of the Amazon rainforest, Malaysia and Indonesia. In contrast to the monocultures, the cocoa and coffee plantations under the tall shade trees (*florestas de sombra*) and what are called *capoeiras* – abandoned Portuguese plantations, gradually recaptured by forest – provide a complex and functional ecosystem. The vegetation is forming several on BirdLife International's Red List. In the past, many grey parrots, one of the world's most popular pet birds and featured on the dobra coins, were trapped and captured for the international pet trade; the legal trade stopped with the island's 2012 UNESCO Biosphere Reserve status. It is thought, however, that on Príncipe some 100 trappers supplement their income with the sale of grey parrots, giving them the local *cacharamba* firewater to drink to keep them quiet on the boat journey across the sea.

São Tomé and Príncipe is a signee to the UNESCO Convention on Wetlands, which protects the seabird colony on Ilhas Tinhosas, a breeding site for more than 300,000 migratory waterbirds on a site just 24ha in area (under threat from seabird harvesting by fishermen), the Malanza mangrove and the highland wetland crater of Lagoa Amélia.

In São Tomé in particular, **litter** is becoming an increasing problem, sitting in heaps along the roadside in some places and starting to spoil some of the northern

dense layers here which protect the soil from erosion. Through their floral diversity, these areas accommodate many animals, especially birds.

However, logging still continues, causing loss of shade cover for cocoa and coffee plantations, and reduced crop quality and quantity. Furthermore, soils are becoming vulnerable, are losing their stability and are exposed to erosion. Degradation risks are increasing and biodiversity is becoming more endangered as a consequence. Thankfully, intrusion into old-growth forest is not yet being pursued very actively. The difficulty of accessibility – steep slopes, long distances, lack of vehicles – and the fear of many local people of the venomous black cobra are the reasons.

AGRIPALMA The biggest environmental story of recent years can be summed up in one word: Agripalma. The Belgian company with 12% of Santomean state capital has been logging local rainforests in the south, replacing them with oil palm plantations on a large scale. Its founders are involved in renewable energies, and Agripalma's story is not a black-and-white one of nature grab versus conservationists, but mirrors a rather complex reality. In a country with a GDP of only US$264 million, and nearly all plantations economically inactive, jobs and investment are badly needed. Yet critics say that the state has signed away far too much land (5,000ha); that watercourses are being blocked by logs and that riverbanks are being eroded as the agreed buffer strips of 40m are not being respected; that the environmental impact study was flawed; that loss or shifts in birdlife is already noticeable; and that workers are employed on precarious contracts with no security. At the centre of Agripalma's operations, around Porto Alegre, workers have protested against the company's bulldozer tactics, with little respect for the local community. Currently operations are continuing at a slower pace as Agripalma is being challenged in the courts, while the Santomean state is under contractual pressure to find land to provide land to Agripalma. The latest news is that in 2013 conservationists obtained a court order forcing Agripalma to respect certain protected zones.

Príncipe presents a more positive picture. The island's UNESCO Biosphere status and its strong pursuit of ecotourism with the current big South African player, HBD, supported by the regional government, provides some protection. Already, turtle meat is illegal, as is parrot-trapping, and the oil palms have not been allowed to make inroads here.

beaches close to the capital. More effort is now being made to clean up the streets, but there is no real understanding of environmental issues and their link with tourism. Despite well-meaning painted signs sponsored by local environment agencies, beer and soft-drink bottles are often left on the beach. I know of only one established recycling scheme, involving liquor bottles, though ecotourism venture HBD have launched an initiative to recycle plastic bottles. As access to sanitary installations is limited, many locals defecate in the *mato*, the forest, or on the beach.

HISTORY

The human history of São Tomé and Príncipe probably begins on **21 December 1470,** (the exact year being uncertain) when the Portuguese seafarers Pedro Escobar and João de Santarém supposedly discovered the island they were to call São Tomé after the feast day of Saint Thomas (in the official saints' calendar, the day has since been moved to 3 July). A replica of the *padrão* stone pillar that marked all Portugal's territories still stands above the beach where Escobar and de Santarém landed, and the men themselves are commemorated by over-life-size limestone statues outside the National Museum in São Tomé.

On 17 January the following year, Escobar and de Santarém discovered a smaller island further north, which they called Santo Antão, after that day's saint. There has been a heated debate on whether the archipelago was populated before the Portuguese arrived. Given the proximity to the West African coastline, it is conceivable that there may have been settlers coming over by boat, and the issue is of great importance to nationalists seeking to establish a Santomean identity independent from the Portuguese settlers. However, to date, no archaeological evidence has been found to prove that early African settlers overcame the considerable navigational challenge, and the scientific consensus today is that the islands were indeed virgin territory when the Portuguese arrived. São Tomé's first administrator, João de Paiva, started to populate the island when he took office in 1485, undeterred by the first settlers in the northwest succumbing to disease. **Sugarcane** was introduced in 1493 with the arrival of Álvaro da Caminha, starting the 'sugarcane cycle'. Príncipe began to be settled in 1500. As early as 1515–17, the Portuguese king, Dom Manuel I, gave the slave men and women of the first settlers, and their common children, their freedom, manumitting them by the *Carta de Alforria*; this also freed their mixed-race (*mestiço*) children. *Alforria* is where the name *forro* comes from, used for the majority creoles on São Tomé island and also the national creole, spoken by some 85% of *Santomense*. This is the source of the *forros'* feeling of superiority, as descendants of free Africans.

In the 15th and 16th centuries, the islands exported sugarcane and became a major **trading post** of the **transatlantic slave trade;** production started around 1510. In 1515, the slave women and mulatto children of the Portuguese settlers were freed, and two years later the first male slaves, who had come to the islands with the Portuguese, were freed too. But there were occasional revolts against the colonialisers, starting in 1517. In 1553, Yon Gato, a blind planter, led a raid against the colonial powers with a group of slaves; today, one of the main squares in São Tomé town bears his name. Legend has it that around this time a ship bearing Angolan slaves was shipwrecked on Sete Pedras, a small group of tall sharp rocks some 5km off the southeastern coast. This gave rise to the widely propagated misconception that those who managed to swim ashore founded the Angolares community along the southeastern coast, around what is today the town of São João dos Angolares. Today, 90% of the fishermen are Angolares, and they have their own language and culture. What is known is that maroons, or runaway slaves, escaped to the deep rainforest twhere these *fujões* had formed settlements called *macambos*, and descended on the town of São João dos Angolares and plantations to take chicken, goats and bananas – and women. In 1585 they burnt down part of the city of São Tomé.

In **1595**, the leader of the most successful slave uprising, Amador, was captured, hung and quartered by the Portuguese. Today, **Rei Amador** is celebrated as a hero of the national struggle and commemorated by a fictitious likeness on all dobra banknotes, by a large bust outside the Historical Archive in São Tomé town and by a commemorative day on 4 January. From the turn of the 17th century, the colony was further weakened by pirate and corsair raids, starting in 1599, when São Tomé town was sacked by a Dutch fleet. But mainly, the superior quality of Brazilian sugar rang in the end of the Santomean sugar cycle. This marked the beginning of two centuries of decline on the islands, during which the people sustained themselves with the cultivation of corn, manioc, yams, vegetables, citrus fruit and sugarcane spirit. In 1641, the Dutch came back, conquered São Tomé, razed over 70 sugar mills and occupied the island for more than seven years. In 1709, São Tomé was attacked by the French. Yielding a much inferior product, sugarcane cultivation was moved across to the better soil and more stable political conditions of Portuguese's largest colony, Brazil. Due to ongoing troubles and raids, the island's capital was transferred from São Tomé to Santo António on Príncipe in 1753. It was nearly a hundred years (1852) before the capital was transferred back to São Tomé. Thus it was to the island of Príncipe that João Baptista da Silva introduced coffee (see box, page 147) from Brazil in 1787. And the smaller island was also the first to see the crop that was to make São Tomé's name: cocoa (see box, pages 20–1). The introduction of these cash crops marked the **second colonisation** of the islands by the Portuguese.

The first wave of settlement had been sustained by convicts, as in the face of rampant malaria, the Portuguese king found it difficult to find settlers willing to colonise these faraway islands. In the second half of the 19th century, however, the Portuguese started to gradually dispossess the *forros*, through land purchases, but also fraud. By the end of the 19th century, 90% of the land was in the hands of Portuguese planters. The labour-intensive cocoa and coffee plantations needed vast numbers of workers, provided by slave labour from the African mainland. After the **abolition of slavery** in Portugal's African colonies in **1869**, tens of thousands of contract workers, *serviçais* ('servants'), mainly from Angola, and later Cape Verde and Mozambique, and indentured labourers continued to cultivate the monocrops, often in conditions virtually indistinguishable from slavery. Workers were rounded up, given a contract they could not read, had their documents taken and promised a return passage that after years of hard labour would then not materialise, as workers had to pay for their own food and lodgings. In the context of slavery (and the later contract work, in many respects different only in name), few of the original African traditions – dances, rituals, songs, stories – of the people forcibly brought to the islands survived intact, but were forged into a new **creole nation**, a cultural blend of the majority *forros*, traditionally occupying the higher positions in society, and the *serviçais* contract labourers and their descendants born on the islands, called *tongas*. Integration of the *contratados*, living separately from the *forros* on the plantations, only started after 1975. One of the cultural legacies slavery has left in Santomean society is a preference for people to work for themselves, to their own timetable, an attitude which still affects the development of a modern work ethic.

Despite the country's geographic isolation, in the wake of burgeoning **independence movements** across colonial Africa, Santomeans, politicians and students had started

1

On São Tomé and Príncipe, the larger plantation estates (*roças*), set up by the Portuguese for the production of cocoa and coffee, were their own self-contained, self-sufficient universes, operating largely outside the colonial administration's remit. The verb *roçar* in Portuguese means to clear land of forest, and the cleared land would stretch up the hill from the sea, to allow for the high altitude needed for arabica coffee. There would be the house of the administrator (*casa do patrão/administrador*), the quarters for administration and book-keeping, coffee and cocoa driers (*secadores*), the workers' quarters (*sanzalas*), a workshop and a nursery. The larger roças had beautiful hospitals; at one point there were over 20 on the islands. A large plantation, such as Água Izé or Rio do Ouro (now Agostinho Neto), would have had 20–30 satellites (*dependências*), connected by a network of railways which transported the beans to town. Transport into town was mainly effected by boat. From there, they would be shipped to Lisbon – where many plantation owners lived as absentee landlords. Many beaches still have the sad remnants of a pier sticking out to sea, and in the grounds of the plantations themselves railway tracks are sometimes just visible still under the grass or forest growth.

Around the turn of the 20th century, there were some 800 plantations on the islands. The *serviçais* from Cape Verde, Angola and Mozambique would work a six-day week; breaking the monotony only with the songs, dances and traditions of their homelands. With independence in 1975, the world of the roças changed forever. The 2,000 or so Portuguese residents left, in fear of reprisals, taking with them the know-how to run the plantations. On 30 September 1975, some 200 plantations were nationalised, to great popular enthusiasm. However, with lack of investment, know-how and experience, production dipped drastically and the buildings and facilities fell into disrepair. Plantations were regrouped into *empresas* but, in the face of volatile world market prices and internal corruption, they could not compete with

to organise resistance, centring their efforts in nearby Gabon. The 1953 **Massacre of Batepá** on 3 February marked a turning point in the islands' colonial history and would in the 1960s be claimed to represent the birth of Santomean nationalism.

Against the background of the ongoing **labour problem on the plantations** under the new colonial governor (1945–53), Carlos Gorgulho, whose prestige rested on logistical construction and other projects (airports, a stadium, cinema) achieved using forced labour, rumours that *forros* would be conscripted by force to work on the plantations led to protests. On 3 February, in Batepá, just north of Trindade (a stronghold of *forro* nationalism), an officer was killed with a machete. During the repression that followed, *forros* were rounded up (some burnt alive trying to hide in a cocoa drier), and many taken to a forced labour camp at Fernão Dias. Prominent *forros* such as Salustino Graça and sympathetic white planters were deported to Príncipe. Physical and psychological torture was used, with the notorious former prisoner Zé Mulato, from the Ponta Figo plantation, the most feared. In one of the most notorious incidents, 46 people were crammed into a cell intended to hold only 10, with only 18 surviving the night. It remains unknown how many died in total; the often-cited figure of 1,032 deaths is taken to be largely symbolic as the last two digits reference the day and month of the beginning of the massacre: 3/2/1953. A young teacher, Alda Graça Espírito Santo (see page 39), took notes from survivors – and went on to become one of the country's foremost politicians and poets. Indirectly, the Massacre of Batepá led to the formation of the cheap cocoa from other producing countries, such as the Ivory Coast. Land reform in the 1990s dissolved nearly all large plantations, distributing the land amongst small farmers; this spelt the definitive end of the plantation economy on STP. Today, most roças belong to the state, but are leased out to private individuals or consortia for business ventures. The majority seem slightly forlorn, as most buildings are dilapidated, not connected to the national grid, and few people are in work. All operate small-scale coffee production for private consumption. Agostinho Neto is maybe the most impressive; Água Izé is great for photography. Monte Café used to be the biggest producer of coffee, a role now taken on by Nova Moca.

A visit to any small plantation, off the beaten track in particular, gives a fascinating insight into a bygone era, much present still in the Portuguese psyche, and a good opportunity to glimpse the legacy of colonialism, not to mention wonderful photographic opportunities: ferns and palm trees reclaiming the land, slowly obliterating the traces of human intervention. The plantations are usually open to visit, though the owner's house is sometimes guarded; there is no system of guided tours locally. Arranged tours focus mainly on Agostinho Neto and Água Izé but, if you are visiting on your own, informal guides are easy to come by and can show you around. On a tour, it can feel slightly exploitative to visit for five minutes, crowded in by curious children demanding sweets or a little money, take pictures and zoom off again, as the locals do not gain anything from living on a tourist attraction. So if you have the chance, wander around and buy a drink or biscuits from one of the shops, or some street food. The larger plantations often also have a *cantina* or *loja* where you can try the local food. If you don't mind roughing it a bit, it is always worth asking whether it is possible to stay the night. In a smaller plantation, ask for the community leader, *responsável*. On São Tomé, plantations such as São João, Bombaim and Monteforte have successfully been turned over to rural tourism, a trend starting in Príncipe too.

CLSTP (Comité de Libertação de São Tomé and Príncipe) in 1960, the forerunner of the MLSTP (Movimento de Libertação de São Tomé and Príncipe) liberation party, recognised by the UN and the Organisation of African Unity. (Other pro-independence parties such as PAIGC and MPLA had been founded in 1956.) Today still, the day is commemorated every year by youth marches, speeches and debates in the media ruminate on the significance and the legacy of 1953.

DECOLONISATION Portugal has the distinction of being the first colonial world power and the last to release its colonies into independence. In the Portuguese **Estado Novo** ('new state'), under the dictatorship of António Oliveira Salazar (1932–68) and Marcello Caetano (1968–74), the colonies were vital to Portugal's existence and role on the international stage, a small country hemmed in by Spain on one side, and the Atlantic Ocean on the other. The church saw its role as the civilising arm of the Portuguese nation. In the late 1960s, the socialist and anti-colonialist Mário Soares was exiled to São Tomé for several months; already in custody, he was called in and told to pack his bags as he was leaving for São Tomé the next day. Once on the island, he was constantly followed around its pot-holed roads by 22 agents of the Portuguese secret police, PIDE, who had started operating on the island in 1953 to investigate the causes of the Massacre of Batepá and who were trying to isolate any dangerous subversives from the population and the country's independence movement, which at that time was coordinated by exiled leader Miguel Trovoada, as Manuel Pinto da Costa was studying in East Germany at the time. When Salazar was replaced by Marcello Caetano in September 1968 (following a brain haemorrhage), Soares was allowed to leave in November. In 1972, Pinto da Costa, freshly returned from East Berlin with a PhD in economics, was elected general secretary of the MLSTP in Santa Isabel (Malabo).

After the fall of the dictatorship on 25 April 1974 in the army-led **Carnation Revolution**, Soares went on to become prime minister (1976–78 and 1983–85) and president (1986–96) of the new democracy. Decolonisation was triggered by the bloodless coup in Portugal; at that point, colonial wars (from 1961) in Angola, Guinea-Bissau and Mozambique had already cost thousands of lives.

CURSE OF THE COCOA?

Few people know that São Tomé and Príncipe was the first African country to cultivate cocoa. Cocoa was first introduced from the Lower Amazon Basin to Príncipe (the Simaló plantation) in 1820, while Brazil was fighting its war of independence, by the Brazilian chief-captain João Baptista Silva (d1837; his bones are kept in a wooden box in the National Museum in São Tomé). Over the following 150 years, the monoculture of cocoa on the 'Chocolate Islands' has been more of a curse than a blessing, but given the trend towards gourmet and single-estate chocolate, together with the possibilities of rural tourism, cocoa could be turned to good use by the archipelago's tourism industry. I met a French couple on honeymoon who were inspired to travel to São Tomé by a chocolate wrapper!

Cocoa, *Theobroma cacao*, originates in the Americas and only grows in a very limited geographical zone: around ten degrees to the north and south of the Equator. The 'food of the Gods' performs best at an altitude of up to 700m.

Today, a third of the islands is covered in cocoa trees, *cacaoeiros*. The cocoa and coffee trees are of a similar height and if you can't see whether they have pods or berries, you can easily distinguish them by their leaves: those of the coffee tree are a shiny dark green, while those of the cocoa tree are various colours. Despite the legend that cocoa was initially only introduced into the country as a decorative plant, João Baptista Silva Lagos introduced the plant purposefully as a cash crop. The story of cocoa cultivation in São Tomé and Príncipe starts in Príncipe, and cocoa took 30 years to reach the bigger island, when the João Maria de Sousa e Almeida (d1869), born on Príncipe of Brazilian parents, started cultivating cocoa at the Água Izé plantation in 1852; he was the first mixed-race baron of any Portuguese colony. Both coffee and cocoa need shade and for this, fast-growing flame trees were imported from South America, *erythrinas* with beautiful orange flowers that are now visible everywhere around the plantations.

With the **abolition of slavery** in 1761 in Portugal, the problem of labour rose ever more urgently. In the early 20th century, the islands were one of the top cocoa producers in the world, but persistent reports of contract workers being employed in conditions of effective slavery were beginning to impact on the colony. In 1908, William Cadbury himself came over to São Tomé to investigate. Despite his Quaker faith and humanitarian concern, he did not have much regard for labour in Portuguese west Africa, but Henry Nevinson's book, *Modern Slavery*, resulted in a **boycott** of Santomean cocoa in 1909 by British and German chocolate producers – Cadbury Brothers in Bournville, Birmingham, Rowntree in Bristol, and Stollwerck in Cologne, Germany. Britain's motives were maybe not completely altruistic, as cocoa from São Tomé was in direct competition with the cocoa from their own

On 5 September 1974, a demonstration in São Tomé and Príncipe demanded independence for the archipelago; only two deaths occurred and these were unrelated to the demonstration. Whilst unrest had started much earlier, immediately after the Carnation Revolution, the Treaty of Algiers was signed between the Portuguese government and the representatives of the MLSTP, accepted by the UN as the sole representatives of the Santomean people. The treaty paved the way for **independence**, proclaimed on 12 July 1975. Don't be surprised, however, if some of the older Santomeans will tell you that things were *much* better during colonial times: there was electricity, there was drinking water, there were proper bus services, and less poverty and disease.

colony, the Gold Coast, today's Ghana. The story of the colonial rivalry between Portugal and Britain is told in fictionalised form in Miguel Sousa Tavares' romance *Equador* (see page 43).

Today, the islands' most famous cocoa comes from **Príncipe** (see page 202). The pods, sprouting directly from the purplish-grey trunk in a range of beautiful colours – burgundy, orange, green, yellow and red – are harvested using a curved knife on a long pole. The pods are opened with a machete, to extract the around 40 fatty seeds (beans) encased in a fresh white acidic-sweet pulp. Children on the plantations love to suck this; try it, it is delicious. A good breaker can open up to 500 pods an hour. Then, the most important part of the process begins: fermentation. The beans, still covered by the pulp, have to be moved regularly in their wooden crates for about six days while the juice drains away ('sweating'). Then, the beans are spread out on long *secadores*, solar drying racks, protected from the rain by plastic covers and regularly moved using little rakes. Then the tiny stem is removed, by hand. To make one pound of chocolate, some 400 beans are needed.

On today's markets, cocoa fetches around US$3,000 per ton, although annual production has fallen from 35,000 tons in the early 20th century to less than 3,000 tons in 2013. More than half of Santomean cocoa is bought by the Dutch. The plantation workers themselves could never afford to buy the chocolate, and have probably never tasted it either, let alone the chocolate bars in the shops. There are some organic cocoa plantations in the north, and Fairtrade ventures have started. The only producer actually making chocolate on the islands is the Italian Claudio Corallo, but with the trend towards vintage chocolate, 'São Tomé' chocolate bars are beginning to appear in shops all over the world. There are more co-operatives appearing, organic agriculture (though nobody has the money to spray anyway, it seems) and even Fairtrade initiatives are on the rise. The Amelonado, a subspecies of Forastero, is still the most widely grown variety. Worldwide demand for chocolate is continually growing, and the country is slowly modernising its production, in a bid to boost exports. Solar driers are replacing firewood-driven ones, with gains for the environment – it might seem hard to believe but São Tome and Príncipe (STP) is exposed to deforestation. The Swiss company **Satocão** (*www.satocao.com*), with headquarters in the capital and an operational HQ near Guadalupe, has started a large-scale operation of recultivating abandoned cocoa plantations and safeguarding varieties, they also provide social security and health care for their workers. (A tourist side to operations might happen in the future, currently you can't visit.)

Some say that STP (the islands' initials) stands for *Somos Todos Primos* ('we are all cousins'), reflecting the family-style dynamics of a small-island population, and Santomean politics are indeed based around prominent people, clientelism and kinship rather than substantial issues, and supposedly a few high-profile *forro* families continue to form the local elite. This cosy – or claustrophobic, if you like – situation has repercussions for the islands' society, politics, economy, judiciary and the media.

When the **Democratic Republic of São Tomé and Príncipe** was founded on **12 July 1975**, with independence from Portugal, the country became a one-party state led by the liberation party MLSTP, with **Manuel Pinto da Costa** (1937–) its first president and **Miguel Trovoada** (1936–) its first prime minister. Da Costa and Trovoada were leading a nationalised (and, from 1979 onwards, centrally planned) economy, with its own secret service and repression of dissent. Marxist–Leninist doctrines and jargon flourished. The **flag** – two black stars on a horizontal three-band of green-yellow-green and a red isosceles triangle on the left echoes the pan-African colours of Ethiopia.

The country's **motto** *Unidade – Disciplina – Trabalho* ('Unity – Discipline – Work') features on the Santomean **coat of arms**: a palm tree topped by a blue star and flanked by a black kite to the left, representing São Tomé, and a grey parrot to the right, representing Príncipe. However, despite the backing of aid from fellow socialist states such as the Soviet Union, Cuba, neighbouring Angola and East Germany, São Tomé and Príncipe's economy struggled from the start. Soon, against the background of collapsing cocoa prices on the world markets, low productivity, mismanagement and internal **power struggles**, the party leadership became increasingly dogmatic and repressive, cutting off the island state even more from the outside world. Political change started slowly as early as 1983–84, but the island's isolation became untenable with the advent of *perestroika* in Gorbachev's Soviet Union in the late 1980s, and the crumbling of old alliances. Seeing its economic fortunes wane with the downward course of its socialist allies, the party engaged in dialogue and change to attract Western donors, and in 1990 São Tomé and Príncipe became a **multi-party democracy**, in a peaceful transition – one of the first countries in Africa to do so! In the same year, in the first, largely free and fair, multi-party elections, the Santomeans provided the opposition Partido de Convergência Democrática (PCD) with an absolute majority, while in the presidential elections they elected the sole candidate **Miguel Trovoada president**. However, the PCD government was dismissed after only three years in office. With the exception of a couple of years, the former ruling sole party, now called MLSTP/PSD (Partido Social Democrático), was to hold on to this post for the next two decades. Elected for five years, for a maximum of two terms, the president has a predominately representative role in Santomean politics, while according to the semi-presidential constitution the prime minister is head of government. In the first **local elections** in December 1992, the MLSTP/PSD took six out of seven districts. Thereafter, local elections were held only irregularly, in 2006 and 2010. In 1995, the year that Príncipe (Pagué) was given self-government, the march of democracy was briefly marred by a short-lived and bloodless **military coup**.

At the **2001 presidential elections**, wealthy businessman Fradique de Menezes was elected president, beating the MLSTP/PSD's Manuel Pinto da Costa, then party leader and former head of state (1975–91). Another military coup in 2003 was again short-lived – in São Tomé, even the coups are *leve-leve* – and did not involve any bloodshed: when President Fradique de Menezes was in a conference in Nigeria, members of the military seized their opportunity. In protest at what they saw as a fake 'democracy' built on vote-buying, amid deteriorating living conditions for both the general population and the army (at that point, the military had not been paid for months), Alércio Costa and Major Fernando Pereira led half of the

PRESIDENT MANUEL PINTO DA COSTA

After two failed attempts in 1996 and 2001 when he lost the presidential elections against Miguel Trovoada and Fradique de Menezes respectively, in 2011 Manuel Pinto da Costa, the country's first president during the socialist one-party state (1975–91) was elected president as an independent candidate after defeating in the run-off Evaristo Carvalho, the candidate of the ADI, with 52.9% against 47.1% of the votes.

Manuel Pinto da Costa was born in 1937 in São Tomé town to Manuel do Espírito Santo Costa and Maria do Sacramento Pinto. His parents and the parents of Miguel Trovoada, his erstwhile friend and later political rival, were close friends. Together with Trovoada he went to primary school in São Tomé, from 1944 to 1948. Thereafter the two friends attended consecutively the seminary in Luanda and grammar school in Lisbon, since at the time there was no secondary education in São Tomé. In 1961 Pinto da Costa left Portugal for East Germany, where he studied economics until 1971 when he earned his doctorate at the Hochschule für Ökonomie in East Berlin. Subsequently, he went to Santa Isabel (now Malabo), the capital of Equatorial Guinea, where he was one of the nine Santomean nationalists who created the Liberation Movement of São Tome and Príncipe (MLSTP) in July 1972. At this meeting, he was chosen Secretary General of the MLSTP. When São Tomé and Príncipe were declared independent on 12 July 1975, Pinto da Costa became president, while Trovoada became prime minister. Soon both leaders became involved in internal power struggles within the socialist one-party state. Finally, in 1979 Trovoada was detained without charge or trial for almost two years. At that point Pinto da Costa had reached the peak of his personal power, simultaneously head of state, head of government, party leader and army chief. However, economic problems forced his regime to gradually liberalise the economy and society from 1985 onwards. Eventually his regime approved the transition to multi-party democracy and, in 1990, the former socialist MLSTP was transformed into the liberal MLSTP/PSD, and Pinto da Costa resigned as party leader.

Following the withdrawal of Pinto da Costa's candidacy to avoid electoral defeat, in March 1991 Miguel Trovoada, who had returned from exile in France, was elected unopposed as president. In 1998 Pinto da Costa returned as leader of the MLSTP/PSD, a position he held until 2005 when he retired from active politics. However, in 2011, 20 years after his departure from presidential office, he declared his decision to run again for the presidency and won. Although Pinto da Costa had been a dictator with far-reaching powers during the socialist one-party state, within the current semi-presidential system he is little more than a representative figurehead. However, in December 2012, he dismissed then Prime Minister Patrice Trovoada – son of Miguel Trovoada – following the approval of a censure motion, the latter accused Pinto da Costa of having dismissed his government by a parliamentary coup d'état.

1

country's 400 soldiers, plus over a dozen former mercenaries, to detain government ministers in the barracks. The coup was universally condemned, and with external mediation, after a week, order was restored. The Nigerian president Olusugun Obasanjo accompanied President de Menezes on his way back to show support. However, the issue of oil (see box, pages 28–9) and the distribution of potentially big revenues, was already looming large in the background.

At the legislative elections in March 2006, the MDFM/PCD (Movimento Democrático Força da Mudança/Partido de Convergência Democrática), a two-party alliance won 23 of the 55 seats in the National Assembly, beating the fathers of Santomean independence and former communists of the MLSTP/PSD. This temporarily ended the awkward cohabitation situation with the MLSTP/PSD – at that point de Menezes's presidency had been plagued by conflicts with six different governments for five years.

The **presidential elections** of July 2006 saw Fradique de Menezes re-elected president, winning around 60% of the vote. The candidate for ADI (Acção Democrática Independente, Independent Democratic Action), businessman Patrice Trovoada (b1962), son of former president Miguel Trovoada, but a controversial figure, tainted by accusations of illegal arms trading and other shady deals, challenged Fradique de Menezes for the presidency and won 38% of the vote. By Santomean standards, the 65% turnout was not high.

In 2006 Fradique's party, MDFM, with its Secretary General, Tomé Vera Cruz, for the first time provided the country's new **prime minister.** Vera Cruz's training as an electrical engineer should have come in handy in solving the ongoing energy crisis in the country, but 2007, in the words of President Fradique de Menezes, turned out to be one of the 'most difficult' years for the young nation in recent history, despite the pardon of the country's debt (see pages 27 and 30) and successes in combating malaria. In July 2007, STP was in the news again for the wrong reasons: an elite police unit, Angolan-trained 'ninjas', protesting for not having received a promised bonus pay, seized the police headquarters, taking the police commander and other officers hostage, but releasing them shortly afterwards.

Political instability remains one of the constants of Santomean public life, as do liberally spread rumours and mutually traded accusations of corruption. When in early 2008, parliament refused to approve the annual budget (*orçamento*), the government was brought down. Amidst **popular discontent** following shortages of staple foods such as rice, sugar and cooking oil, as well as spiralling energy costs, Prime Minister Vera Cruz stepped down, accusing the opposition of making the country 'ingovernable' at an important juncture in its development, on the cusp of the awaited oil flow. At this point, for example, the ANP (Agência Nacional de Petróleo), the body governing the national oil resources, had been without leadership for months and there was a threatening conflict between the World Bank and the government about changes to the oil revenue laws. ADI's Patrice Trovoada assumed the post of prime minister of the country's 12th constitutional government in February 2008, illustrating yet again the circular nature of Santomean politics. (In addition, there had been two governments of 'presidential initiative' in 1994 and 2001 respectively.) By June 2008, however, the opposition led by Rafael Branco headed a new government, as after only three months a vote of no confidence supported by the PCD toppled Trovoada's government, and formed a coalition with the MDFM and the PCD. In August 2010 Patrice Trovoada again took office as prime minister after his ADI party had obtained a majority of 26 seats in the legislative election. However, in November 2012, the majority of MLSTP/PSD, PCD and MDFM in parliament accused Trovoada of mismanagement and dismissed his minority government by a censure motion. In

December, the lawyer Gabriel Costa, who does not belong to any of the three parties, became prime minister of a coalition government of MLSTP/PSD, PCD and MDFM. If you should be on the islands during one of these periodic political crises, you will notice that the vast majority of the population remains unfazed by developments, life continuing much the same as before. Due to financial problems, local elections due in 2013 were postponed to 2014, when legislative elections will be held too.

Elections are, of course, the one time when politicians do like to engage the population. São Tomé and Príncipe has an endemic culture of political clientelism and vote-buying. While the ballot is secret and, despite a few minor irregularities, elections are generally considered free and fair, the practice of *banho* ('bath'), giving presents and cash for votes, is deeply engrained. Around election time, all of a sudden, a fleet of brand-new motor bikes will appear on the streets, a reward for successfully mobilising votes. There is also a dispiriting history of development aid being channelled into personal pockets. In 1996, for instance, 18 new Renault cars for the new MLSTP/PSD/ADI government turned out to have been paid for by the World Bank's structural adjustment credit of over US$3 million, at a time when there was no money to fix the generators and sort out the constant energy provision problems of many of the capital's neighbourhoods. More than ten years later, a local deputy complained to me that foreign donors do not supervise how the money is spent. In 2004, the **corruption scandal** around the **GGA** (Gabinete de Gestão de Ajudas) food aid agency brought down Prime Minister Maria das Neves. In 2009, the corruption-monitoring organization Transparency International (TI) placed São Tomé and Príncipe at joint position 111 out of 180 evaluated countries, the first time the country was ranked. Ministers accused of corruption are often given prestigious postings abroad, or return to government a bit later down the line, as happened during Vera Cruz's cabinet reshuffle in late 2007. As few politicians and public servants are put on trial for corruption, let alone convicted, a sense of general impunity prevails. Despite the absence of significant changes, in 2012 TI improved the country's position to rank 42 out of 176 countries.

On the diplomatic level, São Tomé and Príncipe joined the United Nations shortly after independence and the country is a member state of **PALOPS** (Países Africanos de Lingua Oficial Portuguesa), countries with Portuguese as the official language. With the foundation of **CPLP** (Comunidade dos Povos de Lingua Portuguesa) in 1996, tiny São Tomé and Príncipe joined Angola, Brazil, Cape Verde, Guinea-Bissau and Mozambique in a community of more than 200 million Portuguese-speaking people, which now also includes Timor-Leste, which became independent in 2002. In terms of development, Cape Verde, the island state further north along the African west coast is seen as the model to follow. The country of origin of thousands of contract labourers who were condemned to stay on at independence rather than return to their drought-stricken home is now a successful tourist destination. Portugal remains an important partner in commerce, aid and cultural co-operation. Among the Gulf of Guinea states, Angola has traditionally always been a close ally in terms of financial, logistical and military assistance, but since the emergence of the joint oil exploration with Nigeria, the most populous country in Africa has been successfully vying for influence, promising infrastructural, social and cultural investments. In recent years São Tomé has also strengthened ties with neighbouring Equatorial Guinea. Taiwan has been an important partner since 1997, when Miguel Trovoada swapped diplomatic allegiance to Beijing for Taipei. These days, Taiwan is only recognised by 22 countries worldwide (of which three are in Africa), other small states such as Gambia having severed diplomatic relations in 2013, mirroring the People's Republic of China's growing influence in the region.

1

The overall **human rights** situation in the country is good. However, the judiciary suffers from long delays in sentencing; prisoners often remain in jail without judgement. People's faith in the justice and political system has been eroded amongst accusations and counter-accusations of the 'blue bag', *saco azul*, of corruption. There are occasional protests and demonstrations in the streets of the capital. And, in a sign of the times, the presence of several Facebook groups dedicated to reform in STP reflects the discontent. While the police service is currently being reformed, impunity is a problem many people have commented on to me. In terms of diplomacy, **relations with the US** are excellent: Voice of America radio has transmitted since the early 1990s, and joint military exercises in the Gulf of Guinea (a strategic zone due to its oil wealth) have been conducted for years. In 2006 the US installed a radar system to monitor the territorial waters, and in recent years visits by US Navy vessels have become frequent. In the near-absence of US tourists – apart from day visitors on cruise ships and researchers – the reinstatement of a permanent ambassador in New York (also accredited in Washington DC) seems to herald a renewed political will for a more dynamic co-operation.

ECONOMY

São Tomé and Príncipe's main cash crop for export is still **cocoa**, bringing in US$5 million a year. Most of the cocoa is exported to Portugal, from where is is distributed to France, amongst other countries. Long gone are the days when the islands were the world's leading cocoa producer, but an increase in **co-operative** structures and increased demand for gourmet, organic, single-estate and Fairtrade chocolate is countering the low world market prices for cocoa. Most families live by subsistence farming, bringing in the produce from their yard (*quintal*) to market. As there is not much diversity, most yield the same crops (bananas, papayas, tomatoes, limes, cocoyam, etc), and competition is intense. There are some 50 small and medium-sized enterprises, plus several hundred micro-enterprises, such as restaurants, tailors, shoemakers and carpenters. Micro-credit facilities are still scarce. **Privatisation** since the early 1990s has been slow, hampered by inefficiency, bureaucracy and political meddling. In the fishing industry, a sector with potential growth, attempts are being made to install refridgeration and introduce sanitised handling conditions – most fish today is preserved by salting and drying. Palm oil production is starting up, but not without controversy. **Diversification** is the buzzword, encouraged by NGOs (non-government organisations) and often carried out by Portuguese investors. In the face of logistical challenges, **tourism** is slow to grow, though there are some encouraging sustainable and community-oriented ventures alongside major investments by the Portuguese Pestana Group amongst others.

São Tomé and Príncipe is a member of the Economic Community of Central African States (ECCAS), which is the focus of an increasing number of regional security initiatives. The islands have been an active player in ECCAS's Zone D maritime security exercises, and a participant in the US Navy's Africa Partnership Station ship visits to Gulf of Guinea countries.

US exports to São Tomé and Príncipe include vehicles, electrical machinery, aircraft, and iron and steel products. São Tomé and Príncipe is eligible for preferential trade benefits under the African Growth and Opportunity Act. Despite GDP growth of about 4% a year, supported by tourism and light construction, as of 2012 it possessed one of the world's smallest national economies, with a GDP of US$264 million. Debt, meanwhile, has soared once more to unsustainable levels.

It would be a risky strategy for Santomeans to pin their hopes exclusively on *petróleo*, **oil** (see box, pages 28–9).

DEVELOPMENT In the Human Development Index 2013, São Tomé and Príncipe came in at number 144, out of 185 states surveyed, which means it has fallen since the previous edition. Life expectancy now stands at nearly 65 years, 62 for men and 69 for women. For the first time since censuses have been conducted, there are more men than women. Statistics paint a brighter picture than for many other African countries (over the past few years the IMF has recorded economic growth), but since independence the economy and social indicators have gone down. The country is very rich in fresh water but, due to degraded reservoirs and pipes, some 20% of the population still have no access to clean drinking water, and 85% still lack access to sanitation facilities such as latrines, meaning that, effectively, most defecate in the open air, with dire consequences for public health. Around 1,000 under-fives die each year of infectious diseases like bacterial diarrhoea, typhoid fever and malaria, the biggest killer, though the mortality rate for children under five has come down to 89 per 1,000, due in part to the successful campaign financed by Taiwan. Tuberculosis is still a concern, despite much public health advertising of vaccination campaigns due in part to the successful campaign financed by Taiwan. The cholera epidemic of 2005–6, the first outbreak of cholera for 15 years, caused by dilapidated pipes on a privatised plantation, resulted in three deaths. Whilst there is no hunger, due to the richness of the land, there is very real poverty, and the children with protruding bellies you see everywhere illustrate the lack of balanced nutrition. Over half of the population lives on less than US$1 per day, the official measure of poverty. When STP became a multi-party democracy in 1991, the percentage of the population living in poverty stood at around 35%; there was a steep rise in the first decade of the new millennium, to about 65%, despite an annual GDP growth of some 4%. Meanwhile, the population is growing at an annual rate of about 2%, standing currently at around 190,000 and projected to be 250,000 by 2030. Pressure on resources is growing, as more and more Santomeans leave the impoverished plantations for the capital, which is already home to a quarter of the population. Unemployment, whilst difficult to measure, probably runs at about 50%, the 2012 census features a high percentage of 'inactivity' alongside 'unemployment' of some 30%. Over the years, the cost of living keeps going up – the high rates for water and an unreliable electricity service infuriating the locals – as do crime rates. The government is often perceived as talking a lot and not doing much. A Santomean woman explained the system using the, originally Mozambican, image of *cabritismo*: the *cabra*, goat, of the people is tied to the stack in the middle by a short cord and can only graze what it can reach, whereas the government, grazing on a long cord, is free to take all it likes.

São Tomé and Príncipe receives one of the highest amounts of **aid** per capita in the world, and in 2013 about 90% of the national budget was made up of external aid (US$150 million). Dozens of NGOs are said to operate on these small islands; you'll see many jeeps with 'Cooperação Japonesa' or school buses 'Donated by the Republic of China (Taiwan)' rumbling around the pot-holed streets, and highly paid consultants tapping into their laptops, working on project evaluations and audits in the country's few air-conditioned spaces. Unfortunately, projects are often not coordinated well amongst the agencies.

In 2007, after granting partial debt relief over the years and encouraging the implementation of a tax reform and combat corruption, the World Monetary Fund and World Bank pardoned the vast majority of São Tomé and Príncipe's debt of US$327million under the **Highly Indebted Poor Countries** (HIPC) initiative.

Gerhard Seibert, researcher at the CEI/ISCTE-IUL, Lisbon

Speculations about onshore oil resources in the archipelago already existed in colonial times. However, as exploration drillings on São Tomé island in 1989 were negative, it was presumed that oil could only exist offshore, close to the already discovered offshore oil reserves of Nigeria and Equatorial Guinea. Motivated by this assumption, the small US company Environmental Remediation Holding Corporation (ERHC) became the first to invest in the country's oil development.

The story of oil in STP started in 1997 when the country signed its first oil agreement with ERHC. The company helped the local government to delineate its 320km Exclusive Economic Zone (EEZ) and claim its maritime boundaries. In 1998 the country signed a second agreement with Mobil (now ExxonMobil) on the execution of seismic surveys. Plagued by financial problems, ERHC was not in a position to meet its contractual obligations, so in 1999, the country's government rescinded the contract. In turn, ERHC lodged a request for arbitration at the International Chamber of Commerce in Paris. The problem was only solved when, in early 2001, ERHC was taken over by Chrome Energy Corporation, owned by the Nigerian businessman Emeka Offor. In exchange for a new agreement with ERHC, the company's new owner withdrew the request for arbitration. Around the same time the Norwegian Petroleum Geo-Services (PGS) signed an agreement on seismic surveys with the government.

Aware of the importance of an internationally recognised EEZ, São Tomé and Príncipe had signed bilateral agreements on the delineation of its maritime borders with Equatorial Guinea (1999) and Gabon (2001). However, sea border negotiations with Nigeria failed, because Abuja refused to accept a boundary based on equidistance between the continent and the archipelago. Instead, in 2001 Nigeria and STP established a Joint Development Zone (JDZ) in the waters disputed by the two countries. A Joint Development Authority (JDA) in Abuja manages the 28,000km^2 JDZ. The two countries share the JDZ's profits and costs, in the proportions of Nigeria 60% and São Tomé and Príncipe 40%.

Foreign experts and the local opposition considered São Tomé's oil agreements with ERHC, Mobil and PGS as prejudicial to the country's national interests because they allowed the foreign companies far-reaching financial advantages against inadequate returns. In 2002, US legal experts hired by the government considered the agreements with ERHC and PGS extremely one-sided, since the government received little in return for what it gave to the companies. In the opinion of the experts, only the agreement with Mobil approached similar agreements elsewhere in the international oil industry. As a result São Tomé and Príncipe demanded the renegotiation of all oil agreements.

In early 2003 renegotiated contracts were signed with ExxonMobil, PGS and ERHC. The new agreements with ExxonMobil and PGS were more favourable to São Tomé and Príncipe than the previous ones. In contrast, foreign analysts considered the new agreement with ERHC excessively generous to the Nigerian company. Nevertheless, the renegotiated agreements paved the way for the first licensing round of nine blocks of the JDZ in 2003. Twenty oil companies submitted 33 bids for eight of the blocks. ChevronTexaco offered the highest bid of $123 million for Block 1. Finally, in spring 2004, only Block 1 was licensed to ChevronTexaco (51%), ExxonMobil (40%), and the Nigerian Energy Equity Resources (9%). Reportedly, to avoid assigning the blocks to companies with uncertain capacities, Blocks 2–6 were put into a new bidding round in December 2004, while Blocks 7–9 were withdrawn from the auction. By that time the London-based Equator Exploration had acquired the rights owned by PGS.

In April 2005, the announcement of the five block awards to different consortiums, including dubious small Nigerian oil companies, provoked accusations of irregularities and a lack of transparency. As a result, the Oil Committee of the National Assembly asked the local Attorney General to investigate the block awards. The investigation report confirmed the allegations of irregularities, including vague selection criteria and the awarding of blocks to companies with doubtful technical and financial capacities. Unimpressed by the conclusions of the report, in March 2006 the JDA signed production-sharing contracts with the consortiums that had been awarded Blocks 2, 3 and 4. The signing of the contracts for Blocks 5 and 6 was postponed due to legal questions. Finally, the production-sharing contract for JDZ Block 5 was signed in February 2012. Altogether São Tomé received signature bonus shares of some US$49 million for Block 1 in 2005 and US$28.5 million for Blocks 2, 3 and 4 in 2006.

In 2006, ChevronTexaco drilled the first exploration wells in Block 1. The results of the drillings were disappointing; although the company announced the discovery of oil, the deposits were not commercially exploitable. The news provoked some frustration in São Tomé and certainly dampened the initial enthusiasm about the country's oil prospects. In 2009 the Chinese Sinopec and its subsidiary Addax, the operators of JDZ Blocks 2, 3 and 4 respectively, carried out exploration drillings in the three blocks. Due to consecutive extensions, the exploration phase of the three blocks was only formally concluded in March 2012, with inconclusive results. As a result of the test drilling, most investors, with the exception of ERHC, abandoned the three blocks. In the first half of 2012, Total, which had taken over Chevron's stake in JDZ Block 1 in 2010, drilled new exploration wells in this block. In July 2013, the French company decided to abandon Block 1. The first licensing round for the country's own EEZ launched in March 2010 became another setback, since exclusively third-tier oil companies submitted bids. Finally, in 2011, only one of the seven blocks put in the auction was awarded to Oranto Petroleum, a small Nigerian oil company. Due to preferential rights, ERHC and Equator Exploration were awarded two blocks of their own choice each in the EEZ. In April 2012, Equator Exploration signed a production-sharing contract for Block 5 of the EEZ that included the payment of a signature bonus of $2 million.

While STP still awaits the first discovery of oil, the country has adopted important anti-corruption legislation for the oil sector. Together with the World Bank and the Earth Institute of Columbia University in New York, local lawmakers elaborated a regulatory law of oil revenue management. The government also created a National Oil Agency (ANP; www.anp-stp.gov.st) as the regulating body of the country's oil industry. The agency executes the instructions of the 15-member National Petroleum Council (CNP). As early as June 2004 the then presidents Obasanjo and de Menezes signed the Abuja Joint Declaration on transparency in the JDZ. All information was to be made public on the website of the JDA (http://n-stpjda. com/nstpjda/). However, this has not been done. São Tomé's leaders have on various occasions promised sound management, transparency, accountability and the investment of the possible future oil wealth for the benefit of the people. However, for the time being, nobody knows if the country's leaders really have the political will to meet their promise.

The country is hoping to see a pardon of the remainder. Taiwan continues to be a major donor, having invested an estimated US$100 million in the first ten years of diplomatic relations being established in 1997, financing, for instance, an information technology centre to drive the computerisation of the public administration services. (While mainland China was holding back for years, it is now entering the oil sector.) The leader of the MLSTP/PSD opposition party, veteran politician Rafael Branco has, however, spoken out against Taiwan-supported prestige projects such as a planned multi-million dollar international conference centre; this was since replaced by an electricity plant. The **United Nations**, who have a fairly active office in the capital, are funding social assistance programmes through their Population Fund, investing in poverty reduction, health and women's rights with over US$2 million between 2008 and 2011. Visitors talking to Santomeans will notice that a certain culture of dependency has resulted in much talk of 'the government's' responsibilities to support and help and a certain lack of initiative, born out of a paralysing mix of lack of capital, distrust of empty promises of the past, and Santomean *leve-leve*.

PEOPLE

One of the best things about São Tomé and Príncipe is the **lack of tribal, ethnic or religious strife**. The Santomeans (*Santomense*) are the fruit of a dynamic ethnic mix. The Portuguese colonialists traditionally mixed more with the native population than the English; there is a saying that whereas the English and French colonisers made enemies, the Portuguese made children. Like other Portuguese colonies, such as Angola or Mozambique, São Tomé and Príncipe have a very diverse society. The dominant sector, both in terms of numbers and prestige, are the *forros*, descendants of freed slaves or the product of relationships between Portuguese and local women. They traditionally disdained manual work on the plantations, and in 1953 the rumour of imminent conscription brought on demonstrations, triggering the Massacre of Batepá (see page 18).

Mixed-race Santomeans are called *mulattos* or *bobos* ('yellows'); in contrast to other creole societies they do not necessarily occupy higher positions in society. Prominent mulattos include: President Fradique de Menezes, former prime minister Rafael Branco and former Attorney General Roberto Raposo. *Tongas* are the descendants of African workers born in São Tomé and Príncipe. Those born on Príncipe are known as *minuiê*, but sometimes called *moncós* in a disparaging manner. On Príncipe most of the population (90%) have Cape Verdean heritage. Whites of all nationalities are called *brancos/brancas* or, as I was called in a couple of villages in the south: *colomba*. If you spend a while on the islands, you get used to calls of '*Branco/a, branco/a!*'

São Tomé's rich ethnic mix also contains a **Jewish** element. In 1493, in an attempt to populate the island and to 'whiten the race', an unknown number (according to legend around 1,000) Jewish children aged between two and ten years of age were shipped to São Tomé by order of King Manuel I. Their parents had fled to Portugal a year earlier, when Spain expelled all Jews, but were not able to pay the extortionate poll tax demanded for crossing the border. Three years later, the Jews were expelled from Portugal, too. In São Tomé, the children were converted to Catholicism. Many of them succumbed to malaria and other tropical diseases, but some 600 are believed to have survived and intermarried with members of the creole community. Today, there are few traces of their passing; there is no known Jewish community on the islands, but an international conference in 1995 was the starting point for more research on this little-known part of the island's history.

With the arrival of many **Nigerians** on the oil trail, there has been a fear that Nigerians, indeed far more astute business people than the *Santomense*, are 'taking over', some buying property on the island without even visiting the country. There is also a **Chinese** element on the islands, as evidenced by family names such as Ten Jua or Chong.

With a median age of 17.6 years (2013) – and approximately 40% of Santomeans under 15 – São Tomé and Príncipe is a young society. The urban youth who can afford it wear American-style sportswear, topped with baseball caps, and talk to the world via MSN Messenger.

WOMEN In politics and the judiciary, women occupy a fairly prominent position. A former minister of trade, Maria das Neves (MLSTP/PSD) served as prime minister from 2002 to 2004; though much loved by low-income citizens, she had to step down amid accusations of corruption. Women currently hold 18% of the seats in parliament. In recent memory, during the government of Prime Minister Maria das Neves, who was the first female head of government, the president of the Supreme Court, the governor of the Central Bank, the Secretary of State of Trade and Commerce, the deputy prime minister/Minister for Planning and Finance, and the Minister for Education, Culture, Youth and Sports were all female. Over the recent decade, however, there has been a decrease in the number of women in top positions. Other women occupy senior positions in the more 'traditionally female' sectors of health and culture. Historically, many topographical features, beaches, plantations and mountains bear the names of women, such as Ana de Chaves, who gave her name to the bay of São Tomé, to its second-highest peak and to a river.

In colonial times, many Portuguese settlers had local lovers, euphemistically called **lavadeiras**, 'washer women'. You will notice that in discussions of colonialism, most Portuguese remain proud of their policy of mixing, of 'making children', unlike the more segregationist British or French attitude. Today, despite the **fertility** rate going down, women have an average of five children, and still shoulder a large workload in a male-dominated society. Market traders (*palaiês*), all women, have an important role and manage large budgets. In the fishing community, women have considerable power, and some of the market fishwives are feared for their sharp tongue and rough manners.

The taboo surrounding **domestic violence** in São Tomé and Príncipe is being lifted, and the topic is now discussed in the media and portrayed in community drama. Men often complain of their partners' jealousy, maybe not unfounded, given Santomean men's perceived track record as two-timing *bandidos*. Domestic violence has only been an official crime – thus punishable and a question of public interest rather than something left in the domestic remit – since 2008. UNICEF estimates that about 25% of Santomean women have experienced domestic violence.

HIV/AIDS AND SEXUAL ACTIVITY Only about 10% of 15- to 24-year-old women have comprehensive and correct knowledge of HIV/AIDS. Official figures put the rate of infection at around 1–2%, but this probably hides a higher, increasing rate. A 2012 UN AIDS survey found that STP is one of the few countries where HIV prevalence is higher in rural rather than in urban areas. Also, while there was no clear relationship found between wealth and HIV infection, prevalence decreased unsurprisingly with education. The virus carries an immense **stigma** still, as one local woman who spoke to local television about her condition found. Even with her back turned to the camera, she was identified in her community and ostracised, as was one of her children, also HIV positive. Fearing the stigma, infected patients refuse to go to the clinic to pick up retro-viral medication and infected mothers refuse to use formula milk.

Despite the imaginatively painted panels you see showing the benefits of condoms, and their availability for free at special wooden boxes in bars and clubs, only a third of Santomeans use them regularly. Often women defer to their partner's unwillingness to use a condom – 'one should not eat a banana with its skin', as a popular saying goes – or feel using them would make them seem immoral. The level of sexual education is very low and, while sexual banter is a fixture of Santomean culture, discussing disease and prevention still carries a taboo. *A Saida do Gueto* (*Coming out of the Ghetto*), a TV documentary made by state broadcaster TVS in 2009, 20 years after the first case of HIV infection was recorded here, featured six brave Saotomeans living with the disease.

In the capital, **prostitution** is common in hotels and along the capital's Água Grande canal. A recent newspaper story involved a local businessman looking for a girl, who was surprised to find his own daughter waiting for clients. Some of them, but not all, use condoms, and many are young – *catorzinhas*, literally 'little/sweet 14 year olds'. Already, Santomeans working in the neighbouring Gulf of Guinea states with higher rates of infection, such as Equatorial Guinea, Cameroon and Gabon, are putting themselves at risk. If and when the oil rush takes off, more prostitution and higher infection rates will follow. Under-age sex is common.

The official age for marriage on São Tomé and Príncipe is 14 for girls, 16 for boys. Many young women have their first pregnancy at 14; abortions are illegal, but do take place, using traditional healers. **Homosexual** acts are banned.

RELIGION

The majority of Santomeans are **Christian**, with over 55% Roman Catholic and 20% Protestant, Pentecostal, etc. Many little shops will have names such as 'Deus Quer' or 'Fe-em-Deus' suggesting a God-fearing society. However, the moral teachings of the traditional church – such as monogamy – don't really interfere with the Santomean way of life, and never have, back to the Catholic priests not observing celibacy in early colonial times. **Polygyny** is the norm: men have several women, often cohabiting with a main woman but keeping other lovers and contributing to the upkeep of children. The 'shocking' statistic that the rate of births outside marriage is the highest in the world is down to the fact that few couples marry. Pope John Paul II's sermon during a nine-hour visit in 1992 had little impact. A man with four women is seen as a great guy, *fofo*; for women, the morals don't work quite in the same way.

In the years since the opening up of the country, increasingly, Pentecostal churches offer a counterpoint to the establishment. At weekends, you can often hear gospel songs emanating from places of worship. The Portuguese Maná church has been one of the most successful; sometimes you can see full-body immersion baptisms on the beach next to the museum in São Tomé, with blaring music. The most visible and active faith is the Switzerland-based New Apostolic Church, which started proselytising here in the early 1980s. In addition to this, there are Seventh-Day Adventists, who own the oldest Protestant church on the island and are very involved in development work; a growing number of Jehovah's Witnesses; a growing community of about 200 Muslims; and a similar number of the Baha'i faith. Relations between the religious groups are amicable, though the aggressive money-soliciting of some new churches is now criticised in the media.

In the towns and villages, patron saints are venerated on their feast day with celebrations lasting days and involving processions, dancing, traditional music, food and drink stalls, and *tchiloli* (see pages 44–5). The feast day of São Isidro in Ribeira Afonso at the end of January kicks off the saints' season, followed by São Pedro, the fishermen's patron saint at the end of January, and so it goes on. With a society as mixed as this, animist traditions that believe in the unity of body and soul, and the existence of souls in plants and animals, remain strong and exist alongside Christian rituals. For instance, many Santomeans follow the common magical ritual of *Pagá dêvê* ('pay what you owe', based on the assumption that a problem, such as bed-wetting with children, represents an open debt from a former life that has to be paid off), leaving carved votive figurines near rivers, or believe that rain that falls on 3 May (*Chuva de Três de Maio*) is divine benediction for the fertilisation of the fields and collect this sacred water in containers to drink or to wash in. Practitioners of witchcraft are often members of a major religion. Herbal concoctions are used against the evil eye (*mau olhar*) to make men faithful; and, careful – if you drink a tea made of certain leaves, you might stay on São Tomé forever! Healers (*curandeiros*) are called in to dispel a curse, exorcise a spirit or to cast a spell on a rival. **Djambi** is a spirit-possession cult with the aim of curing illness through communicating with the ancestors, where the healer, the patient and the onlookers enter a state of trance, induced through dance and psychotropic drugs; some participants even cut themselves. With a bit of determination and asking around, it should be possible to get yourself invited to a *djambi*.

EDUCATION

The official literacy rate of 75% is wildly optimistic considering how many people I witnessed struggling to write their names. Until 1952, there were no grammar schools on the islands. Today, the Liceu Nacional in the capital has 4,000 students, studying up to grade 11, age 17; in Príncipe, pupils can only study up to grade nine, and many only get a few years' basic schooling. With children working on the plantations or lacking the money for books, absenteeism is a problem. School uniforms cost money: their introduction for higher education in around 2000 was very controversial. Only about 85% of children go to school – as evidenced by the kids selling necklaces or cakes in the street – and only 80% in Príncipe, where more than 25% of students drop out before the fourth grade. Since 1996, São Tomé and Príncipe has had a higher-education polytechnic, offering degrees. In the late 19th century, São Tomé sent more black students to study in Portugal than any other Portuguese colony. Today, unrest amongst young people is growing, out of frustration with the limited number of study grants to go abroad, and there are stories of nepotism networks ensuring that the few available places go to friends and relations of influential families. Partly in response to this, the private Lusíadas University opened in 2007, offering degrees in business administration and law.

CULTURE

MUSIC Music is the surround sound of Santomean society, the soundtrack to life and love, work and emigration, joys and daily deprivations. In the popular quarters, the *kizomba* beats start early in the morning; even the poorest houses have a stereo, and thumping music will follow you everywhere. Once I saw a father holding a mobile playing a tune to the ear of his baby, and the question whether you like *discoteca, festa, dançar*, is one of the first a traveller will be asked. You might have heard

Tjerk Hagemeijer, Lisbon (author of ST-Portuguese dictionary)

Considering the geographical size of the country, São Tomé and Príncipe exhibits an unexpectedly rich linguistic diversity. The official language and the language of prestige, (European) Portuguese, which is used in administration, education and daily life, is spoken by almost all the inhabitants of both islands. However, the Portuguese language spoken on the islands shows several specific grammatical and lexical traits compared with standard European Portuguese.

The mother tongue of practically all speakers is either Portuguese or one of the creole languages described below. Many speakers have command of more than one language, speaking both Portuguese and one or more creole languages. Although there is no official sociolinguistic data, Portuguese tends to be used more in and around São Tomé town and among younger speakers. The distribution figures below were provided by the National Statistics Office of STP (Angolar and Cape Verdean figures have only recently begun to be officially recorded):

Year	Total	Portuguese population	Santome	Lung'le	Angolar	Cape Verdean
1981	96,661	60,519	54,387	1,533	-	-
1991	117,504	94,907	69,899	1,558	-	-
2001	137,599	136,085	99,621	3,302	-	-
2011	187,356	170,309	62,889	4,224	11,413	14,725

The three local creole languages spoken on the islands, *Lungwa Santome, Lunga Ngola* and *Lung'le*, do not have the status of official language and are not used for administrative and educational purposes. Creole languages are essentially confined to informal environments, such as music, family relations, folk tales, even though radio and television do sometimes broadcast in Santome and Lung'le.

The main creole in terms of number of speakers has several designations, namely Lungwa Santome (literally 'language of São Tomé'), *Santome, Fôlô* or *forro* (historically derived from *carta de alforria* 'letter of manumission', a document granting freedom to slaves), *Lungwa Tela* (literally 'language of the country') and *Dioletu* (dialect) – and is widely spoken and/or understood on both islands, even though it was originally the language of the *forro* population on São Tomé. Santome is the only creole that has enjoyed some written tradition, with the first examples of writings in this language dating from the second half of the 19th century. A handful of contemporary writers has written texts in Santome, such as *Coroa do Mar* (1998) ('Crown of the sea') by Carlos Espírito Santo (see page 235), *Semplu* (2002), a collection of proverbs by Olinto Daio, *Mangungo* (2009), a collections of proverbs, riddles, etc by Jerónimo Salvaterra, and *Paga Ngunu* (1989), consisting of poems by Amadeu Quintas da Graça.

The designations *Angolar, Ngola* or *Lunga Ngola* ('Angolares' Language') refer to the creole language spoken by the Angolares, a closed community that arguably descends from 16th-century runaway slaves with a significant nuclei of speakers in the southern part of São Tomé. However, the fishing tradition of male Angolares resulted in the spread of the community to other coastal areas of São Tomé. Whilst there are still many thousands of speakers, the spread of the speech community and consequent language contact with other languages, especially Santome, and increasing exposure to Portuguese may put the language at risk.

On the island of Príncipe, a very small community of no more than a few hundred people still actively speaks Lung'le (literally 'language of the island'), a language that might well disappear within a few generations, subject to a process of substitution with Cape Verdean creole. In addition to the local creoles, it is worth mentioning *Fa d'Ambô* ('speech of Ano Bom'), the creole spoken on the small island of Annobón (Equatorial Guinea). Today also known as Pagalu, this island, lying 177km to the south of São Tomé, was a Portuguese colonial possession until 1777, when it became Spanish territory (Annobón), until the independence of Equatorial Guinea. Santome, Angolar, Lung'le and Fa d'Ambô descend historically from a common root, a contact language that came into existence on São Tomé by the end of the 15th century, when the island was permanently settled by the Portuguese. This contact language, which evolved directly into Santome, must have stabilised during the 16th century and is the result of contact between the Portuguese and slaves from the African mainland. These slaves were first predominantly recruited in the Niger delta area (Nigeria), with a special role for the old kingdom of Benin (not to be confused with the country of Benin). Quickly, however, slaves from Bantu areas, especially the Congo and Angola, became more dominant around 1520.

Despite the fact that most of the vocabulary of the creoles has its roots in Portuguese, although strongly modified by the phonological rules of African languages, there are also a substantial number of words in the creoles that can be traced back to the African continent, and particularly to the languages spoken in the regions indicated above, namely Edo (Edoid), Kikongo and Kimbundu (Bantu). Lung'le preserved more linguistic features and vocabulary that can be assigned to the Niger delta area, whereas Angolar exhibits significant amounts of Bantu lexicon. Despite these lexical particularities, the three creole languages on São Tomé and Príncipe, as well as Fa d'Ambô, are structurally very similar and all reflect more clearly the impact of Nigerian rather than Bantu languages. Due to the diffusion of the early contact language in time and space, the three creole languages are nowadays not mutually intelligible. The structure of the creoles, very distinct from Portuguese, reflects the strong impact of African languages during its formative period.

In addition to the local creole languages, São Tome and Príncipe has a significant speech community of Cape Verdean creole speakers. This creole, originally spoken on the Cape Verdean islands, is genetically unrelated to the above creoles. It was the Cape Verdean contract labourers in the 20th century who brought along their own creole language, which still constitutes a means of affirmation for the Cape Verdean community on the islands. The majority of Príncipe's inhabitants, for example, are of Cape Verdean descent. There is also *Tonga* Portuguese, a language variety that can still be heard on, for instance, the plantations of Monte Café and Agostinho Neto, where mostly Umbundu-speaking contract labourers from Angola developed a new linguistic code based upon Portuguese. Due to the impact of Portuguese and the unstable nature of this variety, however, Tonga Portuguese is bound to disappear in the near future.

Despite the lesser prestige of the local creole languages, there is a growing interest in their preservation. The publication of Angolar and Lung'le grammars, written by Maurer (1995, 2009) and of a Santome dictionary (Araújo & Hagemeijer 2013), and other studies have helped but there is a need to adopt the official policies concerning the creole languages in order to prevent their disappearance.

'Sodade', the famous ballad of Cape Verdean emigration popularised by Cesária Evora, expressing the emigrants' longing for the homeland (*esse caminho longe, esse caminho para São Tomé?* this long way to São Tomé). Especially on Príncipe, where 90% of the population descend from Cape Verdeans, singers still perform this song with true emotion underlying the haunting harmonies. In colonial times, slaves and later contract workers would use song lyrics to criticise their masters, and expressed the difficulties and the hardships of life on the plantations, working sugarcane, cocoa, coffee, copra and coconuts. Flutes are used, as are *banzas* – a piece of bamboo or branch of a tree called *malimboque* scraped in the way of a *reco-reco*, a percussion instrument much used in South America, and on Cape Verde, too. Different kinds of drums are played, as well as *sacaias* – a small calabash or woven basket filled with grains – you can buy them at the Roça São João (see pages 172–3) – to accompany the *socopé, ussua, Dançco Congo* and *puita* dances. Today, these old styles are struggling to survive, but some groups try to keep the tradition alive; contact English-speaking Edson Andreza (m *990 5013*). Edson belongs to a group of young people performing traditional dances in the capital; they are glad of a donation to finance the costumes, etc. A very popular percussion tradition you will encounter during creole nights (*noites crioulas*), election campaigns and as a tourist attraction, is **bulaué**. Well-known bulaué groups include Marina, Belezinha and Pastelim.

In the 1980s, some bands toed the party line, making propaganda music extolling the virtues of the new one-party state and the bright future. In the 1990s, with the opening up of the country, Santomean musical taste became more open to new influences. The style of popular music you are still most likely to encounter during fairs and religious feasts is **Nacional**, where all generations take to the dance floor. The band Sangazuza still rule the roost; they and their rivals África Negra frequently tour on the islands. On the national music front, the scene is growing day by day, with the emergence of new styles. Singers such as Garrido, Helder Camblé, Leo Bocacopo, Chinha, Sebastiana, or the veterans of traditional *Santomense* music, Pepé Lima and João Seria, give concerts all over the island. Add to these the bands Amigos da Cultura, As Relíquias de STP and O Rock Som. Performing spaces to look out for are the Fundon Pepé, or the Fundon Zé Sardinha. There is always music at popular *festas*, provided by groups such as Equipe Som Master, Banda da Ilha, banda de Marca, As Reliquias de STP, banda Kua Nom or Amisol; check the tourist board website for what's on during your visit or, better still, ask around. At the moment, Príncipe only has one band, Mezcla, and usually has to invite combos from the larger island to animate their parties. Today, **zouk** from the Antilles, **kadançe** from Cape Verde and Angola and **kizomba** from Angola rule the dance floor, reflecting the younger generation's preference for the ear-worm beats and easy lyrics of Loony Johnson and Haylton Dias. *Zouk* and *kizomba* have also been adapted to *forro* and Cape Verdean creole. One of the most venerated and charismatic local *kizomba* singers, **Camilo Domingos**, of Cape Verdean descent and also very successful in Angola, died young. One of his most popular songs is 'A Menina Fala d'Amor' (The Girl Talks about Love). Lisbon-based *zouk* singer Juka regularly visits his home country to perform; big names at the moment are Mesaro and Os Calemas, two young brothers. Popular clubs (*discotecas*), often no more than a wooden shack with a few strobe lights, are a way of life, a place to meet and celebrate and to forget daily worries. First-time visitors might be surprised how sensual the dancing is – bodies rub up very close to each other and seem to move very slowly, particularly during the *tarachinha*, even though this Angolan dance has a fast beat. Western women struggling with the moves and the closeness might be told to 'relax', which is, of course, no great help. Dancing on your own, European-style, is not really done and can feel awkward; men assume that you are waiting to be invited to dance. Young guys, though, will often launch into innovative crazy styles of solo dancing, influenced by Brazilian moves, reggae beats and the São Tomé *puita*. While Santomean men are generally free to dance with whoever they like, women going to a club with their boyfriends are often only allowed to dance with them. Clubs sometimes have live shows by popular singers with a new album out; look for posters and listen to the grapevine. **Kalú Mendes**, who has been singing at the Club Santana weekend barbecues (see page 166) for what seems forever, brought out a new album in 2013, *Boleia*, in honour of the many children by the roadside asking for a lift at the top of their voices. The same year also saw **Os Vibrados** from the São Marçal suburb bring out their first album, influenced by rap and *kuduro*, with urbane social criticism in songs like 'Cacao – Non môle' (2012). They were lucky to have their album sponsored by a big bank – living from music is difficult even in a music-mad society like this. One problem is the lack of author's rights, something the new society of Santomense musicians, **Assomusicos**, was created to address (Association de Artistas e Músicos; Senhor Rivette; m 992 3277). Not all *zouk* and *kizomba* are about luv' and grind. **Tubias Vaniana**'s 'Sofrimento' (2009) tackled domestic violence, and in 2013, his clever 'Arrependimento' told the tale of a young Santomean who moves to Portugal, selling his car (*carro-é*), his motorbike (*moto-é*) and house (*casa-é*) for a dream of a new life – just to find himself crying, without a 'job-é' and hungry ('*fome-é*') in 'Lisbon-é'.

FINE ARTS There was no real tradition of painting on the islands until the early 20th century; more than 30 years after independence, as the economic situation sometimes made it difficult for some artists even to afford paint and brushes. Born in 1894 on Roça Laranjeiras near Santana, Pascoal Viana de Sousa e Almeida Vilhete, **Sum Canalim**, became famous for his naïve, ethnographic paintings of the tchiloli, *Danço Congo* and *socopé* ('only-with-foot'). One of the painters heavily influenced by Sum Canalim was **Protásio Dias Xavier Pina** (1960–99) from Príncipe, whose naïve murals representing the islands' landscapes or traditional dancing are shown in various spaces in São Tomé, including the airport and the Residencial Avenida.

There is a great buzz in the **contemporary arts** scene at the moment. A new generation of very talented painters living and working in São Tomé (or painting Santomean themes from their Portuguese bases) create work that you can find on sale at the only art gallery in the capital (see page 134). One of the most popular painters is the Angolar painter and musician **João Carlos** (Nezó; see page 175), whose distinctive stylised works hang in the Pestana Resort on the Ilhéu das Rolas, as well as at his restaurant in São João dos Angolares, Mionga (see page 171). The abstract oil/acrylic paintings by young artist **René Tavares** make him a universal painter. **Olavo Amado**'s (m 990 7405; e olavo.amado@gmail.com; www. olavoamado.blogspot.com) paintings lead the viewer to guess people and figures through a blurred mist of soft tones and three-dimensional collage elements – you can see his work at the Roça de São João and at CACAU where he is involved in management – whilst **Eduardo Malé**'s dynamic figures in a contemporary context seem to speak up for the times coming to São Tomé. **Guilherme Carvalho** creates beautiful images with sand from the islands' multi-coloured beaches. **Armindo Lopes** (m 991 0358) paints and sculpts fine iconographic African figures, and the abstract paintings of cultural promoter and TV chef **João Carlos Silva** give a taste of richly flavoured colours. **Dário Quaresma Vaz Alves de Carvalho** presents an African take on Cubism, whilst **Adilson Castro**'s powerful colours painted on treated wood featuring doors and small sculpted figures in geometric compositions speak up for symbolism. Living and working in Santana, **Osvaldo dos Reis** (see page 166) uses exuberant colours and playfully energetic geometry to represent timeless Santomean scenes. Also watch out for **José Manuel Mendonça (Zemé)**, **Kwame Souza** and **Oswaldo Gomes**. **Geane Castro**'s metal animal sculptures made out of recycled pieces reveal the creative potential in simple objects, while **Aurélio Silva**'s expressive wood sculptures tap into the spiritual, votive traditions of African art. The vibrant photo-paintings of the island by French artist **Tony Soulié** are available through his gallery (*www.estampe.fr*). A metal-framed print costs €115; standard prints around €30. Meanwhile, art is finding new outlets, on plantations, and particularly in the capital, at the new CACAU arts centre. The fact that there is now a **design *bienal*** (biannual festival) happening in odd-numbered years between November and February to complement the summer Bienal in even years helps artists gain international visibility. The 2013–14 festival showcased much contemporary Angolan art, alongside René Tavares' tchiloli photographs and Geane Castro's haunting figures made from recycled motorbike parts. Inspired by an initial project shown at the festival (www.xerem.org), a Portuguese arts-related eco/community travel agency called Hangar, starting in 2015, aims to show the world through the eyes of artists and local people, who act as guides.

LITERATURE In a society with no bookshops or daily newspaper, oral tradition has always played a major role. Stories featuring animals, such as the clever *tartaruga* (turtle), always after food and his own advantage, and spiritual entities, such as the devil, are told by the *griot* (storyteller). The hunt for food plays a major role in these stories, which also often contain a grotesque element. There are two kinds of stories generally told at night: *Contági* for instance, are based on real events, and are told to keep the memory of historical events, either collective and traumatic events such as the Batepá Massacre or particular situations of everyday life. *Sóia* may contain an element of fiction and are told as entertainment, usually at family meetings. Both are stories that are generally only told at night. Today, storytelling is losing ground to TV soap operas.

Poetry is the dominant form of literary production. The first manifestations of Santomean literature were inspired by the beauty of the islands, such as *Equatoriais* (1896) by **António Lobo de Almada Negreiros**, *Horas d'Ócio no Equador* (1908) by **Manuel Joaqum Gonçalves de Castro**. The motivation of the poets born on the islands was dynamised by their view of society. Most of these poets lived the greater part of their lives in Portugal. Bohemian poet-philosopher **Francisco Stockler**, a Santomean teacher reared in Lisbon, wrote much of his wry, self-deprecating ironic poetry in *forro* creole. More recently, **Mé Sossô** (pseudonym for José Luis Martinho, 1952–) continues this strand, appropriating the image of the 'prodigal son', who travels the world without ever knowing about the death of his family members. A recurrent motif in the romantic poetry of **Caetano Costa Alegre** (1864–1890) is the dichotomy between a fatalistic resignation to the alienation born from the colour of his skin and its valorisation. Inspired by Costa Alegre, the essence of the work of Príncipe-born militant poet **Marcelo da Veiga** (1892–1976), who became an anticolonial activist, is crystallised in the image of the *Ossobó*, the elusive solitary cuckoo of the forest and the name of his major collection. His poem *Evocação* (Ilha do Príncipe) indeed evokes a nostalgic past 'when the island was ours' with 'fine plantations, distant', where, on feast days 'there were no invitations, everyone went', 'canoes without sails / that opened flight like birds with oars only...' While Marcelo da Veiga's first expressions of *négritude* date back to the second decade of the 20th century, they only became known in 1963, more than 20 years after the publication of his *Ilha de Nome Santo*.

The poems of São Tomé-born **Herculano Levy** (1889–1969) are infused with sadness and desire; he frequently returns to plantation life, the *obô* forest and the *Ossobó* bird that lives its treacherous life there. The poetry of the *mestiço* geographer, deputy of the Portuguese National Assembly and author of ethnographic essays on his home country, **Francisco José Tenreiro** (1921–63, see box pages 40–1) is infused with themes of creole identity, pitching a proud and demanding pan-African *négritude* against colonial oppression, but blending in sensual, fertile Santomean imagery; today, his portrait hangs in the National Library in São Tomé and can be found on the 100,000 dobra note. In poems such as '*A ilha te fala*', **Maria Manuela Margarido** (1925–2007) evokes the sensuous sounds and smells of her native Príncipe with arresting yet subtle images: 'The island speaks to you / of wild roses / with petals / of abandonment and fear...', while the poems and dramatic works of **Fernando de Macedo** (1927–2006) focus on Angolar history, giving voice to a marginalised part of Santomean society.

Born in 1926 into the prominent Espírito Santo family from Trindade, **Alda Graça Espírito Santo** was the *grande dame* of Santomean politics and culture. Studying in Lisbon in the 1940s, Alda encountered everyday racism – 'We were called "monkey", and all the rest of it,' she recalled when I interviewed her a few years back – but also made friends with the prime movers of the Luso-African independence movements. One of her best-known poems, *Where are the Men Hunted Down in this Wind of Madness?*, commemorates the 1953 massacre, a fierce lament and demand for justice: 'Blood falling in drops on the earth / men dying in the forest / and the blood dripping, dripping... of the people thrown out to sea...'. The only writer of note to remain on the islands in colonial times, she is venerated by many. As Minister of Culture, she wrote the national anthem, *Independência Total*, and was, up to her death in 2010, president of the Writers' and Artists' Union (UNEAS) and of the Forum for Santomense Women. Equally, the poetry of physician, activist and former guerrilla fighter in Angola, **Tomás Medeiros** is suffused with images of war and exhortations of '*camaradas*' and '*companheiros*'; in '*Aquí estamos*'; '...Here we are with our black back against the sun, / fertilising the soil with our hoes, / with the song of the sun in our breasts without wearying / and the telluric cry that comes from the volcanoes.' A new voice, carrying on some of Alda Graça's themes, is London-based **Conceição Lima** (1962– ; see box, pages 40–1), a journalist and former producer with the BBC, some of whose poems have been translated into English. **Maria Olinda Beja** (1946–) explores themes of *mestiço* mysticism, identity, exile and the poet's place in the world.

One of the few Santomean born-and-bred poets actually continuing to live on the island is lawyer **Aíto Bonfim** (1955–) working with strong, aggressive even, political images. He is also the only playwright the country has, having written three plays for the theatre and a novel, *O Suicídio Cultural* (The Cultural Suicide), a critical assessment of the political *modus operandi* in post-colonial Africa. In the current poetry scene **Frederico Gustavo dos Anjos**, whose poetry exploring metaphysical themes captures the contradictions of the human soul in the island context, has made a name for himself.

Novels While from the early 20th century onwards, narrative has been a reality nourished by metropolitan dwellers enchanted by the islands' magnificent natural world, often resulting in a literature of a more informative kind (narrative

FRANCISCO JOSÉ TENREIRO (1921–63): *ISLAND NAMED AFTER A SAINT* (1942)
Translated by Don Burness

Land!
of plantations of cocoa of copra of coffee
of coconut palms extending as far as the eye can see until they reach the sea
The sea blue like the most pleasing sky in all the world!

Where the pure yellow and round sun shines on the backs of men of women their nerves excited
in a cadence magical yet human: threshing dreaming planting!

Where the women whose arms are stouter and more bent than limbs of the *ocá*
are black like the coffee they gather
working along side their men in muscular labor!
where the little kids watch their parents in a daily rhythm
letting the flavour the warm sap of the ripe *safú* fruit
flow down their moist chins!

Where the star-filled nights
and a full moon round like a fruit
the blacks the kids the extended family
– even the white man and his mulatto lover –
come to the *sócópé* at the lady's place
to hear the guitar played by the vagabond musician
singing to the music!

And the sea echoes the sound…
Where despite the gunpowder in the white man's unlit ship
where despite the sword and multicolored flag
proclaiming power proclaiming force
proclaiming the empire of the white man
this is the land of men singing life
unknown to the white man
this is the land of *safú* of *sócópé*
of the mulatto woman
– ui! Fetish of the white man! –
this is the land of the black man
loyal strong and valiant like no other!

CONCEIÇÃO LIMA (1962–): *AFRO-INSULARITY*
Translated by Russell G. Hamilton
On the islands they left a legacy
of hybrid words and sorrowful plantations
rusted sugar mills breathless prows
resonant aristocratic names
and the legend of a shipwreck on Sete Pedras

Arriving from the North they cast anchor here
by mandate or by chance in the service of their king:
navigators and pirates
slave traders thieves contrabandists
common folk
also rebel outcasts
and Jewish children
so tender that they faded
like sun-dried ears of corn

The ships brought
compasses trinkets seeds
experimental plants heinous acidities
a stone monument as pallid as wheat
and other cargo without dreams nor roots
because all of the island was a port and a road
with no return
all of the hands were pitchforks and hoes

And alive they became stuck on the rocks
like scabs – every coffee tree now breathes
a dead slave.

And on the islands remained
incisive arrogant statues on street corners
more than a hundred churches and chapels
for a thousand square kilometres
and the insurgent syncretism of nativity residences.
And there remains the palatial cadence of the *Ussuá* Creole dance
the aroma of garlic and olive oil
in traditional clay pots
and in the *calulú* the bay leaf mixed with palm oil
and the fragrance of rosemary
and basil from family gardens

And to the ticking of insular clocks were cast
Spectres – implements of the empire
in a structure of ambiguous clarities
and secular condiments
patron saints and demolished fortresses
inexpensive wines and shared auroras

At times I think of their livid skeletons
their fetid hair on the sea shore
Here, on this fragment of Africa
where, facing South,
a word dawns on high
like a banner of distress.

observations, chronicles, memoires, eyewitness accounts, biography, road trips, descriptions of itineraries, diaries and descriptions of journeys), fiction was not a practice much cultivated in São Tomé and Príncipe until the beginning of the 21st century. While most 'Santomean' **novelists** also spent most of their life in Portugal, the universe of the plantation looms large in their work. The stories of **João Maria Viana de Almeida** (1903–?) explored the issue of *mulatto* identity in Santomean society in a tone of mocking irony. **Sum Marky** (1921–2003) was the adopted name of a writer born on São Tomé to Portuguese parents, whose atmospheric novels are still read today. The events of 1953, while little explored in Sãotomense literature, were already in the background of novels such as *Vila Flogá* (1960) and *No Altar da Lei* (On the Altar of the Law, 1962) – the latter had Marky arrested by Salazar's security police – but are at the very heart of his last novel *Crónica de uma Guerra Inventada* (Chronicle of an Invented War, 1999), which takes up the theme of the Batepá massacre, already present in *No Altar da Lei*. In 2006, Manuela Teles Neto took up the theme again in her novel *Retalhes do Massacre de Batepá*, establishing a wordplay between historical scraps and details, *detalhes*).

The novels and short stories of **Fernando Reis** (*Roça, Histórias da Roça, Ilha do Meio do Mundo*) born in the Ribatejo province of Portugal, indulge in atmospheric descriptions of plantation life from a colonial perspective; Reis is arguably the most illustrious colonial writer of São Tomé and Príncipe (together with Luís Cajão, author of *A Estufa*, The Hothouse); he also anthologised traditional stories and added to the catalogue of ethnographic literature (*Povo Flogá, Soiá* and *Soiá II*). The Rosa de Riboque collection of stories by former Minister of Education and Culture, **Albertino Bragança**, explores life in the capital's popular quarter, while his two novels oscillate between history and fiction. However, the honour of the first rendition of post-independence fiction belongs to **Rafael Branco**, former political leader of the MLSTP party and several times leader of the country, author of *Makuta, Antigamente lá na Roça*, a novella written in 1974 and published in 1979, which he was to follow up, many years later (2006) with the novel *Lévélengué: As Gravanas da Gabriela*.

Remaining within fiction, other important names that make up the literary landscape are **Orlando Piedade**, author of *O Amor Probido* (Forbidden Love, 2011), a historical novel fictionalising the early days of Portuguese colonisation on the islands, and writer **Goretti Pina**, the author of two novels: *Viagem* (Journey, 2012) and *No Dia de São Lourenço* (On Saint Laurence Day, 2013).

In recent years, the islands of São Tomé and Príncipe have become a 'transitional' space for Portuguese, with the end of the phase of silencing the impact that the loss of the colonies constituted in Portuguese history. In this way many writers have used the islands as a setting for various events and eras in Portugal's history. For instance, Lisbon journalist **Miguel Sousa Tavares** (1952–) had a runaway success with the atmospheric *Equador* (see box, opposite page). In the same year (2003), the novel *Oríon*, by Porto-born **Mário Cláudio** (1941–), famous Portuguese writer and the author of several award-winning works of fiction, where the island of São Tomé appears like a place where the history of Portugal gains sense – and significance – through the relationships it establishes with Africa. Three years later, another journalist, **Pedro Rosa Mendes**, published *Lenin Oil*, a satirical novel about *realpolitik* in the oil age. Other names such as **Otilina Silva**, a Portuguese who has lived on this island on the Equator for 25 years – the author of *Cores e Sombras de São Tomé e Príncipe* (2000), *Ecos da Terra do Ossobó* (2004) and *São Tomé e Príncipe: Ecos de Ontem e de Hoje* (2006) – are examples of a reorganisation of identity caused by post-colonial dislocation.

Translated by Kathleen Becker

Young Lisbon dandy Luís Bernardo Valença has just arrived on the island to take over as governor, with a delicate political mission (see page 21).

His aim was to do an initial tour of the important plantations on São Tomé island and then go on to Príncipe. This was not a quick task: although the island was small, it only had a few dozen kilometres of open roads where you could circulate in a horse-drawn carriage. Most of the plantations had to be visited on horseback or by boat. Navigating along the coast was in fact, the easiest way to get from the city to the plantations because the *roças* were located mainly in the coastal areas, from where they advanced into the *mato*, as far as deforestation and plant cultivation had reached. The interior of the island was still virgin jungle, just as the Portuguese had found it in the 1400s, with volcanic peaks reaching towards the sky like needles. The highest of them all was the Pico de São Tomé, at 2,042m. But it was only rarely that you could see the top, eternally drowned in clouds and fog. This densely wooded central zone that takes up the majority of São Tomé's surface area is the kingdom of the *obô* – the forest – an inextricable dense labyrinth of giant trees: jackfruit, *ocás*, lianas, *micondó* and *marupiões* trees, mango trees, begonias. Underneath those, around them, desperately climbing above them, straining with the vital effort to reach the light above that eternal liquid cover in suspension, lived the creepers, the *lemba lemba*, the *corda d'água*, the *corda pimenta* and the climbing lianes. Deep in the forest, hanging from the tree branches, ready to let herself drop on to a man passing inadvertently underneath, lived the terrible black cobra, whose bite was the kiss of death, quick and cruel. The old people would say that the only man that ever escaped death from a black cobra was a black fugitive from the Monte Café plantation that now lived in Angolares with one arm missing. When he felt the snake's teeth in his arm, he reacted with the speed of lightning, with two precise and swift strikes of his machete. With the first one, he cut his enemy's neck, with the second, he cut off his own arm below his shoulder – and he survived. Because the *obô* forest is a ghostly territory, where the fugitive black slaves would run to, in a moment of madness, because of a crime committed on a *roça*, or simply in the insane desire for liberty, the forest would readily welcome them, making them free in its liquid shady hug of death. No-one else in their right mind would venture further than a few steps into that opaque and submersed universe …

PERFORMANCE/DRAMA

Danço Congo São Tomé's most popular dramatic representation, Danço Congo, has a frenetic rhythm, and is performed for religious or popular celebrations in the dry season by two dozen all-male dancers wearing elaborate and colourful costumes with frilly trains and ribbons, balloon trousers, knee-high socks and huge headdresses (*capacetes*), wire constructions with fluttering strips of paper. The story can be performed with variations: the owner of a *roça* leaves the plantation to his incompetent sons, *bobos* (literally 'fools') and their wives – wearing large masks. The fools call in the *capitão* (captain) for help. A big party on the plantation ensues, with the *bobos* fooling around and interacting with the audience around them. To the sound of flutes, the seed-filled *sacaia* and the clanging of iron bells, the dancers march in rows of two, stomping fiercely on the ground, and rasping a stick up and down a hollowed-out stick of bamboo or sugarcane. The frenetic choreography is led by the captain, who can be seen throwing his decorated bamboo stick high up

With thanks to Françoise Gründ and Paulo Alves Pereira

Tchiloli or, as it is more commonly called, *tragédia*, is a dramatic and rare spectacle. 'The Tragedy of the Marquis of Mantua and the Emperor Charlemagne' tells the story of a quest for justice in a vibrant performance, blending European costumes and music with African elements, various registers of the Portuguese language, medieval and contemporary literature, and votive imagery. Whilst performances may be adapted to suit place, occasion and audience, the basic chronology remains the same. Dom Carloto (Prince Charles), son of the emperor Charlemagne, and his best friend Valdevinos (Baldwin), the nephew of the Marquis de Mântua, an important vassal of Charlemagne, are out hunting. Dom Carloto, who has designs on Baldwin's wife Sibilla, tricks Baldwin into the dense forest and kills him. The sound of the fanfare announces the entrance of eight musicians, playing *pitu* bamboo flutes and *bombo* drums and shaking *sacaias* filled with shells and seeds. Their dance steps, variations on the waltz, quadrille and contradanse, accompany the beginning of the action, as sometimes the scene of Dom Carloto killing Valdevinos, witnessed by a hermit, is not played out.

Enter one of the key figures: Ganelão, Ganelon of Mayence, Charlemagne's brother-in-law, dressed in white with a gilded riding coat and an elaborate bicorne hat on his head. He commences his dance. The High Court of Charlemagne and his entourage, often elevated and draped with colourful fabrics, is at one end, and the Lower Court of the Mantuans, as vassals of Charlemagne, at the other. Charlemagne, wearing a red robe and a crown made of tin foil topped by a brass cross and a white cotton-wool beard, evokes a medieval figure, though this creole incarnation has little to do with the first emperor in 9th-century Europe. Two more masked men in black: the Dukes Amão (Armand) and Beltrão (Bertrand), appear followed by the group of the Marquis of Mântua, a French nobleman, dressed in black, his sister Ermelinda, mother of Valdevinos, and his niece Sibilla, Valdevinos's widow. They take turns to dance around the small coffin containing the bones of Valdevinos. Sibilla, expressing her grief by twirling round and round, her black skirt ballooning, presents a dramatic image of mourning.

One of the highlights of a tchiloli performance is the appearance of Renaud of Montauban (Reinaldo de Montalvão), also a nephew of Charlemagne, but affiliating himself in the play with the Mântuas. Clad entirely in black, with a crucifix sown into his cloak and a thick black wig with a braid and beard, he begins his spellbinding dance, twirling around his stick, menacing in his anarchic movements.

Dom Carloto wearing a fedora-style hat, meanwhile, marches with rigid steps, reminiscent of a marionette. The Justice Minister, in military uniform, disarms Dom Carloto, and demands the death penalty. Dom Carloto pleads not guilty. Using contemporary Portuguese business language, the Justice Minister telephones the count/defence lawyer, who arrives with his attaché case, sunglasses and white gloves, also effecting a marionette-like dance. The Empress, wearing a large pink crinoline and a crown above her transparent veil and white mask, pleads pity for her son. The entrance of Algoz – a figure dressed in red whose identity is unclear: the devil, a fool, the executioner? – and his duel with Renaud of Montauban, elicit a strong response from the public. Another high point of suspense is reached with the appearance of the page Mosca, holding a letter written by Dom Carloto to Roland, asking for help and admitting his guilt. Amidst much running and commotion, the letter is intercepted by Ganelon and presented to Dom Carloto.

It is suggested that it was indeed Ganelon behind the scheme all along, to get closer to the throne. There is, however, a general reconciliation scene at the end.

In the tchiloli, the participants are all male, even when playing the female roles (the Empress, her maids, Ermelinda and Sibilla), and the roles are hereditary. Masks made from wire, reminiscent of fencing masks, work like a uniform. The rest of the costume is made up of elaborate headgear, sunglasses, mirrors sewn on to the costumes (against the evil eye), ribbons, batons, and kneesocks. The music, with its different motifs for Charlemagne and the Mantuans, follows the heptatonic scale common in Western music, rather than the pentatonic scale characteristic of the Gulf of Guinea region.

How did this spectacle get to São Tomé, and why has it been so successful here? It has traditionally been assumed that the text was brought to São Tomé by Balthasar Dias, a blind poet from Madeira in the mid 16th century, building his 4,000 verses in iambic tetrameter on the 12- to 13th-century Carolingian cycle of historical legends, and the late 11th-century *Chanson de Roland*, telling of Roland's death through Ganelon's treachery, and medieval troubadour romances. However, recent research suggests that the text reached the island only in the late 19th century, in the wake of a renaissance of the 'cordel literature' (literally 'string') pamphlets, telling the story of Charlemagne's rebellious vassal in Portugal. Even the etymology of the word *tchiloli* is not clear. The tchiloli's social function is thought to reflect the need for a burial on plantations, connecting with beliefs of slaves from the continent and as a vehicle for satire and criticism of the colonial powers. Today, in the face of issues such as corruption and impunity, this demand still resonates with many Santomeans.

Catching a tchiloli performance should not be too difficult for travellers visiting in the dry season; they are usually put on for saints' days. On Príncipe, tchiloli performers come over for the St Laurent's festivities in mid-August. Today, there are about nine *tragédias* on São Tomé island. The best-known and most prestigious group is Formiguinha de Boa Morte; another popular one is from Caixão Grande, both suburbs of the capital.

The tchiloli has changed over time, as have the costumes: today faces powdered white with manioc flour and sunglasses often supplant the wire masks; the language is updated to include some *forro* or even English words and contemporary politics find their way into the text. In the current economic situation, the lack of funds for costumes, etc remains a problem but the Formiguinha *tragédia* has travelled to theatre festivals in Europe to introduce Western audiences to this unique Santomean form of dramatic expression. Meanwhile, the fascinating subtexts of this repository of African burial rites, ancestor worship, political expression and exploration of justice keep folklorists and researchers busy.

If you take a taxi out to Boa Morte, ask for *o kinté*, or *o sitio onde se faz a tragédia*, and people will probably be happy to show you; it is only a few hundred metres off the main road (only accessible by 4x4). The rectangle of earth is surrounded by a few traditional wooden houses bedecked with palm fronds, banana trees and washing lines. Taking the little path going off at the top right-hand side leads you to the sanctuary, the little chapel dedicated to Saint John (São João) where on important occasions, such as the saint's feast day on 27 January, tradition dictates that the soil has to be doused with palm wine to honour the ancestors. The new site www.tchiloli.com has beautiful images, plenty of background, and a list of the major groups, with text in both Portuguese and English.

in the air and catching it again. The two singing angels (*anzu cantá*) helping him are said to represent the ancestors. The captain, however, is a traitor who calls in the sorcerer, *feiticeiro* (*fitxicêlu* in creole), to help him usurp power. Dressed in red, the sorcerer arrives with his assistant: the *zuguzugu*. Another central figure is the **Opé Pó** (*pé-pau*, 'wooden foot') on stilts, who comes accompanied by the angel (*anzo mole*). After a fierce struggle for power, the angel is murdered by the *zuguzugu*. Most Danço Congo troupes, however, don't enact this scene, for fear that if the person playing the angel closes his eyes when playing the death, he will die for real. When the sorcerer and his assistant are chased away, the captain calls in the devil (*diabo*), dressed in black, who is also chased away. Finally, the angel is resurrected, and there is a big reconciliation scene at the end.

The action, which can last several hours but is often condensed to about 90 minutes, has been read in many different ways: as denouncing vice and corruption and the pretentions of high office, or as a parable of colonisation and loss of identity, order and disorder. In 1919, Danço Congo was banned by the colonial authorities who were worried by the performance's aggressive character and semiotics (devil killing angel). In the mid-60s, the Portuguese changed their minds, supporting new groups. Today, it is widely performed, and the troupe you are most likely to encounter is the fabulous Aliança Nova company from Neves, an Angolares town in the north of São Tomé island. Their sorcerer is in his nineties! Another active group is Macunjá Consol from Ribeira Afonso. While possibly older than both tchiloli (see box, pages 44–5) and Auto de Floripes (see box, page 190) from Príncipe, in terms of costumes and music, Danço Congo has a lot in common with these other unique cultural manifestations.

2

Practical Information

WHEN TO VISIT

While you can visit the islands at any time of the year, the most popular time is during one of the two dry seasons, either between June and September, or around January or February. Temperatures on the islands hover around 27°C all year round, but the summer months of the long dry season, *gravana*, are the best time for hiking and birdwatching. August visitors in particular have a good chance to catch popular saints' feast days and cultural events, where the streets throng with stalls, open-air discos and entertainment; don't miss the unique tchiloli and Danço Congo dramatic performances. Every other summer (around mid-June to mid-July), in even years, the Bienal cultural festival takes place in the capital. Mid-August, around the St Laurent's festivities, is an ideal time to visit Príncipe, to catch the colourful spectacle of the Auto de Floripes, the biggest celebration on the smaller sister island. To see humpback whales migrating, you have to come between August and October. Another good option is the short dry season, *gravanita*, which lasts from around mid-January to mid-February, including carnival celebrations which are a good opportunity for seeing traditional dances. This period is good for birdwatching too, as the birds are sporting their mating plumage. Between November and March visitors may watch marine turtles laying their eggs, and hatchlings being returned to the sea between September and April. Divers will find best visibility between December and March. However, January, February and March are the hottest months of the year, with the dry and dusty winds blowing sand from the Sahara into the Gulf of Guinea, often clouding the scenery in a 'Harmattan' haze, locally called *bruma seca*. In the rainy season between October and May, hiking becomes tricky on muddy terrain and the air is heavy with humidity, but photographers will find better light, blue skies and brighter contrasts. After finally braving the rainy season with tour groups, I personally would recommend November. Days can be a mixed bag: you might get rain in the morning, then a beautiful afternoon, with blue skies and the air feeling fresh after the tropical downpour, then a more cloudy evening with some rain, or a string of days where it only rains in the afternoons and evenings. The rainy season is best for orchid spotting, but if you want to see orchids and still be comfortable hiking, a lot of the species growing above 800m are still in flower in January. This is also the start of the saints' days season, beginning with São Isidro in Ribeira Afonso on the main island in late January, and on Príncipe with the celebrations of the discovery of the island on St Anthony's Day, 17 January.

HIGHLIGHTS AND ITINERARIES

Hike through dense rainforest to discover the crumbling colonial splendour of plantations, go beach-hopping and birdwatching, rough it at an ecolodge, travel back in time at a plantation house; and relax at Bom Bom Island resort on Príncipe. Taste slow-cooking Santomean specialities and the citrus freshness inside a cocoa pod. Admire majestic tropical flowers and discover a pristine underwater world. Stand on the Equator mark, climb the Pico de São Tomé, and catch performances of the medieval Charlemagne cycle in the rainforest. Replace with elements from other itineraries as preferred.

ONE WEEK

Day 1:	One-day walk of São Tomé town, overnight in the capital
Day 2:	Drive north (Lagoa Azul), plantation visit (Agostinho Neto), crab lunch at Neves, drive to 'end of the road', overnight Mucumbli ecolodge*f*
Day 3:	Beach day at Club Santana (visit Água Izé plantation on the way), overnight Club Santana
Day 4:	Drive to Bom Sucesso, exploring the plantations of Monte Café and Nova Moca, overnight Bom Sucesso
Day 5:	Early morning birdwatching, walk to Lagoa Amélia, overnight in the capital
Day 6:	Head south via Roça São João (lunch), swim at Praia Piscina, overnight at Praia Jalé Ecolodge
Day 7:	Malanza mangrove canoe tour, catch boat to Rolas Island for lunch and visit Equator mark, drive back to capital, stop at Roça de São João for coffee and to pick up souvenirs, visit local *discoteca* in São Tomé town

TWO WEEKS

Day 1:	One-day walk of São Tomé town, overnight in the capital
Day 2:	Drive north (Lagoa Azul), visit Agostinho Neto plantation, crab lunch at Neves, drive to 'end of the road', overnight Monteforte plantation
Day 3:	Drive back to capital and on to Bom Sucesso, exploring the plantations of Monte Café and Nova Moca, overnight Bom Sucesso or Nova Moca
Day 4:	Early morning birdwatching, explore botanical collection, walk to Lagoa Amélia, overnight Bom Sucesso
Day 5:	Hike to Bombaim plantation
Day 6:	Beach day at Club Santana, overnight Club Santana
Day 7:	Drive south from Santana via Roça São João (lunch), overnight Praia Inhame or Jalé Ecolodge
Day 8:	Day trip to Rolas Island, visit to Equator mark and lunch, overnight Praia Inhame or Jalé Ecolodge
Day 9:	Back to capital, visiting Água Izé plantation on the way
Day 10:	Fly to Príncipe, afternoon seabirding trip or half day exploring the plantations, overnight Bom Bom Island resort (or budget option)
Day 11:	Early morning birdwatching, relaxing/snorkelling or walk around Santo António, overnight Bom Bom Island resort (or budget option)
Days 12/13:	Fly back to São Tomé with a couple of days to spare for onward connection home (beach day, souvenir shopping)
Day 14:	Visit Mucumbli ecolodge for a relaxing end to your stay

If no trip to Príncipe planned, replace with three-day cycling tour, Pico de São Tomé, or snorkelling trip to Ilhéu das Cabras and diving baptism.

THREE WEEKS

Day 1:	One-day walk of São Tomé town, overnight in the capital
Day 2:	Drive north via Lagoa Azul, visit plantation (Agostinho Neto), crab lunch at Neves, overnight in the capital
Days 3/4:	Two-day cycling tour (or kayak trip to Ilhéu das Cabras plus organised day trip)
Day 5:	Drive to Bom Sucesso, exploring the plantations of Monte Café and Nova Moca, overnight Bom Sucesso
Day 6:	Early morning birdwatching and explore botanical collection, walk to Lagoa Amélia, overnight Bom Sucesso
Days 7/8:	Climb Pico de São Tomé with one night camping, and overnight at Bombaim plantation
Day 9:	Drive south via Roça de São João (lunch), overnight Praia Jalé Ecolodge or Praia Inhame
Day 10:	Day trip to Rolas Island, with visit to Equator mark and lunch, snorkelling, possibly overnight Rolas
Day 11:	Relax, back to capital, stopping at Sete Ondas beach and/or Água Izé plantation on the way, overnight capital
Day 12:	Beach-hopping along the coast from Praia Micoló, overnight capital
Day 13:	Fly to Príncipe, relax at Bom Bom Island resort, overnight Bom Bom
Day 14:	Early-morning birdwatching, full-day guided visit to plantations
Day 15:	Relax, seabirding boat trip or visit to Santo António, overnight Santo António or Bom Bom
Day 16:	Climb Pico de Papagaio or visit Banana Beach, overnight Santo António or Bom Bom Island resort
Days 17:	Explore the rainforest south of the island with guide, camping
Days 18/19:	Fly back to São Tomé with a couple of days to spare before connection home (beach day/souvenir shopping)
Day 20:	Visit Mucumbli ecolodge or Belo Monte plantation for a relaxing end to your stay

TOUR OPERATORS

Given the high air fares, it often works out cheaper, even for independent-spirited travellers who prefer to organise everything themselves, to book a package (eg: a diving package, with an extension of a week or two). You could sort out the rest once you're there, either through a local operator such as Navetur (see page 112), or by yourself for a lower price, especially if you are resourceful, maybe speak a bit of Portuguese and make some local friends. A tour operator will organise your visa, arrange a pick-up at the airport and assist you with any problems. For people travelling on their own, signing up for a few excursions provides ready-made travel companions. When contacting tour operators, it's best to phone instead of sending an email.

CRUISES Cruise ships such as MS *Amadea*, MS *Bremen*, MV *Hamburg* and Saga Holidays are increasingly including STP in their itineraries. Check www. cruisecompete.com for complete listings.

Road Scholar 11 Av de Lafayette, Boston MA 02111; ✎ 800 454 5768; e registration@ roadscholar.org. This not-for-profit lifelong-learning operation has 1 day on each island as part of their cruise along the West African coast from South Africa to Morocco.

UK

Birdquest Two Jays, Kemple End, Stonyhurst, Lancs BB7 9QY; ☎01254 826317; e birders@ birdquest.co.uk; www.birdquest.co.uk. Birdquest's groups of hardcore international birders hit STP in Jul/Aug, as an extension of their Gabon trip, guided by Nik Borrow, one of the foremost authorities on STP birds. Detailed trip reports on website.

Farside Africa 16 Dean Park Mews, Edinburgh EH14 1ED; ☎0131 315 2464; e info@farsideafrica. com; www.farsideafrica.com. Small Scottish company that can organise anything from camping in the rainforest to a stay at the top-notch Bom Bom Island resort. Good web content, plus voluntary carbon-offsetting initiative.

Greentours Leigh Cottage, Gauledge Lane, Longnor, Buxton, Derbyshire SK17 0PA; ☎01298 83563; e enquiries@greentours.co.uk; www. greentours.co.uk. This company provides a rounded natural history experience for its clients, again as an extension of Gabon. Detailed trip reports on request.

Original Travel 4 Cromwell Pl, London SW7 2JE; ☎020 7591 0300; e info@originaltravel.com; www. originaltravel.com. Catering to the top end of the market, the company is beginning to work with STP as an add-on to Gabon, but can also organise a tailor-made trip with stays at Omali Lodge & Bom Bom, visits to plantations & boat trips, etc.

Rainbow Tours ☎020 7666 1250; info@ rainbowtours.co.uk; www.rainbowtours.co.uk. Established in 1997, this independent Africa & Latin America specialist wins regular travel-industry awards. For instance, Rainbow's 9-day tour staying at Bom Bom and Omali Lodge and starting from £1,970, was selected as one of Wanderlust's best trips for 2014. Check out the excellent website for information about tailor-made tours. See ad in the colour section.

Undiscovered Destinations Saville Exchange, Howard St, North Shields, Tyne & Wear NE30 1SE; ☎0191 296 2674, from the US/Canada 1 800 315 3846; e info@undiscovered-destinations.com; www.undiscovered-destinations.com. This small, friendly adventure travel agency specialising in pioneering destinations offers a 9-day tour (starting from £1,790, inc flights & some meals; land-only rate £835), taking in the Bombaim plantation, hiking to Bernardo Faro, the east coast, the southern beaches, a trip to the Equator & the northeast. Also tailor-made itineraries including the Bom Bom Island resort.

US

Bushtracks 824 Healdsburg Av, Healdsburg, CA 95448; ☎1 800 900 8689; e info@bushtracks. com; www.bushtracks.com. Tailor-made trips organised by family-run Africa experts, supporting conservation & educational projects.

AFRICA
Angola

World Travel Agency Av 4 de Fevereiro, 39 RC Luanda; ☎02 310972, 02 311252; e tour@ wtangola.com; www.agencewta.com. Club Santana resort holidays.

Gabon

Africa's Eden BP 99, Port Gentil; ☎564818; e info@africas-eden.com; www.africas-eden.com

Mistral Voyages Immeuble Diamant, BP-2106, Libreville; ☎760421, 761222; e info@ ecotourisme-gabon.com; www.tourisme-gabon. com. Established agency with offices in Port Gentil & São Tomé, & head office in Marseille. Can also book flights to São Tomé & on to Príncipe.

South Africa

Birding Africa 4 Crassula Way, Pinelands 7405, Cape Town; ☎21 531 9148; e info@birdingafrica. com; www.birdingafrica.com. Whilst STP is offered as an extension to their regular Gabon birdwatching expedition (trip report on website), they are happy to tailor-make an expedition.

Rockjumper Birding Tours PO Box 13972, Cascades 3202; ☎33 394 0225/51; e info@ rockjumperbirding.com, rockjumperbirding@ yahoo.com; www.rockjumperbirding.com. Birdwatching specialist offering STP as an extension to their Aug Gabon trip, including 3 nights' camping on São Tomé & a stay at Bom Bom Island resort on Príncipe. Can book the STP leg only & arrange your own flights.

MAINLAND EUROPE
Belgium

Vitamin Travel Rue des Bouchers 61, 1000 Brussels; ☎02 512 7464; e info@vitamintravel.be

France

Héliades 1 Parc Club du Golf BP 422000, 13591 Aix en Provence; ☎0892 23 15 23; e resaweb@ heliades.fr; www.heliades.fr. This Greece specialist started offering trips to STP in 2012, to complement their Cape Verde portfolio, flying from Paris, Lyon, Marseille, Nice & Toulouse to connect with the TAP departure. Guaranteed departures & choice between chauffeured & self-driven holidays, as well as hiking trips round the plantations, with a night's camping, & relaxing holidays based in Club Santana or Hotel Praia.

Mistral Voyages 111 Rue du Commandant Rolland, 13008 Marseille; ☏04 91 54 73 71; e info@mistralvoyages.com; www.sao-tome. st. Offers 7-night stays in a variety of hotels/ *residencials*/resorts, or 4 themed trips, including an island-hopping circuit, where you get to visit both the main islands & the Equator island. Wed departures from various European cities, including Brussels, Geneva, Paris, Lyon & London. Tailor-made itineraries available too. Partner agencies on São Tomé & in Gabon (Libreville, Port Gentil).

Voyageurs du Monde 55 Rue Ste Anne, 75002 Paris (various other branches); ☏01 42 86 16 00; www.vdm.com. Two 9-day trips, one based at small town hotel Avenida (from €2,500), one at Club Santana resort (from €3,520). A min of 2 people is required. Normally, clients travel via Lisbon, but a stay in Gabon, with passage via Libreville, can be organised too.

Zig-Zag Randonnées 54 Rue de Dunkerque, 75009 Paris; ☏01 42 85 13 93; e contact@zig-zag-randonnees.com; www.zigzag-randonnees. com. 'Sur la piste des plantations' packages, 9-day (from €2,140) & 16-day (€2,740), excellent for keen walkers who also want to discover São Tomé's culture & history.

Germany

Cobra Verde Bauernreihe 6a, 27726 Worpswede; ☏0479 295 2124; e kontakt@cobra-verde.de; www.cobra-verde.de. Pioneers of STP travel offering relaxing beach holidays, 8-day São Tomé circuits, & a 16-day trip to both islands, with the option of an additional beach week.

Ivory Tours Schnieglinger Str 4, 90419 Nürnberg; ☏0911 393 8520; e info@ivory-tours.de; www. ivory-tours.de, www.divingsaotome.de. Africa/ diving specialist offering a 9-day trip with flexible dates throughout the year (min 2 people). Typically, this will include 3 nights in the capital (in upmarket hotels), with an English-speaking programme of a half-day visit of the town & 2 day trips (to Bom Sucesso/São Nicolão waterfall

& the northern beaches), before you go on to Ilhéu das Rolas for diving & other activities such as birdwatching, boat tours, walks, sailing, African dance workshop, volleyball. You can book an additional week on Rolas.

One World – Reisen mit Sinnen Neuer Graben 153, 44137 Dortmund; ☏0231 589 7920; e oneworld@reisenmitsinnen.de; www. reisenmitsinnen.de. This award-winning eco operator offers 2 kinds of 2-week packages, each including both islands: one more based around hiking (including an optional ascent of the Pico de São Tomé), the other more towards relaxation & resort luxury. The award-winning 16-day 'São Tomé Discovery' package (min 6 people) involves travelling on foot & jeep with a city tour & a cookery class at São João, stays at various plantations, & 3 days on Príncipe staying at the remote Abade plantation & exploring the beaches & plantations on foot. German-language tour leader. Full disclosure: the author of this book could well be your guide here. Offset the carbon emissions of your trip (3,760kg!) with a voluntary payment to a climate protection project.

Planeta Verde Dänenstr 15, 10439 Berlin; ☏030 2462 8793; e info@planeta-verde.de; www.planeta-verde.de. Wildlife specialist, offering a beach week at Club Santana as an extension of their Gabon tour.

Italy

With any Italian operator note that prices shoot up in August.

Ekoafrica Via Damiano Chiesa 7/D, 58100 Grosseto; ☏0564 386 222; e info@ekoafrica. com; www.ekoafrica.com. 7 nights (4 at Pestana Equador, 3 Pestana São Tomé), dbl room B&B with flights & transfers start at €1,300 based on 2 people sharing.

Il Viaggio Via Schiaparelli 18, 20125 Milano; ☏02 67 390 001, 02 66 982 915; e info@ilviaggio. biz; www.ilviaggio.biz. Packages of 8 days at Omali Lodge start at under €1,900, 14 days split between Omali Lodge & Bom Bom Island resort at €2,850, including HB, TAP flights, internal flights where applicable, & transfers.

Netherlands

Africa's Eden Westervoortsedijk 71k, 6827 AV Arnhem; e marketing@africas-eden.com; www. africas-eden.com. Ecotourism operator behind the Belomonte plantation on Príncipe. Working with Africa's Connection, the former owners of Bom Bom are offering a one-stop-shop service that includes flexible private charters & packages to Príncipe from São Tomé & the region (Douala, Libreville, Port Gentil, Malabo).

Norway

Espnes Reizer Akersgata 47, 0180 Oslo; ☎47 22 34 70 70; e bb@espnes.no; www.espnes.no.

Portugal

Abreu ☎707 201 840; e directo@abreu.pt; www.abreu.pt. Portugal's biggest tour operator with more than 80 branches across the country selling 9-day packages, combining stays at Omali Lodge, Bom Bom Island resort, Club Santana & Pestana Equador Island Resort on Rolas. Other major operators, such as Solférias (www.solferias.pt), Soltrópico (www.soltropico.pt) or Tagus (☎707 220 000; e telesales@viagenstagus.pt; www.taguseasy. pt) and Entremares (www.entremares.pt) work with the same hotels. These packages are bookable through travel agents such as Atlântida Viajens (Av Columbano Bordalo Pinheiro, 61B, 1070-061 Lisbon; ☎217 228 210; e geral@atlantidaviajens.pt; www.atlantidaviajens.pt).

Fotoadrenalina m 916 944711 (Vitor Costa); www.fotoadrenalina.com. From 2015, this outfit will be running photographic expeditions to STP, with knowledgeable tour leaders who care about sustainability & max contact with locals. While advice will be given, of course, these trips will not be for complete beginners.

Happy Landings Rua da Saudade 15 r/c esq, 1100-582 Lisbon; ☎217 268818/9; m 911 059952; e ets@happylandings.travel; www.happylandings. travel. Run by Eduardo Teixeira da Silva & the Swiss consul in STP, Reto Scherraus (see page 100), this personable agency in the heart of Old Lisbon specialises in the corporate sector but can organise carefully tailor-made packages for independent travellers as well.

Movimento de Expressão Fotografica m 9625 27453 (Luis Rocha); e geral@mef.pt; www.mef.pt. This young, passionate, non-profit association organises documental photographic expeditions to both islands. During 14-day arrangements, you'll be able to stay at plantations such as São João & Bombaim & other local establishments, taking in the best colours, angles & iconic views, with plenty of hiking & contact with local people, including observing the extraction of palm wine, fishing from a pirogue, teaching pin-hole photography to local kids & learning the meaning of living *leve-leve*. Flights are separate.

Terra Africa ☎217 514800; e reservas@ terraafrica.pt, geral@terraafrica.pt; www.terraafrica. pt. Owned by Euroatlantic Airways and offering 2 packages: a 2-centre stay combining Ilhéu das Rolas Resort & Hotel Miramar or Hotel Pestana São Tomé Ocean Resort Hotel starting from €784, & a 1-week stay in the capital only, with the same hotel options or Omali Lodge & Residencial Avenida, starting from €728 pp/dbl room. Flights with TAP or STP Airways (operated by Euroatlantic). Packages bookable through the company or any travel agent in Portugal & abroad. Independent travellers wanting to tack on an additional week travelling around have more flexibility going with TAP; using STP Airways attracts a supplement of at least €116.

Spain

Agrotravel www.turismoresponsable.es. The Basque sustainable travel specialist can facilitate trips.

Casa África Alfonso XIII, 5, 35003, Las Palmas de Gran Canaria; ☎928 43 28 00; www.casafrica.es. Works with the major tour operators & a Spanish traveller I spoke to booked a week at Pestana Ocean Resort, as it was less expensive than just booking the flights.

Cultura Africana c/Santa Inés 4, 28012 Madrid; ☎915 39 32 67; e info@culturafricana.com; www.culturafricana.com. Offers 8-day trips using the most favourable tariff offered by the major operators (Portugal Tours, Lusotours, etc), with the option of more independent travel & private accommodation on request.

Lusoviajes Barcelona; ☎936 58 94 89; www. lusoviajes.com. A 9-day package leaving from Madrid & Barcelona airports. Packages with STP Airways under €1,000, staying 3 nights at Rolas.

Pasaporte a Aventura: Kananga C/Cendra, 30-08001 Barcelona; ☎934 42 49 03; e web@ kananga.com. Also Ambarviajes C/Toledo 73 (access C/Ruda 23), Madrid; m 913 645 912; e info@ambarviajes.com

Portugal Tours Calle Princesa, 90, 2nd floor, 28008 Madrid; ☎915 48 46 00; www.portugal-tours.com. This specialist in lusophone destinations can arrange trips.

Tuareg Viatges Ptge de Mariner 1 bis, 08025 Barcelona; ☎ 932 65 23 91; www.tuaregviatges. es. A 9-day 'Voyage to the Navel of the World' trip starts at €740.

Viajes Dragontours Serreta 17, Cartagena/Avda Doctor Meca 28, Puerto de Mazarrón; Comercial, 30, Urb Camposol (Mazarrón); ☎ 902 19 47 66; e info@dragontours.net; www.dragontours.net. Packages through the same major operators – though there has been little demand for STP as a destination.

Switzerland

A&M Africa Tours Postfach, 8712 Stäfa; ☎ 44 926 79 79; e travel@africatours.ch; www.africatours. ch. Luxury resorts, plantation houses, guesthouses, guided excursions, ecotourism, trekking tours, self drive, etc. Knowledgeable & enthusiastic operator.

Aquaterra Travel Kastanienweg 2, 6353 Weggis; ☎ 41 500 08 45; e info@aquaterra-travel.ch; www.aquaterra-travel.ch. Tailor-made 11-night upmarket trips using Omali Lodge & Bom Bom, with plenty of scope for special requests.

RED TAPE

ENTRY REQUIREMENTS You need a **passport** that is valid for another 12 months after your return date (an unusually long period, so don't be caught out, express passports are costly), a **return ticket**, and a **visa** (see below).

VISAS Unless you are a citizen of São Tomé and Príncipe, you will need a visa (*visto*). Do not attempt to enter the country without one, and don't believe what you see on out-of-date websites, such as, surprisingly, the Foreign Office's.

São Tomé and Príncipe has no diplomatic representation in the UK, despite old contacts circulating on the internet. UK citizens should either go through Brussels (see page 55) or obtain a visa through one of the major agencies such as Navetur (see page 112) or through one of the major hotels, which provide assistance. In the US, the São Tomé and Príncipe embassy, reopened in 2013, is a one-man show, and unless you live in NYC, it might save you hassle to go through a visa service (eg: *www.traveldocs.com*). Australians, New Zealanders, South Americans and the rest of the world can apply to any São Tomé and Príncipe embassy; I would recommend the one in Brussels (see page 55). South African citizens can obtain their visas from the São Tomé and Príncipe embassy in Angola or Gabon. STP has no diplomatic representation in Brazil, and according to the Embassy, visas for Brazilian visitors are best arranged with local support.

It is also possible to apply for a **visa online** at www.smf.st/virtualvisa but the process is far from smooth. In the words of a US citizen resident in STP, 'Most of the bugs have been worked out, but a few of our travellers have had to attempt more than once'. Successful completion of the online application will result in an approval page (Authorization for Entry) that must be printed and presented to the airline in lieu of a visa. The actual visa is paid for and inserted into the applicant's passport upon arrival in STP. It is a good idea to have the correct money to hand, currently US$80, as immigration agents rarely have change.

Even applicants for a tourist visa are asked to provide a '**reference**' in São Tomé; just put 'Direcção Nacional do Turismo, Av 12 de Julho, CP 40, São Tomé, ☎ 00 239 2221542'. If you are using a **tour operator** in your country or locally, they will take care of your visa. For instance, Navetur (see page 112) or Mistral (see page 112) can email you a form to fill in for a 'permission letter' sufficient to obtain a pre-arranged visa payable at the airport (€60 if you are from a country with a visa-issuing São Tomé and Príncipe representation, €50 otherwise). In addition, Navetur also requests a photocopy/scan of the first four pages of your passport.

You might hear through the grapevine that you should be OK to get a visa on arrival if there are a couple of you. This might have happened in the past – the

2

airlines have a duty to take you back to your country of origin and risk a fine, but in practice don't always check visas – but the law has long since been tightened, and tourists arriving without a visa have been sent back, and no offer of paying a fine will help. Don't take the risk.

The immigration services, Serviço de Migraçao e Fronteiras (*São Tomé: Av Marginal 12 de Julho (next to CACAU);* 222 2098; f 222 2695; e *secretaria@smf.st; Príncipe: Delegação Regional Paços do Concelho (City Hall), Santo Antónia;* 225 1183; *deirap@smf.st; www.smf.st*) is where, once in the country, extensions to your visa can be requested. Be aware that there is a dress code – no shorts or skimpy tops – and the attitude is none too helpful. When I needed to extend my stay by a week, I was forced to return three times and only received my passport the day before I was due to travel. For a short period it may be less hassle to incur the fine (about 1,000,000$) at the airport.

Applying in Brussels The very professionally run embassy in Brussels handles visa applications for EU citizens as well as other nationalities (see page 55), the staff there can email you a form. You will usually need to take in or post (registered) your passport (valid up to three months after your return), a passport picture, plus a self-addressed envelope with your details. For a business visa you will need to provide a letter from your company. The visa, turnaround 48 hours, costs €20, urgent (same-day) €30, and is usually valid for up to 30 days. It is, however, not a problem to request a longer validity, maximum 180 days for a business visa. Payment is by electronic transfer, and add another €10 to cover the postage for each passport.

Applying in Portugal You can obtain your visa at the embassy or from one of the consulates (including Albufeira, Funchal and Coimbra) but you cannot apply by post. Bring your passport, a passport photo, the filled-in Modelo 3 form (available on the website) and €20 Monday to Friday between 09.30 and 12.30. The embassy closes at 13.00, but the *senhas*, numbered tickets, are only given out until then. After submitting the completed form, including your address in STP, you can pick up the visa after eight business days. The urgency tax for three business days adds another €10. This 30-day visa is not valid for multiple entries. The 180-day business visas are tricky to get, and you need to provide a letter from your employer. A same-day visa for STP is available only in urgent cases and costs €50, but as there is no entitlement to this service it is not mentioned on the website. If you only have a few hours between the plane that brought you to Lisbon & your onward connection I can think of a less stressful way to pass that time – in which case I would recommend the Brussels option. At the consulate in Porto a visa is €40, or €48 for an emergency visa available within 48 hours. You need to bring two passport photos and you have to deliver your documents and pick up your visa in person; there is no postal service.

Applying in Spain The Spanish consulate offers a same-day visa service; bring or send in your passport, two passport photos, plus €50 in cash. Spanish residents can apply online, which is €30 cheaper.

EMBASSIES AND CONSULATES

ABROAD After years of haphazard diplomatic representation, the opening of a diplomatic representation in both the **USA** and **Cape Verde** is now planned. As for **Portugal**, consulate contact information changes regularly though, so it is best to phone Lisbon for current details.

E **Angola** (embassy) 173 Rua Eng Armindo de Andrade, Mira-Mar, Luanda; ☎ 242 345 677; **e** emb-stp.ango@snet.co.ao

E **Austria** (consulate) Margarethengürtel 1a–3a, 1050 Wien; ☎ 01 545 165 350; **m** 664 355 31 20; **e** gerhard.schiesser@schiesser.at. No visa service.

E **Belgium** (embassy for most European citizens) Square Montgomery, 175 Av de Tervuren, 1150 Brussels; ☎ 02 7348966; **e** ambassade@ saotomeeprincipe.be

E **France** (consulate) 111 Rue du Commandant Rolland, 13008 Marseille; ☎ 04 91 37 58 02; **e** consulat@sao-tome.st; www.sao-tome.st. The dynamic consul, Jean-Pierre Bensaïd, is the owner of Mistral Voyages (see page 112) & is involved in various initiatives supporting the country & fostering Franco–Santomean links.

E **Gabon** (embassy) Bd de la Mer, BP 489, Libreville; ☎ 721527. Only open in the morning; the visa costs 40,000CFA.

E **Germany** (honorary consulate) Marcusallee 9, 28359 Bremen; ☎ 0421 173 6186; **e** rbo@ germanlashing.de. No visa service, & only really responsible for the city-state of Bremen. It's best to call rather than email, though they are in the process of setting up a website.

E **Hungary** (consulate) Szász Károly u 1, Budapest 1027; ☎ +361 2667572; **e** titkarsag@ diplomatamagazin.hu. Visa service.

E **Italy** (consulate) Via Cavour 44, 00184 Roma; ☎ 06 4782 3867; **e** info@saotomeprincipe-roma. it; www.saotomeprincipe-roma.it. The honorary consulate for Rome & the Lazio region is active in humanitarian relief work (collecting donations for medical instruments). They recommend going through Brussels for a visa rather than the e-visto.

E **Netherlands** (consulate) Droogbak 1a, 1013 GE Amsterdam; ☎ 020 711 9000; **e** contact@ visitstp.nl; www.visitstp.nl

E **Portugal** (embassy) Rua 5 Outubro, 1000-017 Lisbon; ☎ 218 461 917/8; **e** embaixada@emb-saotomeprincipe.pt; www.emb-saotomeprincipe. pt (click on Serviços Consulares); (consulate) Av de Boa Vista 1203, 3rd floor, room 303, 4100-130 Porto; ☎ 226 093 436; **e** consulado.stp-porto@ mail.telepac.pt

E **Spain** (consulate) C/Juan Hurtado de Mendoza 13, Apt 505, 28036 Madrid; **m** 626 909 015; **e** ilbrunet@hotmail.com

E **Taiwan** (embassy) 18 Chi-lin Rd, 3rd floor, Taipeh; ☎ 02 28766824; **e** gilandrade67@hotmail. com.

IN SÃO TOMÉ You should not have much reason to contact your embassy, but if you do, accredited embassies (with the exception of Portugal and France) are on the African mainland, in Gabon, Angola or Cameroon. Australians should contact their embassy in Lisbon, Canadians the High Commission in Nigeria, South Africans their embassy in Gabon and residents of the UK their embassy in Angola.

The honorary consuls (usually local businessmen) should be able to direct you, but they are not always available. Most countries' embassy details are on the internet, but much of the information can be out of date; that applies even to the list on file at the Foreign Affairs Ministry, and expats won't necessarily know the contacts either.

E **Angola** (embassy) Av Kwame Nkrumah 45, CP 133; ☎ 222 2376; **e** info@embang.st; www. embangola.st. Embaixada de Angola is a common reference point on this long street.

E **Australia** (embassy) Av da Liberdade, 200, 2nd floor, Lisbon ☎ +351 21 310 1500; **e** austemb. lisbon@dfat.gov.au, anna.marques@dfat.gov. au; www.portugal.embassy.gov.au. Australian Embassy in Portugal:

E **Brazil** (embassy) Av 12 de Julho 20; ☎ 222 6060/1; **e** brasemb.saotome@itamaraty.gov.br; www.saotome.itamaraty.gov.br/pt-br/

E **Canada** 15 Bobo Street, Maitama (PO Box 5144); ☎ +11 234 94 612 900; **e** abuja@ international.gc.ca. High Commission in Nigeria.

E **Cape Verde** (consulate) Rua Damão 10; ☎ 222 2728; **m** 990 6244; **e** consulcvde@cstome. net

E **China** (embassy) Bureau Conselho e Comercial República Popular da China, Av Kwame Nkruma; ☎ 222 1550.

E **France** (embassy) Bairro Quinta Santo António; ☎ 222 1353, 222 2266; **e** patrick.cohen@ diplomatie.gouv.fr. Next to the TVS TV station. I've heard that diplomatic representation may be scaled down in the future.

⑥ Gabon (embassy) Embaixada da República do Gabão, Rua Damão;📞222 4434; m 990 5669.

⑥ Germany (consulate) Honorary Consul Manuel Lima Nazaré (m 990 3306) is also the owner of the Praia Inhame eco-resort; you can get hold of him through the Padaria Moderna bakery on Rua 3 de Fevereiro (📞222 3217; e pamoderna@ live.com). In an emergency, German-speakers are better off talking to the Swiss honorary consul Reto Scherraus (see page 100).

⑥ Guinea-Equatorial (embassy) Fruta-Fruta;📞222 5427.

⑥ Italy (consulate) Av 12 de Julho 978;📞222 2934. Chocolate maker Claudio Corallo doubles up as consul. The embassy is in Angola: Rua Dr Americo Boavida 49, CP 6220, Ingombota, Luanda;📞+244 222 331 245/6; e ambasciata. luanda@esteri.it; www.ambluanda.esteri.it

⑥ Morocco (honorary consulate) Rua de Angola 466, 1st floor📞222 4206; e consmstp@gmail. com. Established in 2013.

⑥ Netherlands (consulate) Rua de Moçambique;📞222 2685, 222 2084; m 990 8457; e farmacabral@cstome.net. Honorary consul is Abilio Afonso Henriques. Embassy in Angola: Empreendimento Comandante Gika, Torre B, Piso 8, Travessa Ho Chi Minh, Alvalade, Luanda; m +244 924 068 802, 923 503 254; e lua@minbuza.nl.

⑥ Nigeria (embassy) Av Kwame Nkrumah;📞222 5404/5; e nigeria@cstome.net; http://

nigeriaembassysaotome.com. Next to the UN building.

⑥ Portugal (embassy) Av 12 de Julho;📞222 1130; e empor@cstome.net, eporstp@cstome.net (though as with most cstome email addresses, their inbox gets full very quickly. Near the Miramar Hotel.

⑥ South Africa (embassy) Les Arcades Bldg, 2nd floor, 142 Rue de Chavannes, Centrville/BP 4063, Libreville;📞+241 77 4 530/1.

⑥ Spain (consulate) Maite Mendizabal; Av Marginal 12 de Julho, Edif Cruz Vermelha/Red Cross building, São Tomé; m 990 3707, 990 3707; e spain.consulado.stp@gmail.com. Embassy in Gabon: Immeuble Diamant, 2nd floor, Bd De l'Indépendance, PO Box 1557, Libreville;📞+241 172 1264; e emb.libreville@maec.es

⑥ Taiwan (diplomatic mission) Av 12 de Julho/ Bairro Banco Mundial;📞222 2671, 222 3529; e rocstp@cstome.net. Near the National Museum.

⑥ UK (embassy) Rua 17 de Setembro 4, CP 1244, Luanda;📞+244 222 334 582, out-of-hours emergency📞+244 222 397 681; e postmaster. luand@fco.gov.uk. Embassy in Angola.

⑥ USA (diplomatic mission) Pinheira;📞222 5519; e ipinto@sto.ibb.gov. Some 5km out of town, on the Voice of America site (📞222 3400). The accredited embassy is in Gabon: Bd du Bord de Mer, BP 4000, Sablière, Libreville;📞+241 01 45 71 00, emergencies: +241 07 38 01 71; e usembassylibreville@state.gov; http://libreville. usembassy.gov/.

GETTING THERE AND AWAY

BY AIR The information below details how to reach STP via Portugal or the African mainland. Visitors may want to combine their trip to STP with a visit to Cape Verde, or spend a few days discovering the city of Lisbon. For information on arriving in Príncipe by air, see pages 189–91.

Via Portugal The most common route for Western travellers is through **Lisbon**, the capital of Portugal. One option is the reliable Portuguese national airline **TAP**, which has recently switched its traditional once-weekly direct flight for a daytime service operating three times a week, with a refuelling stop in Accra (Ghana), returning at night, with the same stopover. This increases TAP's seating capacity to 400 a week for STP. It remains to be seen whether this routing is viable long-term, so always get the latest information from TAP or one of the agencies in STP. The alternative is the national carrier **STP Airways,** which at the time of going to print was operating a weekly direct overnight flight and regularly offers good promotional fares. STP Airways is technically on the European Union's aviation **blacklist** (updated in 2013), which bans carriers from members' airspace for safety concerns or not meeting regulatory standards. In practice, STP Airways gets around this problem by operating with planes belonging to **Euroatlantic Airways**, the Portuguese charter carrier majority-owned by the Pestana Group, the owner of three hotels on São Tomé. It can actually be cheaper to buy a Pestana package with STP Airways, splitting your stay between Pestana Ocean Resort in the capital and the Rolas Island operation, than buying the flights separately!

Round-trip air fares start at around €700 with TAP – economy class gets booked up very quickly. If you are travelling from outside Portugal, it might be cheaper to book your tickets separately, coming in to Lisbon with a budget airline; however, if there's a delay with your incoming flight, without a TAP through-ticket you lose the right to take the next available flight the following week. In any case, make sure on the return flight that you don't cut it too fine between arriving back in Lisbon and your onward connection. Always get the latest information from Navetur, and ideally, plan to spend a couple of days in Lisbon. Whilst I was in STP in late 2013, both the TAP and the STP Airways flight were delayed by a day: one plane had to turn back because a bird wrecked the turbine; the other already came in with an engine problem. At one point in 2013, runway lights at TMS Airport were stolen.

Getting to Lisbon For a full and easy-to-use current list of Lisbon's airport (*www.ana.pt*) connections, search www.wikipedia.org for 'Portela Airport'. For contact details of airlines operating from the UK, Ireland and the US, see pages 60–1.

From mainland Europe TAP fly to Lisbon direct from many European cities, including Barcelona, Bologna, Budapest (via Prague), Frankfurt, Munich, Madrid, Paris, Prague, Venice, Zagreb, as do Lufthansa (Frankfurt, Munich), Air France, KLM (Amsterdam) and Iberia (Madrid). More and more budget carriers are also adding Lisbon to their route network, such as Germanwings (Cologne/Bonn and Stuttgart seasonally) and easyJet (Basel, Berlin Schönefeld, Geneva, Milan Malpensa, Paris CDG and Rome Fiumicino).

From the US and Canada Various carriers belonging to the Star Alliance network (*www.staralliance.com*) fly to Lisbon from the US. TAP has a daily direct New York Newark–Lisbon overnight service (and sometimes, special offers), and United has one daily overnight flight from New York Newark. From Canada, Air Transat flies from both Montreal and Toronto, and the Azorean airline SATA has competitive fares from Toronto (and Boston), as well as Montreal (seasonally) via the Azores. Generelly speaking, in the summer season you can catch a direct flight from Toronto or Boston, at other times you fly via Ponta Delgada. Remember that on flights from North America the rules on taking liquids on board are stricter than when flying from within Europe.

Via Africa From the African continent, the points of entry are Libreville, the capital of Gabon; Malabô (Equatorial Guinea), Accra (Ghana), currently the refuelling stop for all TAP flights from Lisbon; Douala (Cameroon); Luanda (Angola); and Port Gentil (Gabon). Generally, book early, and, as the flight situation can change very quickly, it is probably best to start your research by sending an email to Navetur (see page 112). It is possible to book a through ticket from Europe to São Tomé with Air France but it involves an overnight in Libreville and unless TAP and STP Airways flights are completely booked up the pricing and the potential stopover required probably makes Paris–Libreville–ST less attractive than Paris–Lisbon–ST.

Angola If you want to combine Angola with a trip to STP, there is the national Angolan carrier **TAAG** (*Rua da Missão 123, PO Box 79, Luanda;* \ *+244 222 332 077, 222 332 387;* e *TAAGSAC@flytaag-angolaairlines.com; www.taag.com*), which, while not on the official blacklist, is restricted to only operating certain aircraft within the EU. It is also possible to connect at Libreville (Air France) or Accra (BA has a daily flight), but overnight stops are required for both connections.

There is currently one TAAG flight every week from the capital, Luanda, to São Tomé. Round-trip fares from Luanda start at €200, attracting many visitors keen to relax on the islands. Non-Angolans living in Angola don't have it so easy, as they have to renew their visa each time before re-entry, and Angola is notoriously tricky for visas.

Apart from the daily Lisbon connection, TAAG links Luanda with London (twice a week), Paris, Frankfurt, Harare (Zimbabwe), Johannesburg (South Africa), Lusaka (Zambia), Nairobi (Kenya), Maputo (Mozambique), Windhoek (Namibia), Rio de Janeiro and São Paulo (Brazil), Dubai, Beijing (China), Havana (Cuba) and Sal (Cape Verde).

Gabon The connection between the Gabonese capital of Libreville and São Tomé is served by Equatorial Guinean airline CEIBA. At the time of writing it was flying twice-weekly, and is also on the list of companies not allowed to operate in Europe. This connection could be of interest to those organising a birding holiday independently. Book your **CEIBA** (Quartier Glass, next to SGS; \ 77 35 76, 77 35 77) ticket for around €350, and show it when you apply for your visa. Mistral Voyages (see page 112) or Navetur (see page 112) should be able to help with this.

You can book an (expensive) through ticket to São Tomé with **Air France**, but you will need to stay overnight in Libreville and this is only a good idea if you are planning to combine a trip to São Tomé and Príncipe with seeing Gabon. From London, Air France flies to Libreville via Paris CDG on Tuesdays, Thursdays, Fridays and Sundays, leaving Heathrow at 06.40, for the 10.55 connection to Libreville. Whilst the Eurostar to Paris is the greener option, if there is a delay, without an Air France through-ticket from London, you will have to pay a supplement to get on the next day's flight.

For those staying in Libreville, the closest hotel to the airport (2km) is the Onomo Hôtel (La Sablière, Rte Angondje, Quartier Ambassade US/Aéroport; \ 241 01 45 91 00; e reservation.libreville@onomohotel.com; €90), which offers a free shuttle bus. An inexpensive option is the **Tropicana** (\ +241 731531/32; €20) some 800m further south and a CFA2,000 taxi ride away, CFA4,000 at night. It is also on the beach and has a nice bar and outside restaurant; book early. If you're feeling adventurous, a few hundred metres from Libreville airport is an Aerobar where the pilots fill up; you could try and see whether you can get on one of the South African charter planes going to São Tomé. (You didn't hear it from me.)

Equatorial Guinea Currently two airlines are flying between Malabô and São Tomé, and the flight time is about one hour. Probably the wiser choice is **CEIBA** as although it is also on the European blacklist (see pages 56–7) it has a friendly booking office in São Tomé (see STP Tours, page 61).

South Africa Currently, there are no direct flights to STP, but **South African Airways (SAA)** operate flights from Johannesburg to Libreville, and several times a week from Cape Town and Johannesburg to Luanda. SAA charge from around 8,850R for their twice-weekly flights to São Tomé via Libreville, round

LONG-HAUL FLIGHTS, CLOTS AND DVT

Any prolonged immobility including travel by land or air can result in deep vein thrombosis (DVT) with the risk of embolus to the lungs. Certain factors can increase the risk and these include:

- Previous clot or close relative with a history
- People over 40 but > risk over 80 years
- Recent major operation or varicose veins surgery
- Cancer
- Stroke
- Heart disease
- Obesity
- Pregnancy
- Hormone therapy
- Heavy smokers
- Severe varicose veins
- People who are very tall (over 6ft/1.8m) or short (under 5ft/1.5m)

A deep vein thrombosis (DVT) causes painful swelling and redness of the calf or sometimes the thigh. It is only dangerous if a clot travels to the lungs (pulmonary embolus). Symptoms of a pulmonary embolus (PE) include chest pain, shortness of breath, and sometimes coughing up small amounts of blood. These commonly start three to ten days after a long flight. Anyone who thinks that they might have a DVT needs to see a doctor immediately.

PREVENTION OF DVT
- Keep mobile before and during the flight; move around every couple of hours
- Drink plenty of fluids during the flight
- Avoid taking sleeping pills and drinking excessive tea, coffee and alcohol
- Consider wearing flight socks or support stockings (see www.legshealth.com)

If you think you are at increased risk of a clot, ask your doctor if it is safe to travel.

trip. US travellers wanting to combine visiting South Africa with São Tomé and Príncipe can use SAA, too, departing from New York JFK or Washington Dulles Airport. Fares start at around US$1,650 (breaking up the fare into individual legs is cheaper than a through-ticket), requiring a two-day stopover in Libreville. Once the large runway on Príncipe is finished, there will be much more on offer for South African travellers and São Tomé could then be tagged on to a trip to Príncipe, in a reversal of what happens at the moment, where Príncipe is added on to a trip to São Tomé.

Via Cape Verde Visitors may want to consider combining a holiday to São Tomé and Príncipe with one to Cape Verde. There are many fascinating historical and cultural ties between STP and the arid archipelago, also an ex-colony of Portugal and now a popular tourist and property investment destination, with its own Bradt guide, too. Keen hikers should choose Sant'Antão and Fogo over flat-as-a-pancake Sal. From the UK, there are now direct flights to Sal and Boavista from London Gatwick and Stansted airports, as well as from Manchester with TAP. The national Cape Verdean carrier TACV (*www.tacv.cv*) has flights from London Stansted and Boston, as well as European, Brazilian and African hubs.

Luggage The most important thing to pack is a piece of **carry-on luggage** (keeping within the required dimensions) that contains everything you cannot do without for ten days. If you are going to go snorkelling or trekking, pack all you need for this (wear your hiking boots, for instance), along with your malaria protection and other medication or relevant cosmetics (subject to current restrictions on what you can take). If your luggage is lost in transit in Europe, you might have to wait a while for information, and the office in STP is of limited help. To get compensation, you will have to send in receipts for the bills you incurred as a result of the delay (e *faleconosco@tap.pt*) so make sure you have adequate travel insurance to make up for delays in payment. The problem with delayed baggage that I noted in the first edition is now under control, and TAP recently won the Global Travel award for the Best Airline to South America and Africa.

Departure tax When you leave the country, you have to pay a departure tax before checking in. The counter is at the front of the airport building. The tax is 440,000$, US$21 or €18 (half the amount for children). It's always good to have the exact amount ready, but these days you will usually be able to get change.

Airlines
From Lisbon
STP Airways ✆218 437 040; e reservationslis@ stpairways.st. No representation outside Portugal/STP. The cheaper way to fly, using Euroatlantic planes (owned by the Pestana chain of hotels), STP Airways often runs promotional round trips for €600, the good deal making up for heavier landings & fairly undrinkable wine. See warning on pages 56–7.
TAAG (Portugal) Av do Brasil 31A, 1700-062 Lisbon; ✆213 575 899; e reservas@taag.pt; www.taag.com. There's an office in Porto, too.
TAAG (UK) 259–269 Old Marylebone Rd, Winchester Hse, Suite GF1, London NW1 5RA; ✆020 7170 4343; www.taag.com
TAP Portugal (Portugal) ✆707 205 700; www. flytap.com
TAP Portugal (UK) Brook Hse, 229–243 Shepherd's Bush Rd, Hammersmith, London W6 7AN; ✆0845 601 0932; www.tapportugal. com. Lisbon–São Tomé departure at the time of writing, Thu 23.50.
TAP Portugal (USA) Newark, NJ; ✆800 221 73 70; e tapusa@tap.pt; www.tapportugal.com

UK–Lisbon There is reasonable competition on this route, so take your pick. Double-check the prices of two separate tickets against through-tickets. Whilst TAP maintains it is not cheaper to buy the two legs individually, some travellers have told me otherwise. Some services are seasonal.

British Airways ✆0844 493 0787; www. ba.com, www.britishairways.com. 3 daily flights from London Heathrow.
easyJet ✆0843 104 5454; www.easyjet.com. The no-frills carrier flies daily from London Luton & London Gatwick, Bristol (twice a week) & Liverpool (seasonal).
Monarch ✆087 194 05040; www.monarch. co.uk. Budget flights to Faro (4hrs by train from Lisbon) from London Gatwick, London Luton, Birmingham, East Midlands, Leeds/Bradford & Manchester.
Ryanair ✆0871 246 0000; www.ryanair.com. New connection from London Stansted, several times a week
TAP Portugal ✆0845 601 0932; www.flytap. com. The Portuguese national airline flies daily from London Heathrow & London Gatwick, & several times a week from Manchester.

Thomsonfly ☎0871 231 4787 (Thomson Airways); www.thomsonfly.com. Manchester–Faro (4hrs by train from Lisbon) several times a week. Faro departures, with varying frequencies, also from Bristol, Cardiff, Coventry, Doncaster Sheffield, East Midlands, Exeter, Glasgow, London Luton & London Stansted. Also connections to the Cape Verde islands, such as London Gatwick, Birmingham & Manchester–Sal or Boa Vista, plus Glasgow–Boa Vista, which allows time to explore the Cape Verde Islands for a few days. TAAG service to São Tomé from Praia (Santiago Island).

Ireland–Lisbon

Aer Lingus ☎0818 365 000; www.aerlingus. com. The Irish national carrier offers reasonable fares & a daily Dublin–Lisbon flight.
Ryanair ☎1 520 444 004; www.ryanair.com. The Irish budget airline flies from Dublin to Faro in the Algarve (4hrs by train from Lisbon), & to Porto. Portugal's second city is a short metro hop plus a comfortable 3hr train ride from Lisbon's Santa Apolonia station. A round trip on an open rail train ticket costs about €60 (www.cp.pt), with big savings if you book ahead.
TAP ☎01 656 9162; e tap@apg-ga.ie; www. tapportugal.com. Going to Lisbon with TAP is fairly expensive, only running via London Heathrow or London Gatwick, but the office can help you with your onward booking to São Tomé.

US and Canada–Lisbon

Air France ☎1 800 237 2747; www. airfrance.us. Flights to Lisbon for the TAP or STP Airways connection, or (pricier, so only really of interest to birdwatchers, for instance) to Libreville for the TAAG connection. Air France can book you a through ticket from US airports to São Tomé.
Air Transat ☎1 888 TRANSAT, 1 866 8471112, 1 514 2886705; www.airtransat.ca
SATA (Boston) ☎800 762 9995; (Oakland) ☎408 729 3712; (Toronto) ☎416 515 7188; (Portugal) ☎+351 707 227 282, +351 296 209 720; e contacto@sata.pt, contactus@sata.pt; www.sata.pt
TAP Portugal ☎1 800 2217370; e tapusa@tap. pt; www.flytap.com
United Airlines ☎1 800 231 0856; www.united. com

US Airways ☎1 800 428 4322; www.usairways. com. Philadelphia to Lisbon, with connections from other US cities.

From the African mainland

Air France (UK) ☎0870 142 4343; www. airfrance.co.uk; (US) ☎1 800 237 2747; www. airfrance.us
CEIBA (Gabon) Quartier Glass, next to SGS; ☎77 35 76/77 35 77; (Equatorial Guinea) www.fly-ceiba.com, site under construction.
Gabon Airlines (UK) Jetair; ☎01293 566080; e reservations.gb@gabonairlines.com; www. gabonairlines.com
South African Airways www.flysaa.com; (Gabon) ☎241 724 194, 241 726 081; (UK) ☎0870 747 1111; e voyager@flysaa.com; (US) ☎0861 359722; e saausa@flysaa.com
TAAG www.taag.com; (Angola) Rua da Missão 123, PO Box 79, Luanda; ☎+244 222 332 077, 222 332 387; e TAAGSAC@flytaag-angolaairlines. com; (South Africa) Cape Town; ☎21 936 2742; e cpttkt@taagza.com, cptres@taagza.com; Johannesburg ☎11 450 1116, 450 1117; e taagjnb@global.co.sa

Airline offices in São Tomé

STP Airways Av Marginal 12 de Julho; ☎222 1160; e reservations@stpairways.st; www.stpairways.st. The national airline's office next to the tourist office can sell you tickets to Príncipe (& Lisbon, of course) & change the date of flights for a fee of €100 (Lisbon) or €15 (Príncipe).
STP Tours Av Marginal 12 de Julho; m 986 7131; e reservas@stptours.st; www.stptours. st. The local agent for CEIBA Airways, an airline from Equatorial Guinea connecting Malabo with São Tomé & using Madrid as its European hub. English & French are spoken.
TAAG Av Giovany; ☎224 1150; e neydamascarenhas@hotmail.com; www. taag.com. The Angolan airline flies to Lisbon, Luanda & Cape Verde. Cash payments only.
TAP Rua Santo António do Príncipe (ex-Doutor Luis Machado); ☎222 2307; e tapstp@cstome. net; ☉ 07.30–15.00 Mon–Fri. Office of the Portuguese national airline & they can sell tickets for other Star Alliance carriers too. If you have a problem, ask for the manager, Natasha d'Alva.

BY SEA There are cargo boats operating from Libreville, but they are overloaded, uncomfortable and dangerous – nobody I've spoken to recommends this way of travelling. For details of reaching Príncipe by sea, see page 191.

HEALTH With Dr Felicity Nicholson; special thanks to Dr Gian Meyer and Bibi Braunstein

People new to exotic travel often worry about tropical diseases, but it is accidents that are most likely to carry you off. With the increase in traffic, road accidents are becoming more common in São Tomé and Príncipe, so be aware and do what you can to reduce risks. Try to travel during daylight hours, always wear a seatbelt, and refuse to be driven by anyone who has been drinking.

BEFORE YOU GO Preparations to ensure a healthy trip to São Tomé and Príncipe require checks on your immunisation status, and it is wise to be up-to-date on tetanus, polio and diphtheria (now given as an all-in-one vaccine, Revaxis, that lasts for ten years), typhoid and hepatitis A. A yellow fever vaccination certificate is only required if you are coming from a yellow fever endemic area and the transit time is more than 12 hours. There is a low risk of disease within STP so the vaccine is not needed if you are entering directly.

Immunisation for cholera is not usually recommended for travel to STP unless there is a local outbreak and you are working in poorer areas. The oral vaccine (Dukoral) offers around 75% of coverage for cholera and comprises two doses given at least one to six weeks apart and at least one week before entry for those aged six or over. Younger children require three doses and get less sustained protection.

Hepatitis A vaccine (Havrix Monodose or Avaxim) comprises two injections given about a year apart. The course costs about £100, but may be available on the NHS in the UK; it protects for 25 years and can be administered even close to the time of departure. **Hepatitis B** vaccination should be considered for longer trips (two months or more) or for those working with children or in situations where contact with blood is likely. Three injections are needed for the best protection and can be given over a three-week period if time is short to those aged 16 or over. Longer schedules give more sustained protection and are therefore preferred if time allows. Hepatitis A vaccine can also be given as a combination with hepatitis B as 'Twinrix', though two doses are needed at least seven days apart to be effective for the hepatitis A component, and three doses are needed for the hepatitis B.

The newer injectable **typhoid** vaccines (eg: Typhim Vi) last for three years and are about 75% effective. Oral capsules (Vivotif) may also be available for those aged six and over. Three capsules over five days lasts for approximately three years but may be less effective than the injectable forms if they are not absorbed properly. They are encouraged unless you are leaving within a few days for a trip of a week or less, when the vaccine would not be effective in time. Experts differ over whether a **BCG vaccination** against tuberculosis (TB) is useful in adults, so discuss this with your travel clinic.

In addition to the various vaccinations recommended above, it is important that travellers should be properly protected against malaria. For detailed advice, see pages 63–6.

Ideally you should visit your own doctor or a specialist travel clinic (see page opposite) to discuss your requirements if possible at least eight weeks before you plan to travel.

Travel clinics and health information A full list of current travel clinic websites worldwide is available on www.istm.org. For other journey preparation information, consult www.nathnac.org/ds/map_world.aspx (UK) or wwwnc.cdc. gov/travel/ (US). Information about various medications may be found on www. netdoctor.co.uk/travel. All advice found online should be used in conjunction with expert advice received prior to or during travel.

SUN AND HEAT Remember that you are on the Equator and be sensible when out in the sun. Drink lots of water and note that if you are feeling thirsty, you are already starting to get dehydrated. Mineral water is widely available and using a Platypus/ CamelBak water dispenser while hiking is a great way of accessing water without having to stop and take your daypack off. The glare and the dust can be hard on the eyes, too, so bring UV-protecting sunglasses, individual doses of sterile saline solution, and, perhaps, some soothing eyedrops.

Protection from the sun The incidence of skin cancer is rocketing as Caucasians are travelling more and spending more time exposing themselves to the sun. Keep out of the sun during the middle of the day and try building up exposure gradually from 20 minutes per day. Sun exposure ages the skin and makes people prematurely wrinkly, so cover up with long, loose clothes, wear a hat when you can, and don't forget the suncream. Be especially careful of sun reflected off water and wear a T-shirt and lots of waterproof suncream when swimming; snorkelling often leads to scorched backs of the thighs and shoulders, so wear bermuda shorts and a T-shirt if you're going for more than a quick dip.

In the capital of São Tomé, the Intermar supermarket (see page 124) sells various suncreams up to factor 30 but if you need one with a higher sunblock factor, bring your own. Thanks to the Santomean haze, the sun does not have a relentless feel to it, but don't forget you are on the Equator.

MALARIA IN STP with Philip Briggs

Although diminishing on both islands (on Príncipe in particular), *paludismo* is still the biggest killer of children under five. The rates of infection are steadily going down thanks to an intensive fumigation campaign inside houses, and education on impregnated mosquito nets, with many donated or sold at a symbolic price. A few years ago, São Tomé hospital had to cram two children into one bed, now there are far fewer cases and Príncipe is in the pre-elimiation stage of malaria. The *Anopheles* mosquito that transmits the parasite is most abundant near marshes and still water, where it breeds, and the parasite is most prolific at low altitudes. Malaria-carrying mosquitoes tend to live in the walls of houses, and a campaign to spray houses with permethrin is gradually covering the whole island.

The ambitious plan is to carry out three rounds of *fumigação/pulverização*, then test the whole population and treat the positive cases, thus gradually eliminating the disease. In mid-altitude locations, malaria is largely, but not entirely, seasonal, with the highest risk of transmission occurring during the rainy season. Those heading for moist and low-lying areas, such as the capital and along the coast, and, of course, anyone spending long periods deep in the forest, are at high risk throughout the year, but the danger is greatest during the rainy season. Even if this does not apply to you, all travellers to central Africa should assume that they will be exposed to malaria and should take precautions throughout their trip.

Prevention   There is not yet a vaccine against malaria that gives enough protection to be useful for travellers, but there are other ways to avoid it and since most of Africa is very high risk for malaria, travellers must plan their malaria protection properly. Seek current advice on the best antimalarials to take: usually mefloquine, Malarone or doxycycline. If mefloquine (Lariam) is suggested, start this 2½ weeks (three doses) before departure to check that it suits you and stop it immediately if it seems to cause depression or anxiety, visual or hearing disturbances, severe headaches, fits or changes in heart rhythm. Side effects such as nightmares or dizziness are not medical reasons for stopping unless they are sufficiently debilitating or annoying. Anyone who has been treated for depression or psychiatric problems, who has diabetes controlled by oral therapy, who is epileptic (or who has suffered fits in the past) or has a close blood relative who is epileptic, should probably avoid mefloquine: discuss this with a heathcare professional.

In the past doctors were nervous about prescribing mefloquine to pregnant women, but experience has shown that it is relatively safe and certainly safer than the risk of malaria. That said, there are other issues, so if you are travelling to São Tomé and Príncipe while pregnant, seek expert advice before departure.

Malarone (proguanil and atovaquone) is as effective as mefloquine. It has the advantage of having few side effects, can be started the day before travel and need only be continued for one week after returning. However, it is expensive and because of this tends to be reserved for shorter trips. Malarone may not be suitable for everybody, so advice should be taken from a doctor. There is no limit to the length of time Malarone can be taken, as long as it is tolerated. There is now also a generic form which is slightly cheaper. Paediatric tablets for children are also available, prescribed on a weight basis.

Another alternative is the antibiotic doxycycline (100mg daily). Like Malarone it can be started one to two days before arrival. Unlike mefloquine, it may also be used in travellers with epilepsy, although certain anti-epileptic medication may make it less effective. In perhaps 1–3% of people there is the possibility of allergic skin reactions developing in sunlight; the drug should be stopped if this happens. It is also unsuitable for children under 12 years. It may be used in early pregnancy (before 15 weeks) where there is nothing else suitable.

Chloroquine and proguanil are no longer considered to be effective enough for São Tomé and Príncipe, but may be considered as a last resort if nothing else is deemed suitable.

All tablets should be taken with or after the evening meal, washed down with plenty of fluid and, with the exception of Malarone (see above), continued for four weeks after leaving. Despite all these precautions, it is important to be aware that no anti-malarial drug provides 100% protection, although those on prophylactics who are unlucky enough to catch malaria are less likely to get rapidly into serious trouble. In addition to taking anti-malarials, it is therefore important to avoid mosquito bites between dusk and dawn. Keep your repellent stick or roll-on to hand.

There is, unfortunately, the occasional traveller who prefers to 'acquire resistance' to malaria rather than take preventive tablets, or who takes homeopathic prophylactics thinking these are effective against this killer disease. Homeopathy theory dictates treating like with like so there is no place for prophylaxis or immunisation in a well person; bona fide homeopaths do not advocate it. It takes at least 18 months residing in a holoendemic area for someone to develop some immunity to malaria so travellers to Africa will not acquire any effective resistance to malaria. The best way to prevent infection is to prevent mosquito bites in the first place and to take a suitable prophylactic agent.

A minimal kit contains:
- A good drying antiseptic, eg: iodine or potassium permanganate (don't take antiseptic cream)
- A few small dressings (Band-Aids)
- Suncream
- Insect repellent, anti-malarial tablets, impregnated bed-net or permethrin spray
- Aspirin or paracetamol
- Antifungal cream (eg: Canesten)
- Ciprofloxacin or norfloxacin, for severe diarrhoea and a product to re-establish the intestine flora, such as ultralevure
- Tinidazole for giardia or amoebic dysentery (see page 67 for regime)
- Antibiotic eye drops, for sore, 'gritty', stuck-together eyes (conjunctivitis)
- A pair of fine pointed tweezers (to remove hairy caterpillar hairs, thorns, splinters, coral, etc)
- Alcohol-based hand rub or bar of soap in plastic box
- Condoms or femidoms
- Digital thermometer if you are in more remote areas
- Antihistamine for allergical reactions to insect bites
- Sterilising hand spray/wet wipes – useful in between counting dobras to pay for food and touching your food to eat it
- Sterile container for stool/urine sample
- Digital thermometer

Diagnosis and treatment Even those who take their malaria tablets meticulously and do everything possible to avoid mosquito bites may contract a strain of malaria that is resistant to prophylactic drugs. Untreated malaria is likely to be fatal, but even strains resistant to prophylaxis respond well to prompt treatment. Because of this, your immediate priority upon displaying possible malaria symptoms – including a rapid rise in temperature (over 38°C), and any combination of a headache, flu-like aches and pains, a general sense of disorientation, and possibly even nausea and diarrhoea – is to establish whether you have malaria, ideally by visiting a clinic.

Diagnosing malaria is not easy, which is why consulting a doctor is sensible: there are other dangerous causes of fever in Africa, which require different treatments. It is easy and inexpensive to arrange a malaria blood test but even if you test negative, it would be wise to stay within reach of a laboratory until the symptoms clear up, and to test again after a day or two if they don't. It's worth noting that if you have a fever and the malaria test is negative, you may have typhoid or paratyphoid, which should also receive immediate treatment.

Travellers to remote parts of São Tomé and Príncipe would be wise to carry a course of treatment to cure malaria. With malaria, it is normal enough to go from feeling healthy to having a high fever in the space of a few hours (and it is possible to die from falciparum malaria within 24 hours of the first symptoms). In such circumstances, assume that you have malaria and act accordingly – whatever risks are attached to taking an unnecessary cure are outweighed by the dangers of untreated malaria. Experts differ on the costs and benefits of self-treatment, but agree that it leads to over-treatment and to many people taking drugs they do not need; yet treatment may save your life. There is also some division about the

Practical Information HEALTH

2

best treatment for malaria, but either Malarone or Coarthemeter are the current treatments of choice. Discuss your trip with a specialist either at home or in São Tomé and Príncipe.

COMMON MEDICAL PROBLEMS Air conditioning often brings on an irritated throat through dry air, abrupt changes in temperature and dirty filters. On my first visit, I picked up a throat problem that stayed with me for two months and eventually turned into tonsillitis – don't do as I did and self-medicate but go and see a doctor.

Travellers' diarrhoea Travelling in São Tomé and Príncipe carries a risk of getting a dose of travellers' diarrhoea; perhaps as many as half of all visitors will be affected and the newer you are to travel, the more likely you will be to suffer. By taking precautions against travellers' diarrhoea you will also avoid typhoid, cholera, hepatitis, dysentery, worms, etc. Travellers' diarrhoea and the other faecal-oral diseases come from getting other peoples' faeces in your mouth. This most often happens from cooks not washing their hands after a trip to the toilet, but even if the restaurant cook does not understand basic hygiene you will be safe if your food has been properly cooked and arrives piping hot. I remember plenty of lukewarm plates of food, so if in doubt, ask for your meal to be re-heated (*faz favor, pode aquecer mais um pouco?*). Even if this presents some hassle for your waiter/waitress, the locals do usually realise that a tourist's stomach, *barriga*, is more vulnerable. The maxim to remind you what you can safely eat is:

PEEL IT, BOIL IT, COOK IT OR FORGET IT.

This means that fruit you have washed and peeled yourself, and hot foods, should be safe but raw foods, cold cooked foods, salads and fruit salads which have been prepared by others, ice cream and ice are all risky. Ask for your drink without ice, *sem gelo*. That said, plenty of travellers and expatriates enjoy fruit and vegetables, so do keep a sense of perspective: food served in a fairly decent hotel in a large town or a place regularly frequented by expatriates is likely to be safe. If you are struck, see below for treatment.

Water sterilisation It is much rarer to get sick from drinking contaminated water but it happens, so try to drink from safe sources such as bottled mineral water. Alternatively, water should have been brought to the boil (even at altitude it only needs to be brought to the boil), or passed through a good bacteriological filter; chlorine tablets (eg: Puritabs) are also adequate, although theoretically less effective and they taste nastier.

Treating travellers' diarrhoea It is dehydration that makes you feel awful during a bout of diarrhoea and the most important part of treatment is drinking lots of clear fluids. Sachets of oral rehydration salts (ask for *soro* at a pharmacy) give the perfect biochemical mix to replace all that is pouring out of your body, but other recipes taste nicer. Any dilute mixture of sugar and salt in water will do you good: try Coke or orange squash with a three-finger pinch of salt added to each glass (if you are salt-depleted you won't taste the salt). Otherwise make a solution of a four-finger scoop of sugar with a three-finger pinch of salt in a 500ml glass. Or add eight level teaspoons of sugar (18g) and one level teaspoon of salt (3g) to one litre (five cups) of safe water. A squeeze of lemon or orange juice improves the taste and adds potassium, which is also lost in diarrhoea. Drink two large glasses after every bowel movement, and more if you are thirsty. These solutions are still absorbed well if you are vomiting, but you will need to take sips at a time. If you are not eating you need to drink three litres a day plus whatever is pouring into the toilet. If you feel like eating, take a bland, high carbohydrate diet. Heavy greasy foods will probably give you cramps.

If the diarrhoea is bad, or you are passing blood or slime, or you have a fever, you will probably need antibiotics in addition to fluid replacement. A dose of norfloxacin or ciprofloxacin repeated twice a day until you are better may be appropriate (if you are planning to take an antibiotic with you, note that both norfloxacin and ciprofloxacin are available only on prescription in the UK). If the diarrhoea is greasy and bulky and is accompanied by sulphurous (eggy) burps, one likely cause is giardia. This is best treated with tinidazole (four x 500mg in one dose, repeated seven days later if symptoms persist). Some people react to malaria with diarrhoea, so most local doctors will expect you to have taken a malaria test before you come to see them, just to ensure that hypothesis can be eliminated.

Insect bites Aside from avoiding mosquito bites between dusk and dawn, which will protect you from elephantiasis and a range of nasty insect-borne viruses, as well as malaria (see page 63–6), it is important to take precautions against other insect bites. During the day it is wise to wear long, loose (preferably 100% cotton) clothes if you are pushing through scrubby country; this will keep off ticks and also tsetse and day-biting *Aedes* mosquitoes which may spread viral fevers. São Tomé and Príncipe is thought to have *Aedes aegypti* mosquitoes that are not as yet carriers of dengue fever, but given the lack of serum diagnostic facilities, it is difficult to say with certainty. Mosquitoes and many other insects are attracted to light. If you are camping, never put a lamp near the opening of your tent, or you will have a swarm of biters waiting to join you when you retire. In hotel rooms, be aware that the longer your light is on, the greater the number of insects that will be sharing your accommodation.

Tsetse flies hurt when they bite and it is said that they are attracted to the colour blue; locals will advise on where they are a problem and where they transmit sleeping sickness.

Tumbu flies or **putsi** are a problem where the climate is hot and humid. The adult fly lays her eggs on the soil or on drying laundry and when the eggs come in contact with human flesh (when you put on clothes or lie on a bed) they hatch and bury themselves under the skin. Here they form a crop of 'boils' each with a maggot inside. Smear a little Vaseline over the hole, and they will push their noses out to breathe. It may be possible to squeeze them out but it depends if they are ready to do so as the larvae have spines that help them to hold on. In putsi areas either dry your clothes and sheets within a screened house, or dry them in direct sunshine until they are crisp, or iron them.

Jiggers or **sandfleas** are another flesh-feaster, which can be best avoided by wearing shoes. Known locally as *bichô*, they latch on if you walk barefoot in contaminated places, such as beaches used by pigs, and set up home under the skin of the foot, usually at the side of a toenail where they cause a painful, boil-like swelling. They need picking out by a local expert.

The *larva migrans* **hookworm** sometimes hitches a ride with STP tourists. Transmitted by water contaminated with dog faeces and accompanied by an annoying itch, as the 'geography worm' burrows map-like tracks under the skin. The parasite is treated with either an ethyl choloride spray or carbon dioxide freezer spray (used for warts). If neither is to hand, mix a few crushed thiabendazole tablets with a bland skin cream and apply it to the area for 12 hours under a waterproof dressing.

Dengue fever This mosquito-borne disease may mimic malaria but there is no prophylactic medication available to prevent it. The mosquitoes that carry this virus bite during the daytime, so it is worth applying repellent if you see any mosquitoes around. Symptoms include strong headaches, rashes, excruciating joint and muscle pains, and high fever. Dengue fever lasts only for a week or so and is not usually fatal. Complete rest and paracetamol are the usual treatment; drinking plenty of fluids also helps. Some patients are given an intravenous drip to prevent dehydration. It is especially important to protect yourself if you have had dengue fever before, since a second infection with a different strain can result in the potentially fatal dengue haemorrhagic fever. The good news is that whilst dengue fever cannot be discounted, it has not been reported on São Tomé and Príncipe for more than ten years.

Avoiding insect bites As the sun is going down, don long clothes and apply repellent on any exposed flesh. Pack an insect repellent containing at least 50–55% DEET (roll-ons or sticks are the least messy preparations for travelling). You also need either a permethrin-impregnated bednet or a permethrin spray so that you can 'treat' bednets in hotels. Permethrin treatment makes even very tatty nets protective and prevents mosquitoes from biting through the impregnated net when you roll against it; it also deters other biters. Otherwise, retire to an air-conditioned room, burn mosquito coils or sleep under a fan. Coils and fans reduce rather than eliminate bites. Travel clinics usually sell a good range of nets, treatment kits and repellents.

In case you do get bitten, be sure to bring a soothing medicated gel for mosquito bites. I know of only one place in São Tomé which occasionally sells anything like that – Economax supermarket in the capital – see page 124, and it's not very effective. A gel such as Fenistil is also good for sunburn.

Bilharzia or schistosomiasis
With thanks to Dr Vaughan Southgate, Natural History Museum, London
Bilharzia or schistosomiasis is a disease that commonly afflicts the rural poor of the tropics. Two types exist in sub-Saharan Africa – *Schistosoma mansoni* and *Schistosoma haematobium*. It is an unpleasant problem that is worth avoiding, though it can be treated if you do get it. The most risky shores will be close to where people use the water a good deal, wash clothes, etc.

It is easier to understand how to diagnose it, treat it and prevent it if you know a little about the life cycle. Contaminated faeces are washed into the body of water, the eggs hatch and the larva infects a certain species of snail. The snails then produce about 10,000 *cercariae* a day for the rest of their lives. The parasites can digest their way through your skin when you wade, or bathe in infested fresh water.

Winds disperse the snails and *cercariae*, and the snails in particular can drift a long way, especially on windblown weed, so nowhere is really safe. However, deep water and running water are safer, while shallow water presents the greatest risk. The *cercariae* penetrate intact skin, and find their way to the liver. There, male and female meet and spend the rest of their lives in permanent copulation. No wonder you feel tired! Most finish up in the wall of the lower bowel, but others can get lost and can cause damage to many different organs. *Schistosoma haematobium* goes mostly to the bladder.

Although the adults do not cause any harm in themselves, after about four to six weeks they start to lay eggs, which cause an intense but usually ineffective immune reaction, including fever, cough, abdominal pain, and a fleeting, itching rash called 'safari itch'. The absence of early symptoms does not necessarily mean there is no infection. Later symptoms can be more localised and more severe, but the general symptoms settle down fairly quickly and eventually you are just tired. 'Tired all the time' is one of the most common symptoms among expats in Africa, and bilharzia, giardia, amoeba and intestinal yeast are the most common culprits.

Although bilharzia is difficult to diagnose, it can be tested for at specialist travel clinics. Ideally, tests need to be done at least six weeks after likely exposure and will determine whether you need treatment. Fortunately it is easy to treat at present.

Avoiding bilharzia
- If you are bathing, swimming, paddling or wading in fresh water which you think may carry a bilharzia risk, try to get out of the water within ten minutes.
- Avoid bathing or paddling on shores within 200m of villages or places where people use the water a great deal, especially reedy shores or where there is lots of water weed.
- Dry off thoroughly with a towel; rub vigorously.
- If your bathing water comes from a risky source try to ensure that the water is taken in the early morning and stored snail-free, otherwise it should be filtered or Dettol or Cresol added.
- Bathing early in the morning is safer than bathing in the last half of the day.
- Cover yourself with DEET insect repellent before swimming: it may offer some protection.

Skin infections Any mosquito bite or small nick in the skin gives an opportunity for bacteria to foil the body's usually excellent defences; it will surprise many travellers how quickly skin infections start in warm humid climates and it is essential to clean and cover even the slightest wound. Creams are not as effective as a good drying antiseptic such as a spray, dilute iodine, potassium permanganate (*permanganato de Potassio*; a few crystals in half a cup of water), or crystal (or gentian) violet (*cristales de violete de genciano*). One of these should be available in pharmacies. The most common problem with insect bites on the islands comes from something as banal as scratching yourself with dirty nails (women in particular) and getting infected wounds, often on the ankles. Hand hygiene and self-control work well. If the wound starts to throb, or becomes red and the redness starts to spread, or the wound oozes, and especially if you develop a fever, antibiotics will probably be needed: flucloxacillin (250mg four times a day) or Augmentin (250–500mg three times a day). For those allergic to penicillin, erythromycin (500mg twice a day) for five days should help. See a doctor if the symptoms do not start to improve in 48 hours.

Fungal infections also get a hold easily in hot moist climates, so wear 100% cotton socks and underwear and shower frequently. An itchy rash in the groin or flaking between the toes is likely to be a fungal infection. This needs treatment with an antifungal cream such as Canesten (clotrimazole), which is sold in pharmacies. If this is not available try Whitfield's ointment (compound benzoic acid ointment) or crystal violet (although this will turn you purple!).

Eye problems Bacterial conjunctivitis (pink eye) is a common infection in Africa; people who wear contact lenses are most open to this irritating problem. The eyes feel sore and gritty and they will often be stuck together in the mornings. They will need treatment with antibiotic drops or ointment, difficult to obtain in São Tomé and Príncipe so consider bringing it from home. Lesser eye irritation should settle with bathing in salt water and keeping the eyes shaded. If an insect flies into your eye, extract it with great care, ensuring that you do not crush or damage it, otherwise you may get a nastily inflamed eye from toxins secreted by the creature. Bring your own contact lens solution and include a couple of starter packs (under 100ml) in your hand luggage in case of lost baggage. Better yet, unless you wear hard/gas-permeable lenses, are those that can be disposed of on a daily basis.

Prickly heat A fine pimply rash on the trunk is likely to be heat rash; cool showers, dabbing dry and talc will help. Some people react well to Lauroderm in powder (used for babies' nappy rash/diaper skin), which can be found at local pharmacies. Treat the problem by slowing down to a relaxed schedule, wearing only loose, baggy, 100% cotton clothes and sleeping naked under a fan; if it's bad you may need to check into an air-conditioned hotel room for a while.

OTHER MEDICAL ISSUES
Meningitis This is a particularly nasty disease as it can kill within hours of the first symptoms appearing. The telltale symptoms are a combination of a blinding headache (light sensitivity), a blotchy rash and a high fever. Immunisation protects against the most serious bacterial form of meningitis and the tetravalent vaccine ACWY is recommended for central Africa, but if this is not available then A+C is better than nothing. Other forms of meningitis exist (usually viral) but there are no vaccines for these. When meningitis occurs on São Tomé and Príncipe, no analysis is made of the particular type; treatment is purely by antibiotics. Local media normally report localised outbreaks. A severe headache and fever should make you run to a doctor immediately. There are also other causes of headache and fever, one of which is typhoid, which can occur in travellers to central Africa. Seek medical help if you are ill.

Tropical amoeba This is a tiny organism, transmitted through faeces. Often, there are no symptoms at all, but amoebae can cause dysentery or a liver abscess up to a year after travel. Stay alert to changes in your body/health after your return.

Sexually-transmitted diseases The risks of sexually transmitted infection are high in São Tomé and Príncipe, whether you sleep with fellow travellers or locals. About 80% of HIV infections in British heterosexuals are acquired abroad. If you must indulge, use condoms or femidoms, which help reduce the risk of transmission. If you notice any genital ulcers or discharge, get treatment promptly since these increase the risk of acquiring HIV. In São Tomé and Príncipe, where HIV rates are low still, syphilis and gonorrhea, as well as candida and trichomonad infections are more cause for concern. Although there is a family planning organisation in the capital, the morning-after pill is only intermittently available and the level of information can be sub-standard – you might have to read the leaflet yourself. If you do have unprotected sex, visit a clinic as soon as possible (the Policlínica in São Tomé is recommended, see page 128); this should be within 24 hours, or no later than 72 hours, for post-exposure prophylaxis for HIV.

Rabies Rabies is not normally present in São Tomé and Príncipe, but animal or bat bites should always be assessed carefully.

Snakes, spiders and other biters Apart from a bee or wasp crawling into your drink, the only real wildlife hazard present on the islands is the **black cobra** (*Naja melanoleuca*), originally introduced to combat the rats eating the cocoa pods. The cobra preta's neurotoxic (nerve-destroying) venom results in paralysis if not immediately treated. First symptoms are paralysis of the eye muscles (usually the eyelid dropping), with the danger then of respiratory arrest, which cannot be treated on the islands. The juvenile black cobra is completely black, the adult has yellow-white scales at the front. The snake is fairly common in the southern and eastern parts of São Tomé island and on a six-hour forest walk I saw two: a juvenile, her head aggressively raised, and an adult, around 1.8m long, sunbathing – plus a headless adult dangling from the hands of a palm wine worker. Don't panic though, as while there are many stories involving the black cobra (people chopping off their arm with their machete in order to survive), hikers being bitten are unheard of and deaths by cobra bite are extremely rare on the island as a whole. Like all snakes,

MEDICAL FACILITIES IN SÃO TOMÉ AND PRÍNCIPE

There is no general phone number for medical emergencies. Most villages have a first aid post, but these *postos de saúde* do not have much equipment and can only deal with small injuries. In an emergency, head straight for the hospital. Apart from the central hospitals in the capitals of both islands (proper A&E services only in São Tomé), there is one in São João dos Angolares in the south of São Tomé island, and in Neves in the north, but neither is equipped to deal with major injuries. The only pharmacies (*farmácias*) are in both capitals and Trindade. You will probably need some Portuguese, although you may manage in French or English. There are about 40 doctors practising on São Tomé and Príncipe, amongst them a number of competent Cuban doctors. Few medical staff speak English, but most will have some French, others some Spanish or German from training in Cuba or the former East Germany. I've been given unreliable medical advice on both islands. Add to that the hazards of communicating in a foreign language, and it is probably best to bring somebody who can translate for you, or to find an English-speaking medic; on São Tomé this means the Taiwanese Medical Mission in the capital.

Divers should make enquiries with the Pestana Ocean Resort about whether the planned decompression chamber on the main island is now in place. Although there is a *câmara hiperbárica* in Libreville, Gabon, 250km away, evacuation takes many hours – so don't run any risks. Most diving accidents are due to human error.

Commonly required medicines such as ibuprofen, antiseptic sprays and common antibiotics are widely available in pharmacies, but bring a couple of high-strength (+50%) DEET insect repellent sticks/sprays, a good cream/gel (*pomada*) for insect bites, and if you have sensitive teeth bring your own toothpaste. Treatments for malaria are best bought in advance – in fact it's advisable to carry all malaria-related tablets on you, and only rely on their availability locally if you need to restock your supplies.

If you are on any medication prior to departure, or you have specific needs relating to a known medical condition (for instance if you are allergic to bee stings or you are prone to attacks of asthma), then you are strongly advised to bring any related drugs and devices with you.

black cobras rarely attack unless provoked. As a precaution, however, wear stout shoes and not too tight clothing, including long trousers in the forest, watch your step and look where you're putting your hands. A guide will alert you to any danger.

Locals will usually kill black cobras immediately as, if bitten, chances of getting to the hospital in time (within 30 minutes to two hours) for the antivenom are slim. And, according to local guides, the antivenom will only delay death for a couple of days – probably due to the fact that the hospital in São Tomé held the wrong one for years. By the time you visit, however, the correct one should be in place, though it seems impossible to ascertain whether they do or don't have it. Tour guides do not carry the antivenom. If it makes you feel safer, you can order the (expensive) Saimr polyvalent snake antivenom from SAVP (*Modderfontein Road 1, 2131 Sandringham, South Africa;* \ *+27 11 386000 (emergency);* e *meagans@savp.co.za*) and donate it to the hospital when you leave. Be aware though that the antivenom cannot simply be injected into a muscle, it has to be injected intravenously, diluted in short infusions under supervision for allergic reactions that may occur. Early anaphylactic shock is a documented issue. It also has to be kept cool, which is impossible in the south of the island.

If bitten, snakes will dispense venom in only about half of their bites. Keeping this fact in mind may help you to stay calm. Many so-called first aid techniques do more harm than good: cutting into the wound is harmful; tourniquets are dangerous; suction and electrical inactivation devices do not work. The only treatment is antivenom. In case of a bite that you fear may have been from the black cobra:

- Try to keep calm – it is likely that no venom has been dispensed.
- Prevent movement of the bitten limb by applying a splint.
- Keep the bitten limb BELOW heart height to slow the spread of any venom.
- If you have a crepe bandage, bind up as much of the bitten limb as you can, but release the bandage every half hour.
- Evacuate to a hospital which has antivenom – in São Tomé and Príncipe, only the capital.

And remember:

- NEVER give aspirin; you may offer paracetamol, which is safe.
- NEVER cut or suck the wound.
- DO NOT apply ice packs.
- DO NOT apply potassium permanganate.

Happily, the black cobra never made it to Príncipe, nor to Ilhéu das Rolas. See www. africanreptiles-venom.co.za/snake_courses_snake_handling_c.html for more details on the black cobra.

The brown *samangungú* **tarantula** is one of the largest spiders in Africa, but you don't come across very many. Locals will tell you that the *samangungú* might jump you if they feel attacked. If you are bitten, locals will tell you not to drink water; left untreated, the bite will be painful, but that's all. Wash any bite with soap and water or similar, protect against infection and monitor for changes/ anaphylactic reactions (breathing difficulties/chest pains).

There are a couple of nasty, beautiful **fire worms** on the islands, and very few **scorpions**: you'd have to go and seek them out in the cracks of a basalt wall near Lagoa Azul. *Aliança* is a tiny yellow **ant** whose small size stands in no proportion to the painfulness of its bite.

African ticks are not the prolific disease transmitters they are in the Americas, but they may spread Lyme disease, tick-bite fever and a few rarities. Tick-bite fever is a flu-like illness that can easily be treated with doxycycline, but as there can be some serious complications it is important to visit a doctor if you think you have contracted it.

Ticks should ideally be removed as soon as possible, as leaving them on the body increases the chance of infection. They should be removed with special tick tweezers that can be bought in good travel shops. Failing that, you can use your finger nails: grasp the tick as close to your body as possible and pull steadily and firmly away at right angles to your skin. The tick will then come away complete, as long as you do not jerk or twist. If possible douse the wound with alcohol (any spirit will do) or iodine. Irritants (eg: Olbas oil) or lit cigarettes are discouraged since they can cause the ticks to regurgitate and therefore increase the risk of disease. It is best to get a travelling companion to check you for ticks; if you are travelling with small children, remember to check their heads, and particularly behind the ears.

Spreading redness around the bite and/or fever and/or aching joints after a tick bite imply that you have an infection that requires antibiotic treatment, so seek advice.

Toxic plants At contact with the innocuous-looking *folha ganhoma*, a type of nettle called *lochiga* locally, the skin will come up in harmless but painful blisters. Guides can point it out to you and will often chop it with their machete. One traveller I met had a leaf attach itself to her upper arm; when peeled off, it left the skin scarred for a week. The locals use palm oil, but a wash and an antiseptic is probably a better idea. A string of tiny sticky leaves that can cause a slight reaction on the skin is the *pega-pega*. If you are travelling with small children, watch the tropical plants in resort gardens; ask locally which are toxic.

Marine dangers Before assuming a beach is safe for swimming, always ask local advice. It is always better to err on the side of caution if no sensible advice is forthcoming, since there is always a possibility of being swept away by strong currents or undertows that cannot be detected until you are actually in the water. Accidents due to undercurrents and human error have been reported from Club Santana, Ilhéu das Rolas, and due to violent waves and human error from Bom Bom and Jalé, as well as from Praia Piscina (very sudden violent waves). On the last two beaches, caution is important, as, unless you are part of a group, during the week you are likely to be on your own there. Watch out for sea urchins (*ouriços*); the spines of the big *ouriço gallo* can give you fever.

Snorkellers and divers should wear something on their feet to avoid treading on coral reefs, and should never touch the reefs with their bare hands – coral itself can give nasty cuts, and there is a danger of touching a venomous creature camouflaged against the reef. On beaches, never walk barefoot on exposed coral. Even on sandy beaches, people who walk barefoot risk getting coral or urchin spines or venomous fish spines in their feet. You might also get your toes pinched by one of the many crabs, so consider bringing water sandals or buying some cheaply in the market.

If you do tread on a venomous fish, soak the foot in hot (but not scalding) water until some time after the pain subsides; this may be for 20–30 minutes in all. Take

Practical Information HEALTH

2

the foot out of the water to top up, as otherwise you may scald it. If the pain returns, re-immerse the foot. Once the venom has been heat-inactivated, get a doctor to check and remove any bits of fish spine in the wound.

When swimming in the ocean, you'll occasionally experience a fine prickling, which is likely to be the sting of a jellyfish, known as *mãe d'água* (*alforreca* in Portuguese). They are not a big problem, although they do tend to occur in large numbers during full-moon high tides. The most common ones I've seen are small and have a blue filament. You might get away with just a few harmless blisters, but en masse their sting is painful and fiery. The effects, thankfully, pass after about an hour.

The risk of **shark** attacks on tourists is practically zero, as any big whites live hundreds of miles out to sea, though there have been occasional run-ins with local fishermen on the stretch of coast between Angolares and Ribeira Peixe. The only shark in these waters to be a bit wary of is the tiger sand shark, who likes to feed at river mouths and, incidentally, is the only shark known to adjust its buoyancy by 'burping'. Lucky divers might find beautiful, fierce-looking, curious – and harmless – barracudas swim towards them to investigate.

SAFETY

Generally, São Tomé and Príncipe is a very safe place indeed for travellers. There is very little violent crime, and armed robberies and rapes are rare still. Where else in Africa can you walk around the streets of the capital at practically any time of the day or night, the only danger a raspy throat from answering so many questions? *Não temos fronteira*, you'll hear as an explanation, we have no border – nobody can just jump on to the next plane to immunity. There has, however, been a rise in petty crime. Mobile phone theft was hardly heard of a few years ago but unfortunately, today, nicking *telemóvels* has become common. You won't get mugged for a mobile phone, but don't leave it unattended for an opportunist thief to take advantage. I had two stolen, one on each island, and both times from inside a bag, the thieves leaving money and other things behind. Clubs and beaches are the most common place for this to happen; a beach that might look completely deserted to you might not be. Lock your valuables in the car and if you don't have one, carry your money/mobile phone in a waterproof pouch (available from outdoor shops back home, not on the islands) that you can sling over your neck and take into the water. Other possibilities might be to pay locals a few dobras to look after your things, or to hide them under palm leaves or suchlike. If you do have a *telemóvel* stolen, people will probably suggest you go to the National Radio station to appeal for information; unless you are staying on for a while, I wouldn't bother though.

There have been instances of theft from hotel rooms, especially on Príncipe. If you have a lock on your case/backpack, use it – especially if you are staying in a place where the door doesn't lock. The humidity can affect locks and sometimes keys go missing. If you are planning to claim on your travel insurance, go to the police to try to obtain a report for your insurance; if you are not planning to claim, again, I wouldn't bother.

If you want to report a crime to the police, take your passport and a Portuguese-speaker with you, and draw up a short text in Portuguese and English beforehand, detailing what happened, and ask the duty officer, *chefe de serviço*, for a stamp and signature, so you have something in black-and-white. 'I need this for the insurance company' is *preciso disso para o seguro*. One other precaution: if you give people lifts, move much-coveted items such as torches out of sight to remove temptation. The general phone number for the police (24 hours) is ☏ 113.

If you go out at night, be aware that with the exception of a couple of places in the capital, there is usually no provision for left items in clubs; people leave their belongings in their cars or carry a handbag. Even in the most isolated fishing village, if you leave your daypack in somebody's house while you go out on a boat, for instance, it's best to bring a little padlock.

WOMEN TRAVELLERS Since this guide was first written the situation has changed and women travellers should prepare for gentle harassment, hissing and hailing in the street, and also be careful on their own on beaches, especially close to towns. In the past I have felt perfectly safe moving around at all hours and even the most persistent chat-ups or drunken ramblings were never threatening. However, exercise the usual caution in an unfamiliar place and be aware that a white woman, especially, on her own is seen as a potential adventure, or even a potential second or third *mulher*. A friendly chat or a desire to learn about the country and its culture is easily misconstrued as romantic interest. Expect to be repeatedly asked the following: whether you are travelling on your own (*sozinha*), where you are staying (*onde estás hospedada?*), whether you have a boyfriend (*namorado*) or a husband (*marido*; to be married is *casada*) and where the boyfriend/husband is, plus how many children (*filhos*) you have. Santomean men like to tell women travellers without children that they must at least have one! If you are asked for your phone number (*contacto*) and give it out, in my experience hardly anybody, men or women, actually calls; it seems more of a friendly ritual to type your number into their mobile phone. Wearing a ring will ensure a quieter life, and even better might be to invent a jealous (*muito ciumento*) Santomean boyfriend (*namorado Santomense*).

In line with things generally being more rough and ready on Príncipe, some men there have a tendency to try to boss women travellers around, assuming, for instance, that giving you a lift somewhere stakes some kind of claim on you, and lecture you on how impolite it is not to then stay glued to their table. If this kind of thing happens, just thank them politely for the lift/drink and walk away. More worryingly, two female students were harassed on a beach trip organised by two male acquaintances; trust your instincts. Again on Príncipe, a passing motorbike rider once shouted at me to go back to my own country, whilst in a couple of villages in the south of São Tomé some kids called me *colomba*, a derogatory term for white colonials. However, these were the only times I encountered anything resembling hostility. This is the advice from a long-term expact: 'Do think about the way you dress; the local dresscode changes from place to place, from situation to situation, from social group to social group'. Look around and take your cue from the local girls.

WHAT TO TAKE

Those items listed in square brackets ([]) are things that not all travellers will need, but that are difficult or impossible to get on the islands.

- Adapter (3-pin to 2-pin from UK, US 2-pin to European 2-pin from the US)
- Plenty of memory cards/rolls of film and batteries. Chargers.
- Waterproof dry bag/case for keeping your camera dry when hiking or on the water

2

- Strong mosquito repellent (2x)
- Mosquito-bite relief gel
- Sunscreen
- Permethrin spray for mosquito nets
- Head torch (2x if you are planning to do a lot of hiking)
- [Contact lens solution/glasses]
- [Platypus/CamelBak hydration pack for hiking]
- Binoculars for birdwatching
- Hiking boots with a good grip
- Small padlock
- Small dry bag to keep car keys/mobile safe when swimming
- Water-/windproof matches
- Photos of family to show
- Small fold-out map of the world to show where you live
- Small presents: notebooks, pens, picture books, Portuguese–English phrasebooks, mini dictionaries
- Photocopies of passport with visa, credit cards, flight tickets

MONEY

The official currency on São Tomé and Príncipe is the **dobra** ($). One dobra equals 100 *cêntimos*. There are notes of 5,000 (purple), 10,000 (green), 20,000 (red), 50,000 (brown), and 100,000 (green/purple), and coins of 100, 200, 500, 1,000 and 2,000 dobras. The dobra is not traded on international markets, but you can convert online on most currency converter websites (eg: *www.xe.com*), or the useful site of the Central Bank of STP (*www.bcstp.st*). The dobra is pegged to the euro (as in Cape Verde). In 2013, the rate of inflation was running at around 7–10%, with the price hike in essential consumer goods such as cooking oil and rice affecting the population badly; no wonder you will frequently hear that life is a bit *complicado*, or *difícil*, 'difficult'. An agricultural worker takes home about the minimum wage of around 450,000$ a month. Office clerks earn about 500,000$; at the big hotels, waiters earn €30 a month, receptionists around €12.

As regards travellers, the **euro** is much more common than the US$ and is the **lead currency** now. Generally, wherever prices are displayed in euros or dollars, you pay more. There are a number of **banks** in the capital and one on Príncipe. **Credit cards** are still hardly used. In inimitable *Santomense* style, the day the National Investment Bank launched the first Santomean American Express card, after two years of preparations and negotiations, the bank's assets were frozen under suspicion of fraud. The only hotels on the island where guests can pay by credit card are the Miramar, Omali Lodge, Club Santana, Pestana Equador on São Tomé; and on Príncipe, only at the Bom Bom Island resort. However, don't rely on this. I've had both my Portuguese Visa and German MasterCard refused at Santana and Bom Bom for no reason. There seems to be an issue with the handling agency REDUNICRE (✎ *+231 21 313 2929*) receiving fraud warnings. So the only place credit cards reliably work is the Pestana and the Omali.

There has been talk of **ATM** machines coming to both São Tomé and Príncipe for a while, but so far the few available in the capital dispense only dobras, and only to local account holders with a **Cartão 24**. More relevant for travellers, at the **Banco Internacional de São Tomé and Príncipe (BISTP)**, again in the capital, you can use your Visa/MasterCard/Diners debit/credit card to arrange a **money**

	$
Local snack (bar/restaurant)	25,000–55,000
Fish and bananas (lunch/dinner)	45,000–150,000
Pizza	55,000–150,000
Small piece of jackfruit	5,000
500g tomatoes from the market	20,000
Bread	25,000
Palm wine	1000/litre
Beer	20,000–30,000
Coca-Cola	15,000–50,000
Coconut on the beach	1,000–3,000
Cooking oil	40,000
1.5l bottle of mineral water	20,000–50,000
Imported butter	55,000
Imported cheese	40,000–300,000
Imported wine	100,000–1,000,000
Príncipe biscuits	10,000
Imported biscuits	35,000
Gourmet Santomean chocolate	90,000–300,000
500g Santomean coffee	40,000–450,000
500g gourmet Santomean coffee	90,000–500,000

transfer in about ten minutes, with your passport. If you are staying for longer it is quite easy to open a BISTP account, just bring a photocopy of your passport (if you are opening the account on Príncipe, have one ready in your luggage, as you might not find a working photocopier). You will be issued with cheques that you can use in some, but not all, shops and restaurants on the islands.

When buying from street vendors or from the market, **change** (*troco*) is a constant issue, so it is a good idea to keep 5,000$ and 10,000$ notes handy, as well as plenty of coins. Especially in the market, prices are often given in multiples of *contos*, ie: 1,000$. So a piece of jackfruit might be *três contos*, a clutch of ripe bananas *cinco contos*. A colloquial word for money is *verba*, *cacau*, or, more refined, *meios*.

BUDGETING

These daily budgets are per person on the basis of a couple sharing, and rates are approximate. Bear in mind that the prices for many goods and services go up about 7% each year.

LUXURY Staying at a top hotel/resort, hiring a car with guide, eating at resort/top-end restaurants: £125/€150.

MID-RANGE Staying at a small hotel/city guesthouse, one organised activity with picnic, one meal at an upmarket restaurant: £75/€90.

BUDGET AND SHOESTRING Staying at a basic guesthouse, getting around by shared taxi or bike, hiring a local guide, eating street food and one meal at a popular restaurant: £40/€50.

For more information on getting around on Príncipe, see pages 191–2.

BY CAR The country has about 1,100km of roads (1,000km in São Tomé, 100km on Príncipe, 250km sealed and 850km unsealed), supplemented by countless dirt tracks. Whilst there are a fair number of pot-holes on the capital's roads, the **roads** inland and north from the capital are pretty good overall and, in particular the north and south coast roads, navigable by ordinary saloon car. The interior road goes past the suburb of Madre de Deus to Trindade and leads up 1,000m to the botanical gardens at Bom Sucesso and the Monte Café plantation. You can access these by saloon car, though it will get badly rattled. The northern road – due to be resurfaced in 2015 – which runs from Guadalupe to Lagoa Azul and hugs the coast to Neves until eventually fizzling out into a grass track a few kilometres past Santa Catarina on the northwest coast. The road south towards Angolares and Porto Alegre that in the past was diabolical and full of pot-holes has been remade – though from Porto Alegre onwards it is still the same. Meanwhile, the number of cars and motorbikes is increasing, as are accidents; as a pedestrian in towns, watch out when crossing the road. Traffic signs were introduced on a large scale in 2013, but signs indicating destinations are mainly limited to the capital, pointing out the main roads south to Angolares or north to Neves. People are happy to give directions and sometimes they might ask for a lift, *boleia*. Santomean drivers sound their horns frequently, Italian-style, to alert other road users. While traffic drives on the right, outside the city, cars coming from different directions are often competing for the same bit of road with the fewest pot-holes.

Car rental is still expensive, or alternatives are **motorbikes** and **bikes**. For details of car hire companies in the capital of São Tomé see page 111. Most Santomeans travel by shared **yellow taxis** and these can also be hired individually (called a *frete*), paying for all the seats.

BY BIKE At the moment there is no official bike hire on São Tomé island, though you can contact Navetur (see page 112) or the Cycling Federation (see page 93) to see whether that has changed. **Mucumbli ecolodge** near Neves (see pages 144–6), owned by the president of the Cycling Federation, has bikes. You could buy a bike to use for the duration of your stay and sell it on (to another expat probably) when you leave. A large store on Rua de Angola in São Tomé, **Martins & Azevedo,** (℘ *222 2156; ⊕ 08.00–12.30, 15.00–17.30 Mon–Fri, 08.00–13.00 Sat*), sells bikes (EMT brand) for around €135.

BY BOAT A great way to see São Tomé island is by boat. Navetur (see page 112) can take you on a *volta a ilha*, with two nights beach camping and excellent birdwatching opportunities. You can also try Tropic Venture (see page 89), or arrange a trip through your hotel.

Accommodation on the islands ranges from a beach shelter made out of palm fronds by your guide and basic dives for €10, through city hotels and restored plantation houses to a five-star resort. Although São Tomé and Príncipe does not have a developed backpacker infrastructure, there is now a great deal of choice for a range of budgets, with new places springing up all over the place. Options include guesthouses in the city, ecocamps, B&B stays with expats, and four- or five-star international standard hotels and resorts. The high season is August and the Christmas/New Year period. You shouldn't need to bring a mosquito net, as it is provided free of charge in nearly all hotel/hostel rooms. However, the nets might have been hanging there for years, losing their permethrin impregnation, so bring a permethrin spray to treat them. When you get to your room, it's a good idea to check everything is working: that the taps are running and the loo flushing, and that there is toilet paper.

Rate-wise, single travellers get heavily penalised although often the difference in price is very small. If you want to book online, try the www.logitravel.pt website. There is no formal set-up for **staying with local families** yet, but try Navetur (see page 112) for contacts or guides like Luis Mário Almeida (see page 159) may be able to put you in touch with Santomean families and/or a plantation. Ask around and explain that you want to experience how 'normal' Santomeans live, *conhecer a vida do dia em dia dos Santomenses*; as a guideline, a fair rate to offer for B&B is €20, though you will probably be asked for €25.

You can **camp** anywhere on public land in the islands (ask for permission for the Obô National Park) but have to bring nearly all your own equipment. Also, in practice, unless you know exactly what you are doing with a compass, etc, it is always better to have a guide. The Navetur agency can arrange tent and sleeping bag hire (see page 112) but you are better of bring what you need. I've found that in the dry season a hammock with mosquito netting and strong poncho-style rain flaps is enough, so you can get away without carrying a tent. If you find yourself stuck, build a shelter from palm fronds. Some travellers staying for longer periods of time choose to rent a cheap room to use as a base, where they leave their stuff while off on camping trips.

EATING AND DRINKING

The staple item of the Santomean diet is **fish** – *grelhado* – grilled, baked (*asado*) or to a lesser degree cooked/boiled (*cozido*). The most popular are flying fish (*peixe voador*), and you will see these cut open and laid out to dry on the beach or drying sheds in large quantities. They have a delicate taste, but aren't seen much in restaurants as they are full of little bones. One of the most popular fish you will be served in restaurants is the red grouper (*cherne*). Another is the sea bass (*corvina*), with firm flesh and great flavour, associated in *forro* culture with prestige, luck and knowledge. A good option for a **beach lunch** is to buy a fish directly from the fishermen, around midday. Expect to pay around 20,000$ for a big fish, and ask whether you can grill it over the fisherman's fire (*pode-se grelhar o peixe?*); if you bring a lime and some salt from town, you can have yourself a real feast.

In *forro* culture, to be well-fed is a sign of wealth and status, and two words commonly used to describe people outside the norm are *massabruta*, meaning a portly person, and *socanina* used to describe a very thin person. For breakfast or *matabicho* (literally 'kill the little beast', the hunger inside), most Santomeans reheat the remains of the previous evening meal (*jantar*), and only eat a snack for lunch (*almoço*), while a standard tourist breakfast is rolls, jam/cheese and fresh papaya. Currently, 90% of food is imported but small agricultural ventures, often funded by NGOs, are trying to promote more self-reliance.

Small **eating establishments** – *petisqueiras*, *churrasquerias*, *quitandas* and *quiosques* – might not be immediately visible to you as they often look like small wooden shacks. For those with a sweet tooth, *pastelarias* are a welcome Portuguese heritage and serve a selection of homemade pastries. At lunchtime, in every village, there should be at least one person who will serve simple cooked food; you just have to ask *Onde há comida quente?* The food, mostly fish or chicken with manioc, fried banana or jackfruit, is often very tasty. I have, however, heard of travellers being charged a hefty 300,000$ for a simple dish at some of the plantations on both São Tomé and Príncipe island already used to visitors. Be sure to discuss prices beforehand.

Roadside food – grilled corn-on-the-cob, *safú* fruit, stews from big pots – can be an excellent and cheap choice. Expats will usually warn you off street food and eating dangerous food items such as salads, but everybody's stomach reacts differently; try to acclimatise it gradually to the unfamiliar bacteria (see page 66).

TRADITIONAL SANTOMEAN DISHES The grilled fish 'belly', *barriga de peixe* (usually *peixe andala*, Atlantic sailfish), is frequently served with rice (*arroz*), breadfruit or manioc. Beans (*feijão*) are a staple food. Another staple is *banana cozida* (cooked banana), the blandness of the banana offset by wonderful spicy sauces, like the red malagueta piri-piri sauce found in every restaurant, or a green parsley *salsa* sauce at more upmarket places. The Santomean signature dish is **calulú** (see box, opposite, page for a recipe): dried smoked fish in a delicious sauce made from *ocá* leaves, palm oil, lady's fingers (okra), malagueta chilli and watercress, plus a variety of fresh herbs, resulting in a multi-layered flavour. *Calulú* takes about five hours to prepare. Other similar dishes are *blablá* and *djogo*, and *cachupa* is a popular Cape Verdean dish cooked with corn, green and broad beans. It is not that easy to find these time-intensive traditional specialities and in most places you have to request them a day in advance; the upmarket restaurants tend more towards Portuguese cuisine and fish dishes. I only know of one place where you can just turn up and have a *calulú* – in the market building in the capital. If you've made friends locally, you could ask them whether you could try specific dishes at their house. I've usually bought a few beers from the local *loja* (shack store) if I found myself invited for some food in a village. Beach picnics on agency excursions are an opportunity to try cocoyam (*matabala*), papaya, banana snacks, etc. At popular celebrations (*festas*), such as saints' days, you will get the opportunity to try delicacies like *estufa de morcego*: bat stew. The

With kind permission from the author and publishers of Na Roça com os Tachos *and* Façam o Favor de Ser Felices. *Translated by Kathleen Becker.*

The following recipe for the Santomean signature dish *calulú* is taken from João Carlos Silva's cookbook accompanying his 2006 RTP Africa TV programme *Na Roça com os Tachos*, 'On the Plantation with Cooking Pans'. The owner of the rural tourism venture at São João dos Angolares and the CACAU space is now advisor to the government, too. You can get all the ingredients listed here at the market; the vendors will love the idea of a *branca*, or better even, a *branco*, trying their hand at cooking this dish! Palm oil is essential to Santomean cuisine; in the West, it is usually available from ethnic stores, or you can buy some on the islands to take home.

INGREDIENTS *Galinha fumada* (smoked chicken), *óleo de palma* (palm oil), *maquêquê* (a green tomato-like fruit), *tomate* (tomato), *cebola* (onion), *quiabos* (lady's fingers), *pau pimenta* ('pepper wood'), *óssame* (a red bulbous fruit), *mosquito* herb, *couve* (kale cabbage), *gimboa/jimboa* herb, *malagueta* (chilli), *folha de louro* (laurel), *pimento* (pepper), *cominhos* (cumin), *beringela* (aubergine), *mússua* (hibiscus), *fruta-pão* (breadfruit) or *farinha de trigo* (wheat flour), *bananas*.

PREPARATION Chop all the vegetables, including the pieces of breadfruit, and cook them in a saucepan with palm oil until all the ingredients turn into a big 'soup'. Add the smoked chicken, cut into pieces. Pull out the breadfruit after cooking and mash it in a small mortar, to thicken the sauce. If you don't have breadfruit available, you can get a similar result using wheat flour. Leave everything 'to fall in love, until you smell the aroma of a kiss …' A few moments before serving, pull out the *mosquito* twig. Serve accompanied by an *angú* of bananas (see below), or rice and manioc flour. Be creative and replace the *gimboa* with spinach or the *mosquito* with basil or any other aromatic herbs. Instead of the chicken, you can use fish or other smoked meats.

For the *angú* accompaniment, peel green bananas and leave them to cook until slightly soft. Then beat them in a mortar until you have a paste, which, using a spoon, you can form into the number of patties you like.

poorest sections of society, lacking the money to buy fish, often eat forest/sea snails (*búzio*) as a source of protein. Don't follow suit unless in an emergency, they are harmful. You'll see the yellow-red flowering wild **manioc** by the wayside sometimes; its roots are a popular food, ground into flour and made into a pudding. Sold occasionally by kids on plantations, the fluffy starchy white heaps don't honestly taste of much.

VEGETARIAN FOOD You won't get any hassle for being a vegetarian, and you will eat fairly well, but the food may be a bit on the boring side. If you eat fish, you're in heaven of course. Western-style restaurants are used to vegetarians, but in a popular eating place, to say that you are a *vegetariano/vegetariana* does not mean much to people, and the person serving you might panic and say they have *nada*, nothing, for you! Just explain that you don't eat meat or fish, *nem carne nem peixe*, and know what to ask for: *feijão* (beans), *arroz* (rice), *tomates* (tomatoes), *banana frita* (fried banana). As long as you trust the storage facilities for eggs, an omelette (*omelettes*) is a good fallback – just make sure to ask for an *omelettes simples*, or *omelette de queijo*, cheese omelette, otherwise you might find bits of *chouriço* sausage in it as a well-meant treat. Occasionally you can get an omelette with fresh herbs (*ervas frescas*). Try asking for an *omelette de micôcô*; this famous thyme-like herb is a Santomean favourite. And there are always chips/French fries (*batatas fritas*). Some other **vegetables** you can ask for are *cenoura* (carrots), *pimpinella* (a white tree vegetable) and *couve* (cabbage). They'll usually come boiled (*cozidos*) so use hot malagueta sauce or green salsa to spice them up; if you would prefer them grilled ask for them *grelhados* or *salteados*. Less commonly available in restaurants are peppers (*pimentos*), aubergine (*berengela*) and *maquêquê* (a green tomato-like fruit). If you're staying longer and know an informal eatery, you could try bringing in your own vegetables for them to prepare. Sometimes you will be able to get cabbage (*couve*) or other local greens like the delicious *lossua* which grows around Monte Café; the only proviso here is that they are likely to have been prepared with chicken stock, *caldo de galinha*, as that's the one on sale here. Consider bringing your own vegetable stock. For **vegans**, the choice is similar, as dairy products don't really form part of the Santomean diet anyway.

FRUIT Most people's favourite is **jackfruit** (*jaca*), a big, ballooning, pock-marked yellowish-green fruit, sold along the roadside, the pieces covered with banana leaves to keep the flies away. In Europe, a whole *jaca*, if you can find them, can cost up to €40. Here, it might only set you back 150,000$. The only problem is the fruit's incredibly sticky sap: bring a plastic bag if you want to take a piece (*pedaço*) back to the hotel/hostel. Jackfruit sellers always keep a cloth and oil for cleaning the sap off their hands; at worst, use moisturiser or suncream. Be prepared that people think it's incredibly funny to see a Westerner, women especially, eating a piece of jackfruit on the go. A new discovery for me was that you can also eat the large seeds. Cooked or roasted they taste a bit like chestnuts and are very nutritious. Few Santomeans make use of them, however. **Mangoes** (*manga*) grow in most plantations, but it's difficult to find homemade mango juice. *Cajamangas* have a lovely fresh acidic taste, but are very fibrous. *Safú* is a small oblong fruit of a beautiful purply blue with a taste reminiscent of olives and artichokes. The basic way to prepare *safú* is to top and tail them, scratch off a few strips of the skin (*casca*) and boil them in salted water for a couple of minutes. It is sometimes eaten in the morning with butter, or to accompany bread or breadfruit; often sold grilled along the roadside. Kids break open **cocoa** pods with stones to eat the citrusy-tasting flesh, and suck on **sugarcane** (*cana*), which is sold cheaply at the roadside and at the market. In the 16th century, sugarcane, brought to Europe by returning Crusaders, became the island's first cash crop, turning São Tomé and Príncipe into the second African producer of sugarcane after Cape Verde, which had less success with the crop. Probably the most important fruit on the islands is the **breadfruit**, the spiny *fruta pão*, with starchy spongy whitish flesh; the trees often grow next to erythrinas on cocoa plantations. Originally from the Pacific region, the breadfruit was brought to São Tomé and Príncipe in the mid 19th century by the first baron of Água Izé. It is eaten with fish dishes and used to mop up palm oil, or as a dessert; Santomeans travelling to Lisbon often carry a few in their luggage. The prize for the weirdest-looking fruit could go to its cousin, the **African breadfruit**, *izaquente*. Originally from equatorial Africa and looking like a huge spiky, slightly squashed, green football, an *izaquente* can weigh up to 10kg. Once it has fallen off the tree, it is left to go off for a while until ready. You sometimes see the seeds being washed in the river, waiting to be made into a paste and a sweet pudding, or into a savoury dish with palm oil. Kids eat the fresh seeds of the oblong fruit of the **carozeiro**, one of the most common trees in urban areas. The taste is not unpleasant and is similar to coconut. The fruit of the *coleira* tree, coca nuts, are also eaten; they contain caffeine and stave off hunger. A tropical fruit much in evidence on the islands is, of course, the **banana**, introduced to Africa 2,000 years ago, and a good source of potassium. Generally, *banana madura* (ripe) is the yellow one which you can eat as it comes. Various varieties grow in São Tomé and Príncipe. The green plantain banana you will eat cooked (*cozido*) and fried (*frito*) are *banana prata*, the 'silver banana' and *banana pão* ('bread banana'), which is larger, with dark yellow flesh, and the most used for frying. For snacking and dessert, the popular small *banana maçã*, 'apple banana', has a lovely appley taste. Much coveted, too, are the less-common *banana d'ouro*, 'golden banana', whose skin has a red colour, and the *Gran Michel*. Even though banana plants are found in every *quintal* in the country, their cultivation is labour intensive. Banana plants grow fast, their large elliptic leaves unfurling from the stem at the rate of one a week, but they need regular watering and removal of excess shoots to channel all the plant's energy into fruit production. Also, they are easily toppled by the weight of rainwater – when you're out hiking, you'll occasionally hear one of them come crashing down. Each stalk produces one huge flower cluster on a violet trunk that bears the fruit – tightly packed clusters of small, square-looking bananas – and then dies, new stalks growing from the underground rhizome (bulb). Bananas are made into all kinds of snacks: *banana seca*, shrink-dried whole bananas with a smoky flavour; a small sausage-shaped banana snack called *fios*, made with corn flour; and the Príncipe speciality *bobofrito*, a delicious high-energy snack made with ripe bananas fried in coconut oil. Other popular **snack foods** are *gigumba* (peanut brittle), sometimes sold in bars and restaurants – usually by the bottle only – and *palla-palla*, sweet or savoury crisps made of banana or cocoyam (*matabala*).

A common **street food**, corn-on-the-cob (*milho*) costs around 3,000$. *Arroz doce* is sweet rice prepared with coconut and sweetcorn traditionally eaten for breakfast. Street kids sell it for 2,000$ in sawn-off soft-drink cans. My favourite sweet snack is *açucarinhas*: patties made from coconut and sugar fried in palm oil. Sold outside bakeries for about 1,000$ they work especially well put inside a corn roll (*broa*). Some prefer the coconut a bit burnt (*queimada*). Another desert is *aranha* ('spider'), filigrane sugar strings stuffed with food colouring, prepared with eight coconuts to 1kg of sugar. For **dessert** (*sobremesa*, 'on the table'), chocolate mousse is a favourite (as in Portugal), and as it's nearly always made from a packet, you don't have to worry about raw eggs spending ages sitting in the shop in the heat.

Self-catering is a great idea. Buying fresh produce from the market gives you a real experience of Santomean culture and contact with the people, and when complemented with forays to Western-style supermarkets, you can eat well and cheaply. The only minor problem is power cuts disabling fridges and electric hobs. Also, if you don't want ants crawling around your cereals, make sure you put all opened food in the fridge.

DRINKS The ubiquitous refreshing Sagres lager (you will notice blown-up bottles as decorations in restaurants) and the slightly sweeter Super Bock are imported from Portugal. The national Rosema beer, Nacional, brewed in the north of São Tomé, comes in big bottles with no label; easier to drink is their Pilsner-style Criollo. Wines sold in the cheap restaurants/shops are usually Portuguese table wines such as Faisal or the light Casal Garcia *vinho verde* ('green wine'). Upmarket restaurants and supermarkets have a large selection of Portuguese wines (including a pleasant red Capote Velho), plus French and South African vintages and even champagne. At the other end of the scale, on Príncipe I came across white wine mixed with Sprite. Wine is usually sold by the bottle (*garrafa*); it's difficult to get wine by the glass (*copo*) and that combined with the hot humid climate turned me into a dedicated Sagres drinker. *Aguardente* (from *agua ardente*, 'burning water') is made of sugarcane, as is Gravana rum, and if you come across an artisanal distillery, you can see it being produced and buy some cheaply. Locals often drink the hard-hitting cheap *cacharamba* gin-style firewater. Less commonly available is *ponche*, a basic cocktail made from *aguardente* and honey; other versions are made with white rum, quinine leaves and lemon. Mé-Zóchi is a sweet liqueur (43%) that comes in various flavours such as orange (*laranja*), *cajamanga* and pineapple (*ananas*). Cocoa liqueur is a popular newcomer and miniatures make a nice souvenir, but few shops sell them.

The national drink, however, is **palm wine**. *Vinho de palma*, or *vim pema* in creole, comes in three qualities; the purest, most undiluted variety is made at high altitude, decreasing in quality the closer to town you get. Buy a small bottle (sealed with a bit of twisted palm leaf or newspaper) from a street stall for around 500$ or, even better, buy some straight off a palm wine worker in the forest. Bring your own container/thermos cap, as the sawn-off mineral water bottles or beer cans used can be pretty filthy. The wine ferments during the day. In the morning, it is like milk (*doce*, sweet); the longer the liquid ferments, the more acidic it becomes, turning into what is called *ussuá*. Come night, a cork will come flying out of the bottle, champagne-style, and the increased alcohol content makes it more explosive, too. Unfortunately, alcoholism is a growing problem on the islands, in the wake of a degradation of living conditions and loss of trust in the future over the past decade.

Don't be surprised if your waiter/waitress asks whether you want them to open your drink (*posso abrir?*). The reason for this cautious approach is to reassure the customer that the bottle hasn't been tampered with. In the past there have been cases of poisoning on the island when romantic scores or workplace grievances needed to be settled; tourists were never involved. **Soft drinks** all go by the same local name here: 'Sumol' (passionfruit, orange or pineapple, lemonade, even Coca-Cola sometimes). The main type of juice is mango juice (*sumo de manga*), imported from Lebanon. If you would like/rather not have ice in your drink, ask for *com/sem gelo*. Fresh **coconut water** is not often sold commercially, but it's usually easy to ask somebody on the beach to find a green coconut and open it for you. The contents, *dawa,* is meant to be incredibly healthy, but the slightly sour juice didn't agree so well with my stomach at least. As for **coffee**, in Western cafés on São Tomé you can find the range of Portuguese-style variations: *café, garroto, carioca*. A *galão* has more milk than coffee (my favourite is a *galão escuro*, with two shots of espresso, which is like a *latte* or *latte macchiato*). On Príncipe (apart from places like Bom Bom), coffee means a pot of the local earthy brew. Unfortunately, few hotels and cafés actually serve Santomean coffee, but you can always try and ask for local coffee (*café de cá*). **Tea** (*chá*) is available in Western hotels/restaurants and in some local places too, often the Lipton brand, and in varieties such as peach or green tea. You can ask for milk (*leite*) or a lemon (*limão*) – which here means lime. *Chalela* or *erva de Príncipe* is the local lemongrass tea, lovely! Or you could try asking for a delicious alternative common in Portugal used to treat colds: *carioca de limão*, hot water with lemon peel.

PUBLIC HOLIDAYS Check at the tourist information office and ask around locally for details of events/celebrations, etc, and for the many saints' days.

1 Jan   **New Year's Day** Santomeans gather on the beaches to celebrate; there is a tradition of putting on a new set of clothes after a bathe in the sea to represent the new year.

3 Feb   **Heroes' Day** Commemorations mark the anniversary of the 1953 Massacre of Batepá on 2/3 February, with dancing, oral history, a march by secondary-school pupils, wreath-laying, etc.

1 May   **Labour Day** International Workers' Day.

12 Jul   **Independence Day** Celebration of independence from Portugal in 1975. Festivities centre around Independence Square in the capital and start on the eve of 12 July, but the big gathering for speeches, cultural performances, etc, is held in a different town each year.

6 Sep   **Armed Forces' Day** Parades through the streets of the capital.

30 Sep   **Agricultural Reform Day** Celebration of the 1975 nationalisation of the largest plantations.

26 Nov   **Algiers Agreement Day** Celebration of the 1974 decolonisation treaty between Portugal and the MLSTP (see page 19) that paved the way for independence.

21 Dec   **São Tomé Day** Discovery of São Tomé island in around 1470.

25 Dec   **Christmas Day**

OPENING HOURS Most shops and services observe the regular opening hours of the 'English week', *semana inglesa*: 08.00–12.30 and 14.00–17.30 Monday–Friday, 08.00–13.00 Saturday, with variations. Restaurants usually stay open late until around 23.00, in Príncipe until about 22.00. In the capital, banks and a few other places relevant to tourists, such as the TAP agency, close early and institutions such as libraries are only open on weekdays, while the phone exchange stays open until 21.00 and the central petrol station until midnight. There are a few nominally '24-hour' kiosks/shops. All opening hours quoted have to be taken with a pinch of salt, not least to accommodate the frequent power cuts.

SHOPPING AND SERVICES

If you don't want to buy something because you've already got it, you can say *Obrigado/a, ja tenho*. Otherwise, just say *Obrigado/a, não quero* ('Thanks, I don't want') or *não preciso* ('I don't need').

MARKETS AND SHACK STORES Fresh fruit and vegetables and many other items such as shoes, clothes, stationery and cosmetics are sold at markets. Small shack stores (*lojas*, sometimes called *cantinas*) exist in countless numbers – every plantation and fishing village has at least one – selling very much the same basic foodstuffs, including biscuits, cheap wines, soft drinks, tomato paste and cooking oil.

SOUVENIRS One of the greatest pleasures on the islands is discovering the range of unique produce and quality crafts available – just watch your luggage allowance (though even STP Airways will normally grant you an extra 5kg). **Coffee** and **chocolate**, as well as **vanilla**, are the most obvious souvenirs to take home; children will enjoy a wooden rattle or carved boat. Príncipe, while not great for souvenir

Practical Information   SHOPPING AND SERVICES

2

shopping, is the home of **bobofrito** (see page 83), and you can pick it up very cheaply (25,000$). *Bobofrito* keeps well and makes a welcome present for friends on the main island, and for hillwalking friends back home, as an exotic high-energy snack. Some of the airport vendors, and my favourite shop on São Tomé, Qua-Tela, now sell it in prettier packaging than the traditional big brown sausage-shape and chopped into pieces.

It is easier than it appears to take some of the majestic **tropical plants** home, including the waxy pink porcelain roses (the signature flower of São Tomé, if not endemic); the amazing bright-red endemic giant ginger, *bordão de macaco*, which has a new yellow flower appearing every day; and various varieties of 'parrot beak' heliconias. On the day of your departure, you can pick up a bunch for €5 (residents pay only 100,000$) but note that bouquets are usually incredibly heavy! In the capital, a new central nursery called **O Horto da Bita** (*just off Av da Independência;* m *993 9940*) sells flowers and is planning to open to visitors for guided visits. Aromatic vanilla is produced by the **PAPAFPA co-operative** (*222 2037*) based at Nova Moka; by the time you visit there might be organised plantation visits to Novo Destino; ask the agencies.

To remember nights at the discoteca or to give to friends with an interest in music, buy some CDs recorded at a recording studio (*estúdio de gravaçao*) found on both islands; at only around 60,000$, these make a great souvenir. A range of T-shirts, towels, flags and caps with the national flag (*bandeira*) or with slogans of the 'Kiss me, I'm São Tomean' and 'I'd rather be in Príncipe' variety are available at the local market, as well as online.

In the capital, **necklaces and bracelets** made of brown, grey, black or red seeds are on sale in hotels (expensive) or touted by kids in the centre of the capital for around 40,000$. If you like **DIY souvenirs,** try to find some *salacontas* beads (red or grey) on a guided walk, and have them made into a collar on the islands or back home. Visit **Praia Sete Ondas** (see page 168) for beautiful 'sea cookie' sea urchin shells. On the slopes of the *obô* forest you will find leaves eaten into a filigree shape by a caterpillar, and these look lovely on a card, for instance, or pasted on to gift-wrapping.

CHOCOLATE In 2011, the Italian *Corriere della Sera* newspaper called **Claudio Corallo** chocolate (*www.claudiocorallo.com*) 'the best in the world'. Who exactly used that epithet first, and when, is lost in the mists of time but in any case, it is kind of true. On the islands, the best place to pick up chocs is after a **Corallo tour** (see page 132), which takes place on the days before flights. My visit was an epiphany. This chocolate can be truly mood-altering, in the best sense of the word, with a friend of mine even claiming 'gastronomic orgasm-inducing qualities!' While prices are roughly the same as in the shops, the wares are kept in better conditions and the price of the very worthwhile tour is discounted from your shopping.

In Europe, the deservedly famous Corallo chocolate is sold through top-end retailers such as Fortnum & Mason in London, Printemps in Paris and in an increasing number of shops in Portugal, but at about twice the price.

Chocolate lovers should try the following websites:

www.boaboca.pt From their base in the UNESCO-listed historic centre of Evora in the Alentejo (fantastic holiday region, and Evora is only a short hop from Lisbon by train), Boa Boca sell a range of beautifully packaged chocolate products, such as brandy-soaked raisins, orange, sugar crystals, and cooking chocolate. They sell Saotomean coffee too.

www.cafedirect.co.uk Luxury Fairtrade drinking chocolate from STP, 300g for under £3, available from various supermarkets and online ethical stores.

www.chocolatetradingco.com Sells Callebaut 2.5kg chocolate chips for baking, etc, alongside Cluizel bars.

www.chocolats-pralus.com The 75% Forastero bars from this French chocolatier have been getting rave reviews and also feature in the beautiful 'Tropical Pyramid' collection. 'Quite unlike what is usually found in Africa ... a result of the trees' genetic purity'.

www.cluizel.com The 67% cocoa chocolate bars and miniatures made from the Trinitario cocoa variety (a mix between Criollo and Forastero) have 'subtle grassy and liquorice notes'. Paris-based chocolatier Michel Cluizel prides himself on not using child labour on his Vila Graçinda plantation near São João dos Angolares. Check the website for retailers; in the UK the chocolates are available through www.seventypercent.com (see below) and www.chocolatetradingco.com, n the US from Amazon and other online stores.

www.enricrovira.com Chocolates and hot chocolate made with cocoa from Príncipe by Barcelona chocolatier Enric Rovira, who is the author (with Corallo) of a book homage to cocoa and who has been called the 'Dalí of chocolate'.

www.lakechamplainchocolates.com 85g 'Sao Thome' 70% cocoa (fruity vanilla) vegan kosher bars for €4.

www.neuhauschocolates.com Chocespresso hot chocolate with Saotomean cocoa. You can order online for delivery throughout mainland Europe, to the UK and even the US.

www.revillonchocolatier.fr Fancy Christmas chocs made in Lyon since the end of the 18th century – the story goes that the tradition started with a Lyon patisserie apprentice who would secretly give chocolates wrapped in love notes to his beloved. These Grandes Origines beauties are made with 70% Santomean ganache, and the love notes have been replaced with quotations.

www.saotomeprincipe.eu/chocolate/chocolate/chocolatestp.htm Not up to date, but a long list of brands using cocoa from STP.

www.seventypercent.com Sells Cluizel chocolate in the UK, and offers chocolate tasting certificates. Here's what one expert has to say about the Vila Graçinda bar (available for just under €5), giving it 9 out of 10: 'The aroma is deep and quite brooding with soft molasses, liquorice, damp tobacco, espresso and some spicy high notes ... the delivery is quite surprising. A light touch of fennel accompanies raspberry jam and a hint of fresh fig before darker aspects slowly begin to take hold; the coffee, tobacco and oaken spices being most prominent. The finish is even and sustained, all on faint tannins, anise and a figgy back note.'

HAIR AND BEAUTY Visiting a Santomean salon is great fun and an inexpensive cultural experience, especially having your hair braided (women) or an interesting pattern shaved (men). The artificial hair (*postiço*) woven into braids (*tranças*) and the little transparent or multi-coloured beads (*missangas*) can usually be picked up cheaply in a shop or market. Braiding takes time, but is a morning or afternoon well spent, listening to the women's gossip and banter. Apart from being a great conversation item, this style is practical in the tropical heat. If you have Caucasian hair, especially if it's fine, a style that will hold for months on local ladies' heads will start unravelling after two weeks. In any case, for most people, enthusiasm for African hairstyles usually unravels just before boarding the plane home; keep in mind that unbraiding (*distrançar*) takes a good while, too. Make sure you communicate what you want – I had an odd fringe cut in one place and some hair colour I'd brought in just slopped on to my head. You can usually get other beauty treatments like waxing at salons, too.

Both islands are ideally suited to hiking, sports fishing and diving (with restrictions). Hikes can range from gentle walks to waterfalls and a few hours' beach-hopping to rainforest treks lasting several days. Cycling, surfing and kayaking are only beginning to take off, but at the time of going to press STP's first parapente course was being organised by Portuguese guide Amilcar (m *998 6597*; see below).

HIKING GUIDES In general, a proper guide is worth having, and rainforest hikes are practically impossible without a guide. Be wary though, most impromptu 'guides' on plantations, for example, can tell you very little about the history of the place (even in Portuguese).

Some guides like to take control a little, marking up prices and shielding you from finding out about real taxi costs, etc. You will also find that many locals call themselves *guia* or guides but in many cases all they do is act as *accompagnantes,* keeping you company but without knowing much background. You will often be approached at the airport with the question of where you are staying, and self-professed guides will then turn up at your hotel. Even teenagers have got in on the act.

São Tomé The Navetur and Mistral agencies employ excellent guides who usually speak French (some of them English); some are available for private work, too. At Mistral Voyages, reliable, calm and collected **Agostino Espírito Santo** (m *991 1881*; e *edalessanto@hotmailcom*) is a good bet for Francophone and Anglophone visitors. Working for Navetur, **Nilton Paquete** (m *993 9452*; e *nilton1900@ hotmail.com*) has good English and loves to share his knowledge. Taxi driver/ guide **Joaquim Ribeiro** (m *990 6491*) is very experienced; he has some French and a bit of English. **José Spencer** (m *991 9305, evenings*), based at Mucumbli (see pages 144–6), near the Ponta Figo plantation, is a very knowledgeable hiking guide who runs trips to the Pico, around the northern waterfalls, and treks along the remote southwestern coast/island crossings; he only speaks Portuguese. Other excellent forest guides are **Lucio Primo** (m *990 4468*), your best choice for orchid hikes, and his younger brother **Brice Monteiro** (m *991 0060*); both are based at the Monte Café plantation and speak French and some Spanish. Brice has little English still, but is a very experienced, knowledgeable and caring guide – I have climbed the Pico a few times with him and can unreservedly recommend him. A new English-speaking entry is **Amilcar Pina Silva** (m *998 6597*; e *ecolevestp@ gmail.com*) or Blanko Fôlo ('white *forro*'), a maverick motorised Portuguese guide who can take you to all kinds of places that you'd never find on your own (€70/day), such as off-the-beaten-track plantations and underground market bars. Some local guides have no phone and have to be contacted via a neighbour, invariably in Portuguese.

The **Monte Pico guide association** (e *montepico@yahoo.com.br; www.montepico. blogspot.com*) has 50 members and is involved in looking after the main island's botanical garden and the Obô National Park. Its dynamic president, **Luis Mário Almeida** (m *991 1670*; e *lumanovamoca@hotmail.com*) speaks good French and very basic English. There is no office as such, and Luis Mario is based at Nova Moka where he rents out basic accommodation, so he can be difficult to contact and it's best to send enquiries to both email addresses. Monte Pico's General Secretary is Joël Santos (m *991 1117*), based at Monte Café (see pages 158–9). The **Associação dos Guias**, or Guides' Association, was formed in 2013, and its president is Walter Martinho (m *991 6617*).

Príncipe There are now more English-speaking guides on the island, but activities are most easily organised through the Bom Bom Island resort.

DIVING The bumpy underwater relief of the islands' volcanic ocean floor mirrors the archipelago's mountainous surface. Enjoy the undisturbed natural beauty of a habitat where the equatorial currents at the meeting point of the eastern and western Atlantic host a wealth of species, including sharks, rays, turtles, fan corals and many fish you won't see anywhere else in the world. If you are spending any time in Lisbon before your onward flight, visit the magnificent **Oceanarium** (❧ *+351 218 917 002; www.oceanario.pt*), one of the biggest in the world, for a flavour of what you could see. However, don't come with a tick-list of big fish, but with a spirit of discovery. The agreeable water temperature, averaging around 26°C, is unusually warm for the Atlantic. The only times when diving is hampered somewhat by choppy waters are the months of March and April.

The biggest improvement to diving services would be a (mobile) decompression chamber; at the time of going to print, the Pestana group of hotels was trying to have one set up.

There are plenty of good dive sites dotted around the coast of São Tomé as well as near Club Santana and Ilhéu das Rolas, just off the southern tip of the island. Príncipe has less human intervention and even fewer fishermen, trawlers and dragnets disturbing the marine fauna and flora of the shallow littoral than ST. At night, with the coral flowering, it turns into a garden. However, there is no dedicated diving infrastructure here yet, as the big player, the HBD company, are taking the cautious approach and will not offer diving without the presence of a decompression chamber.

Dive centres

ᵢⱼ⤳**Costa Norte** www.costanorte.pt. New (2013) outfit operating out of the Pestana Ocean Resort (see page 115) & Pestana Equador on Ilhéu das Rolas (see page 179). It operates a keen pricing structure, & offers all PADI instruction levels. Volta a ilha €65 with a min 8 people. Ask about the so-called live-aboard adventures, leaving Pestana in the morning to visit the Tinhosa Islets.

ᵢⱼ⤳**Sete Pedras Diving Centre** ❧ 224 2400 (Club Santana reception); m 990 4424; www.setepedrasdivingcenter.com. Well-equipped diving centre, formerly called Club Maxel (which used to be where Tropic Venture is now). This PADI centre offers Discover Scuba Diving & the regular range of diving courses, exploring the abundant warm waters for moray eels, trumpet fish, butterfly fish, barracudas, sand sharks & turtles. Manager Alberto Miranda has the PADI Master Scuba Dive Trainer grade & apart from English & French is a good bet for speakers of Italian & Spanish in particular, as he undertook some training in those countries. His dream is to establish a diving base in his hometown of Santo António, Príncipe. Ask to see the copy of the Atlantic fishlife guide. The centre

can also organise snorkelling trips by boat, sport fishing & hikes with local guides.

ᵢⱼ⤳**Tropic Venture** Praia Lagarto ❧ 222 8006; m 993 4199 (João Santos); e helpro.js@gmail.com; www.tropicventure.com. This is now the longest-established diving centre, & they organise dives all over the island, with a favourite spot at Club Santana. Dives cost €40, whether with your own or hired equipment, though prices go down to €30/dive if you buy a package of 10. You'll be taught by João Santos, a Portuguese PADI instructor with 30 years' diving experience & who is passionate about his work. With diving, trust is essential; & João provides a personalised experience, sharing meals & travel tips with his clients, rather than just dropping them off at the end of the day. I took my diving baptism here (see pages 90–1). Talk to Tropic Venture about snorkelling, fishing trips, jetskiing, wakeboarding, boat hire & other activities. If you can find enough people to spread the cost, a boat spin around the island, *volta a ilha*, on the *Léve-Léve* catamaran costs €500.

Dive sites

For Ponte da Baleia and Sete Pedras, see Ilhéu das Rolas page 183; for Príncipe, see pages 208–9.

São Tomé

ϟ Diogo Vaz Initial flat section down to 15m, with a rainbow-coloured garden of small fan coral at 10–12m, then a drop down to 40m, & another to 65m – for experienced divers only. Scuba diving at this depth is touching the absolute limit of what is recommended; bear in mind that at the time of writing there is no decompression chamber on the island. Large red, yellow, brown & black fan corals, red carp, jackfish, butterfly fish & rock fish around walls & big rocks on brown sand.

ϟ Kia 2 levels, 2km off Ilhéu das Cabras: 12m & 22m, with red carp, a nursery of moray eels & red snappers, manta rays, rock fish, yellow, green & orange tubular coral, & sometimes a nurse shark. Even sand sharks of up to 6m in length

have been seen here. Good night diving.

ϟ Lagoa Azul This popular snorkelling spot with good visibility also accommodates different levels of scuba diving. Complete beginners can do their 1st scuba dive down to 3m. The next levels go down to 8–20m & 20–45m. Expect to see intense marine life along the lagoon's reefs including various hard & soft corals, including fan corals (mind the rare 'black' coral – which actually, is white – it stings!), red snapper, butterfly fish, large red carp, pork fish, soldier fish & sometimes even turtles. This is also one of the most beautiful sites on the island for advanced divers, who can explore a 10m rock wall, looking for moray eels & barracudas. Excellent night diving.

ϟ Morro Peixe 12–20m depth, small caves

TAKING THE PLUNGE IN SÃO TOMÉ

Thanks to João Santos, Tropic Venture (see page 89)

With their warm and usually clear waters, and no crowds, the islands are an excellent place to kick-start your diving career. After too many divers had paraded their underwater shots on their cameras at dinner, I was ready to take the plunge myself. The best preparation you can do for the PADI Discover Scuba Diving is to go for a few snorkelling sessions, *mergulho livre*, until you're comfortable keeping your head under water for a while, looking around to enjoy the wildlife. Practise diving straight down a metre or so pinching your nose tight and unblocking your ears – you need to know how to do this when scuba diving, otherwise you could do serious damage to your eardrum. Then you'll be in a better position to enjoy your first *mergulho com garrafa*, 'with bottle'.

My Discover Scuba Diving session took place on a beautiful clear January day, with the calmest of seas. At the diving centre there was a brief theory session and a questionnaire about safety, medical conditions and legal issues. You also get to put on the mask and practise breathing through the tube – this might sound basic, but some people fail at that stage. One of the first things you have to learn then is the sign language: unlike in day-to-day life, where making the thumbs-up sign means 'everything OK!', under water it means quite the opposite: that you want to head up to the surface. It's a habit difficult to lose!

Next we head out to Ilhéu das Cabras by boat, where the first big surprise awaits: the way you unceremoniously enter the water. Basically you secure your mask with your hands, cross your legs and are tipped into the sea backwards. The second surprise is just how noisy it is underwater: every exhalation seems amplified, resulting in a myriad of noisy bubbles, instead of the zen tranquillity I'd somehow expected. The first breaths might be nervous and hectic, but as I began to start floating along, hands linked with the instructor, I began to calm down.

with big red snappers, nurse sharks & hawksbill turtles.

🤿 **Santana** Diving around the islet of Santana just off the resort on the east coast, goes down to a depth of 35m & offers good visibility. The islet is traversed by a wide channel of 6m depth; on the channel's seaward side, a small cave extends about 8m into the rock. Expect to see barracudas, red carp, red snapper, turtles, the rare cusk eel, the electric-blue deepwater cardinalfish & various corals. Diving through the tunnel at a depth of 12–19m is especially rewarding at night, as you see very large fan corals.

🤿 **São Miguel** A star dive site where you are likely to see turtles, nurse sharks, barracudas, & various jackfish, which can be reached from both the capital & Ilhéu das Rolas.

🤿 **Uba-Budo** A new discovery, there are 2 sites (8–25m), with lots of butterfly fish & angelfish, plus many different small fish.

KAYAKING In theory, you can paddle all around the islands. In practice, there is a shortage of kayaks. At the time of writing, on São Tomé island only Club Santana is currently able to arrange commercial kayak hire and trips on a turn-up-and-go basis.

On Príncipe, the Bom Bom Island resort is now offering kayak hire and guided kayak trips. Once the problem of lack of kayaks is solved, trips on both islands may be organised, from a gentle half-hour paddle in a double kayak for complete beginners, and crossings between Porto Alegre and Ilhéu das Rolas in the south, to expeditions along the Príncipe coast. Try contacting João Costa Alegre (m *990 3278*), president of the Kayak Federation.

Then come the exercises. At only 2–3m below the surface, you have to kneel on the ocean floor and practise taking your mask off and putting it back on, and – the Big One – take out your mouthpiece. These are vital skills to have; if the fins of a fellow diver or a rock knocks off your gear, you need to know how to rectify the situation without panicking. I can't be the only one to feel this: it requires a real leap of faith to take out the mouthpiece, exhale slowly with your lips puckered, and retrieve the piece the right way, without panicking or getting entangled in the oxygen lead. With the next exercise, tapping your diving buddy for oxygen, I finally understood that you'll always have access to oxygen even if your own supply fails – resolving an irrational fear that had stopped me taking the plunge for many years.

That sorted, we head out to one of the sunken ships in Ana Chaves Bay for the fun part. Going down, going down ... trying to regulate my buoyancy by breathing in different ways, I make out sea snakes, fluffy and colourful, grumpy-looking moray eels in their lairs, spherical balloon fish, starfish and many kinds of other marine life crowding around the rusty metal structure. It's a truly magical experience. When João taps on his watch, which says '12', I'm thinking it's midday and we need to go up. But no, it's to say that we're down to 12m, which is the maximum depth you should go on a first dive. What a thrill that is. Slowly we make our way up to the surface, stopping at intervals to decompress, and when we emerge, the grin on my face reaches from one ear to the other.

My next step was the Open Water course, at the end of which you receive a card that you can show at PADI centres all over the world to prove that you know the basics. Instead of the crash course that is the *baptismo de mergulho*, this is 3–4 days of picking up the basics – and who knows, with the chance of seeing barracuda, dolphins, a turtle even!

OTHER WATERSPORTS

Swimming At the time of writing, English-language swimming lessons are still held at the Hotel Miramar pool in the capital. One day, the **Club Nautico** might be ready. Once refurbished, the historic watersports club on the capital's coast road, incorporating the saltwater pool where many Santomeans learnt to swim, will offer various activities and facilities, from jetskiing to a disco.

Surfing *Thanks to Bastien Loloum of MARAPA, author of a guide to adventures in STP due to be published 2014*

Endless Summer? So far, few surfers have made it to São Tomé and Príncipe, although a handful of French and US surfers started exploring the islands in the 1990s, provoking the glee of fascinated local kids joining them on wooden floats around Ilhéu das Rolas and Porto Alegre. The population of the fishing villages still find the whole thing hilarious. One crew left a surfboard propped up against a house in Porto Alegre in the south of São Tomé and the local kids now use it to paddle around the bay. Others used left-behind boards to perfect their art. Due to the lack of serious waves, São Tomé and Príncipe will always be more of a novelty attraction than a fixture on the surf circuit. Summer, the so-called *gravana* between June and September, and August in particular, has the best swell, while February/March time also works. The predominantly southerly wind works its way along the coast, flattening the waves, and the best time in the day to surf is either early in the morning, between 06.00 and 09.00, or in the afternoon between 15.00 and 18.00 when there is less wind. You will have to bring all your gear and there is no coastguard or lifesaving equipment. Currently, the president of the kayak federation, João Costa Alegre (see above), also looks after surfing.

Surfing spots The south and west coast are the best bet for vaguely regular waves, including the sweeping southern beaches of Micondó, Sete Ondas and Praia Grande, and Ilhéu das Rolas. River breaks are available along the coast but carry the risk of effluent. Given the microclimates and changing tides, a swell can turn up at any moment. Consult the www.shomar.fr site for sea conditions.

• **As antenas**: This right-hand wave surges atop a rocky reef (take care at low tide) right in front of the Voice of America (VOA) transmission masts. Head for Praia Pomba, following the coast north and swimming some 500m to the break. As this can get fairly tiring, you may want to hire a *piroga* (wooden dug-out canoe) ride with fishermen from Pantufo who will drop you off right on the wave.

- **Iô Grande**: A fishing village in the southern Caué district. This long right-hand wave forms in the mouth of the country's longest river. Watch out for sharks though: don't surf on rainy days!
- **Porto Alegre**: At the end of the road, enter the water in front of the fishing village. This wave unfolds beautifully in Iogo-Iogo Bay, providing fantastic views of Budu Baxana and Vila Malanza. Sea urchins are a problem here though. In Porto Alegre, look out for Xun, a young local surfer who featured in the only surf movie made about São Tomé, *The Lost Wave* by Paul George (available on Amazon).
- **Ribeira Afonso:** A peaceful spot with a fishing-village vibe. This right-hand wave forms in the river's mouth.
- **Santana:** Enter the sea in front of the church and follow the coast south behind the cliff. You might want to set up a session with Marlin, an experienced surfer who knows this beach like no-one else (no telephone contact available, ask around locally). To take advantage of this wave, consider renting the COD apartment (see page 166). Careful of the sea urchins!
- **Sete Ondas:** Despite its name, the Beach of the Seven Waves is only really suitable for playing in the whitewater – which makes it ideal for beginners and children. Do watch out for the currents here though, the sea here is not as calm as it looks.

CYCLING Cycling on the islands might be hot work occasionally, but is a great way to explore the landscape, due to the lack of serious traffic and variety of terrain, from the flat coast road to strenuous inland hills, plus exciting off-road tracks used in the national championship races, Volta do Cacau (*http://voltadocacau. blogspot.pt*).

You can **rent a bike** fairly cheaply in the capital and from the Roça São João in the south (with advance notice) and at Mucumbli in the north (see pages 144–6). In general, if you ask around, somebody will probably know somebody who can hire out a bike to a tourist. Consider cycling to one of the plantation houses and stay overnight or just cycle around exploring; this mode of transport will ensure you get plenty of interaction with Santomeans more used to Westerners in 4x4s. The area around the capital is fairly flat, to the south in particular, but as soon as you go any distance, you will find gentle hills and some steep inclines too. At the time of writing, the French-run São Tomé Bike project was on hold. On Príncipe, biking is harder work and the choice of bikes is less good.

In São Tomé, the **Cycling Federation/Federaçao de Ciclismo** (*Tiziano Pisoni* m *990 8737;* e *aliseistp@cstome.net/tizimari@hotmail.com*) has started offering a number of routes for all abilities, exploring plantation houses or beaches, or a combination of the two. Every route can be customised. In the north of the island, Tiziano and Mari Pisoni speak basic English, and they hire out bikes from their lovely Mucumbli ecotourism place in the north (see pages 144–6). **Sample itineraries** starting from the capital are: Plantations and Beaches of the North (40km, 3–4hrs); São Tomé's Popular Quarters and Fishing Village (25–30km, 2–3hrs); Plantations and Beaches of the East (35km, 4–5hrs). Taking the bikes by car opens up the West Coast route (40–50km, 5–6hrs), and the Bombaim plantation/waterfalls route, with two options for the return journey, depending on ability. Experienced cyclists can **cross the island** from the northwest (town of Neves) to the east (Água Izé plantation). Count €10 to rent a hybrid bike per day, plus €10 for the guide. If you want to set out on your own, you will be given a **roadbook** to help you navigate. Bike trips of varying durations are possible too, for example:

- **Day 1:** São Tomé–Monteforte plantation house, via the northern beaches (35–40km)
- **Day 2**: Monteforte–Chamiço plantation house (usually very difficult to access) via Agõstinho Neto plantation (1,000m ascent, 35km)
- **Day 3**: Chamiço–Bombaim plantation house, via the historic Monte Café plantation (45km)
- **Day 4**: Bombaim–São Tomé through the rainforest (30km)

This itinerary can be extended:

- **Day 5:** São Tomé–São João dos Angolares (45km)
- **Day 6:** São João dos Angolares–Praia Jalé Ecolodge (40km)

ARTS AND ENTERTAINMENT

In the near-absence of formalised cinema or theatre, much of Santomean art happens on the street: from murals and bulaué music to the islands' unique dramatic traditions of Danço Congo (see pages 36–7), tchiloli (see pages 44–5), and Auto de Floripes on Príncipe (see page 190). Popular entertainment revolves around **dancing**, in a discoteca or a public dance area (*terraço*). You will find *capoeira*, the Brazilian martial art dance born out of slavery. At the time of writing, there were rehearsals every Friday and public holidays on Yon Gato Square or Independence Square at 15.00, and Monday, Wednesday and Friday between 18.30 and 20.00 in front of the Marcelo da Veiga cinema (see page 123) as well. Ask locally for classes. If you run out of **reading** matter, there is no real bookshop on the island, but the former Portuguese cultural centre, Instituto Camões (see page 127), and the Alliance Française (see page 127) have books for persusal. The excellent arts centre in the capital, CACAU (see page 134) also hosts music sessions, film screenings and festivals. The 'Centre for Arts and Utopias' sometimes makes its large library of books available for reading there (with plenty of foreign editions).

PHOTOGRAPHY

In a way, the archipelago is a photographer's dream: the majestic trees of the rainforest, the picturesque colonial architecture, the colourful cocoa pods and flowers of the plantations, cultural spectacles in bright colours, the smiles of

Santomean children, and, for the specialists, rich birdlife and an underwater world. However, as you will see when you look at São Tomé and Príncipe pictures on the web, the country is not actually the easiest for photographers. Often, a haze hangs over the islands, especially in January/February, but also during the main tourist season from June to September. Whilst the high-level cloudforest yields magical shots, beach shots can end up disappointing even if you manage to exclude that annoying corner of grey 'nothing' sky. In theory, the rainy season is better for taking pictures of dramatic skies and strong contrasts; in practice, trekking becomes difficult. Digital photography allows great interaction and children in particular are delighted to see their smiling faces (though you often end up taking photographs of large groups, as they all come running) or their *capoeira* martial arts' manoeuvres. Try to keep dirty hands off the screen (*Cuidado!* Careful! *Não mexer!* Don't touch!). With adults, there is a marked difference. You should ask before you take photographs of anything that isn't a general scene (*Posso tirar foto?*), especially for a close-up. At the market in particular, vendors are often reluctant to be photographed and it's better to first establish contact by buying something. Apparently, there is still a belief that a photo takes away the soul of the person but I have also had a few fruit-sellers ask to have their photograph taken – and then ask for money. If you are particularly keen on people/portrait photography, make sure you visit Príncipe, as people there see far fewer tourists and are generally more open to having their picture taken. In general, if you have the chance to have a couple of pictures printed off (on São Tomé only in the capital and Trindade, on Príncipe only in Santo António) and give them to the person you took a picture of, this will be immensely appreciated. A photographer friend of mine even travelled with a portable printer! If you promise to send prints at a later date, try and actually do it.

Take care with your equipment; digital cameras in particular are very vulnerable to humidity, especially in the mists of the higher ranges, so pack them into a separate plastic bag. I carried my compact Panasonic Lumix on a two-day hike where it rained most of the time and forgot to put it in a waterproof bag, so water entered the camera body corroding the contacts. More recently, another Lumix died on me on the Pico, this time the focussing mechanism took a hit or fell victim to the dreaded humidity, and my companion's cameras also stopped working temporarily. (Be careful with laptop computers as well, limiting their exposure to the humid air.) If you are shooting on print film, take more rolls of film than you think you will need; Sensia 100 is one of the best.

MEDIA AND COMMUNICATIONS With Mário Lopes of Global Voices and TEDx

Communication is second nature to Santomeans, who love to talk and banter mercilessly with each other. In a society that runs on gossip and networking, most news still travels 'mouth-to-mouth', *radio BB*, *boca-a-boca*. There is no daily newspaper and the weekly *Correio da Semana* closed in 2010, with the demise of the Rafael Branco government.

However, São Tomé and Príncipe is embracing new technology and the country hosted its first **TEDx** conference on 20 June 2013, which was a big coup for the country's media entrepreneurs. TEDx events take place on a yearly basis, and aim to bring together the makers and shakers from various areas to exchange ideas. The STP event's motto 'Get Connected to the World' summed up its mission to connect the two small islands with the rest of Africa and the world. Eminent authorities from diverse fields came together, including specialist in medicinal

2

herbs Maria do Céu, naturalist Robert Drewes, the new force behind Príncipe ecotourism Mark Shuttleworth, Angolan journalist Aoni d'Alfa and Estonian arts entrepreneur Kris Haamer.

PUBLICATIONS *O Parvo* ('the Idiot', on sale at the Passante café in the capital) is a weekly publication. Its founder Ambrósio Quaresma made it a polemical publication, with its incisive politics and use of caricatures. Now less of a reference, you can consult it in the National Library or Mediateca, and more easily online (www.parvodigital.info). There is good access to French-language publications but it is usually impossible to get hold of journals or magazines in English. *Kê-Kuá* is a free weekly paper that has been published since 2011; the name is a typical Santomean expression of surprise.

Online There is still a lack of a **daily online newspaper** updated as things happen. The ones that are available serve mainly Santomeans in the diaspora and other interested parties. The 'father', if you like, of online newspapers here is *Telá Nón* (*www.telanon.info*), founded on Independence Day 2000 and still under its founder–director Abel Tavares da Veiga, with the same layout, which covers politics, economy and sports. When things 'get hot' on the islands, this is the reference source for first-hand news; however, it does not use social networks.

Founded by young entrepreneur Karlley Frota, a Santomean who trained as a journalist in Portugal, the **STP Digital platform** (*www.stpdigital.net*) boasts a strong database reuniting information on history, culture, demographics, etc, and serves as a source of reference, concentrating mainly on what is happening on the islands and with stories about Santomenses around the world, but also including content from other lusophone countries. STP Digital was the first to make proper use of the major social networks (Facebook, Twitter, Instagram, Linkedin, Pinterest) and its Facebook page (*www.fb.com/stpdigital*) boasts over 6,900 followers, no mean feat in such a small country and making it the company with the most Facebook followers on the islands.

The STP Press **news agency** (*www.stp-press.st*) is a state-owned information organ, with near-daily updates. Due to long years of inactivity, it hasn't yet got the following amongst Santomense *internautas* it deserves.

According to its website, **Reporter Info** (*www.reporterstp.info*) sees its role as a public interest site aiming to celebrate a pluralist view of what happens in São Tomé and Príncipe and the world.

Global Voices Lusofonia (*www.pt.globalvoicesonline.com*) is a community uniting more than 500 bloggers and translators around the globe who work together to produce articles, reportage and civic media from all over the world. Giving emphasis to the voices, places and people that can be heard in international media, they also provide extensive coverage of São Tomé and Príncipe.

For details of radio stations broadcasting online, see below.

Radio and TV For daily news, radio and TV are the most important sources reaching all but the most isolated localities.

The national radio, **Rádio Nacional**, with its headquarters on the Marginal, is an important community medium, broadcasting 24/7 news and useful information on daily life such as health campaigns, lost and found items, death notices and so on, all with plenty of national and international music thrown in (FM93.7, PM114.7). To the disgruntlement of many in the diaspora, Rádio Nacional's programmes are not available online and its official site at the time of writing had already been unavailable for a long time. There are also a number of **private radio stations**, such as **Rádio Jubilar** and **Rádio Viva FM**. **Rádio Somos Todos Primos** (*www.somostodosprimos.net*) is currently the only radio station streaming online 24/7, offering various programmes on culture, news and entertainment, as well as rebroadcasting some Rádio Nacional podcasts.

The state-owned Portuguese **RTP** (*www.rtp.pt*; podcasts available) broadcasts via satellite a 24-hour mix of programmes produced in Lisbon, with local content by the delegation of **RTP África** (São Tomé: FM92.8; Príncipe: FM101.9). **Rádio França Internacional** (RFI 1 Afrique; *www.rfi.fr*) broadcasts 24 hours a day on FM102.8. **Rádio Difusão Portuguesa RDP** (www.rdp.pt) is available locally, and **Voice of America** (see pages 92–3) broadcasts from a huge local station. On the islands, the English programme is broadcast via MW 1530.

READING Reading is still not a common habit, though there are now more books published in Sáo Tomé that lusophone readers can consult in the Historical Archive and UNEAS (União Nacionais de Escritores e Artistas Santomenses); the latter has been working together with Ulaje (União Literária Artística e Juvenil) to promote reading. To pick up foreign books, try CACAU (see page 134), Roça São João (see pages 172–3), or the lounge at Omali Lodge where I've done informal book swaps with English and German-language novels; if you read Afrikaans, this is the place to go (see pages 114–15). In the capital, the Pastelaria/Restaurant Central (see page 120) honours *Santomense* poets with moving extracts from their poems (Portuguese only) and portraits. Although very few books are read, poets are held in high regard. For more on poetry, see pages 38–9.

TELEPHONE
Mobile phones The use of mobile phone (*telemóvel*) is growing (about half of the population own one), and **network coverage** is fairly good overall. On São Tomé island you can call home from the highest mountain on the island, but you may still encounter patchy areas if driving south or north, as well as on Príncipe. All *telemóvel* numbers start with 9, and calls from mobile to mobile cost 2,400$ per minute. You can't leave messages on people's phones yet, though these days most people send text messages. Since 2014, former monopolist CST is being challenged by Angolan Unitel-STP, owned by Isabel dos Santos, daughter of the Angolan president.

If **buying a mobile phone** in São Tomé and Príncipe expect to pay at least €30 for a new handset with charger and SIM card. By asking around, however, you can probably get hold of a **secondhand handset** and sell it on or donate it before you leave. Hiring a mobile phone is no longer worth your while. If you're not staying for longer than a couple of weeks' holiday, you won't really need a mobile. Any longer than that, it does make sense to have one, especially if you are researching something and have to make arrangements with guides, etc. I have found though that Santomeans and expats alike are reluctant to make firm appointments and they will ask you to give them a ring nearer the time ('Ring me tomorrow', *Liga para mím* (or *Dá-me um toque amanhã*).

A *Cartão Beijo* SIM card with 100,000$ credit costs 315,000$. Top-up cards, *cartão de recarga* (values 50,000$, 100,000$ and 300,000$) are sold by the **Companhia Sãotomense de Telecommunicaçoes (CST)** and several small shops or kiosks that usually have a sign up. To top up your phone credit, follow the instructions on the back: scratch to reveal your recharge code (*código*), call the *recarga* number (m *990 2021*), type in the code, and press '1' to confirm.

If you've brought your own phone note that a US phone will not be useable due to the different bandwidth and it has to be *disbloqueado*, **unlocked**, with specialist equipment that does not work with all models. Some European mobiles don't need to be unlocked. Ask at CST who can *disbloquear* your phone for you. CST staff can also often sell you phones and give you general advice. If using your own phone, however, be prepared for haphazard service.

For information on keeping your phone safe, see page 74.

Contacting São Tomé and Príncipe from abroad If you need to contact somebody urgently in São Tomé and Príncipe call them, even though it's expensive. Calling São Tomé and Príncipe from the UK on a BT **landline** costs more than £1 per minute, and even with a provider such as Lycamobile you won't get anything below about €0.80.

Few Santomeans use **Skype** yet, and at €1.15 per minute to landlines and mobiles alike (€0.09 per minute for a text message) there isn't much incentive to use the service. Connections can also be extremely haphazard.

From the UK, try Telestunt (*www.telestunt.co.uk*), where calls to STP landlines cost £0.35 per minute, calls to mobiles £0.40 per minute. Be careful, however, as you will be charged even if the other party doesn't reply or the line is engaged. From Portugal, PT's »Hello« cards work out best, at €0.50 per minute to both landlines and mobiles, with good line quality and an option for instructions in English. They can be used from public phone boxes and PT landlines, and are sometimes sold in promotion with two available at a discounted price. Current low-cost favourite Lycamobile charges €0.79 per minute.

From some countries such as Germany, calls to STP mobiles can only be connected through the operator, for an additional operator fee of more than €5 – per call! For price comparison checks, see www.voip-call.info/isocode/ST.

Calling within/from São Tomé and Príncipe When you're in the country, the easiest way to call home is from the CST (see above), which is half-owned by Portugal Telecom, half by the state. There is a CST in the capital, in São João dos Angolares, and in Santo António on Príncipe. There are public phones in most larger places, and often private ones in shops; look for the sign *Telefone aquí*. Public phonecards are sold to the value of 50,000$ and 150,000$, but they don't last long on calls abroad and you hear an annoying beep after each unit (*impulso*).

STP is one of the most expensive places in the world to call from and to. Calling the UK from São Tomé and Príncipe costs around 13,000$ per minute, the US 15,000$ per minute; there is no on/off peak period. Calling the UK from a hotel can cost €3 per minute.

Call the International Operator on 100, for Portugal direct 102 or 104, Directory Enquiries on 103, and for a Portuguese-language weather forecast (*meteorología*) call 151. Both landlines and mobile telephone numbers recently required an additional digit, a 2 for landlines, and a 9 for mobile phones.

INTERNET AND EMAIL Since the arrival of the fibreoptic cable in 2013, internet access has improved considerably, even allowing telemedicine operations with Portugal. There are a dozen public places to access the internet, of which two are on Príncipe, and a few wireless areas, mainly attached to hotels and some public institutions. Around 22% of Santomeans are internet users, and Facebook usage is under 5%.

If you're writing long emails in an internet café, make sure you save frequently to ensure that you don't lose them if the power goes down suddenly. Many email addresses with the national provider CST (*www.cstome.net*) have very limited storage capability, and your emails are likely to bounce (and may take days to do so). Most Santomean internet users have a Hotmail account.

Although some Santomeans do use the internet, they don't necessarily reply to emails; this can even happen with people working in tourism or a plantation with tourist accommodation.

LANGUAGE

People are friendly and most will make the effort to understand what you are saying, even if you don't have a single word of Portuguese. French and Spanish will definitely help somewhat – many visitors get by in *Portunhol* – but I can't stress enough how much more fun you'll have on the islands if you make the effort to pick up some Portuguese before you go. I've found it very helpful to do some one-on-one conversation classes before I went. Contact your local university or ask at a Portuguese café/restaurant. There are Portuguese communities in most larger towns in the UK, the US (New Jersey, New England, California) and Canada (Ontario, Quebec, British Columbia), and about half a million Portuguese people in South Africa. The Portuguese cultural institute, Instituto Camões (*www.instituto-camoes.pt*), operates language centres all over the world, including in the UK (Edinburgh, Newcastle, Oxford), the US (Newark), South Africa (Johannesburg), France (Lille, Lyon, Poitiers), Germany (Hamburg) and Hungary (Budapest).

Of the **self-taught language courses**, Manuela Cook's *Teach Yourself Portuguese* (paperback & CD, 2004) and Hugo's *Portuguese in Three Months* (2003) come recommended. Listen to the dialogues on the CDs over and over. Even if you already speak French and/or Spanish, the Portuguese nasal sounds and 'sh' sounds, together with fast speech and a joy of word play can make it difficult to understand. One tip: if you need receipts or even if you're just buying a phonecard, you usually need to give your name, so it's handy if you know how to spell (*aletrar*) your name in Portuguese. Another good resource is www.learningportuguese.co.uk.

As most travellers will pass through Lisbon on their way to São Tomé and Príncipe, consider combining **language classes** in the Portuguese capital with sightseeing and getting to know the country that colonised STP for 500 years. Whilst not the easiest language to learn, Portuguese is the fifth-most spoken language in the world – used by some 200 million people – and the third-most used language on the internet! So if you're planning ever to travel in Angola (gradually opening up to tourism, with a Bradt guide available), Brazil, Guinea-Bissau, Mozambique, the Cape Verde islands or indeed Portugal, learning the language is an excellent investment for your travels. I've heard good reports of **CIAL** (*Av da República, 41–8° Esq, 1050-187 Lisbon;* \ +351 217 940 448; *www.cial.pt*), and a good option is to take the three-hour course in the morning and a one-to-one lesson in the afternoon. CIAL also has an Algarve branch in Faro, three hours from Lisbon (*Rua Almeida Garrett, 44 r/c, 8000–206 Faro;* \ 289 807 611; e *algarve@cial.pt*), if you want more sun with your language learning.

By the way, every Tuesday at 12.30, Santomeans, former colonial staff and others interested in the country meet for an informal lunch in the unpretentious **Inhaca restaurant** (*Rua das Portas de Santo Antão 8;* \ +351 213 477 039) on central Lisbon's restaurant mile.

If you want to combine learning Portuguese with your stay in São Tomé and Príncipe, so far this can only be done informally, although a few accommodation providers are planning to offer it in the future. In the capital, ask the Instituto Camões about contacts for informal Portuguese classes, put a note up at Xico's café (see page 119) or try to set up a **language exchange** with an English-speaking student or a member of the hotel staff; many now want to improve their English. If you want to **learn** *forro*, ask around and somebody will oblige.

Learn some basic **greetings and small talk** and even if you have very few words, starting questions with *Faz favor* is a good idea, then you can always explain the rest with your hands and feet.When greeting someone, *oi!* does not have the impolite connotations that it does in English. In the street, Santomeans attract attention in different ways: the French *Monsieur/Madame* is commonly used for tourists, and *Amigo/a!* ('Friend!') for a younger person, tourist or local. Hissing is used to hail friends. If you hear this, it could be a bunch of schoolkids who want to get a wave and a smile from you, or, if you're female, a generic response to a white woman walking around on her own.

For more on language, see pages 219–32.

BUSINESS

Due to the *leve-leve* factor, a slow and politicised bureaucracy and problematic energy provision, you need a strong vision and unflagging stamina to do business in São Tomé and Príncipe. You need to be outgoing, too; a lot of deals are down to personal introductions. Personal contacts are very important so get hold of as many contacts of the local movers and shakers as you can. Find a phonebook (*lista telefónica*), learn Portuguese and be prepared to do a lot of networking. Local entrepreneurs face interest rates of nearly 30% and complain that the state does not support the private sector. Some of the sectors where the state is looking for investment are tourism, transport and alternative energies. However, due to the amount of red tape, statistically, setting up a business in São Tomé and Príncipe takes 192 days. Foreign investors face the added difficulties of government whims dictating the allocation of plots of land or the granting of permits. Dynamic São Tomé-business consultant, Swiss honorary consul and plantation owner Reto Scherraus (*www.scherraus.com*) offers advice in English, French, German, Spanish and Portuguese (as well as in Russian, written only). Another useful platform is www.businessinstp.st. Amongst the regular population, some have bright ideas but no funds, and some have ideas and some funds but are still wary of committing to anything, given the general instability. For business advice, a good contact could be the Guiché Único, literally a 'single counter', run by notary Ilma Salvaterra (*Av Amilcar Cabral;* m *991 7711;* e *ilmasal3@gmail.com; www.gue-stp.net*).

Last but not least, check www.juristep.com for the laws of the land (tax, constitutional, oil, labour, etc), most are translated into English. The UK Yahoo group dedicated to STP http://uk.groups.yahoo.com lists a number of companies.

BUYING PROPERTY

Buying property or land is only really an option to individuals with (dual) STP citizenship. The few available apartments sell for around €90,000. Expect to pay €150,000 for a house near the sea within easy reach from the capital, less in zones further away, where there is more choice still. Plots of land within a radius of 5–10km from the capital sell for €20,000–40,000. Prices shoot up, of course, if it is known that a foreigner is buying. A useful contact is Reto Scherraus (see above).

Condomínio Vila Maria ☎222 3600; e vilamaria@pestana.com; www.pestana.com. Connected with the Pestana Hotel across the road, this luxury residential complex has some 50 villas with pool, for personal use, investment or for buy-to-let. There is a games field, & residents have free access to the hotel facilities & casino.

TOURISM

In 2013, just under 13,000 visitors entered São Tomé and Príncipe. The majority of these were Portuguese, followed by the Angolans, who have recently started taking advantage of cheap air travel and are looking for relaxation in security, as well as the good diving. Far behind on the list of nationalities visiting STP come the French, who have a long tradition of development aid and cultural exchange with the country. On my visits, I have met German, Hungarian, Italian, Spanish, Dutch, British, US and Israeli travellers. Generalising wildly, the Portuguese were more after the beach and bar experience, the other Europeans, in particular the Germans and the few British, more in search of an active rainforest adventure. Given the ongoing vagaries of flight connections and self-sabotaging attitudes, the tourism authority's target of 25,000 visitors per year by 2014 is far off target, but if the country can preserve its natural beauty, manage the potential oil wealth in a socially sustainable way, and bring down the prices of flights, tourism could become a more dynamic part of the economy. Things are definitely on the move as long-established hotels that were beginning to look a bit tired are getting spruced up in the face of sudden competition, and new guesthouses, rural tourism ventures and restaurants are springing up all over the place, including, gradually, the towns outside the capital. As for Príncipe, the potential for *turismo rural* on its romantically crumbling plantations is only now being discovered. Over the next few years, quite a few beaches that today have only a couple of fishermen's shacks on them will be ringed with holiday developments, and the first cruise ships have started to include São Tomé on their tours of the West African coast. However, as long as flights and accommodation costs stay relatively expensive, São Tomé and Príncipe will never be a mass tourism or backpacker destination.

At the moment, few people speak English and never underestimate the *leve-leve* factor. Essentially, don't be discouraged if nobody, apart from established agencies and hotels, replies to your emails, and be aware that much online information is out of date. If you are independent-minded and not in a mad rush, just book your first couple of nights' accommodation to get your bearings, and organise the rest once you arrive. As a general rule, going to an office in person is always better than ringing, and ringing is nearly always better than emailing. The big resorts are never full, but book early for some popular favourites, such as the Avenida guesthouse in the capital (see page 116), or places with very limited space, such as the Praia Jalé Ecolodge (see pages 175–6) in the south of São Tomé island. Both the CNN network and the *Guardian* newspaper chose São Tomé as an up-and-coming destination for 2014, and with the number of flights from Lisbon increased to four a week, who knows it might finally happen?

CULTURAL ETIQUETTE

Santomeans in general are friendly and relaxed, and very helpful when you are driving around on un-signposted roads or walking on plantation trails. There are no cultural no-nos in terms of clothing or topics of conversation, even though the recommended answer to the enquiries as to of what you think of the country is probably *muito lindo*, 'very beautiful'. While speaking some Portuguese greatly enhances your experience, travellers can have a fantastic time even just communicating with hands and feet. One thing the Santomeans really appreciate is if you are willing to try unfamiliar things, such as tasting a local fruit, mixing on the dance floor, or showing curiosity about the local language or traditional remedies. If you are planning to stay longer than just a short holiday, small island society gossip is an occupational hazard.

I've found the best response to children's persistent cat-calls of *Brancaaaa!* ('white woman') is to acknowledge them with a *Tudo bem?* (All OK?) and a smile and wave. Have a few simple phrases in Portuguese for children, such as asking their name (*como é que te chamas?*) and age (*que idade tens?*). Many will be pleased to try out their French on you, or you could teach them a couple of words of English. If you need information on anything, ask for the oldest, *o mais velho*. For adults, too, a few basic words of greeting go a long way, especially if you pick up a couple of local expressions. Replying *leve-leve* (literally 'slowly-slowly', meaning 'I'm fine') to *Tudo bem?* always gets a positive reaction.

BEGGING There are few beggars in STP, but children in the villages have quickly learnt to shout for sweets (*Doce, doce!*), money (*Dá-me dobras/dinheiro!*) or, less often, for a lift (*Boleia!*) when you drive by. While it is less harmful to give biros (*esferográphicas*; children will often specifically ask for them), notepads or balloons than sweets, local NGOs and others will tell you that giving presents to individuals divides families and communities – tourists should not encourage begging. If nothing else, it makes life more difficult for the travellers that come after you. At Agostinho Neto plantation, for example, visitors are already routinely asked for gifts.

It is true that with the tourists' money usually just going to the tour company, the people living on the plantations and serving as living attractions and photo opportunities are not getting anything out of it. It's also understandable that travellers want to give gifts and help, that presents help to establish contact, and, seen from the Santomean perspective, all white people seem to have money. If you are taking pictures of an amateur cultural performance such as dance or *capoeira*, you might be asked for *patrocinio*, sponsorship and this seems fair enough. Giving indiscriminately, however, encourages a mentality of expectation that is already, some would say, quite developed in São Tomé and Príncipe. As a responsible traveller, try to establish a relationship in a different way. Say *Não tenho* ('I don't have') or *Não temos* ('We don't have'). Some travellers like to ask what they will get back in return, *Que me vai dar?* If you want to make a donation, give it to the community leader or an NGO (see below).

TRAVELLING POSITIVELY

Buy local goods and use local services wherever possible. Buying a piece of jackfruit or sugarcane, a sip of palm wine, or some wild strawberries helps the local economy and is a good way of starting a conversation. For travellers with a bit more time, **voluntary work** is an excellent way to engage with the country. Teaching English, for instance, would do enormous good in helping Santomeans earn some of the money that tourism is bringing in, by enabling them, for example, to work as guides on the plantations and get better-paid jobs generally, a better education and offer a way for them to engage more successfully with tourists. If you are resourceful, you might be able to set up a placement informally through a school or a plantation, funding yourself. Consider choosing Príncipe, which is still behind its larger sister island in development and should offer a very rewarding experience. More than 80 NGOs are represented here, most of them Portuguese; check which humanitarian organisations in your country might have ties with São Tomé and Príncipe. The South African **HBD** ('Here Be Dragons', the owner of Bom Bom Island resort, amongst others, see pages 207–9) ecotourism venture also runs a number of projects. On both islands, the churches can distribute unwanted clothes to those who need them most.

In Portugal, contact details for humanitarian and friendship associations for both islands can be found on www.imigrantes.no.sapo.pt/page2comunidades1.html. The northern coastal town of Aveiro has been twinned with Santo António, capital of Príncipe, since 1988. There are various ways to get involved from the north of Portugal, but try contacting **António Martinho** in Oporto (m +351 969 347 983; e toveracruz@portugalmail.pt), as he can put you in touch with projects in education, health or working with youngsters or elderly people. Other towns twinned with Santo António are Odivelas and Oeiras. In Lisbon, the **Casa Internacional de São Tomé & Príncipe** (Rua da Assunção 40, 3rd floor left; e cistp2013@gmail.com, info@cistp.com; www.cistp.com) is a new meeting space for the Santomean community in Lisbon. It is currently only open for special events such as book launches, debates and workshops, but contact Danilo Salvaterra, and he will point you to who/what you need. You can also try the **Associação da Comunidade de São Tomé & Príncipe em Portugal** (ACOSTP; m 9682 7447; e acostp@hotmail.com). The **French consulate** in Marseille has a charitable association too (see page 55).

The local conservation NGO, **MARAPA** (see pages 113–14) can probably find you some informal volunteering work cleaning beaches or helping with turtle patrols, staying below the ecomuseum in Morro Peixe. Since 2011, ST has also had an **International School** at primary level (Campo de Milho, in the former Al Gharb restaurant; m 991 8701; e escolainternacionalstp@mail.com) and there might be opportunities for volunteering there as well. In Coimbra, the **Association of Santomean Students** would be a good contact (look for Associação de Estudantes de São Tomé e Príncipe em Coimbra on Facebook) for Portuguese speakers interested in volunteering.

NGOS

Adventist Development and Relief Agency (ADRA) Praia Emilia; ✆222 4324; www.adra.st, www.adra.org. Any US citizen, regardless of faith, can apply to volunteer in the areas of health, marketing, computers, English teaching, monitoring & evaluation. ADRA International covers travel costs & offers other benefits. To apply locally, contact the dynamic Nigerian (English-speaking) head, Ugo Tchuku Watchuku, direct. ADRA STP can provide accommodation in its compound & an allowance. Donations are welcome for primary school meals, libraries, glasses, etc, & it is possible to sponsor a child as part of a successful long-term community project in the south of the island. Through ADRA Canada, you can sponsor a fruit tree (CAN$6).

Alisei/Nuova Frontera Rua Barão Água Izé; ✆222 3346; m 990 8737; e nuovaf@cstome.net, tizimari@hotmail.com. For volunteering with this Italian NGO involved in various projects in the areas of agriculture, education & sexual health, contact Tiziano & Mari Pisoni (see also page 144–6). Basic Portuguese required.

Caritas Bairro Quinta St António; ✆222 2565; e caritas_stp@cstome.net. This Catholic relief organisation runs an orphanage & offers the opportunity to sponsor individual children or to volunteer.

Embaixada da Ordem Ecumenica de Malta OSJ Bairro Campo de Milho (subject to change); ✆222 7513; e embassy-stp@osi.com.es; www.osi.com.es. The Ecumenical Maltese Order can accommodate volunteers in various projects on both islands. Work with young girls at risk in Santana, older people or children in the capital or on the Diogo Vaz plantation in the north, or with a public health project on Príncipe. Divers can get involved in a new project training Santomean coastguards.

English Students Association of São Tomé and Príncipe ✆991 5353; e quintino_stepup@yahoo.com. With plenty of goodwill, but practically no money for teaching materials, young Santomeans give up their free time to teach English summer classes.

ESCOLA + http://escolamais.webs.com. A successful co-operation project for secondary education on the islands, with the IMVF (see below), the Ministry of Education & Culture in STP & the Portuguese Institute for Development Support working together.

FONG – STP Rua Barão de Água Izé; ✆222 6754, 222 7552; e fong@cstome.net; www.fong-stp.org. Next to the Quá-Téla shop, this is the Federation of Santomean ONGs (NGOs).

Happier Children www.happierchildren.org. Founded in 2012 by the owners of the Shiadu guesthouses in Lisbon & Porto (www.shiadu.com) as part of their Corporate Social Responsibility concept, this small educational NGO works with primary schools in the southern Caué district – 'don't just teach how to count, teach them what counts'. The aim is to provide an educational experience in partnership with Portuguese schools, online exchanges with schools in Portugal via webcam & eventually real life exchanges too. Volunteers should have some Portuguese language skills. If you want to fundraise for the NGO, get in touch with them for information on how to hold fundraising dinners, *jantares solidários*, anywhere in the world.

Instituto Marquês de Valle-Flór (IMVF) Saúde para Todos, Bairro 3 Fevereiro; ✆222 2199 (health), 222 7911 (education); www.imvf.org. Well-established NGO present in all lusophone countries, working in health, education & culture, including the documentation of plantation history.

Médicos do Mundo Vila Dolores; ✆222 7960. The 'Doctors of the World' NGO places Portuguese-speaking medics on short-term missions. The office can be found a few doors down from StepUp (see opposite page).

Missão Católica Rua de Santarém; ✆225 1067; e parsenio@iol.pt. Volunteers are welcome Jul–Sep to help with training, games & activities for children, assist with development work on the plantations or to undertake social work with the disabled on both islands. Through the Sisters of the Holy Family you can also sponsor (become *padrinho/madrinha*, literally 'godparent') a child or an old person to receive a daily meal & necessary medication. Padre Senio speaks good English.

Santa Casa de Misericordia Rua Juventude; ✆222 7311/2. The São Tomé branch of Portugal's oldest charity is involved in social care & collects leftover medicines that travellers don't want to take home. You can support the charity's work by stopping for some ethical souvenir shopping at the attached Ossobô shop (see page 125), just across from the National Museum, where you can also drop off your unwanted medicines. Contact the friendly Dona Mila for work on volunteering in

Ribeira Afonso, Neves & Trindade, or on Príncipe. Alternatively, stop for a meal from the old people's home next to the hospital, as the proceeds go to the charity. Food is served every day except Sun (↘ 990 6772). The menu changes regularly & features dishes such as Portuguese duck rice, fish curry or Angolan *moamba*.

StepUp Vila Dolores; ↘ 222 1285; m 991 5350; e ned_stepup@yahoo.com; www.stepup-stp. org. The director of the StepUp NGO, US-American Ned Seligman, can find you volunteering work at his English school. You'll receive pocket money & stay at Ned's house, & you don't have to speak Portuguese to apply. StepUp also sell a lovely educational colouring book for children depicting the island's wildlife, & a set of playing cards. You can also contact Ned's assistant Quintino (m 991 9359), who runs SAPEL (Society for the Promotion of the English Language) at the Canossian Sisters, next to the CST phone exchange in the capital.

Part Two

SÃO TOMÉ

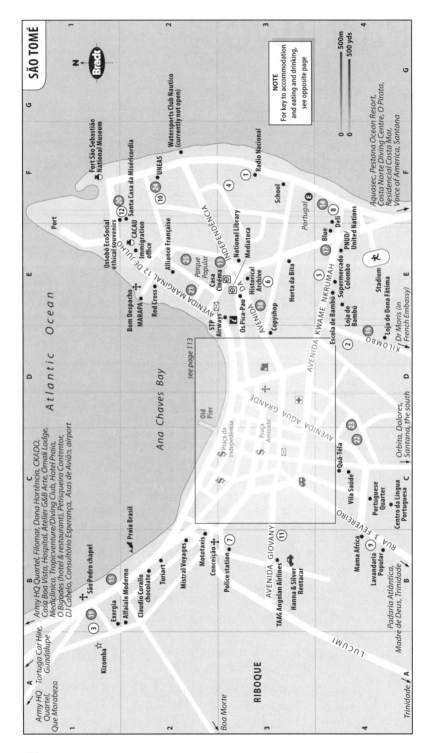

SÃO TOMÉ

N

Bradt

NOTE
For key to accommodation
and eating and drinking,
see opposite page

0 _____ 500m
0 _____ 500 yds

Atlantic Ocean

Ana Chaves Bay

Army HQ Quartel, Filomar, Dona Hortência, CK-DO,
Casa Boa Vista, Hospital, Atelier G&B Arte, Omali Lodge,
Mediclínica, Tropicventure/Diving Club, Hotel Praia,
O Bigodes (hotel & restaurant), Petisqueira Contentor,
DJ Cabelo, Consultório Esperança, Asas de Avião, airport

Army HQ
Quartel,
Que Morabeza

Tortuga Car Hire,
Guadalupe

Kizomba ☆

3

19

São Pedro chapel

Exergia

Alfaiate Moderno

Claudio Corallo
chocolate

15

Praia Brasil

Port

Ossobô EcoSocial
ethical souvenirs

CACAU

Immigration
office

Alliance Française

20

12

Santa Casa da Misericórdia

24 UNEAS

10

Fort São Sebastião
National Museum

Watersports Club Nautico
(currently not open)

1

Radio Nacional

Turiart

Mistral Voyages

Mototaxis

Conceição

Police station

7

see page 113

Old
Pier

Bom Despacho

MARAPA

Red Cross

STP
Airways

Os Pica-Pau

18

Praque
Popular

25

Casa
Cinéma

13

National Library

Mediateca

Historical
Archive

6

Horta da Bita

21

INDEPENDÊNCIA

AVENIDA MARGINAL 12 DE JULHO

AVENIDA 3 DE

Copyshop

Portugal

Blue

17

School

E

Deli

14

8

PNUD/
United Nations

Supermercado
Colombo

5

Escola de Bambú

2

Loja de
Bambú

Stadium

E

16

Dr Moris (in
French Embassy)

KILOMBO

AVENIDA KWAME NKRUMAH

Loja de Dona Fátima

Aquasec, Pestana Ocean Resort,
Costa Norte Diving Centre, O Pirata,
Residencial Costa Mar,
Voice of America, Santana

Praça da
Independência

Praça
Amizade

AVENIDA ÁGUA GRANDE

Quá-Tela

23

22

Vila Saúde

Portuguese
Quarter

Centro da Língua
Portuguesa

Orbita, Dolores,
Santana, the south

RUA 3 FEVEREIRO

RIBOQUE

Boa Morte

AVENIDA GIOVANY

TAAG Angolan Airlines

11

Hanna & Silver
Rentacar

Mama Africa

9

Lavandaria
Popular

LUCUMÍ

Padaria Atlântica,
Madre de Deus, Trinidade

Trinidade

A   B   C   D   E   F   G

1

2

3

4

3

São Tomé:
the Capital

Established around the wide sweep of Ana Chaves Bay in 1493, São Tomé became the capital of the island when, according to legend, the Portuguese left their first settlement Anambó, 30km further north. Some 50 years after São Tomé was granted city status in 1535 by the Portuguese king, João III, the cathedral and the fort of St Sebastian were built. Today, many of the old colonial buildings, with their carved wooden wraparound balconies running around the houses, arched windows and balustrades are falling down, while others have been restored in pretty bright or pastel colours. With market traders pulling along a swordfish by its beak, street vendors selling cheap watches, hair bands and brushes, jackfruit sellers, music blaring from a car stereo or a shack shop, and a lot of chat and laughter, the city has a Caribbean feel to it.

In the streets, yellow taxis vie for space with buzzing motorbikes and mud-caked jeeps; the pavements are populated with teenagers in baseball caps, businessmen and functionaries in suits. Moneychangers chat on corners, schoolchildren in uniform mingle with older men and street vendors sporting torn and faded election T-shirts and mothers carrying babies in a sling on their backs. Stray dogs rummage in rubbish on dusty streets, black kites divebomb the harbour for fish, while the citizens negotiate the broken pavements on the broad avenues leading towards the odd imposing architectural relic of 1950s Salazarist aesthetics, garden villas and small white stone residences with red tiles. The sea spray crashes on to the

SÃO TOMÉ
For listings, see pages 114–22

🛏 Where to stay
1	Casa Amarela	F3
2	Casa Arnaldo	D4
3	Cocoa Residence	B1
4	Dona Delfina	F3
5	Elitneide Casa de Turismo	E4
6	Hotel Agôsto Neto	E3
7	Hotel Residencial Baia (currently closed)	B3
8	Miramar	F4
9	Navetur Apartment	B4
10	Poiso Alto Guesthouse	F2
11	Residencial Giovany (currently closed)	B3
12	Santa Casa Apartments	F2

Off map
	Casa Boa Vista	B1
	Hotel O Bigodes	B1
	Hotel Praia	B1
	Omali Lodge	B1
	Pestana Ocean Resort	F4
	Residencial Costa Mar	F4

✖ Where to eat and drink
13	B24	E3
14	Café Passante	F4
15	Contentor Azul/ Paraíso dos Grelhados	B1
16	O Kilombo	D4
17	Papa-Figo	E4
18	Pico Mocambo	E3
19	Piroga de São Pedro	B1
20	Plê-Museu	F1
21	Roulote Ultima Estação	E2
22	Sombra da Coleira	C4
23	Sombra do Caroceiro	D4
24	Tété	F2
25	Tia Leo	E2

Off map
	Asas de Avião	B1
	Dona Hortência /Os dois Pinheiros	B1
	Filomar	B1
	Petisqueira Contentor	B1
	Que Morabeza	A1

wide boulevard of the Marginal running around the bay, past sandy inlets strewn with black rocks. A short walk out to the other side of the city towards the popular Riboque neighbourhood reveals traditional wooden houses on stilts, humble shacks with zinc roofs propping each other up, and, in between, delicately carved wooden roofs reminiscent of Swiss chalets.

HIGHLIGHTS

Explore the commercial and political heart of the country, see contemporary Santomean art and the collections of the National Museum, and taste your way through local specialities, from fried banana to the national dish, *calulú*. Dive into the buzz of the market, sip coffee on a seafront terrace, learn how to dance *kizomba* and stock up on delicious chocolate and coffee. And, within a short drive of the city, discover atmospheric plantations, snorkelling and diving, and rainforest hikes.

GETTING THERE AND AWAY

São Tomé Airport/Aeroporto de São Tomé (✆ *222 1877*) is 15 minutes' drive out of town. There is no public transport link, but if you have booked with an agency, somebody will meet you there and this is the easiest option if you're arriving on your own. On the other hand, there is no problem getting a **shared taxi** for about 20,000$ – or offer €3 as you probably won't have any dobras yet and your luggage will most likely take up a whole seat. A private run will cost about €10 as you will have to pay for all the seats. Even if your phone works here (see pages 97–8), there is no taxi company that you can ring, but a few taxis will always be waiting to fill up with passengers outside the terminal building. The taxis do not have a meter.

GETTING AROUND

TAXIS One of the first things that strike you about the city is the abundance of **taxis** – all yellow, New York-style, and mostly Toyota models of varying ages and sizes. You can get a ride to almost anywhere on the island from the central **market square** (*praça de taxis*). You can also easily flag down taxis from the road. Very few taxi drivers speak English, though some will know French. There are no taxi companies, but some of the taxis on the square have signs up on the roof with their destination, often nearby suburbs. These will wait until they're full before they leave and cannot be hired for an individual ride. The locals use them to transport chickens, fish, petrol, car parts, electrical goods, pots and pans. I once saw a tied-up live goat being heaved into the boot of a cab, bleating. If you're not in a hurry and if you want to travel as the locals do, this is a very cheap way to get around. Sample fares are: ST–Neves 20,000$, ST–São João dos Angolares 20,000$, ST–Porto Alegre 30,000$. A white person, especially a woman, will usually be given the front seat. Try to have the correct change. At the end of a journey, you can always ask the driver to take you to a specific location and pay a bit more. If you choose to hire a taxi for yourself, to go *em frete* (French: *une course*), you will pay a lot more, effectively as much as the driver could have earned if all the seats were taken (and a lot of people can fit into these taxis) – plus the return journey, even if you're only going one way.

There are many *motoqueiros* now providing a **motorbike taxi** service, offering cheap and fast rides mainly in the city, but also to other places on the island, even those that taxi drivers might not consider because of the state of the road. However, because of the dust on the roads and the discomfort of a long ride, they're best for short runs in the city. If you speak Portuguese, you can organise your ride back with them. They are often keen to give you their contact details, and if they are reliable you have a dedicated motorbike taxi network set up. Bear in mind, however, that no helmets are available, and that there have been accidents; ask to go *devagar*, 'slow'. A lift to the Pestana Hotel from the city centre will cost around 20,000$, to the airport 35,000$. Motorbike taxis can be found at the western side of the taxi square, at the bottom end of Rua 3 de Fevereiro. Another bunch of *mototaxistas* work from the former Feira do Ponto market, right next to Residencial Baia.

CAR AND MOTORBIKE HIRE Car hire is expensive. Expect to pay at the very least €30 per day, though the average is more like €50–60. Fuel costs extra, and there is usually a 5% consumer tax to pay on top of the total. Make sure you have insurance included and ensure your travel insurance covers you for third-party damage. By and large, you get what you pay for. Make sure you have dobras to pay for the fuel, to avoid detours. **Navetur** and **Mistral** (see page 112) hire cars; Navetur can sometimes do you a deal. A group of young men hire out motorbikes of different sizes (€20, negotiable) from the square next to the Conceição church. Other hire car options to try are:

🚗 **Elisio Costa** c/o Foto Ramos Costa [113 A3], Rua 3 Fevereiro; 222 4233; m 990 3317. The friendly owner of the photography shop can arrange jeep hire for €35/day.

🚗 **Exergia** [108 B1] Mártir Pinto da Rocha; 222 1400; m 991 0167; www.exergia.st; 08.00–18.00 Mon–Fri, 08.00–noon Sat. The company has 17 scooters available, prices starting at a very fair €10 for 3hrs. Min age 17. The scooters have a 50cc engine, so a regular drivers' licence is sufficient. Electric cars are planned, too. Price includes helmet & insurance.

🚗 **Hanna & Silva Rentacar** [108 B3] Rua 3 Fevereiro, up from the TAAG office; 222 6282; m 983 9188; e hannaesilva-rentacar@hotmail. com. Run by Nelsy Sousa from the Tourist Authority, who speaks English, this company offers possibly the lowest rates on the market, starting at €35/day for 1 of their 10 cars. In the words of an English traveller: 'More importantly Wagner, the manager, was a great chap & very helpful. He speaks reasonable English & acted as a guide for us for ... a very relaxing & interesting day. ... We managed to get diesel into the petrol tank in São João dos Angolares but within about 1½hrs he arrived with a mechanic & sorted it all out for us, all without any fuss.'

🚗 **Turiart** [108 B2] Av Marginal 12 de Julho; 222 5339; e turentacar@cstome.net; www. turentacar.st. Turiart, near Mistral Voyages, offers a range of cars from a Suzuki Jimny to a 10-seater Toyota Prado, & are the only company where you can pay by credit card – with the usual STP proviso, of course, that sometimes cards are refused. A guide/driver costs an extra €15/day. Daily rates, decreasing for rentals of 5–10 days & over, start from €52. Turiart's staff speak English & offer a 24hr service. Other services include airport transfers (€10/couple), São João dos Angolares (€25/couple) & Porto Alegre (€50/couple).

There is also a shop opposite Omali Lodge (08.00–12.30 & 14.00–17.30 Mon–Fri, 08.00–13.00 Sat) that sells Havaianas flip-flops, bikinis, beach bags, etc, and also hires out jeeps for €150 per day with a guide, and two **electric mopeds**. With a reach of 50km, mopeds won't take you very far around the island, but are perfect for short distances. Beautifully quiet and comfortable, they cost €20 for the day and only €10 for three hours, which is plenty for a spin round the city and its environs; a car driving licence is sufficient for rental.

Filling up The most reliable and central **petrol station** in town is the one with the BP sign on Praça de Amizade e Solidaridade entre los Povos; it stays open till midnight and there are usually money changers around to convert your euros/dollars – as well as youngsters taking advantage of stationary motorists to push seed collars and bracelets.

TOURIST INFORMATION AND TRAVEL AGENCIES

TOURIST INFORMATION
Obô National Park m 990 8888 (Aurélio Rita); www.obopark.com

i Posto de Turismo [108 E3] Av 12 de Julho, CP 40; ☎ 222 1542; e turismo@turismo-stp. org; www.turismo-stp.org; ⏱ 08.00–17.00 Mon–Fri, 08.00–noon Sat. The tourist office on the Marginal, next to the STP Airways office, sells a good, inexpensive map, a handful of books & postcards, & presents a wide selection of crafts without actually selling them. At the moment staff can only give very general advice, not book hotel rooms or find contacts for you that go beyond the mainstream. According to travellers' reports, even directions to common tourist attractions outside the capital seem difficult. Also, the phone service is not always that helpful or friendly, & they don't really speak English. Because the tourism authority is only gradually waking up to tourists' needs & until training programmes start providing results, travel agencies are a better bet.

LOCAL TRAVEL AGENCIES
Gold Tours & Services [113 B3] Rua de Moçambique, CP 501; ☎ 222 4598; m 994 7516; e reservas@goldtours.st, info@goldtours. st; www.goldtours.st. Friendly agency run by Carvalho de Mendezes, the owner of the Poiso Alto Gold Guesthouse (see pages 116–17), with website in Portuguese & English. Can facilitate visas, book hotels & plantations, flights & airport transfers, & arrange excursions & car hire with or without a driver. The agency's speciality is tailor-made trips, & though the office is not always staffed, you will find a dedicated personalised service here, just drop them an email. Carvalho de Menezes is also setting up a website, www. pousadas.st, which aims to be an online guide to staying at the historic plantations on the islands, & will be available in English. He has a particular interest in finding a wider audience for plantation history, much of which still needs research.

Mistral Voyages [108 B2] Av Yon Gato, CP 297; ☎ 222 1246, 222 3344; hotline m 990 4050; e mvoyages@cstome.net, vilanova@cstome.net; www.mistralvoyages.com. Situated next to the former Feira do Ponte market, Mistral is the best point of contact for French speakers. The smaller sister of the Libreville, Port Gentil & Marseille operations can sell & confirm air tickets for TAP, TAAG & STP Airways & arrange car hire (up to a 14-seater minibus with driver). Excursions include a half-day city tour; trips to Bombaim, to the south, including a crossing to Ilhéu das Rolas; early-morning sport fishing for marlin, sailfish, tuna & barracuda; boat trips to the beaches of the north, including Ilhéu das Cabras & Lagoa Azul; & visits to Príncipe. 'A la carte' excursions can be organised too. It's best to send your enquiries to both email addresses, & phone if you haven't heard back. The office manager's name is Carlos Vilanova. A good guide for English-speakers is Albertino (Edgener) Espírito Santo (m 991 1881; e edalessanto@hotmail.com); he also has excellent French & is available for research. Costs per day are €15.

Navetur-Equatour [113 A2] Rua Viriato da Cruz, CP 277; ☎ 222 2122; logistics co-ordinator Suzana m 991 5750; e navequatur@cstome.net, navetur@ cstome.net; www.navetur-equatour.st; ⏱ 08.30–12.30 & 15.00–17.30 Mon, 08.00–12.30 & 15.00–17.30 Tue–Fri, 08.00–12.30 & 15.00–17.00 Sat. Located in a lovely ochre-grey colonial building & run by Santomean Luís Manuel Beirão, Navetur is the most dynamic travel agency in town, & their website is the most helpful to tourists before they set off. For English speakers, the best person to talk to is Luís (though he's not always around), or Miguel. Navetur's friendly staff can confirm air tickets for TAP, TAAG, STP Airways, Ceiba to Lisbon, Libreville, Príncipe, Luanda & Douala, & book tickets for STP Airways flights to Príncipe. You can book stays at the plantations of São João, Bombaim, Monteforte, Praia Inhame & Abade, as well as the Praia Jalé ecolodge & Mucumbli ecolodge (near Neves), trekking, sailing trips, diving, sightseeing

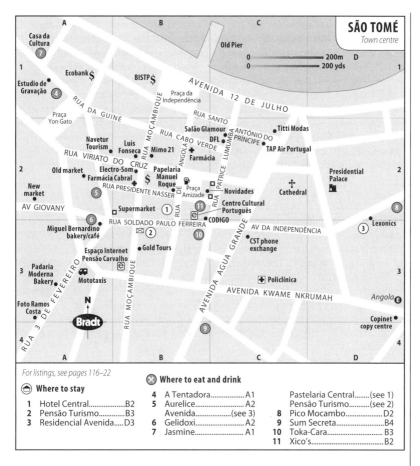

SÃO TOMÉ
Town centre

Old Pier

0 —————— 200m
0 —————— 200 yds

Casa da Cultura ⑦

Ecobank $
BISTP $
Estudio de Gravação ④
Praça Yon Gato
Praça da Independência
AVENIDA 12 DE JULHO
RUA DA GUINÉ
RUA SANTO
Salão Glamour
ANTÓNIO DO PRÍNCIPE
DFL
Titti Modas
Navetur Tourism
Luis Fonseca
Mimo 21
Farmácia
TAP Air Portugal
RUA CABO VERDE
RUA MOÇAMBIQUE
ANGOLA
RUA VIRIATO DO CRUZ
RUA PATRICE LUMUMBA
Old market
Electro-Som
Papelaria Manuel Roque
Presidential Palace
New market
Farmácia Cabral $
⑤
RUA PRESIDENTE NASSER
Praça Amizade
Novidades
Cathedral ✝
AV GIOVANY
Supermarket ①
⑪
Centro Cultural Português
⑧
Miguel Bernardino bakery/café ⑥
RUA SOLDADO PAULO FERREIRA
✉ ②
CODIGO
AV DA INDEPENDÊNCIA
Lexonics ③
Espaço Internet
Pensão Carvalho
Gold Tours
⑩
CST phone exchange
RUA AGUA GRANDE
AVENIDA AGUA GRANDE
Padaria Moderna Bakery
Mototaxis
RUA MOÇAMBIQUE
Policlínica ✚
RUA 3 DE FEVEREIRO
Foto Ramos Costa
AVENIDA KWAME NKRUMAH
Angola ⓔ
N
Bradt
⑨
Copinet copy centre

For listings, see pages 116–22

🛏 **Where to stay**

1 Hotel Central.....................B2
2 Pensão Turismo..............B3
3 Residencial Avenida.....D3

✗ **Where to eat and drink**

4 A Tentadora.................A1
5 Aurelice.........................A2
 Avenida..................(see 3)
6 Gelidoxi.........................A2
7 Jasmine.........................A1
8 Pico Mocambo...................D2
9 Sum Secreta........................B4
10 Toka-Cara..........................B3
11 Xico's.................................B2

Pastelaria Central........(see 1)
Pensão Turismo...........(see 2)

& trips to Ilhéu das Rolas. If you want to go to an out-of-the-way plantation or beach, the staff will try everything they can to make it possible. You can get a 2-week holiday for a couple in Jan, staying at a variety of hotels & plantations on both islands, with a 3-day trek including the Pico de São Tomé & Rolas & a 3-day car hire with guide, for under €2,000, excluding flights. The guides are always knowledgeable & the picnics thoughtfully put together, with lots of local produce to try. The agency is also a good contact for scientists planning a research trip, as well as for cruise operators. 'Glamping' facilities are planned at Praia Zongonhim beach with its sand of changing colours: a couple of comfortable tents measuring 6m x 6m & sleeping 3 or 4 people are especially good for birdwatching trips. In 2013, Navetur acquired a new AC bus for airport transfers & a new 12m x 7.5m boat seating 20 passengers for trips around the island, to Ilhéu

das Rolas, Lagoa Azul or Santana/Cabras. The company sells guidebooks (this one, as well as its Portuguese-language translation & the Pocket Tropics title), postcards & the Pocket Tropics map (€3). Ask about renting the new Navetur apt, see page 118.

LOCAL CONSERVATION AGENCIES

MARAPA [108 E2] Bom Despacho; ☎ 222 2792; e marapastp@gmail.com; www.marapa.org. Friendly, long-established NGO protecting artisanal fishing & the marine environment, including sea turtles. Contact them for information on the ecomuseum at Morro Peixe turtle beach (see page 139) & Operação Tunhã whale-watching trips (see page 139). Think of these as marine wildlife watching trips though, as the one I went on featured a large shoal of bottlenose dolphins (tunhã meaning 'dolphin' in Santomense dialect), flying fish (their performance eliciting an 'aaaahhhhhh' from us every time), white-tailed tropic birds &, especially, bridled terns, known locally as kaié. Costing around €20–25, the boat trips run either out of the capital (where a larger boat is available) or from Morro Peixe in the north & Porto Alegre in the south. Though the rides are fairly smooth, if you're prone to seasickness take precautions. MARAPA also runs the ecolodge at Praia Jalé (see pages 175–6) & can advise on hiking & surfing options (consider a donation, this is not the tourist office but staff are probably better informed). MARAPA can also advise on turtle watching/patrols & trips to watch turtles laying their eggs or the release of hatchlings. Multi-lingual project co-ordinator Bastien Loloum is a long-term resident & a fount of information, as well as the author of a Portuguese-language activity guide to be published in 2014. With an emphasis on using conservation to benefit the people of STP, this is a worthwhile organisation to support.

WHERE TO STAY

HOTELS In São Tomé town, accommodation ranges from €15 hovel-like establishments to €200 a night international-standard hotels, with the few B&Bs probably the best value for money. If you are staying for a while, there is the option of renting an apartment. Take one star off the regular star-rating system for hotels.

There is no real backpacker infrastructure in São Tomé. Most of the cheap places have ancient mattresses that dip in the middle and if you are basing yourself in one of these for a longer period of time, but still want a good night's sleep, it might be worth buying a mattress, *colchão* (around 800,000$) from the old site of the Feira do Ponto market, next to Conceiçao church, and donating it or selling it on before you leave.

Luxury

Omali Lodge Luxury Hotel (formerly Marlin Beach) (30 rooms) Praia Lagarto, CP 463; 222 2350; e reservations@omalilodge. com; www.omalilodge.com. On the airport road in front of Praia Lagarto, this resort-style complex, set in a tropical garden with pool, is a favourite with South African guests & has a friendly, service-oriented atmosphere where English is spoken as a matter of course. All suites are either on the ground or 1st floor & have AC, en-suite bathrooms with bath &/or shower, phone, satellite TV, fridge – &, probably unique in STP, tea- & coffee-making facilities. Prices range from €100 to €350. There is a business centre & a conference centre. Under its new owner, the HBD company, the hotel was refurbished in 2013 as a boutique hotel, with a more up-to-date 'modern Africa' look. Whilst fairly close to town, the beach has a bit of litter & is separated from the hotel by the busy airport road, but it pleasant enough & never gets crowded, apart from on Sun when the locals come out for a swim, fortified by the fresh coconuts for sale on the beach. The hotel restaurant has a famous b/fast (6.30–10.00) & good international cuisine for lunch (noon–15.00) & dinner (19.00–22.00), with attentive service. The 'Léve-léve' bar has a snack menu (burgers, pizzas, etc) & stays open till 01.00. Prices have now switched from US$ to €, although you can pay in US$ & dobras at the day exchange rate; credit-card payments are accepted from €50 upwards. Omali Lodge has a pleasant pool (open to day visitors for 125,000$, very handy & the only day it gets crowded is Sun), which is also used for the pool-based lessons of Tropic Venture's diving courses (see page 89). It also has the only tennis court on the island, free to use for guests & tennis club members (€15/month, including pool use); for lessons, contact Tropic Venture's João Santos (m 992 7059). Floodlit, the court is open to non-residents too, & a racket & balls can be hired for a few euros. Kids will enjoy the bouncy castle. A shop connected with the Santa Casa charity sells Santomean produce & this guidebook. Birdwatchers can scan the garden for weavers, the São Tomé thrush, São Tomé prinia, harlequin quails & white-winged widowbirds. In Jan/Feb, there are plenty of bats too, chattering in the treetops. Omali Lodge's sister operation is the Bom Bom Island resort on Príncipe (see pages 207–9). A taxi into town & back should cost about 70,000$. Owner Mark Shuttleworth, the 1st South African in space

('Homem na Lua', man on the moon), prides himself on paying above-average salaries & supporting social justice & conservation. **$$$$**

🏠 **Pestana Ocean Resort** (105 rooms) Vila Maria; ✆ 222 3600; e reservas@pestana.com; www.pestana.com. While this is the island's only 5-star resort hotel, you do have to take 1 star off in your mind, as with all establishments on the islands. Opened in 2008, the hotel was built on the spit of land across from the Parliament, around the foundations of the historic São Jerónimo fort established by the Dutch during their occupation in the mid 15th century. Pestana is Portugal's biggest group of hotels, & the opening of this hotel spelled a sign of confidence in São Tomé tourism. Rooms are modern, comfortable & spacious, with good bathroom facilities. Staff are always friendly & professional, & receptionists & waiters always made me feel welcome despite the fact I'm more of a budget tourist. The hotel features an outdoor saltwater pool, a very small private beach (of sorts, when the tide is in), the Costa Norte diving & fishing centre (see page 89) offering all kinds of nautical adventures & who use the pleasure-boat jetty, & a small gym. The fine spa has lovely sea views. Packages available with STP Airways (majority-owned by Pestana) are an inexpensive way of getting to the islands with accommodation already thrown in. Independent travellers can then commute between 2 worlds, taking advantage of the fine hotel b/fast in the mornings & exploring the 'real' São Tomé during the day. Be careful not to let high bar prices drive up your bill. The (mainly buffet) food is nothing special, sadly, as it lacks imagination & local produce. The octagonal building next door houses the casino & an in-house nightclub, which has a fine sound system & beautiful ocean terrace. At the time of writing, Sat was the best night (but enquire with reception), while on Fri, entry fees came right down, as Pirata next door was the place to be that night. The Wi-Fi signal is excellent in the lobby (non-residents pay 50,000$/hr) but is not as reliable in the rest of the hotel. I had bad mobile phone reception in my room; if you're not happy, ask to switch rooms. While ecotourism isn't top of the list of priorities here, the hotel's social commitments include donating food to an old people's home run by the Red Cross. The shop is expensive & sells few things actually made on the islands. The hotel can organise all the usual guided trips for you, as well

as car hire. If you see the author of this guide in the lobby, it's probably to take advantage of the credit card cash advance facility, less expensive here than at the bank. **$$$$**

🏠 **Hotel Praia** (30 dbl, 4 suites, 3 bungalows) Praia Lagarto; ✆ 222 2623; e hotel.praia.hotel@gmail.com; www.hotel-praia.com. Opened in 2009, this 4-star hotel on the airport road, owned by Santomeans, is the country's prestige hotel project & it has huge rooms, excellent food, a large swimming pool set in a large green space & (usually) a strong Wi-Fi signal to recommend it. The *praia* (beach) of the name isn't that great, though by the time you visit, the marine pool complex at the tip of the new jetty across the road from the hotel should be ready. This is a good place to meet business people & NGO staff on missions, but the place is still lacking the soul that comes with history. For all its Santomean ownership, I found the ambience a bit strange & hushed, presaged by the freezing-cold reception room. There is a good selection for b/fast. Lunches & dinners, served at huge tables, come with occasional quirks you wouldn't expect from a 4-star place: you might find only one portion of ketchup & mayo to go round, for instance. Gym facilities & massage – guests qualify for 1 free massage a week. There is also an internet terminal for guests. **$$$$**

🏠 **Miramar** (60 rooms, 5 suites) Av Marginal 12 de Julho, CP 69; ✆ 222 778, 222 511, 221 346; e hmiramar@cstome.net; www.miramar.st. For years, most business visitors, diplomatic representatives & development consultants fetched up in the oldest 4-star hotel on the island, built in 1986 & twice renovated since by the new owner, the Pestana Group. The hotel is equipped to an international standard, with all modern amenities, & has very friendly staff with excellent English. Credit cards are accepted. About half of the rooms have a sea view. The airy Café Passante is one of the best features of a hotel that's still a bit rustic-dark in décor. The Barracuda Bar (🕐 08.00–midnight) is good for a nightcap, but has a slightly fusty atmosphere & most people seem to prefer to sit in the comfortable lobby, a popular meeting place for the local elite & where expats come to take advantage of the Wi-Fi to check their emails. The Baron restaurant offers international cuisine, & is where a sumptuous b/fast is taken with a view of the garden. Some visitors stay just

1 night before flying home & on those days b/fast is served very early, from 04.00. The friendly receptionists can organise most things for you such as guided tours, trips to Príncipe, etc. Head receptionist is Wanderley Costa (m 993 0850). Business facilities include a conference room. If you don't have your own transport, the hotel can call you an (expensive) taxi into town; walking only takes 15–20mins. The shops attached to the hotel sell spangly party dresses, linens for men & women & swimwear. The 600m² pool with waterfall is set in a 10,000m² tropical garden, excellent for birdwatching, & making up for the lack of a proper swimming beach nearby. $$$

Mid-range

🏠 **Hotel Agôsto Neto** (16 rooms) Rua Amilcar Cabral, off Av da Independência; 📞222 3584, 222 6728; e netagosto@cstome.net; www.hotelagostoneto.com. Opened in 2007, this small & friendly central hotel is prettily furnished with lively colours. Rooms start from €70, with AC, TV, radio, telephone, minibar & a tea kitchen. An ample b/fast is included, served with a smile & with the option of locally produced coffee. Wi-Fi throughout, plus 1 terminal for guests. To discuss long-stay discounts, speak to the manager. I wouldn't recommend Room 101, it's a bit of an overflow option & you can hear reception traffic. Free airport transfer. $$$

🏠 **Cocoa Residence** (9 rooms) 33b Rua Padre Martinho Pinto da Rocha; 📞2222 7276, 9915588; e cocoaresidence@cstome.net, www.hotelcocoasaotome.st. This friendly guesthouse run by affable and dynamic Alfredo Gaspar is a good choice for solo travellers in particular, as there are 6 sgl rooms (just over €50), plus 2 dbls (€65) & 1 suite with internet terminal (€75). Rates include airport transfer. While not smack-bang in the centre (10-mins' walk or 2-mins' *motoqueiro* ride), it's opposite the popular Kizomba club, so the way to your bed after a night out dancing is short. Wi-Fi day use for residents and non-residents is €4, and the airy restaurant/bar section is great for meeting other travellers. Lunches and dinners are served (best booked in advance). At the time of writing, the wine policy was BYO (a friendly store selling refrigerated vinho verde for instance is only a few steps away), though beers were available. Take advantage of the good car-hire rates. There's a lovely initiative in occasional workshops in *puita* dancing, beadwork

or making an African handbag; you pay 100,000$ to register but get your money back on the day.

🏠 **Hotel Central** (16 rooms) Rua de Angola, CP 836; contact via Pastelaria Central on the ground floor (see page 120). Opening in 2014, this is a very central option, with comfortable, spacious & light dbl rooms, with AC, veranda, satellite TV & Wi-Fi. $$$

🏠 **Residencial Avenida** (18 rooms) Av da Independência; 📞224 1700; e ravenida@cstome. net; www.residencialavenida.net. Owned by Santomeans, this small light-blue hotel right opposite the Presidential Palace was the 1st guesthouse on the island & was refurbished in 2010. With its nicely tended garden & good standard of accommodation, the Avenida remains deservedly popular with a good mix of tourists, politicians & business travellers, & makes you feel very welcome. Book as early as you can. All rooms are on the ground floor, with AC & private bathroom, mini fridge, hot water, TV & room service. Prices range from a sgl for just under €65 & a dbl for just under €80 (B&B) to a trpl suite for up to €155 FB. That the rooms don't get much natural light is the only thing you might not be happy with. The personal & friendly service extends to the bar. At reception you can buy maps, & use the internet terminal; it's free for residents, but bring a jumper as the AC is always on full. Free Wi-Fi for residents in rooms, bar & restaurant. For last-minute craft souvenirs, there is a stall next to the bar, though the selection isn't great. Bernardino & Paulo at reception are old hands & very friendly. $$$

🏠 **Hotel Residencial Baia** (13 rooms) Av da Conceição; 📞224 2100, 222 1155; e hotelrbaia@ cstome.net. This is a central base, if a bit stuck in time & noisy due to its position right next to the busy market. At the time of writing this hotel was being renovated & was up for sale. $$$

🏠 **Hotel O Bigodes** (20 rooms) Bairro Hospital; m 990 4937, 995 2442 (António Lima); e idbigodes@hotmail.com. Associated with the (expensive) Bigodes restaurant with several verandas (& a children's play area), this B&B hotel near the airport has 10 dbl rooms & 10 twin rooms; ask for a sea view, as the price is the same. Wi-Fi throughout. B/fast is taken on the large veranda with sea view. $$

🏠 **Poiso Alto Guesthouse** (5 rooms) Rua da Palma Carlos (antiga Rua Adriano Moreira),

CP 501; 📞 222 4008, 222 4598; 📱 994 7516;
📧 info@poisoalto.st; www.poisoalto.st. Located
off the Marginal (taking the 1st street to the
right coming from the city centre, just past the
Museum), this is one of the top recommendations
I give travellers asking me for a good place to stay.
Functional bedrooms with en-suite bathrooms in
a welcoming former family home. The large cosy
sitting room where b/fast is served has comfy sofas
& a selection of books you might actually want to
read. The large kitchen is fairly well equipped, &
there is Wi-Fi throughout. Carvalho de Menezes,
the owner, is quick to respond to email enquiries,
which is not always the case on the islands. The
main draw here is the friendly welcome by staff &
the owner, who also runs Gold Tours in town (see
page 112). **$$**

Budget

🏠 **Elitneide Casa de Turismo** (12 rooms)
Av Kwame Nkrumah; 📱 990 3317, 990 6742;
📧 elitineidetur@hotmail.com. Rooms of variable
standards, with prices ranging from between
€25 for Room 4 (little light & pretty smoky) to
€40. Friendly owner & staff. Smoking is allowed
throughout the hotel, which might be off-putting
for some. Can be booked through Navetur (see
page 112). **$$**

🏠 **Pensão Turismo** (7 rooms) Rua Soldado
Paulo Ferreira; 📞 222 2340. Very central location;
5 rooms share 2 bathrooms. There are 2 additional
rooms in a different building at the corner of
Rua Santo António do Príncipe, opposite the
Presidential Palace – which is where I stayed,
very comfortably. B/fast, taken in the restaurant
with its beautiful stained-glass windows, doesn't
start before 08.15. Overall, pretty good value for
money. **$$**

Shoestring

🏠 **Residencial Costa Mar** (6 rooms) São
Gabriel; 📞 222 1113. At the excellent price
of €20pp, these light-blue repainted beach
cottages (plus 2 more rooms in another seafront
building) next to the popular Pirata restaurant/
club on the Pantufo road are a good proposition.
The rooms have either AC or a fan, & a shower

without curtain. The place can't, however, shake
off rumours of casual prostitution. B/fast must be
pre-booked & is €5, lunch & dinner can also be
arranged (steaks, chicken), but the darkish dining
room isn't that convivial, & you're probably better
off next door at the (expensive, of course) Pirata
or at a local place in the Pantufo fishing village
along the road leading south. The bar is open
08.00–23.00. **$**

🏠 **Residencial Giovany** (18 rooms)
Av Giovany; 📞 222 3929; 📱 996 1869 (Onório).
Currently closed for refurbishment, this place is in a
central location. In its previous incarnation it was not
that clean & my mattress was pretty ancient but on
the plus side there was hot water, a pleasant balcony
& friendly staff. B/fast can be arranged. **$**

B&B

🏠 **Casa Amarela** (2 rooms) Av 12 de Julho;
📞 222 2573; 📱 990 4492; 📧 norarizzo35@
hotmail.com. The 'yellow house', a colonial villa
next to the National Radio building, comes
thoroughly recommended. The price of €40
sgl/€50 dbl gets you a tastefully furnished
room with fan & a beautifully presented b/
fast, including various breads, homemade
papaya jam, fresh fruit & freshly squeezed
pineapple juice (when Nora is there, if she's
away, Café Passante is very close). There is an
equipped kitchen for self-catering & a living
room. Laundry is included. The whole house
can be rented too. The lovely garden with palm
trees & orchids is overlooked by a porch with
deckchairs, where you can sit & relax, listening
to the waves. The beach across the road is not
really a swimming beach, but sometimes people
set up a volleyball net there, & it's on the expats'
running/powerwalking circuit. Casa Amarela is
a favourite with visitors who have an interest
in culture & sustainable tourism, as having
lived here for 20 years, the Argentinian owner,
architect Nora Rizzo, knows the island intimately
& can give you advice on tailor-made holidays,
whether you are interested in plantations,
popular culture or gastronomy. Reservations are
made by paying a deposit into Nora's Portuguese
bank account. **$$**

APARTMENTS Living in an apartment gives you great independence, and being
able to cook means you don't have to rely on restaurants and can also try cooking
some Santomean dishes yourself. The drawback of living like the locals is that if

the power or water fails in your district, you will have the same problems. Long-term apartment rentals start at around €250 per month. Ask around, look at the noticeboard in the Coconote supermarket (see page 124) or put a notice up at Xico's (see opposite); somebody might know somebody who is at the end of a contract and leaving their apartment.

🏠 **Casa Arnaldo** Quilombo; m 990 8775; e arnaldosposten@hotmail.com; www. casaarnaldo.saotomeprincipe.eu. There are 2 houses available for long-term rental (€350 & €400/month), plus 3 clean private en-suite rooms (€25 sgl/€30 dbl) with AC, fridge, b/fast & airport transfer. The neighbourhood has a lovely vibe & is a 5mins' walk from the centre. The only downside could be that smoking is allowed in the houses. The house nearest to the road can be a little noisy. A new apt is being built on top of the private rooms. **$$**

🏠 **Casa Boa Vista** (2 rooms) Bairro Hospital; 🖄222 3003; m 984 6461; e joachimkerstin@web. de, kejo-news@email.de. Run by friendly German missionary couple Kerstin & Joachim, who arrived on the island in 2011, this is, for my money, the best budget option. It is certainly the cleanest, & offers a large kitchen plus a communal room with a large table. This is a quiet residential place, with the odd Bible class going on, & is great for families.It's not intended for parties, but nor will the owners try to convert you to their beliefs. The issue of occasional power cuts will probably be solved by the time you arrive. Wi-Fi, TV/DVD & board games. The couple can hire out bikes, a moped & a jeep to guests. Kerstin is a qualified nurse & can point you to good local medics. Non-smoking throughout. Occasionally lunches on request. **$$**

🏠 **Dona Delfina** (2 apts) Rua Caixa; m 990 4689. Apts in a residential area, 10 mins' walk from the centre: one with kitchen, but without natural

light (€30); one without kitchen, but with natural light (€25). The cost for dbl occupancy is only €5 more, so it's good value for couples. **$$**

🏠 **Navetur Apartment** (3 rooms) Rua 3 de Fevereiro; 🖄222 2122; e www.navetur-equatour. st. A recently refurbished clean dbl room with AC, on the 1st floor of a house in a popular neighbourhood, a few mins' walk from the market square, costs €25/night (€35 in high season, Jul, Aug & Easter), or €20 for sgl occupancy (€30 in high season), less on a weekly/monthly basis. Outside, ladies sell fruit & veg in the mornings (usually jackfruit, too), & corn on the cob & *safú* fruit by candlelight in the evenings. You can survey proceedings from the balcony, with a beer. The house is next to the popular local shop/bar Pedra-Pedra so it can get a bit noisy at night, whilst in the daytime the occasional toddler likes to take a nap in the doorway. A leaflet in the cupboard explains what to do to the taps if there is a power cut, which also disables the electric hob. The meticulous & radiant *empregada*, Nini, comes in every morning Mon–Sat to wash up your kitchen stuff, tidy & fetch water if necessary. She can wash & iron your clothes for 10,000$ per item. Can be booked through the Navetur agency, see page 112. **$$**

🏠 **Santa Casa** (2 apts) Above the Ossobô crafts shop (see page 125); e scmstp@gmail.com. Sgl €30, dbl €50 but prices drop for long-term rental, starting at 1 month. All profits go to supporting the work of the Santa Casa da Misericordia, Portugal's oldest charity. **$$**

✖ WHERE TO EAT AND DRINK

If you are in the city on Thursday, **CACAU** (see page 134) hosts a set price Grand Buffet, which will enable you to try most of the island's specialities.

Restaurants

✖ **Avenida** Av da Independência; 🖄224 1700; ⏲ 08.00–22.00 daily. Unlike the popular bar of the same name, I've never seen this restaurant exactly buzzing. With its fairly standard fare for the money, it's more of a default option for hotel

guests, offering national & international dishes (€9–15 for main dishes such as steak or cod). The fish dishes are good though & the place is airy, with linen tablecloths, murals, & a TV. You can order *calulú* & other typical dishes the day before, & even the vegetarian *lossua* & *folha de mússua*,

I'm told. Strict vegetarians should request *caldo de legumes* (vegetable stock) be used, & you might have to insist a bit on these specialties that are not on the menu; give plenty of advance notice & you might have to request it with management rather than the staff. $$$$

✗ O Bigodes Praia Francesa; \ 222 3944; m 991 8916 (Luis Gomes). This expensive restaurant with a spectacular setting on a platform sticking right out into the ocean, on the road towards the airport, caters for expats & wealthy Santomense & the clients of the pousada (hotel) next door (see page 116). Vegetarians are offered a couple of pasta dishes, but should ring ahead to make sure there actually is pasta in the house (or BYO). $$$$

✗ O Pirata Estrada de Pantufo; \ 222 7821; ⊕ 09.00–midnight daily. Great location on an airy wooden porch full of artworks, & right on a palm-fringed beach just past the Parliament, with a picturesque shipwreck rusting away in the middle distance. The new management has brought in a new menu, with a good selection for vegetarians & some nice touches using local ingredients (sap-sap fruit mousse). Service is attentive; some of the waiters speak English. There is art everywhere, including changing exhibitions by local artists. On days when there is a party on, *festa*, there might be an entrance charge, for men anyway. At the time of writing, party night was Fri. $$$$

✗ Dona Hortência/Os dois Pinheiros Campo de Milho (behind IDF army barracks); m 990 5825. Book in advance for excellent Portuguese & African home cooking. For vegetarians, Dona Hortência can make a lovely vegetable tart (*torta de hortaliza*). As is often the case with these family places, you might be the only one dining. Make sure you ask the way, either when you book or get your hotel to explain the route to you. $$$

✗ Filomar Bairro Hospital; \ 222 1908; ⊕ lunch & dinner daily. Run by Cape Verdean Filomena, this restaurant is a popular choice with ministers, expats, couples & tour groups on their last day. It serves various local fish, chicken drumsticks, an omelette with vegetables for vegetarians, & fresh fruit for afters. There is an AC inside dining space &, a more preferable option in the evening, a nice ventilated terrace with view over the bay but beware of mosquitoes. The small top terrace is nice for romantic dinners. Service is OK, but mineral water only comes in huge

bottles, wine is also by the bottle (Casal Garcia *vinho verde* & Alentejano wines) & fruit juice only comes in 1-litre packs. The dilapidated sign for the restaurant is hard to spot; when you come down Hospital Hill from town, the turn is a dirt track on your right. $$$

✗ Sum Secreta Av Kwame Nkrumah; \ 222 4604; ⊕ 07.00–22.30 Mon–Sat, could be earlier. Great place for value-for-money food eaten around big, round, linen-covered tables on a spacious & covered terrace with a constant cool breeze. Santomean specialities such as *calulú* (80,000$) & *blablá* are only available if you ask for them in advance. Service is friendly if sometimes slow. 'Mr Secret' is popular with the locals, visiting groups & courting couples for a sorbet ice cream. For 40,000$ they can prepare you a selection of vegetables with rice. The *pastelaria* section has a good selection of cakes, but nowhere near as nice an atmosphere. $$$

✗ Xico's Praça de Amizade; \ 222 1557; m 995 7464; e calhaurolado@gmail.com; ⊕ 05.30–22.00 Mon–Sat. Excellent coffee, sandwiches, salads & much more in a central location. While still popular with expats for watching football on the giant screen (the place will usually open for the big matches even if it's Sun, check beforehand) or the occasional cultural event like *fado* nights, the former 'Café Companhia' is no longer the must-stop place it used to be. Vegetarians should order a great gratin dish from owner Francisco (Xico in Portuguese) the day before. Internet by USB sticks, €5/hr. Cosy colourful décor, if slightly bored service. $$$

✗ Piroga de São Pedro Av 12 de Julho, opposite the fishermen's chapel dedicated to St Peter; m 980 6020; e modetecbs@hotmail.com; ⊕ 10.00–22.00 daily. Opened in 2013, this airy space alongside the main seaside drag serves good fish & meat in a straw-lined interior. They are open to suggestions, & as with most places, vegetarians should ring a day ahead. $$–$$$

✗ A Tentadora Praça Yon Gato; m 998 6737; ⊕ 07.00–21.00 Mon–Sat. DJ Pekagboom, real name Percio Silva, recently came back from spending a dozen years in Portugal & was determined to set up a restaurant that would be a bit different from the usual fish-n-banana fare, & more dynamic. The owner of this cosy, family-run courtyard restaurant even goes round the market sometimes, he told me, & tells people what the soup of the day is (watercress, for example, or *micôcô*). B/fasts are served till 11.00 (there might be cake), wine is available by the glass (well, they'll hold your bottle for you), & they can make a vegetarian dish such as omelette with *makêkê*, or *fuba* with green beans to please the Angolans, & will sometimes throw in a free pudding. Percio will also keep your dinner bottle of wine cool for you if you're coming back for lunch the next day. $$

✗ **Pensão Turismo**   Rua Paulo Soldado Ferreira; ☎ 2222 340. Once you've found the entrance (opposite the pharmacy with the BAYER sign; go up the stairs at the back), this family-run affair is a good choice for lunch or dinner, which you can see being prepared in the open kitchen, though you can feel a bit isolated if you don't speak Portuguese. In the corner stands a bust of Lenin from the olden days, when STP was a 1-party state. $$

✗ **Tété**   Av 12 de Julho; m 990 4353; ⊕ 18.00–22.00 Mon–Fri, but larger groups should phone ahead. Unmarked, very popular, family-run fish restaurant on the Marginal, behind a hibiscus hedge & a cajamanga tree next to the UNEAS office, with *concón* or flying gurnard a speciality. *Calulú* & other specialities can also be ordered. Again, phone the day before, as they are usually full & especially as Dona Tété is planning to move to another site. $$

✗ **O Kilombo**   Bairro Quilombo; m 991 9588; ⊕ 9.30–22.30 Mon–Sat, occasionally Sun. Mário will take care of vegetarians as well, just give him a day's notice. Lovely coconut rice! $

✗ **Que Morabeza**   Budo-Budo neighbourhood (near the quartel army headquarters); m 991 0035; ⊕ lunch & dinner daily, but ring ahead. 'Morabeza' is the iconic Cape Verdean concept of hospitality, & Gina's friendly Cape Verdean restaurant is a local favourite for a quick lunch with the local NGOs for example. $

Cafés and Pastelarias

🖳 **Café Passante**   Av 12 de Julho; ⊕ 08.00–21.00 daily. The outdoor *esplanada* next to Hotel Miramar has good coffee, plus cakes & pastries, hamburgers & pizzas. There are a couple of indoor tables, but it's much nicer to sit outside & watch the sea. In this favourite meeting place for both locals & expats, the Great Café Passante Challenge is to try to open a book & actually read more than a few lines before somebody you know turns up. $$

🖳 **Jasmin**   Rua Municipio; ☎ 222 7130;

⊕ 07.00–23.00 Mon–Sat. This new pleasant tea salon with an airy terrace, situated in the beautifully restored Casa de Cultura (now slowly starting to actually show some culture), has become immediately popular. Hamburgers, shwarma, pizzas, etc, are served, & thanks to a generator, power cuts don't affect operations. $$

🖳 **Pastelaria Central**   Rua de Angola; m 985 1732 (Inês); ⊕ 07.00–20.00 daily. Little Portugal in the centre of town! Opened in 2013, this AC space (the former Le Paguê restaurant) offers fine Portuguese homemade pastries, even *pastéis de nata* (custard tart). This is the current daytime meeting place of choice. $

Snack restaurants

✗ **Asas de Avião**   Bairro Aeroporto; ☎ 222 6950, 222 8033; ⊕ 08.00–22.00 Mon–Sat. This bar/restaurant situated under the wings of a stranded plane next to the airport is one of the most curious places for a snack meal or some late-night fried bananas & a beer. There are a few tables right under the wing, with the TV & bar within view, while strings of little light bulbs lead to more private tables, often, it seems, used by couples on a secret assignation. Access to the pool costs 30,000$. This place is vaguely surreal when you're on your own, but gets busier around departure time. There are actually 2 stranded planes and the story behind them is fascinating; these Lockheed Constellations, 'Connies', were used during the Biafra war (1967–70) to transport vital food aid & to evacuate people. The Portuguese government supported the breakaway Nigerian province, while the Soviets & the UK supported Nigeria. São Tomé became the centre of the relief operations & more than 5,000 relief missions were flown from São Tomé to a dangerous makeshift airstrip in Biafra. While the Barcelona-based CAUÉ Association were campaigning for the 2nd plane to be turned into a museum to this humanitarian relief effort, an indoor restaurant & disco opened here, & the whole thing has suffered a bit too much additional building work instead. The management don't seem very interested in the planes' illustrious history, but you can see photographs of the rebuilding work on the walls. $$$

✗ **Aurelice**   Old Yellow Market, off Rua Município; m 990 9810, 990 4031; ⊕ 08.00–21.00 Mon–Sat. It took me a while to find this small, inexpensive restaurant because the name on the wall outside is completely different, the sign reading 'Ristorante Delice'. Right inside the yellow market building, it's a bit dark, but you can pre-order an inexpensive calulú. Another delicacy is *kisaká* (*manioc* with smoked fish), sold for 20,000$ at one of the entrances to the market; ask around. $$

X **B24** Parque Popular; m 992 2222; ⊕ 07.30–23.00 daily. This is currently the most popular of the shack restaurants in Parque Popular. Owner Iola is a genial mix of Cape Verdean, Angolan & Brazilian, & this heritage is reflected in her cooking. $$

X **Contentor Azul/Paraíso dos Grelhados** Av 12 de Julho; m 999 4005; ⊕ 09.00–23.00 Mon–Sat. Operating out of a blue ship container right on the seafront, this informal, popular & friendly BBQ place is good for sitting at one of the ourside tables to watch the daily catch coming in. A popular starter is chunks of marinated marlin stomach, the speciality main is the flying gurnard fish, concón, with grilled breadfruit & *malagueta* chilli sauce, washed down by local Rosema beer. No toilets. $$

X **Plê-Museu** Rua Juventude; m 991 2019; ⊕ 08.00–20.00 Mon–Sat. Handy stop for a quick snack between the National Museum & the Ossobô souvenir shop, though they seem surprised to see tourists. Proper meals, such as *calulú*, have to be ordered in advance. It gets very hot at lunchtime outside. $$

X **Petisqueira Contentor** Av 12 de Julho; ✆222 4018; ⊕ 08.00–23.00 daily. Off the beaten track, this unpretentious restaurant on the main road opposite the Bigodes turn also has a couple of tables outside, serving a changing menu (eg: pargo snapper fish or chicken). $$

X **Sombra da Coleira** m 990 6992, 992 0581; ⊕ 08.00–22.00 daily. This place has changed greatly since I first visited. There can still be a good atmosphere when there's a football match on or films on a big screen under the cola-nut tree. Only snacks are on offer, & food now has to be ordered in

advance & includes dishes such as filet steak, pork (*lombinho de porco*) for 140,000$, veal (*de vaca*) for 180,000$ & pork cutlets (costoletas de porco) for 130,000$. Feel free to order an ice cream as the Portuguese owner assures me that they never have a power cut, as they're on the same electricity feed as the police next door. Opposite you'll find a juice bar, Sombra da Fruteira. $$

X **Sombra do Caroceiro** m 993 2849; ⊕ 24hrs, to be taken with a large pinch of salt. Right next to Sombra da Coleira & it's perfectly OK for a plate of rice & beans & a beer. The menu changes daily & can include sea snails, fried banana, *polvo* (octopus), chicken thigh & fried fish. $$

X **Toka-Cara** Rua Patrice Lumumba; ⊕ 08.00–21.00 Mon–Sat. Small informal eating place for a quick snack of fish & rice, across from the Instituto Camões. I've often had an early evening Sagres & a plate of fried bananas here & usually ended up chatting to curious passers-by. Toilet facilities (in a barrack opposite) are pretty dire. $$

X **Papa-Figo** Av Kwame Nkrumah; ✆222 7261; ⊕ 07.00–23.00 daily, often later. Popular with both locals & staff from the UN HQ across the street, this friendly terrace snack bar gets nicely busy in the evenings. The *shwarma* for 50,000$ (also take-away) is very popular. My favourite is the ripe *banana frita madura*, when they have it, so much nicer than the regular fried banana. $

X **Roulote Ultima Estação** Parque Popular; m 985 6591; ⊕ 09.00–03.00 daily. Usually stationed outside the Parque Popular, this licenced van sells burgers & kebabs to stem those late-hour hunger pangs. Another one can usually be found off Av da Independência. $

X**Tia Leo** Parque Popular; m 991 2967; ⊕ 08.00–23.00 Mon–Sat. A recommendation of the Spanish honorary consul, 'Aunt Leo' serves a daily changing menu of chicken curry Santomense style, with coconut milk & *cajamanga*, *calulú* (70,000$), Caboverdian *cachupa*, or a jardineira pork and vegetable stew. $

3

ENTERTAINMENT AND NIGHTLIFE

Bars

♀**Bar Avenida** [113 D3] Av da Independência. This round bamboo-furnished bar/café, attached to the Residencial, is a meeting place for politicians, functionaries & journalists – São Tomé's 'second

parliament' – plus tourists & assorted regulars. In the daytime there is a craft stall outside, in the evenings there is (fairly loud) TV with news & football matches, *boca-a-boca* news and gossip passing by word of mouth, & Wi-Fi (payable for non-residents, free for guests). Open late & always friendly, with excellent coffee & a selection of teas as well as snack food such as rolls with salad garnish. There are some plastic tables outside too. This is also a handy toilet- &/or phone-stop en route between the centre & the Hotel Miramar area; both amenities are located next to the hotel reception.

♀ **Pico Mocambo** [113 D2] Amilcar Cabral, off Av da Independência, 1min from Hotel Agôsto Neto; ☏ 222 7506; m 984 5961, 986 5770; e picomocambo.geral@gmail.com; www. facebook.com/pico.mocambo; ⊕ 08.00–midnight daily. At the time of writing, Godi & Hélène's central, atmospheric & airy bar is the place to be, the true successor to the now defunct Café &

Companhia. The cocktails are fab – many different ones made with rum & tropical fruit, for instance, & the national version of a mojito with gravana rum is a good deal. There are gin evenings, too. Pizzas can be ordered in from Jasmin (see page 120) & take about 20mins to arrive (don't expect an Italian job but they'll do for mopping up the booze). Look out for special events such as the cheese & wine tasting – that's the French touch for you – & the b/fasts starting in 2014. Can-do approach, friendliness, international vibe & free Wi-Fi. There is an *artesanato* craft shop below. Fluent French-speaker Garrido Odair, who runs the shop, sometimes offers workshops; talk to him about one-to-one lessons.

CLUBS For young Santomeans, nightlife usually means a club (*discoteca*) and you should try and go at least once to see what the local dancing culture is all about. Local women will sometimes tell you that there is too much *confusão*, a commonly used word meaning 'trouble', in clubs, but for a tourist, even as a woman on your own, there is no problem. If you enjoy dancing, you will get a lot more out of the experience if somebody shows you a few steps in advance. **Dancing lessons** can be arranged informally through CACAU, or contact suave Junior (m 995 7936; e *junior.ginbulu@ hotmail.com*), who speaks Spanish and charges €10 an hour per person.

Below are some listings but 'what's hot' changes quickly, so ask around locally.

☆ **Asas do Avião** [off map, 108 B1] Next to the airport; ⊕ Fri & Sat 20.00–02.00. Club attached to a restaurant/bar, playing a mix of music & with unofficial spaces for 'privacy'. There is a small pool too. Free entry for women, men pay 50,000$.

☆ **Beach Club** (see Pestana Ocean Resort, page 115) [off map, 108 F4]

☆ **DJ Cabelo** [off map, 108 B1] Bairro de Saton (direction Airport, ask locally for directions); m 990 5484; www.transparencia.st/ publicitcabelo.htm; ⊕ Thu 21.00–03.00. DJ Cabelo is the man of the moment & offers his recording mixtape services on Praça Yon Gato. When I visited I found the sound system a bit overstretched.

☆ **Dolores** [off map, 108 C4] Bairro Dolores; m 991 4090; ⊕ 21.00–03.00/04.00 Wed–Sat, 18.00–midnight Sun. Currently only sporadically open in the Fruta-Fruta neighbourhood (head for Bom Bom), with the obvious advantage over Orbita (see below) that it's closer to the town centre. There is a chance of taxis outside waiting to take clubbers back into town. If you don't want

to rely on that, arrange a pick-up with a driver beforehand, go with friends, or, at worst, ask for a lift (*boleia*) from a car with a mixed group of men & women. Entrance charges vary between 20,000$ & 50,000$, depending on the day & your gender.

☆ **Kizomba** [108 A1] Rua Martíres Pinto Rocha; m 990 5355; ⊕ 21.00–04.00 Wed, 21.00–03.00 Sat, 18.00–23.00 Sun. Taking its name from Santomeans' favourite style of dance, the Kizomba has a young clientele, especially on Sun, the day recommended by the locals. Within walking distance from the centre on the road parallel to the Marginal, the club gets unbearably hot on popular days. Entry is 15,000$ for women, 20,000$ for men.

☆ **Orbita** [off map, 108 C4] San Guembú; m 994 5439, 991 6429; ⊕ 21.30–03.00 Fri & Sat, 18.30–22.00 Sun. At the end of a dirt track, some 4km south of town on the Angolares road, past Bom Bom. A taxi costs about 80,000$; the return might be a problem as there are no taxis waiting to take clubbers back to town.

OTHER ENTERTAINMENT The lively **Parque Popular** [108 E2] is a common venue for concerts, competitions and shows. In terms of the little **cinema** [108 E2] available, the Santomeans prefer actions films, the more dead bodies the better – and it's true that I did once meet a baby boy called Van Damme! In the bars, restaurants and small shops, Santomeans crowd around the **TV** screen to catch Brazilian soap operas, *telenovelas*, while the news shows the latest from the other former Portuguese colonies: Guinea-Bissau, Angola, Cape Verde, Mozambique, and, incongruously, the rush-hour traffic snaking around Lisbon. The bar at Residencial Avenida is a cosy place to watch the news at night and listen to the comments. Of the countless music videos on TV, most are blatant male fantasies of girls writhing around the singer; the less professionally produced ones might feature impromptu bands of goats scuttling past between the cameraman and the recording artist.

Men play a card **game** called *bisca* or checkers with beer bottle caps. *Oril* is a Cape Verdean game played on a board with holes, made from *pau feijão* with chips made from black wood, *pau preto*.

Cultural institutions in the city also organise a number of events, for details see page 127.

Casa Cinéma/Teatro Marcelo de Veiga
[108 E2] Praça Cultura. Despite the name, this impressive building, built with forced labour in the 1950s & restored with Taiwanese money, has not hosted any theatre productions or films for a while, but is now a venue for fashion shows, political rallies, Igreja Universal gatherings & music events. It also houses a branch of Banco Equador. The balcony is normally locked but can be opened up on request, & it offers a magnificent view of Ana Chaves Bay.

SHOPPING

Check the Navetur agency website for current details of shops and initiatives selling local produce, palm oil and bread, both in the capital and further afield.

CLOTHES If your luggage was not on the same plane as you, there are various places to shop for replacements. Open-air markets sell a variety of clothes, fabrics and shoes: there are various locations, including Praça Yon Gato; secondhand clothing is sold on Rua Giovany.

Blue [108 E4] Av Das Nações Unidas, Loja 604 (opposite Hotel Miramar); m 987 3084. Designer clothes for men, women & kids, plus accessories & interior design items.
Mimo 21 [113 B2] Rua Viriato da Cruz; ☎222 3993. Good selection of clothing & shoes, & helpful staff.
Novidades [113 B2] Praça Amizade; m 994 0411; ⊕ 08.00–12.30 & 15.00–17.30 Mon Fri.

I found a couple of pairs of linen & cotton trousers here that were a good fit & good value. Friendly owner.
Titti Modas [113 C2] Rua Santo António do Príncipe. Expensive young fashions. There are always far more sales staff in here than customers, but if you're looking for something for the *discoteca*, this is the place. Prices are displayed in euros.

FABRICS Several places sell the West African fabrics in lively colours, most are synthetic but some cotton (*algodão*) is available too, at a higher price. You'll always find some fabrics for sale on the first floor of the new yellow market building next to Taxi Square, **Luis Fonseca** [113 B2] has some (pricier) fabrics, and I like the shack **Loja de Dona Fâtima** [108 D4] in the Quilombo neighbourhood, opposite the water font and washing tank (25,000$/m). For a dress you'll need several metres.

FOOD AND DRINK

Carla Charcuteria [108 F4] Av Kwame Nkrumah; ✆222 5192; ⏰ 09.00–12.30 & 15.00–18.30 Mon–Sat. Slightly stuffy deli, with a selection of beverages, dairy products, cereals, olives, nuts & fairly expensive local coffee/chocolate, etc. Aimed at those staying at Hotel Miramar around the corner.

CKADO Av Marginal [off map, 108 B2] 12 de Julho✆222 2135; ⏰ 08.30–13.00 & 15.00–20.00 Mon–Thu, 08.30–20.00 Fri–Sat. Huge supermarket; its opening was hailed as a blessing by many expats. You can find a good selection of Corallo coffees & chocolates kept in good conditions. For some reason you have to show your till ticket at the exit – don't be alarmed.

Coconote [113 C2] Praça Amizade;✆222 6031; ⏰ 08.30–12.30 & 15.30–19.00 Mon–Sat. Supermarket selling an enticing selection of French specialities, as well as cookies, wine, coffee & local dry snacks at good prices. No AC.

DFL Supermercado [113 C2] Rua Moçambique; ✆222 5181; www.dfl.st; ⏰ 08.00–23.00 Mon–Fri, 08.00–midnight Sat, 08.00–23.00 Sun. With long opening times, a good selection of groceries & phone credit, this is one of the very few supermarkets open on Sun.

Economax [113 B2] Rua Soldado Paulo Ferreira; ✆222 4626; ⏰ 08.00–12.30 & 15.00–21.00 Mon–Fri, 08.00–20.00 Sat, 09.00–13.00 Sun. French wines, Belgian beers, a large selection of cosmetics & household goods, fresh cheese, stationery & sometimes certain things you will find nowhere else, like 'Marie-Rose' cream for mosquito bites (*pomada para picadas*) & repellent (350,000$). Handy for its late opening hours. The owner is always friendly.

Gelidoxi [113 A3] Rua do Município (Mercado Municipal, next to Padaria Miguel Bernardo);

m 980 8035 (for orders); ⏰ 06.30–20.30 Mon–Thu & Sun, 06.30–22.00 Fri–Sat. The new darling on the scene, selling ice creams & pastries, fresh fruit juices & yoghurts. Their motto 'Gósto cu plazé di télá non' translates as 'flavours & pleasures from our lands', & their tamarind, mango & *safú* ice creams are spectacular.

Intermar [113 C2] Praça Amizade;✆222 1250; e intermar@cstome.net. The most popular local supermarket sells a wide range of foodstuffs, including Portuguese dairy products (butter, cheese), cosmetics & a good selection of local chocolates & coffees that you can pay for in US$/€ if necessary.

Miguel Bernardino [113 A3] Market Sq. While a bit noisy, this place is good value & a favourite meeting place for b/fast, as well as operating as a bakery. Lazy beginner birders can snap cordon bleus picking crumbs here.

Padaria Atlântica [off map, 108 B4] Rua 3 de Fevereiro, towards Riboque. Bread & rolls for sale 24hrs.

Padaria Moderna [113 A3] Rua 3 Fevereiro; ✆222 3217; ⏰ 03.00–21.00. Long-established bakery selling fresh rolls (*pão*), bread (*pão de forma*, white & with cereals), French-style pastries (*pain au raisin* & *pain au chocolat*), dry cakes (*quêque*) & coconut-topped sweet rolls (*pão de Deus*), etc.

Supermercado Colombo [108 E4] Av Kwame Nkrumah; m 980 1904; ⏰ 08.00–12.30 & 15.00–19.00 Mon–Fri, 08.00–13.30 Sat

Ubaga-Tela [off map, 108 B2] Towards the airport;✆222 323; m 990 3476; ⏰ 06.30–19.00 Mon–Sat, 07.00–13.00 Sun. If you're heading out towards the airport & don't fancy going to CKADO (see above), this friendly grocery is next to the pretty green church. Open Sun mornings, too.

POSTCARDS For the nicest postcards, *postáis* (15,000$), go to the central post office (see page 131); they have a good selection featuring plants and birds. Hotels such as the Miramar and Avenida sell postcards, too, but they're more expensive. Navetur sells cards with images of waterfalls and plantations that will convey some idea to friends and family of where you've been. For more arty cards, visit G&B Arte (see opposite page). Consider printing off your pictures at the copycentre and making your own.

SOUVENIRS People will sometimes just stop you in the street and offer crafts, and there are a few stalls dotted around selling little carved boats (some more polished than others), coconuts carved into cups, spoons and bags, seed collars, etc. The tourism office (see page 112) on the Marginal can't sell you its good selection of *artesanato*, but can point you to where you can purchase them. French jewellery designer **Valérie** (m *995 0217*; e *valerie32@hotmail.fr*) sells her colourful natural bead jewellery; she also uses the beautiful sea urchin shells from Praia Sete Ondas. For a wide selection of crafts or if you want something more enduring, stop at the **CACAU** art gallery (see page 134).

Atelier G&B Arte [off map, 108 B1] Hospital Hill; m 991 1286; e guilcar7@hotmail.com; ⊕ 14.00–18.00 Mon–Fri, or by appointment; it's best to call ahead to make sure somebody is there to receive you. Beautiful sand postcards & paintings, & paintings by local French-born artist Bruno Spagnol (now mainly based abroad, but keeping his hand in) & artist-musician Guilherme Carvalho. Heading towards the airport from town & going up Hospital Hill, look for a yellow wooden house on the right-hand side of the road, level with the quartel army complex on the left.

Escola de Bambú (ETMAD) [108 E4] Av Kwame Nkrumah; ☏ 222 2592; ⊕ 08.00–17.30 Mon–Sat. Watch bamboo furniture being made at this 'bamboo school', & order a piece to take home. A varnished table will set you back 350,000$. Choose your chair model carefully & try to pick the most ergonomic one, as I've found most bamboo furniture pretty excruciating to sit on after a little while.

Loja de Bambú [108 E4] Around the corner from ETMAD (see above); ⊕ 08.00–12.30 & 15.00–17.30 Mon–Fri, 08.00–13.00 Sat. Small shop selling banana products, coffee from Trindade, dried jackfruit & small crafts such as palm fans.

Mama Africa [108 B4] Rua 3 de Fevereiro; m 986 5770; e mamafricastp@gmail.com; www.mamafricastp.blogspot.com; ⊕ 10.00–20.00 Mon–Fri, 10.00–18.00 Sat & Sun. Nice selection of handicrafts – they are strong on the bags front – & other souvenirs, with friendly Rasta staff. Examples can be seen at Omali Lodge, for example. Also sells foodstuffs, & brightly coloured clothes, which can also be made to measure if you want to choose your own fabric. The furniture item of the moment is bamboo lampstands made by ST–Guinean Godi, who used to work here before taking over the Pico Mocambo bar (see page 122). Free shipping to Lisbon, shipping to other places on request.

Os Fidos Riboque; ask locally, they moved recently. 'The reliable ones' craft shop sells beautiful objects made out of coconut: coffee pots & cups, jewellery boxes, cooking spoons, etc. Come & buy direct to get the best price. Note that coffee spoils in the untreated coconut cups so unless you want just to look at them or use them as storage containers for spare change & suchlike, try to find a food-neutral varnish to treat them when you get home.

Os Pica-Pau [108 E3] Praça da Cultura, next to the large former cinema building housing the Mediateca and banks; ⊕ 08.00–17.00 daily. An association of 24 artisans, friendly guys selling wooden boxes & carved tableaux of Santomean scenes, cocoa-pod sculptures, jewellery made from a variety of local seeds, &, my favourite, beautiful trays (300,000$) with intricate designs made from different local woods, such as cedrela. The only tortoiseshell items now for sale are antique pieces, so thankfully this (widely banned) merchandise is on its way out. With the development of the cinema building, the location of the shop may change.

Ossobô EcoSocial [108 F1] Praça de Juventude; ☏ 222 7933; www.ossoboecosocial.org; ⊕ 09.00–18.00 Mon–Fri, 09.00–13.00 Sat. This is a highly recommended 1-stop souvenir shop with a social conscience – it's attached to the Santa Casa de Misericordia charity. Sells Corallo chocolate (various flavours, including coffee, ginger & orange) & coffee, jams (such as banana prata with vanilla), dried fruit, little bags of pepper, books & CDs, clothing, bags, & beautiful crafts such as wooden inlaid trays, rings, bracelets & hair accessories using cow horns instead of tortoiseshell for a similar effect.

Quá-Téla [108 C4] Rua Barão de Água Izé; m 990 4114, 990 8737; e quatelastp@hotmail.com; ⊕ 08.30–12.30 & 14.30–19.00 Mon–Fri, 09.00–15.00 Sat. Working with various small producers, my favourite souvenir shop has a great selection of edibles, including coffee, pala-pala chips, spices, jams & Django's cocoa liqueur. Radiant Catarina actually knows how to cook the odd items for sale such as *izaquente*. She offers a catering service, too. While there is a sign pointing to the shop – '100 metros' – from the large Avenida Nkame Krumah, many don't know where it is, so look for the road between the blue-&-white Patrice Lumumba school & the Igreja Adventista temple, & it's to your right, slightly set back.

MISCELLANEOUS

Estudio de Gravação [113 A1] Praça Yon Gato. You'll see signs for Estudio de Gravação, where about 60,000$ will buy you a mixed CD. Or try Electro-Son on Rua Moçambique, opposite Banco Equador.

Foto Ramos Costa [113 A3] Rua 3 de Fevereiro; ☎222 4233. Senhor Costa offers digital services & sells memory cards (1GB for 700,000$). You can have passport pictures taken, your images burnt on to CD & paper prints made from any Nokia mobile phone. You'll spot the yellow Kodak sign of the shop from the market square.

Horto da Bita nursery Rua 3 de Fevereiro, just off the roundabout; m 993 9940, 994 9876 (Vivalda, speaks English). Dynamic Bita sells beautiful ornamental plants, some of which she brings in especially from Angola, but also pots of local herbs such as *micocô*. Prices start at 100,000$. A young member of the family, Vivalda, a presenter with local broadcaster TVS, speaks English. There are plans to open up the nursery to visitors on certain days of the week, in the meantime, phone ahead to visit. There is another small nursery on Avenida Kwame Nkrumah.

Luis Fonseca [113 B2] Rua Moçambique; ☎222 1039. Shop selling hardware & useful items like torches (but for batteries you have to go to Intermar), snorkelling gear, backpacks, shoes, etc.

Papelaria Manuel Roque [113 B2] Rua Moçambique; ☎222 1120; ⊕ 08.00–12.30 & 15.00–17.30 Mon–Fri, 08.00–13.00 Sat. On the corner with Rua Nasser, this is one of the bigger stationery shops in town.

OTHER PRACTICALITIES

COMMUNICATIONS

Phone Use the CST phone exchange. Otherwise, look for '*Telefone aquí*' signs, for example around the market square.

CST [113 C3] Av da Independência; ☎222 2226, 222 2982; ⊕ 07.00–21.00 Mon–Sat daily, 07.00–19.00 Sun. By day, CST is a hub of activity, with people chatting into the 6 posts. This is the procedure: go to one of the posts, lift the receiver & dial 555, then wait for the tone. You will be asked to type in, *marcar*, the number you want & press the hash key (cardinal). The line is often crackly, but this will clear once you're connected. You will already be charged while the connection is being made. Should you hear 'Este posto não está activo', call back to the counter 'Número/Cabina ... faz favor!', giving the relevant number (above the post) & staff will activate the phone for you. You pay afterwards at the counter; local calls cost 2,500$/min, but international calls are expensive, ranging from 13,000$ to 21,000$. You can also ask to be called back (☎222 1101). Make the 1st call from one of the inside cabins.

Internet Public **Wi-Fi** spots are the lobby of the Hotel Miramar, and the lobby of the Pestana hotel (*50,000$/hr*). At Xico's café (see page 119), the former Café & Companhia, you pay a staggering €5 per hour for internet. The Cocôa Residence charges a day rate of €4 for use of its fairly OK connection. Your best bet is the free Wi-Fi at CACAU (see page 134).

Although the number of dedicated internet cafés has fallen to more or less one, a number of the cultural institutions offer access to the internet, some with up to one hour free using the in-house terminals. There is also Wi-Fi in the National Library. For details, see opposite page.

🖳 Espaço Internet Pensão Carvalho [113 B3] Rua Moçambique, corner with Av Kwame Nkrumah; ☎222 6007; m 990 3737; ⊕ 07.30–21.30 Mon–Sat, 10.00–20.00 Sun. This small space with 10 terminals is very popular. The guesthouse is no longer open, but the name has remained. Rates start at 3,000$ for 5mins, 1hr costs 22,000$ & 1hr 20mins 27,000$.

COMPUTERS AND PHOTOCOPYING

Some of the cultural institutions also offer printing and photocopying services, see below.

CODIGO – Sistemas de Informação [113 B2] Rua Patrice Lumumba; 222 4204; e codigostp@gmail.com; 08.00–12.30 & 15.00–17.30 Mon–Fri, 08.00–13.00 Sat. Computer repairs, & accessories such as print cartridges & the odd computer for sale.

Copinet [113 C3] Av Nkrame Krumah; 222 5001; e copinet_digna@cstome.net; 07.30–19.00 Mon–Fri, 08.00–19.00 Sat–Sun. Large operation with high-quality copies, including A3, & scanning services. Some office supplies are on sale too.

Lexonics [113 D3] Av da Independência, corner with Av Amilcar Cabral; 222 2644; 07.30–19.00 Mon–Fri, 08.00–17.00 Sat. A few mins' walk from the National Library.

CULTURAL AND RESEARCH INSTITUTIONS

Alliance Française [108 E2] Aliança Francesa; Rua Gago Coutinho; 224 2300; e informations@astp.org; www.afstp.org; 07.30–noon & 14.30–17.00 Mon–Fri. This is the French Cultural Institute. The library has a few STP titles on display, alongside French books & DVDs to buy & borrow. There are also a few CDs of Santomean music. If you're staying on São Tomé for a while, it's worth getting a reader's card (*cartão*) for 100,000$, but even without one you can surf the net on 1 of the 5 terminals. You can watch DVDs, & there's a photocopier here too. This is the place to meet young ambitious Santomeans taking French classes, especially now there is an outside garden café, which should be Wi-Fi enabled by the time you read this. Activities include cinema sessions on Wed night, art exhibitions & salsa classes.

Centro Cultural Português/Instituto Camões [113 B2] Rua Soldado Paulo Ferreira; 222 1455; e ccp@cstome.net; www.instituto-camoes.pt; 08.00–12.30 & 14.30–17.00 Mon–Fri. A nice, cool space in which to sit down, it has a wide range of books & magazines in Portuguese, with some French titles, too. There are sometimes books by local authors for sale & exhibitions of work by local artists. Free 30min internet access at 8 terminals, but none too fast.

Centro da Lingua Portuguesa [108 C4] Bairro Quinta Santo António; 222 4244. This cultural centre in the ISP polytechnic building near the French Embassy has occasional cultural activities.

Historical Archive [108 E3] Arquivo Histórico; Praça Cultura; 222 2306; e ahstp@cstome.net; 08.00–noon & 14.00–17.00 Mon–Fri. The best place to buy books on STP & there are some magazines you can browse too. The Historical Archive holds the Câmara Municipal records of the city. If you would like to do some research, access is refreshingly informal. In 2013, a UNESCO-supported plan for the digitalisation mainly of the records pertaining to the 16th & 17th centuries was announced; paper records of the recruitment & distribution of slaves to the various plantations, for instance, are vulnerable to decay.

Mediateca [108 E3] Praça da Cultura (entrance at the side where the Pica Pau craftspeople are); 224 3106; e medbistp@cstome.net; 08.00–noon & 14.00–17.00 Mon–Fri, 08.00–15.30 Sat. Serene, AC study space, with shelves of reference books on economics, politics & sociology, & copies of African magazines such as *Africa Today* (*Africa Hoje*) & newspapers to be read in comfy chairs. You can access the DVD & CD library, & various databases. Olga & Vanya at reception are very helpful. There is no Wi-Fi, but 10 computers that you can use free of charge & unsurprisingly, the service is very popular. You are entitled to 60mins of surfing the net (*navegar*). You have to sign up & leave your bag with reception. Printing costs 1,000$ black-&-white, 2,000$ colour.

National Library [108 E3] Biblioteca Nacional; Praça da Cultura; 222 6013; 08.00–17.00 Mon–Fri. The giant plastic breadfruit outside the entrance was used as the central prop in the film *Frutinha do Equador* (see page 241). At the time of writing, it wasn't possible to get a reader's card (*cartão de leitor*). Don't expect a vast selection of STP-related books. If you want to photocopy something, Lexonics office services is nearby (see above). There is free Wi-Fi, which can also be used out of hours if you stand in front of the building.

DRY CLEANING AND LAUNDERETTES

Aquasec [off map, 108 F4] Vila Maria; ✆222 5025; m 990 4770; ⏱ 07.30–noon Mon–Fri, contact management for Sat opening times. A few doors down from the National Assembly. Dry cleaning a pair of trousers costs 20,000$.

Lavandaria Popular [108 B4] Rua 3 de Fevereiro, next to the Navetur apt. Launderette.

HAIR, BEAUTY AND MASSAGE

Salão Glamour [113 C2] Rua Patrice Lumumba; ✆222 3294; ⏱ 08.30–18.00 Mon–Sat. My favourite beauty salon, which always has a fun vibe between the clients & the girls working there. Dona Nanda is hairdresser to the expats, but prices for cutting, waxing, pedicures & manicures are fair. There is no sign outside; go up the stairs of the yellow building next to the DHL supermarket.

Santa Casa da Miséricordia [108 F2] Lar Dona Simôa Godinho (old people's home), Bairro Hospital; ✆222 2367; m 990 6772 (Elsa); ⏱ 17.00–20.00 Mon–Fri, 16.00–19.00 Sat. Relax & do a good deed as profits from the 80,000$ spent on a 45min *leve-leve* massage by a therapist trained in Portugal go to this charity's work. Call one day ahead to book.

Vila Saúde [108 C4] Rua Barão de Água Izé; ✆222 6520; m 990 4971; e vilasaude@cstome. net, crisdoria90@hotmail.com; ⏱ 08.00–18.00 Mon–Sat. Health centre offering a bit of everything: therapeutic massages (300,000$), detox, Reiki sessions (250,000$) & natural beauty treatments (steam bath 150,000$). The snack bar is brightly painted & nicely decorated, with a shaded outside seating area and is a handy rest stop for an ice cream, juice or hot dog. Owner Cristina Dória sells tropical flowers too.

MEDICAL FACILITIES

✚ **Consultorio Esperança** [off map, 108 B1] Carvalho Campo de Milho; m 990 3212; e efcarvalho1@live.co.pt. Dr Carvalho, who speaks French & Spanish, was recommended to me by several expats. Her surgery is signposted on the road out to the north, past the Cape Verdean Cultural Centre just over the brow of the hill.

✚ **Dr Moris** [off map, 108 D4 Embaixada da França; m 990 4826; e moris.ganev@undp.org. Originally from Bulgaria, this friendly GP works out of the French Embassy, which sponsors the consultations so you only pay 100,000$.

✚ **Hospital** [off map, 108 B1] Dr Ayres Menezes Bairro Hospital; ✆222 1222. In an emergency, 24hr service is given by the hospital up on Hospital Hill. In 2007, a brand-new 24hr A&E (*banco d'urgência*) unit with X-ray, plastercast & surgery services opened. Treatment at this is free. Don't phone for an ambulance, which can take a while; it's best to get the injured person straight here. In the extremely unlikely event of being bitten by the black cobra, this is where the anti-venom should be held (see page 71). The hospital is named after Dr Ayres Menezes (1894–1965), son of the island's first black doctor & anti-colonial activist.

✚ **Mediclinica** [off map, 108 B1] Praia Lagarto, opposite the pontoon; m 983 2551. This clinic groups together several Cuban doctors.

✚ **Policlínica Água-Grande** [113 C3] Av Kwame Nkrumah; ✆222 7258, 222 1991, 222 1212, Taiwanese Medical Mission ✆222 7766, 222 4074, 222 4075, 222 7084; e missmedicardis@cstome.net. For non-urgent general medical services, from dentistry to gynaecology, this central *policlinic* is preferable to the hospital – despite stray dogs wandering in & out. Appointments can be made by turning up at reception around 14.00. A list of treatments with prices is displayed, & there is an on-site pharmacy, where medicines with a prescription are cheap. The Policlínica is also a good bet if you want an English-speaking medic or dentist, as the Taiwanese medical mission, Missão Médica Taiwan, is based here. *Análises* of blood/urine/stool are cheap here, about 10,000$, but make sure you check your slip as you might have to hand in your urine sample, for instance, at 07.00 the next day. Sterile containers are not always available, so try the pharmacies or, as a last resort, the Taiwan mission's official headquarters towards the airport.

PHARMACIES The pharmacies take it in turn to open at night. The cheapest, with queues, is the Armazém de Medicamentos on Rua Patrice Lumumba.

✚ **Farmácia Cabral** [113 B2] Rua Moçambique; ✆222 2084. Old-fashioned pharmacy housed in a recently repainted pink-&-blue corner building. Look for the black-&-white BAYER sign. The Cuban GP who works here is called Doutora Montes.

A CONSULTATION WITH A TRADITIONAL HEALER

If you would like to do as the locals do, go to see a herbalist practising *medicina tradicional*. Experienced herbalist and bone-setter Mestre Horatio works from his home, a herb garden with aloe vera and other medicinal plants at the back, and treats stomach infections and ulcers, hepatitis B, haemorrhoids, and many orthopaedic cases. When I visited, one patient was having heated drinking glasses applied over judicious cuts around the knee, to suck out the 'bad' blood from the haematoma suffered during a fall. The blood gradually congealed in the glass, and afterwards, the cuts looked amazingly neat and didn't bleed. Meanwhile, another patient, a young woman, was having her knee reset, wailing and screaming; nothing for the faint-hearted. I came away with free advice for travel bug diarrhoea: to buy a certain herb called *barbosa*. Mestre Horatio's speciality concoction, however, is an aphrodisiac that also fights intestinal infections. The Mestre's claims of successful cancer treatment might ring hollow to Western ears, but his patient agreed that bone-setting works much faster than hospital treatment. Many patients come to Mestre Horácio with conditions that have not improved with conventional medicine (as happens in the West); others with serious diseases have to wait too long to go to hospital. To get to Mestre Horácio's house, take the Água Porca road parallel to Rua 3 de Fevereiro, turn right at a shoemaker's shack in front of the *prédio* (a taller stone-built house), and follow the dirt track about 200m down. Look for a ramp on your left; most people will be able to direct you. Mestre Horácio is a Christian, '*do livro*' ('of the book', the Bible), not a traditional healer but, if you're interested, it should not be too difficult to find a *stlijon* if you ask around.

Mestre Horácio Riboque; m 993 0365; ☉ 09.00–16.00 Mon–Fri

✚ **Farmácia Epifánia de Franca** [113 B2] Rua de Angola; m 991 4050; ☉ 08.00–20.00 daily. Well-stocked pharmacy in a beautiful white colonial building. Pharmacist Senhor Damião is very friendly & will do his best to summon some English.

✚ **Farmácia Pantufo** South along the coast, near the church (ask for directions), Pantufo; ☏ 222 7638; ☉ 08.00–12.30 & 15.00–17.30 Mon–Fri, 08.00–13.00 Sat. The best-stocked pharmacy in town I'd say, even if it's not exactly in town, but in the suburb/fishing village of Pantufo. It stocks Cégripe, which is a miracle flu fighter (€240,000), or at least the Portuguese swear by it. You can order medication that isn't in stock, which makes a nice surprise to the frequent response of *não temos* (we don't have it) or *esgotado* (out of stock), though it will take a few days to come in. It also sells the morning-after pill, but as with most things in STP, it is wise to phone ahead to check.

MONEY

Banks A dozen banks cluster around Praça da Independência. The Banco International de São Tomé and Príncipe (BISTP) is the most reliable. With your Visa, MasterCard or Eurocard (both debit and credit cards) you can arrange a money transfer (cash advance) in ten minutes. Bring your passport. Travellers' cheques are cashed too, if with a bit of reluctance. Queues can get long. Do check your pile of dobras carefully as in the rush currencies can get confused, and once I found a 5,000$ note in between a wad of 50,000$ notes. BISTP can check banknotes for you, too. In recent years, there was a problem with fake banknotes, in particular

US$100 and notes of €5 and €50, handed out on occasion even at reputable places. I once heard about an American traveller who was given some fake notes at one bank and then had several notes refused at the airport when he needed to pay his departure tax. New security measures have now curbed the problem somewhat.

$ Banco Equador [113 B2] Rua de Moçambique 3B; ✆ 224 1950; e be@bancoequador.st; www. bancoequador.st; ☉ 08.00–15.00 Mon–Fri & 08.30–12.30 Sat, other branches have reduced hours.
$ Banco International de São Tomé and Príncipe (BISTP) [108 E3] Praça da Independência; ✆ 224 3100, 224 3108; www.bistp. stp; ☉ 07.45–15.00 Mon–Fri.
$ Ecobank [113 A1] Travessia do Pelourinho,

opposite INDUS; ✆ 222 2141, 222 5002; e ecobankstp@cstome.net; www.ecobank.com; ☉ 07.30–15.30 Mon–Fri, 08.00–noon Sat. Santomean branch of Togo-based pan-African bank with excellent connections for African transactions & with agencies in more than 20 countries on the continent. At the moment, the cash mashine dispenses dobras only, unfortunately, & only to account holders. More services are planned.

Money changers Money changing is tolerated and there are many money changers, *cambistas*, in the city touting for business (US$/€) on the corners of central roads and elsewhere in the centre of São Tomé town. One who is very friendly and reliable is **Gualter** (m *994 4472*), who has a ready smile despite his limp. If you don't want their services, just say '*Ja está*' ('already done') or '*Não preciso, obrigado/a*', 'I don't need it, thanks'. The rates are more advantageous than those at the bank, but be aware of the current exchange rate and count the notes that you are given. You will get a low rate if you change small US$ notes as the money changers have to pay a charge for banking them. If you have a chequing account with BISTP and run out of money at the weekend, most money lenders can advance you money against a personal cheque, but they will ask for about 20% commission. If you are looking to change larger sums, ask around and people will come to your hotel.

Wire transfers If you don't have access to a Visa or MasterCard account and need to have money wired quickly, there are **Western Union** (*www.westernunion. com*) services at Banco Equador and Ecobank. This only costs the sender.

Cashback My personal hot tip is to take your credit card to Pestana Ocean Resort (see page 115). Even non-residents may use their cashback service, which is direct and doesn't go through REUNICRE, avoiding the common embarrassments of non-authorised cards. For this to be possible, they have to have money in the till (*caixa*), which means early evening is a good time; you can ring in advance to check the situation. The fee was about €10 when I last used it, and you don't even need to bring your passport. Be polite, as this service is a courtesy for non-residents.

POLICE To report a crime, the relevant station in São Tomé is the **Polícia de Investigaçao Criminal (PIC)** [108 B3] (*Av Conceiçao*; ✆ *222 1622*; ☉ *24hrs daily*), next to Residencial Baía. The police service is being reformed, but, for the time being, you will struggle even to get a crime report for your insurance company. Bring your passport and somebody who speaks Portuguese and stress that you will be leaving soon. Be prepared to answer all the questions (name of father and mother, number of children), but don't agree for the paperwork to be sent to your home address; it's not going to happen. In the case of my stolen phone, it was retrieved months afterwards by a friend, having been sold on six times. In case of emergency, call ✆ 113; fire service ✆ 112.

POSTAL AND COURIER SERVICES The **central post office** [108 E2] (*www.correios-stp.st*; ⊕ *07.00–noon & 14.00–17.00 Mon–Fri*) on the Marginal, next to the tourist information, offers a whole range of services and has a separate room with a good selection of postcards for sale, many of them of the birds of the islands. You can also buy quite beautiful postage stamps, some with STP wildlife, others wildly inappropriate, featuring Lady Di or huskies. There is a postbox, *caixa de correio*, outside. The smaller post office (⊕ *07.30–noon & 14.00–16.30 Mon–Fri*), on Rua Soldato Paulo Ferreira has recently been refurbished and is a bit more central. The friendly lady working there also sells a few postcards and envelopes alongside stamps, but there is no postbox outside.

Postcards to Europe cost 22,000$, to the rest of the world 25,000$, but sometimes if they don't have the right postage (as happened to me on Príncipe), you might have to pay 25,000$ anyway, even only to Europe. Club Santana and the bigger hotels will take care of your mail.

For urgent mailings or valuable documents, **courier** DHL has a representation in the Mistral Voyages office [108 B2] (☏ *222 3344*; m *990 4050*; ⊕ *07.30–noon & 14.00–16.00 Mon–Fri*). Expect to pay around €40 for sending a document to Europe. What locals and expats do, however, is to use a carrier (*portador*), a person they trust who is travelling back to Lisbon. These things are even arranged via social media sites such as Facebook these days.

TRANSLATIONS AND INTERPRETING
Flatela 012B Bairro Dolores; m 991 3126; e flatela@flatela.com; www.flatela.com. Agency offering all combinations of languages. Translation rates start at €0.04 per word.

WHAT TO SEE AND DO

CATHEDRAL [113 C2] (*Lg Água Grande;* ☏ *222 2209;* ⊕ *05.30–10.00 & 15.00–19.00 Tue–Sun, 05.30–07.30 & 15.00–20.00 Mon; Mass Sun 06.00–07.30, 10.00–11.30 & 17.30–19.15*) Who would have thought that one of sub-Saharan Africa's oldest cathedrals was the **Santa Sé** here in São Tomé? Across from the presidential palace, Nossa Senhora da Graça (Our Lady of Grace) was built and rebuilt over the course of 400 years, from 1576 to 1958. The impressive cathedral occupies the dividing line between the business part of the city and the administrative part. The story of its construction is the story of São Tomé itself.

In 1493, Álvaro de Caminha, the island's third feudal lord, had a stone and quick-lime chapel built on the site of the present cathedral. Dedicated to the Virgin Mary – maybe as a thank you for not succumbing to malaria as the first settlers had ten years before – it was finished in 1499, only to be destroyed when pirates sacked the town. Rebuilt in 1505, the new Avé-Maria church was elevated to the status of *Sé*, 'cathedral', for the newly created Diocese of São Tomé and Príncipe in 1534, and renamed Nossa Senhora da Graça. A new Dutch/French incursion in 1562 destroyed the building, and construction of the current cathedral did not start until 1576, by orders of the pious Portuguese king, Dom Sebastião (1557–78), when the whole building was moved closer to the river. When Portugal and its territories fell under Spanish rule in 1580, work carried on, but renewed invasions in 1599 left the cathedral badly damaged. This was the beginning of the legends that have attached themselves to the cathedral over the years, and one told that if the cathedral was ever finished, the island would sink below the waves. The first mixed-race marriages in sub-Saharan Africa were held here, as members of the different ethnic groups on the island – *forros*, *mulattos* and colonials – carried on mixing. In

3

1814, the frontispiece and the roof fell in. In 1937, the towers were raised by another 10m, and raised again in 1952.The cathedral was only completed in 1958.

Today, the spacious interior has a beautiful frieze of simple **blue-and-white tiles** (1970); one of the 200-year-old originals is kept in the sacristy, together with the valuable ivory crucifixes and silver liturgical instruments. Ask for Padre Lionel and if he is around, he will be happy to show you. More blue-and-white *azulejos* form a large **fresco of the Holy Trinity** above the main altar. It is said that under the altar lie the (transferred) bones of Ana de Chaves, a local noblewoman who died in 1566, giving her name to the bay. To the right, a **statue of St Thomas** holds a palm frond, a symbol of martyrdom. The stained-glass windows are recent, as are the Stations of the Cross in bas-relief which come from Madrid, and the paintings of the Annunciation and the Sacred Heart of Jesus, from Braga in Portugal (1950s). At the back of the cathedral, the marble baptismal font is kept behind an Art Nouveau-style grill.

The diocese's bishop, the Portuguese Reverend Dom Manuel António Mendes dos Santos, worked as a missionary on the islands in the 1990s. The cathedral's feast day is 24 March or the following Sunday. Friendly custodian Hilário Mapanga (m *991 9370*), of Caboverdian descent, understands a bit of French.

CLAUDIO CORALLO CHOCOLATE FACTORY [108 B2] (*Av Marginal 978;* ❜ *222 2236;* m *981 5284 (Nicola), 990 6130 (Claudio Corallo); www.claudiocorallo.com*) Fabulous in-depth tasting sessions of what has been called 'the best chocolate in the world' are available here on the days before international flights, just after 16.30 when production stops. Forty years of passion and care about the exact calibration of the ingredients are much in evidence here, and new flavours and new products are continually being developed. The slight, grey-haired, Italian Claudio is passionate about providing a counterpoint to 'sick' industrial chocolate, where the beans are roasted to cinders, with the purest chocolate experience from his Terreiro Velho plantation on Príncipe (see page 202).

Buy your ticket (*bilhete* or *senha*) on the day, at around 15.00 or 15.30. You can only book the tastings at the factory, not through the agencies and it is not possible to ring and make a reservation by phone. The 100,000$ price of entry is discounted from what you buy – and you'd have to have an iron will not to buy anything. Tastings only really happen if Signore Corallo is here and not on his Príncipe plantation, for instance. However, you can contact Nicola to see if an individual tour can be arranged outside the usual times, at a cost of €5 (which can be set against chocolate purchases, too). If you want to buy chocolate on a day the factory is not open for tours, check at the gate with the *segurança* if you can buy chocolate anyway (*faz favor, para comprar chocolate?*).

The quality of the experience depends a bit on whether you're with a huge group or with a handful of people. In the latter case you might end up sipping 77%-proof cocoa *aguardente* from a bowl in a communal experience, smacking your lips to avoid burning your throat and trying improbable delicacies such as cocoa anchovy paste. Note that Claudio has little English, so a member of the group usually translates.

The chocolate offered for sale is not actually cheaper than at the supermarket, but is certainly lower in price than at the airport, and it is kept in better conditions.

MARKET The *Mercado Grande* [113 A2] is held in and around the large yellow **Mercado Municipal** building plastered with posters on the Taxi Square. Negotiating the narrow walkways between pyramids of limes, tomatoes, charcoal, spices, chillis, garlic and onions, and stacks of aromatic herbs, tourists will often be urged to look at a particular vendor's produce with cries of '*Amiiiigo/a!*' or

'*Monsieur/Madame!*'. Agencies such as Mistral offer a tour of the market as part of their half-day exploration of São Tomé town, but the best way to see it is to come when you actually have some shopping to do, as goods are very cheap, and the experience is a lot more fun. Buying small quantities can be difficult, and it helps if you know roughly what the prices of the produce are (see page 77) and then you can just offer the 1,000 or 2,000 dobra coins, *moeda*, rather than handing over a large note and then fighting for your change or being handed a large clutch of bananas or such like that you didn't want. If you see a vendor pulling her ear it means 'it's good!' Also on sale are very nice sugary doughnuts, buttered corn bread, *milho*, cakes, etc.

The **Mercado Novo** [113 A2], officially Côcô-Côcô, located in a yellow market hall on Avenida Giovany was built with Taiwanese money and inaugurated in 2007. It has improved hygiene conditions. Fish is landed on **Praia Brazil**, right opposite the former Feira do Ponto market. Wandering amongst the women offering fish, charcoal, rice, etc, and pulling sailfish by their long bills along the (pretty dirty) foreshore is interesting, but not exactly one of the highlights of São Tomé. From early in the day, palm wine is drunk from plastic cups, and in the afternoon inebriated market traders line the Marginal celebrating the end of the working day.

NATIONAL MUSEUM [108 F1] (*Museu Nacional; Av 12 de Julho;* \222 1874; ☉ *08.00–noon & 14.00–16.00 Mon–Fri, 08.00–13.00 Sat; admission 500$ locals, 5,000$/€2 tourists*) A must if you have any time in the city. Since 1975, the Museu Nacional has been housed in the striking cream-coloured former fort of St Sebastian, built by the Portuguese in 1576 on this strategic point to guard against the frequent attacks on the island by the French and the Dutch. Looking from the museum entrance at the tall statues of the Portuguese seafarers who discovered the archipelago, Pedro Escobar is the one on the right, with the Prince Ironheart haircut. Alongside is the island's first administrator (1485–90), nobleman João de Paiva, and João de Santarém. The statues were temporarily dismantled after independence. Opposite the entrance is a **chapel** dedicated to the Roman martyr and favourite Portuguese saint, Sebastian, in honour of the pious Portuguese king, Dom Sebastião (1557–78), who had this fort built. As you enter the museum itself, look up; through this opening hot oil used to be released on to enemies' heads. The museum office to the left as you come in sells a handful of postcards. No photography is allowed inside the museum. The current director's name is Ernesto Lima.

A declaration by the country's first president, Manuel Pinto da Costa, reminds visitors of the tragic history of human enslavement, and items from five centuries of Portuguese colonialism and 30 years of independence are spread over two storeys. The few explanations are, unfortunately, only in Portuguese. You have to visit with a guide, who might speak French, less so English. If you can arrange an outside translator/guide (through Navetur or Mistral agencies, for instance), your experience will be greatly enhanced, as a lot of the objects will mean very little otherwise.

The **first room**, displaying sacred art and liturgical garments, illustrates the continued presence of the church during the two centuries of decline between the sugarcane cycle in the 16th century and the beginning of the coffee/cocoa cycles in the 19th century. The niche between rooms one and two has a sandstone sculpture of the Virgin and Jesus with Sant'Ana, the island's female patron saint.

Also on display is a collection of impressive **dark-wood furniture** in the Indo-Portuguese style, originating from the pharmacy at Bombaim plantation. The **agriculture room**, dedicated to coffee and cocoa cultivation, has portraits of João Baptista da Silva, who introduced coffee to Príncipe in 1800. Sadly, however, visitors no longer get to see the bones of Brazilian-born João Maria de Sousa e Almeida, who first brought cocoa to the islands in around 1820, which were kept in a wooden casket. A black-and-white photograph shows Santomeans' joy at the nationalisation of the plantations in the autumn of 1975. The **turtle room** has a lot of information on São Tomé and Príncipe's marine turtles, with ping pong balls not doing such a bad job representing turtle eggs. There is also a life-size reproduction of an *ambulância* leatherback turtle.

There are **great views** out to sea and down to Praia Museu from the parapet running around the top.

PRESIDENTIAL PALACE [113 D2] (*Palacio do Povo; Av da Independência;* ℡ 222 1143) The guards of the impressive 'Pink Palace' – the former governor's palace from the more recent colonial past – wear impassive faces, and if they feel you are coming too close to the office of the President of the Republic they will make it clear that you should keep your distance. Alternatively, they have been known, in the unprofessional way of many Santomean officials, to whistle at women walking past on their own. Despite its official name of 'the People's Palace', the guards will try everything to stop you from taking photographs of the building – probably a security hangover from the military coups of the none-too-distant past.

CACAU [108 E2] (*Largo das Alfândegas;* ℡ 222 262; m 984 2473; e info@ cacaucultural.com; www.cacaucultural.com). Known by its initials (Casa das Artes, da Criação, Ambiente e Utopias) and housed in a former public works storehouse, the new venture of gastro-artistic maverick and cultural councillor João Carlos Silva (JCS) is an exhibition space, café, bar and restaurant. Unless there is an arts Bienal going on, for instance, various shops here sell excellent crafts such as horn jewellery, prints, irresistible bookshelf supports in the shape of egrets or porcelain rose, and little stools. There are also edible souvenirs produced at JCS's plantation, or a collection of René Tavares's beautiful illustrations on the tchiloli theatre. Come here on a Wednesday for a jam session or Thursday to join expats and travellers for the *quinta tradicional* Grand Buffet (€15) allowing you to try most of the island's specialities (enough of them vegetarian to make it worth your while if you don't eat fish or meat). They will often show a fascinating black-and-white documentary film on plantation life.

ONE-DAY WALKING TOUR Start your day with a coffee and a pastry on the **Passante** terrace next to the Miramar Hotel. Walk along the seafront towards the centre, between almond trees, past the secondary school and the National Radio to the **National Museum** at the fortress of São Sebastião, and spend a couple of hours discovering the history of the country through the collections of paintings, photographs and sculptures. From the battlements, there are fine views out to sea. Carry on along the seafront, pick up some colourful stamps at the post office (postcards are sold next door), sort out your ticket to Príncipe at STP Airways if you're planning a trip to the sister island, and take the small road to the left of the post office up to **Praça da Cultura** ('Culture Square'), the hub of Santomean cultural activity and home to the Mediateca, the Historical Archive and the National Library. Look out for the giant breadfruit outside the library, and the fictitious likeness of Rei Amador, the 'slave king' who in the late 16th century led the most successful revolt against the exploitative plantation economy, outside the Archive. Once you've done the round of the square, turn into the **Parque Popular**, where a collection of brightly painted snack sheds surround an artificial lake and a children's playground. Stop here for an inexpensive lunch (for instance, at the *barraca* number 24).

Coming back out of the Parque Popular entrance, take the second road to the right, broad Avenida da Independência. After a few hundred metres, to your left, a marquee signals the light-blue Residencial Avenida, with its shady bamboo bar that is also a good place for a post-lunch coffee stop. Coming out of the bar, turn left to carry on along the Avenida da Independência again, and head for the nearby **Cathedral** where you can admire the frieze of blue-and-white Portuguese tiles and the statue of St Thomas to the right of the altar. On exiting, try your luck taking a snap of the pink **Presidential Palace** before the guards warn you off. The fairly filthy canal here is where the Água Grande, 'big water' (Santomeans often call rivers just *água*), runs into the sea; Água Grande gave its name to the capital district. The source of the river is near the Nova Moca plantation up in the hills.

Carry on along the seafront to reach, very soon, **Independence Square**, where in 1975 independence was proclaimed. Every 11–12 July the square is the focus of Independence Day celebrations, and after musical and Danço Congo performances on the night of the 11th the president enters at midnight, accompanied by a torch-lit parade that comes from Batepá (see page 158), and makes a rousing speech. Out in the bay, it's difficult to tell which of the ships are picturesque wrecks left to die, and which are tug boats out on harbour business. Pick up some jackfruit – prepared in a bag, if you're feeling lazy – from the fruitselling 'amigas' on the square.

Amongst the banks clustered around the square, the splendid white colonial building across from the BISTP (the important one for travellers, see page 130) is the country's central bank BCSTP, which in the late 1990s was implicated in fraud, embezzlement and other assorted scandals marring the country's reputation. Take Rua de Angola towards the brightly painted colonial houses surrounding **Praça Amizade**. Turn left, left again and then right to reach Rua Soldado Paulo Ferreira, one of the main thoroughfares. This will lead you to the **Praça dos Taxis** or 'Taxi Square', where hundreds of yellow taxis vie for business. Put your camera away and spend some time wandering around the fruit and vegetables, spices, herbs and other wares displayed inside the yellow **central market** and, if you're hungry, grab a buttered *broa* corn roll, a *banana madura* or an *açucarinha* sweet to go (have small change ready). Rejoin the Marginal coast road passing Conceiçao and, turning left, carry on along Praia Brazil, where the fish is landed around midday. A bit further along, the chapel of **São Pedro** was built in the early 1960s, its sail design homage to St Peter, the patron saint of fishermen. Inside, you can see two statues: one of St Thomas, the second, smaller, of St Laurent, patron saint of Príncipe (with Santo António). Senhor Deti who has been looking after the chapel since 1991, might well ask you for a contribution for a candle.

Further along, to your left, look out for the **Sporting Club**, set slightly back from the Marginal. This pretty, green colonial building was a focus for the Santomense drive for independence. Under cover of a football club founded in 1940 (Sporting is the name of one of the most famous clubs in Lisbon, with green kit), nationalists met and schemed resistance against the colonial government. Reward yourself with a beer and the catch of the day at the famous 'blue container' snack shack if it is open, or catch a motortaxi to CACAU for a local snack, to take advantage of the fastest internet connection in town, and to shop for some crafts.

3

4

The North and Northwest

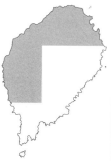

On the northern coastal strip, some of the best beaches on the island lie within 30 minutes' drive from the capital, and the relatively flat coast road makes this good terrain for biking. Past the town of Guadalupe the real savannah landscape begins, with dry open plains dotted with small baobab trees, their branches reaching for the sky, their distinctive stems dangling downwards. This area is home to plentiful birdlife, many introduced by settlers, such as the conspicuous black-winged red bishop, but also endemics like Newton's yellow-breasted sunbird and the São Tomé prinia. Past Neves, the landscape changes again, as the road, lined by waterfalls in the wet season, leads past black basalt beaches.

HIGHLIGHTS

Go shell-hunting at Praia das Conchas, snorkelling at Lagoa Azul and swimming at Praia dos Tamarindos. Drive the winding coast road through the baobab and tamarind savannah, stopping for a crab lunch in Neves, until you hit the end of the road – and maybe explore even further. Admire the archipelago's most impressive plantation, Agostinho Neto, and hit the roof of the archipelago on a two-day climb up the Pico de São Tomé.

GETTING AROUND

The northern road to Neves from the capital is well served by yellow **taxis**; a shared one-way ride costs 25,000$ and takes about an hour. You can ask to be dropped off anywhere *en route*.

NORTHERN BEACHES

Due to a large fishing village here, the vast **Praia Micoló** turtle beach is unfortunately pretty dirty these days, but, as it's served by yellow taxis from the capital, it makes a good starting point for **beach-hopping** along the coast, swimming, or looking for sea and shore birds, starting with the palm swifts building their nests in the coconut palms. You can pick up a picnic lunch at the village market. The next beach along, **Fernão Dias**, holds special significance for the Santomean collective memory and the independence movement, as during the repression of the 1953 insurrection (see page 18) there was a labour camp here, and the bodies of killed *forros* were dumped into the sea from the pier. Other prisoners were shackled together and forced to fetch sand for construction, or, in a pointless, humiliating exercise called 'emptying the sea', had to collect seawater in a pail on their heads and empty it on to the beach. For many year son the night of the **2–3 February**, traditional music was played, and the *puitá* was danced, and the events of those days were re-told by storytellers in

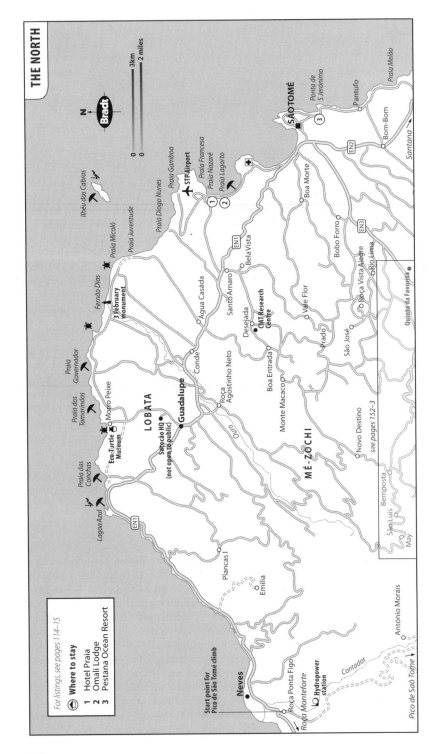

0 3km
0 2 miles

N

For listings, see pages 114–15

Where to stay
1 Hotel Praia
2 Omali Lodge
3 Pestana Ocean Resort

Ilhéu das Cabras

Praia Micoló
Praia Juventude
Praia Diogo Nunes
Praia Gamboa

STP Airport
Praia Francesa
Praia Nazaré
Praia Lagarto

SÃO TOMÉ
Ponta de S Jerónimo
Pantufo
Praia Melão

Bom-Bom
Santana

EN2

Fernão Dias
3 February monument

Praia Governador

Praia dos Tamarindos
Morro Peixe

LOBATA

Praia das Conchas

Eco-Turtle Museum
Sotecão HQ (not open to public)

Guadalupe

Lagoa Azul

EN1

Agua Casada

Conde

Roça Agostinho Neto

Santo Amaro
Bela Vista
EN1

CIAT Research Centre
Desejada

Boa Morte

Vale Flor
Prado
Bobo Forro
EN3

Boa Entrada
Monte Macaco

São José
Roça Vista Alegre
Rio Lima

Novo Destino

MÉ-ZOCHI

Quinta da Favorita

see pages 152–3

Outro

Plancas I

Emília

Bemposta
São Luís
May

Start point for Pico de São Tomé climb

Neves

Roça Ponta Figo
Roça Monteforte
Hydropower station

Contador

António Morais

Pico de São Tomé

commemoration (*soiá*). The next day, a procession of high-school pupils marched from the capital, wreaths were laid and speeches made. Fernão Dias was chosen as the potential site for the deep-water port that would have been a central feature of the Free Trading Zone, a project for the area that was subsequently abandoned.

Visible out to sea from the coast, **Ilhéu das Cabras** is geologically the oldest part of the archipelago. Boat, snorkelling and diving trips (see page 89), and possibly kayak excursions, go out to 'Goat Island'.

Through the sand-dredging operation alongside, the small **Praia Governador** has lost a lot of the appeal that made Portuguese author Miguel Tavares use it for some central scenes in his bestselling *Equador* novel (see page 43), but there is good shell-hunting next to the sand-digging machinery. The next proper beach along, **Praia dos Tamarindos**, is one of the best on the island, fringed by tamarinds, an indigenous African tree with edible if acidic fruit and high-quality wood used in cabinet-making and joinery; the leaves are cooked to expulse intestinal parasites. Unless you're unlucky and a cluster of jeeps from the capital descend on it, this is a quiet and clean stretch of white sand. Herons and egrets like to sit in the tree tops. It is only the area around the stagnant water to one side that is fairly littered; I once spent a lot of time stalking a green-backed heron with my camera, but couldn't get a frame without a beer bottle floating in front of it. **Praia Morro Peixe** is OK for swimming, though a bit close to the village (don't leave your mobile phone on the beach). Also exercise caution on Tras Morro Beach; locals rightly advise not to go on your own and there have been thefts. To get to Morro Peixe from the main coast road, turn right at the big monument at the end of Guadalupe. (You will pass the headquarters of **Satocão** on your left, the Swiss cocoa corporation that is currently revitalising cocoa plantations all around the island. Just before the village, unmarked turn-offs to the right lead to Praia dos Tamarindos island. Morro Peixe is a turtle beach, and **Casa Tatô**, an **ecomuseum** dedicated to the marine turtles nesting on this strip of coast, was inaugurated in 2007 right at the beachfront. For information on visiting or taking part in turtle patrols (see page 12), ask for Hipólito Lima (m *991 3792*), or contact the MARAPA conservation NGO in the capital (see pages 113–14). City-based co-ordinator Bastien speaks English. Accompanying the release of hatchlings (*filhotes*) costs €5, as does a trip looking for egg-laying turtles. The activities usually run September to April. Simple meals are served, too; phone Hipólito on the above number. You can volunteer here for a month or so; it's a rewarding experience, even if conditions are very basic.

Morro Peixe is also the main beach for MARAPA's **whale-watching trips** and you need to book in advance. Another good swimming beach is the next one along, **Praia das Conchas**, reached from the main road by taking a right turn at a large baobab tree. Just ten minutes rummaging between the cracks in the rocks at the end of the beach shows you why this beach is called 'shell beach', as it yields broken shells in various colours, including pink, yellow and red. At the weekend, it can get a bit crowded. Prominent politician Patrice Trovoada has a house here, bought off another former president, Fradique de Menezes.

About 30 minutes' drive from the capital, **Lagoa Azul** ('blue lagoon'), surrounded by baobab trees and fossilised corals, is a favourite spot with visitors; you can see its turquoise waters peeking out as you approach on the coast road. The clear water and shallow gradient make Lagoa Azul a great snorkelling spot, especially over on the right-hand side of the lagoon. Local kids will love trying out your snorkelling mask if you let them, and take you up to the little outcrop to the left to play in the branches of the baobab. Sadly, Lagoa Azul's popularity has been attracting muggers recently, and tourist cars, left unattended during snorkelling sessions, have been broken into. The tourist authorities are now planning to place security guards there.

GUADALUPE TOWN

The capital of the Lobata district, with some 6,000 inhabitants, is said to be the most Catholic town in the country. The pretty church, **Nossa Senhora da Guadalupe**, completely rebuilt in 1939 and containing statues of St Joseph and St Benedict flanking one of Our Lady, is worth a visit. The key is held by the Franciscan sisters (❨ *223 1124*), based at a large house at the entrance of town on the left, opposite the New Apostolic church. Home to the dance company Leoninos, Guadalupe is a stronghold of the MLSTP party (see page 19). The city made huge headlines in 2011 when hysteria about 'spirits' in the secondary school resulted in one death – of the faith healer who died at the climax of his Djambi trance – and resulted in the closure of the school for six months.

Half way to Guadalupe, consider turning off towards Madalena to have a look around the **Boa Entrada** plantation with its Art Nouveau veranda.

WHERE TO STAY

Celvas Residencial (10 rooms, 1 suite) Main road; m 993 5849, 991 3417. Easily overlooked (marked only by a painted knife & fork & the name in filigree metal above the entrance), this pleasant guesthouse with restaurant has

rooms between €35 & €50, & a family suite. Friendly & amenable owners Celeste & Vasco put their first names together to name their venture. B/fasts are lovely, with good coffee, guava jam, cheese & scambled egg. You can arrange for one of

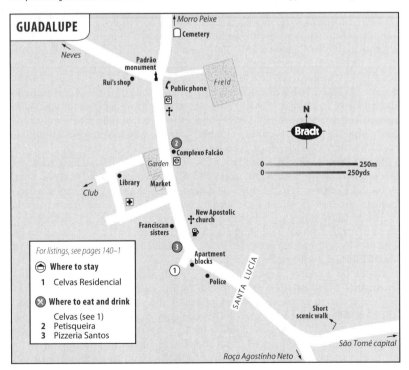

GUADALUPE

↑ *Morro Peixe*
☐ Cemetery

Neves

Padrão monument

Rui's shop
☏ Public phone

Field

☖
✝

N

Bradt

❷
● Complexo Falcão
☖

Garden

0 ——————— 250m
0 ——————— 250yds

Library   Market
Club
✚

New Apostolic
✝ church
Franciscan ●
sisters

❸
Apartment
blocks
❶
Police

SANTA LUCIA

Short
scenic walk

São Tomé capital

Roça Agostinho Neto

For listings, see pages 140–1
⊖ **Where to stay**
1   Celvas Residencial

⊗ **Where to eat and drink**
    Celvas (see 1)
2   Petisqueira
3   Pizzeria Santos

their employees, kind & dynamic Nani, who lives on the Agostinho Neto plantation nearby, to act as a guide (starting from €10). At the time of writing Wi-Fi was still slow, 'swimming instead of surfing', so check when booking. Otherwise, the street has plenty of internet options. When you go out at night, make sure you have the contact number of the owner in case the door is shut & the guard asleep. Bring earplugs as the local dogs have fierce barking parties. **$$$**

✗ WHERE TO EAT, DRINK AND DANCE Pick up something from the **market** on the main road in the centre of town or the little **shop** run by Senhor Vera Cruz's wife, on the left-hand side of the road just after the monument marking the turn-off to Morro Peixe. The famous Paladar restaurant is shut, unfortunately, but a couple of new restaurants have recently opened.

✗ Celvas Main road. Attached to the guesthouse of the same name (see above) & a big addition to the island's gastronomic circuit – you just wouldn't expect such a place here. Fine local cooking, friendly service & large wine list, all under a shady canopy. The pet parrots might be munching on starfruit as you eat. Vegetarians can request a tofu dish or similar with a day's notice. Prices range from €12 *menu turístico* to €15 à la carte, for traditional dishes such as *calulú* with medicinal herbs, smoked fish or even wild crab. **$$$**

✗ Pizzeria Santos Main road, a couple of doors down from Celvas; m 980 5795; ⊕ 07.00–21.00 daily. Fresh pizzas with various toppings, 1 is enough to share. Santinho, the friendly owner, can take orders for a delicious banana cake, for instance, for the next day. Cakes cost 200,000$. **$$**

✗ Petisqueira Main road. Watch the Neves traffic go by, with some grilled fish or a plate of rice & beans. **$**

For entertainment, you have the **Complexo Falcão** on the main road and **Socorro club** (ask for directions) which is open Saturday and Sunday.

OTHER PRACTICALITIES
✚ First aid Área de saúde ☎ 223 1155. There's a 24hr *urgência* service at the back.

🖳 Internet There are various options along the main road, including Coleira Net (Main road; ⊕ 09.00–20.00; 10,000$/hr, 20,000$/3hrs), & Kiosque do Terry & Loja Padrão (⊕ 07.00–22.00 daily. Wi-Fi works with so-called *senhas*, paper slips issued by the CST telecommunications company, although they might not always be available. Also, while Guadalupe feels like internet café central, take opening hours with a pinch of salt.

Miscellaneous Complexo Falcão sells a bit of everything, including phone top-ups, etc. Some Fri & Sat nights local heroes, the Sangazuza band, might be playing.

Police/Polícia Main road; ☎ 223 1168

WHAT TO SEE AND DO
Roça Agostinho Neto The biggest (3,380ha) and most impressive plantation on São Tomé might seem familiar as it features on the back of the 5,000$ note. Built in typical Portuguese colonial style, this plantation was once one of the biggest producers of cocoa, alongside bananas, wood, coffee and copra. Originally called Rio do Ouro ('golden river'), the plantation was renamed Agostinho Neto in 1979 after the first Angolan president and poet (1922–79) to celebrate the political, military and financial help his government gave to the young republic; his bust still greets visitors on arrival. Most of the people living here are descendants of Cape Verdean contract labourers. Various tracks lead to the plantation off the main road: either take a left at an unmarked crossroads before you reach Guadalupe, or wait for the left-hand turn just after entering the town (look for a big panel with educational health drawings next to a pink shack).

On arrival you might be surrounded by a flurry of children and/or adults asking for money or a present as you ascend the sweeping avenue up to the imposing

hospital. Following the old railway tracks up, the drive is lined with offices and workshops once used by the colonial administration. The government is planning to restore the hospital, unused for the past dozen years, and maybe turn it into a campus for São Tomé's new private university. From the upstairs window you get a sweeping view of the plantation. Behind the hospital are the former kitchen quarters and the mortuary. The key to the pretty **chapel** beside the hospital, over 200 years old, is held by Dona Fatima, who lives in a blue house with the number 35 on it, or a visit can be organised by Du, who lives two-thirds of the way up the big avenue in a light-blue house with the number 031 on it; he works as a *motoqueiro* and might be off somewhere. Nani from the Celvas guesthouse in town lives here and can show you around. He can also take you around the impressive botanical garden or to the **waterfall** (*cascata*) about a 30-minute walk away, which not many visitors take the time to explore. To stay at the *roça*, ask for Senhor Asunção; when I visited he was building a wooden house to receive tourists. The **botanical garden** is great for relaxing in the shade but as it now houses the provincial government administration, you have to pay to get in (a donation of 25,000$ per person, ask to be shown round). A few of the trees have labels, but it's better to bring or find a guide who knows about their medicinal properties and other uses. **CIAT** (Centro de Investigação Agronómica e Tecnológica) \ 222 3342. Situated on the road connecting Santo Amaro with Madalena, at the point where the road turns off to Boa Entrada (and Roça Monte Macaco), this agronomical research institution issues the export certificates for tropical flowers and cocoa/coffee plants (with 72 hours advance notice) and carries out microbiological research. Visits are best arranged in advance, ask for manager Jacob Monteverde. Navetur (see page 112) can also arrange a visit for you.

Hiking Coming from the capital, some 500m before you reach Guadalupe, a dirt track turns off to the right for a gentle 1–1½-hour hike up a hill, *morro Mu* or *Quim Quim*, to the telecommunications mast, with great views of Guadalupe and Agostinho Neto. The local name for this area is Canavial. Early on in the walk, after passing a field of sugarcane on your right, look out for an artisanal **aguardente production** operated by a friendly bunch of workers. Watch the sugarcane stems being squeezed through the metal rollers, the liquid distilled in a large cast-iron container and through a cooling tube, and buy the resulting clear alcoholic drink for a few hundred dobras. Bring a clean container. As you continue walking up, every now and then you'll see small edible orange fruit on the ground: *guégué*, the African grape.

Marked 'Muquinquin', the Canavial entrance is opposite the new clay-built houses that inspired the development at Praia Jalé but are still waiting to be inhabited; the first of them are already suffering damage. The local Roça Caldera supports five artesanal *aguardente* productions. I'm sure somebody can lead you to one; check with guide Nani at Celvas (see pages 140–1).

FROM GUADALUPE TO NEVES

The northern road winds along the coast, overlooking rocky beaches, and out to sea, wooden *pirogues* plough through the waves, while closer to the shore the occasional lone snorkel can be seen sticking out of the water. Taking a right turn-off from the main coast road (marked by a big almond tree) brings you to **Anambó**, where the first Portuguese explorers are thought to have landed in the late 15th century. The white stone pillar decorated with the Portuguese coat of

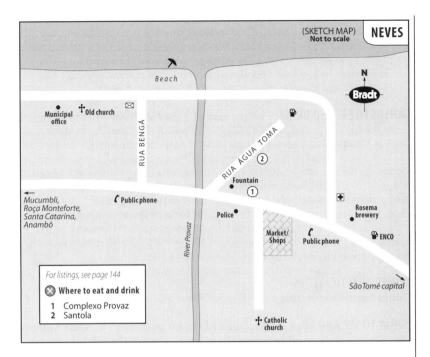

Beach

Municipal office

† Old church

RUA BENGÁ

N

Bradt

RUA AGUA TOMA

②

Fountain

①

Mucumbli,
Roça Monteforte,
Santa Catarina,
Anambô

☎ Public phone

Police

River Provaz

Market/
Shops

☎ Public phone

Rosema
brewery

ENCO

For listings, see page 144

⊗ **Where to eat and drink**

1   Complexo Provaz
2   Santola

São Tomé capital

† Catholic
church

arms and topped by a cross is a 1939 copy of the monument (*padrão*) that marked every Portuguese landfall since 1483. The monument stands on a square framed by almond trees, near the mouth of the river that the first settlers called *agua bom*, 'good water' (safe for drinking). In colonial times, Anambó was a popular place for society events such as tea on Friday afternoons, swimming, picnics and dancing. Mountain bikers can brave an old colonial road now in much disrepair, leading past the Água Sampaio waterfall to Neves; contact the Cycling Federation (see page 93). A proper seaside restaurant has opened here called **Mar e Sol** (m *990 3809*, $–$$), serving freshly grilled fish.

NEVES

Populated mainly by Angolares, this town has some 5,000 inhabitants and shelters the harbour where all diesel and petrol supplies come in by ship from Angola. One of the few factories in the country, the **Rosema brewery** (☎ *223 3158*) employs some 200 people in the production of Nacional beer. Up until the late 1950s, Neves was a whale-fishing port, with a Norwegian company processing 1,000 tons of oil out of 100 animals caught in the record year of 1946. In 2007, São Tomé and Príncipe drew the wrath of Greenpeace by expressing interest in a Japanese whale-hunting proposition.

The town's most famous daughter is Maria dos Ramos (1916–?), who was taken prisoner and deported to Príncipe with her Portuguese husband for protesting against the arbitrary injustices of the colonial government in the run-up to 1953 insurgency. Her daughter, Angela, still lives locally. Neves is also the home of the island's oldest and most famous **Danço Congo** ensemble, Aliança Nova (see page 46). The name comes from a tiny yellow ant with a painful bite, suggesting the frenetic quality of the dance. Try asking for Aliança Nova president, Senhor Urbano, who can probably tell you where to catch a performance.

The North and Northwest   NEVES

4

The hills above Neves are excellent **trekking country**, in particular because they are in a semi-arid zone. Roça Ponta Figo (see page 146) is a good starting point. Just before you get to the Ponta Figo turn (coming from the capital), crossing the Contador river, look out for a good early morning view of the Pico de São Tomé.

There are some places to stay not far outside Neves (see below).

✗ WHERE TO EAT AND DRINK Visit the **market** at the entrance to town as you arrive from the capital, or pick up something from one of the countless roadside stalls such as bread rolls, coconut or sugar sweets, corn on the cob, etc.

✗ Santola Rua Água Tóma; m 990 5562, 9953 811; ⏲ 10.00–22.00 daily. Famous restaurant serving huge red crabs (170,000$/kg) & other local dishes, such as *búzios do mar* (sea snails) or fish (70,000$). Downstairs is a little dingy; go upstairs to enjoy a bit of a breeze. The kids outside are only too happy to pose for pictures, but can also be quite cheeky. Coming from the capital, take a sharp right at the fountain (there is a sign), just before you reach the River Provaz. **$$**

✗ Complexo Provaz Main road, on the right just before you get to the Santola turn; m 992 6076, 997 1896. This newly opened restaurant serves local fare. **$**

OTHER PRACTICALITIES
District Hospital/Área de saúde ☎ 223 3173   Police ☎ 223 3167

WHAT TO SEE AND DO Neves had the first church on the islands, **Nossa Senhora das Neves**, 'Our Lady of the Snows' (feast day 5 August or the following Sunday), next to the Água Ambó River. After extensive restoration in 1939, not much remains of the original structure, and it is not in use any more. Coming from the capital, you reach the old church by taking a right into Rua Bengá. Ask for the key at the house next to the church. When the Franciscan Sisters, Irmãs Franciscanas Hospitaleiras da Imaculada Conceiçao (☎ 223 3115) arrived on the island, they built a new, much bigger church. To get to it, take the first left past the Rosema brewery, Rua Madre Santa Clara. The church, featuring a wooden cross and some stained-glass windows, is only open at Mass times, but the Sisters can give you the key.

NEVES TO THE END OF THE ROAD

AROUND NEVES From Neves, the road winds on around the coast, past various waterfalls (for example at kilometre markers 40/41), which are at their best, of course, in the rainy season. **Roça Diogo Vaz** is the first major working plantation after Neves. As you enter, to the right-hand side are the cocoa driers, with the pigeon tower in the background.

⌂ Where to stay and eat

⌂ Mucumbli (6 chalets) m 990 8737, 990 8736; e mucumbli@gmail.co, tizimari@hotmail. com. Opened in 2013 near the Ponta Figo plantation, these new wooden chalets with their extensive veranda overlooking the sea are my personal little slice of paradise. A large mucumbli tree provided the name, sunbirds & weavers flit about, bamboo loungers & a hammock invite you to dive into true *leve-leve* relaxation, & the beach of dark sand is a 10min walk away. The water here is not crystal-clear but still offers plenty of interest for snorkellers. There's hot water & comfortable beds, local materials & crafts, & you'll discover unexpected design touches. Owners Tiziano & Mari Pisoni came to the island 20 years ago to work for an agricultural NGO, & the food they serve here is just what you'd expect from Italians passionate about good home-cooking & local ingredients. Vegetarians are well served with *carozeiro* pesto, & in season you could ask for a *safú* risotto, or a

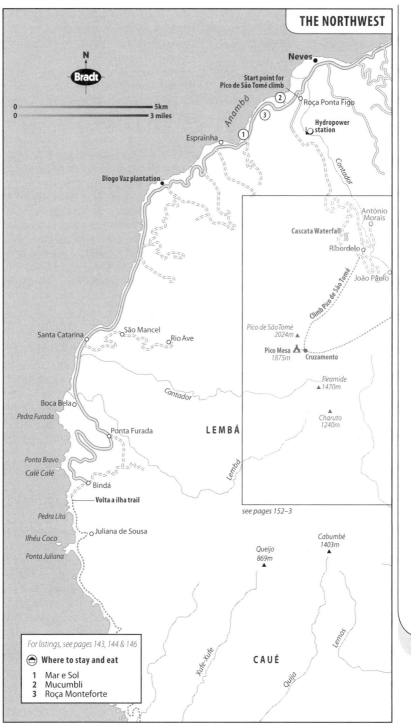

Neves

Start point for
Pico de São Tomé climb

②

Roça Ponta Figo

③

Hydropower
station

Anambó

①

Esprainha

Contador

Diogo Vaz plantation

António
Morais

Cascata Waterfall

Ribordelo

João Paulo

Climb Pico de São Tomé

Pico de São Tomé
2024m ▲

Pico Mesa ▲
1875m

Cruzamento

Santa Catarina

São Mancel

Rio Ave

Cantador

Piramide
▲1470m

Charuto
1240m

Boca Bela

Pedra Furada

Ponta Furada

LEMBÁ

Ponta Bravo
Calé Calé

Bindá

Volta a ilha trail

Pedra Lita

Ilhéu Coco

Juliana de Sousa

Lembá

see pages 152–3

Ponta Juliana

Cabumbé
1403m

Queijo
869m
▲

Cabumbé
▲

CAUÉ

Xufe-Xufe

Quija

Lemos

For listings, see pages 143, 144 & 146

🍴 **Where to stay and eat**

1 Mar e Sol
2 Mucumbli
3 Roça Monteforte

0 ———————— 5km
0 ———————— 3 miles

N

Bradt

mango risotto. Non-residents can book for lunch or dinner (€10–15). Meals are quite filling (pasta followed by main dish & a chocolate cake), so take your time, no-one will rush you. The banana seca you see in the solar driers is excellent &, at 25,000$, possibly the cheapest on the island. The garden is full of surprises, & Tiziano might bring his pet civet, lagaia, over from town. Tiziano is a keen cyclist, involved with the annual bike race Volta do Cacau around the island, & has bikes for guests to use. In the future these will be available to non-residents too. The owners can also organise hikes & boat trips. Mucumbli is a handy base for climbing the Pico (see pages 147–8) & other excursions, such as the Volta a ilha (see page 78). The road up here is scheduled for tarmacking by 2015. Last, but not least, another thing I really like about this place is that the staff are clearly happy & are treated well, something that's often missing in other places. **$$**

🏠 **Roça Monteforte** (7 rooms, 3 more planned) m 991 1362. Small, quiet plantation house under an hour's drive from the capital that offers nice-looking rooms. Ask the manager, Senhor Jerónimo, for the *quarto da ponta* at the corner: the best room, with a sea view. Sea views can also be had from the balcony; enjoy them from the comfy armchairs, keeping an eye on wandering pigs & birds flying over the trees. Monteforte is a good base for exploring a working plantation, for birding expeditions & for trips around the north of the island. A guide can be arranged locally, even English-speaking, though I'd recommend some advance planning. Our intrepid Italian photographer for this edition tackled the Pico de São Tomé from Monteforte on his own, just taking local guide Cuco to the first waterfall & continuing without a guide – don't be tempted to emulate him! He found the Pico 'almost impossible during the rainy season'. He did, however, warmly recommend the tasty *calulú* and conversations with patriarch, Senhor Jerónimo. Lunches & dinners ($) on the upstairs terrace are relaxing, but service can be on the slow side. Monteforte beach has fine black sand. **$**

What to see and do

Roça Ponta Figo This plantation used to be a nursery, providing plants to other *roças*, and has a beautiful church. One of the best treks you can do on the island leads through São Tomé's deepest valley to an impressive but fairly unknown **waterfall**, the Cascata Angolar (or Contador). Eight **tunnels** are dotted around the area; let the bats (*morçegos*) escape first before you go in, and keep your head down. Local guide José Spencer will lead you (m *991 9305, evenings; if you don't speak Portuguese, you can get a message to him through Mucumbli ecotourism, or Navetur*). José can also organise informal, cheap accommodation on the plantation, with running water and electricity. On the 2½-hour walk taking in the waterfall and six tunnels, and crossing a bridge with huge trees fallen across it, you will see plenty of interesting plants and birds; I got tantalisingly close to spotting the elusive *ossobó* bird. There is the option early on to do a short detour to see the ruins of **Communidades**, a satellite of Ponta Figo. If you haven't got your own transport, the easiest way is to get a taxi (around €25 for the return trip) to drive you to Ponta Figo, pick up the pre-arranged guide and drop you both off further up. If you want to save money, start early in the day, take a shared taxi and start walking from the plantation, leaving enough time to catch a return taxi towards the capital. Bring a picnic to share near the end of the walk, at the working hydraulic plant. Here you have a great view down to Neves, across the hills and out to sea. After lunch go downhill back to the pre-arranged taxi pick-up point. Even if you just turn up, you should easily be able to find a guide, and there is a **shop/canteen** for a meal or quick snack.

Ponta Figo used to be the most popular **starting point for the Pico de São Tomé**, and is also the start/end point for a three-day northwest–east **crossing of the island** via Bombaim and the Pico towards Água Izé (rarely undertaken, as far as I know; contact José Spencer for details). A possible **bike** excursion could run to the **Manuel Morais** plantation; contact Tiziano Pisoni at Mucumbli ecotourism (see page 144).

Santomean coffee is expensive; not because it is the best – in fact, the robust taste of some of the basic Santomean brews isn't everybody's cup of coffee – but because it is so rare. The coffee plant originates in Ethiopia. In São Tomé, arabica coffee can only be grown in a narrow horseshoe belt, at an altitude of between 800m and 1,400m around the Pico de São Tomé. Robusta coffee bushes, with a higher number of coffee cherries and bigger leaves, can be grown at a much lower altitude; this coffee has about double the caffeine. Robusta is used to give bulk; what provides the quality is arabica. The small coffee trees bear white coffee flowers, with a scent not unlike jasmine. Coffee berries take eight to nine months to ripen and they are hand-picked when they are ripe and red. The main season for this is the *gravanita* (mid-January to mid-February). The cherries are pulped, then fermented, revealing the two seeds inside, the coffee 'beans'. These are washed and dried in the sun, raked every few hours, but only lose their green colour with roasting. Most Santomeans pick, roast and grind their own coffee, without blending. Claudio Carollo sells two qualities, Jambo and Selecção, and also grows *liberica*, a niche, low-yield coffee, on Nova Moka.

Climbing the Pico de São Tomé (2,024m) Climbing the island's highest point (also, on old maps, called 'Pico Gago Coutinho' after the colonial admiral who first measured what, in 1918, was the highest mountain in the Portuguese empire), is one of the most physical and rewarding things to do on the island. You will hike through different types of forest, with views of misty peaks in the distance, and see amazing plants, trees and orchids close-up. Even experienced hill-walkers have found the climb demanding, unrelenting even, but the determining factor here is the weather. If you hit a lot of rain, the Pico is a tough walk indeed, slip-sliding your way up and/or down, carrying a backpack laden with water and overnight gear. Otherwise, the Pico is a perfectly possible proposition for anybody in good physical condition who doesn't mind using roots and lianas to get ahead.

There are **two ways** to climb the Pico. The **first route** leaves from above the **Ponta Figo** plantation (see opposite page), for a fast and steep climb to camp at Pico Mesa (1,875m), from where it is only an hour or so to the summit. The following day, you descend via **Carvalho** (1,595m), with the only slightly exposed part of the walk involving a bit of scrambling. At the Carvalho rest area, ask the guide to point out a mature *cubango* tree; its bark is burnt to chase bad spirits away. On the way down, listen out for the metallic cries of the São Tomé oriole and look around for the São Tomé giant sunbird and the maroon pigeon. You finish (or overnight) at the **Bombaim** plantation house (see pages 156–7). This route is preferred by the tour operators because it is less steep and you see more on the way up.

The **second route** leaves from the botanical gardens at **Bom Sucesso** (see page 160), reaching Carvalho after about three hours, with camping at Estação Sousa/Mesa. Look for tall fig trees and the endemic *pinheiro-de-São-Tomé* pine, bearing round green fruit, amongst the (introduced) quinine trees. The next day you climb the Pico via Carvalho and descend towards **Ponta Figo**. It is possible to do a night climb from Ponta Figo, to see the sun rise from the Pico, but only privately as far as I know, not through the agencies. It is also possible, if you are more interested in the physical challenge than the local fauna and flora, to climb the Pico in one

When the driver rang the doorbell at 04.30 to pick us up, it was still dark in São Tomé town. Luckily, the bakery down the road was already open, so Helmut and Karin from Germany and I picked up some warm *pains au chocolat* and fresh rolls for the drive north. Shuttling through the spreading daylight, there was little conversation as we drove up past the Ponta Figo plantation, picking up the guides, José and Brice, to our starting point at about 500m altitude. While we loaded up with bottles of water, Nilo the driver rustled in the forest nearby, trying to drag a *pimpinela* vegetable within his reach; whenever I see him, he is always collecting herbs and plants for food or to make up some remedy for a member of the family, in true *forro* style.

On the long slog up, through big, ancient trees, light-green ferns and dangling lichens, Brice kept us entertained: he carved off some bark from a tree and held a match to it, lighting it with a steady flame that carried on burning on its own. This was the oil tree, *pau d'óleo* – handy to know if you should ever find yourself stuck in a rainforest with no dry wood. Not that I would recognise the tree the next time I saw it; you could spend a lifetime learning tree recognition on these islands.

Growing under our feet was *capim colchão*, mattress grass, and after a few hours' hiking, it looked inviting! As we climbed, José taking the lead, once in a while we heard a crash from below: a banana plant falling over, weighed down by rainwater. Suddenly, a shout! There is only one thing that could make a guide cry out like this: the black cobra. And indeed, a *cobra preta*, seeing its escape route blocked, had hurled itself through the air to get out of our way, right past the guide, who, understandably, thought it was going for him. Meanwhile, the forest was changing around us, as the trees became more stunted and the canopy more open. We were entering the mist forest, its subtly reduced colour range of nebulous greys and greens creating a magical atmosphere.

At some 1,850m, we reached the campsite at **Mesa do Pico de São Tomé**, surrounded by lots of white-blossoming *kata d'obô* trees covered in tree ferns, a quinine tree and a passionfruit tree. We collapsed on to the grass in the sun, eager to save our energy for the last bit up to the top. At some 1,300m, this was already one of the longest ascents I'd ever completed in a day, and I couldn't believe my luck as we hadn't had a spot of rain. One more hour on a steep overgrown path got us to the summit of the Pico. As there is not much of a view, we took pictures of ourselves. Back at camp, shamefully, we didn't do anything, while the guides prepared a dinner of spaghetti with fish and vegetables. I dropped hints about 'celebrating in style', fishing for a swig of Karin's Bell's whisky. Unfortunately, this apparently very effective family remedy to ward off

day, in an 18-hour round trip, again from Ponta Figo. Whichever way you choose, bring a couple of changes of clothing; they don't weigh much, and it is sheer bliss to change into a dry T-shirt and trousers half way through a day's rainy hike. The most important item to bring, however, is walking boots with a good grip, especially as the route up has suffered degradation over the past few years.

THE END OF THE ROAD Not many visitors seem to make it to **Santa Catarina**, the last village on the west coast and it will always stay in my mind as the only place in the whole country where, I guess, my unfamiliar skin colour made young children shriek and run away! If you're planning an end-of-the-road picnic, pick up bread rolls, *chouriço* sausage and jackfruit here. Near the Baptist church, the **Escola de**

stomach bugs was strictly rationed. An electric storm rumbled over the hills somewhere as we crawled into our tents.

The next day, after a breakfast of coffee and rolls, it was time to switch the camera to macro mode for a bit of orchid photography. Right under the wooden sign pointing the way to the Pico sits a *bobofilho* ('yellow son', a local name with no claims to botanical correctness), and a one-minute walk up through the grass yields a beautiful epiphyte *polystachia* orchid clinging to the trees. Unfortunately, we soon found out that we were not going to be so lucky with the weather. The rain started as we began to trudge along towards Carvalho, and continued for three hours, soaking us through and through. All of a sudden, like a flash, José's machete came down on something: a small *samagungú* tarantula, hairy, brownish and dead. Apparently, if you are bitten, it's not a major problem, but don't drink any water. On the way down from Carvalho the view occasionally opened up to reveal the top of Ana Chaves and other peaks in the mist. Possibly we should walk a little faster, I thought, as behind me Brice managed to carve a spoon out of a piece of wood picked up on the way as he walked. Continuing down past rows of bright-red monkey flowers, through bamboo forests, and crossing a couple of rickety bridges, we were only too glad to see Nilo waiting to take us to the Bombaim plantation, where a cold beer on the balcony beckoned.

Seven years on, I have climbed the Pico again several times, in the rainy season and the other way round, starting from Bom Sucesso, with tour groups. The first time, the rain started at Lagoa Amélia and did not stop for eight hours, completely soaking the sleeping bags and mats. We didn't get to the Mesa campsite as planned, only making it to Estação Sousa, and it was too wet to light a fire. If that happens, you're looking at a two-hour walk the next morning, before a 45-minute climb to the top. That last bit you can do without luggage, leaving your backpack at the sign to Ponta Figo (a descent of about seven hours). One of the lessons I learnt from this was not to attempt the Pico if you have major knee issues, as the up and down, and getting caught in the rootwork and slipping on mossy planks of cut wood is merciless. Another is to wrap everything in extra drybags or bin liners. Bring a cooling gel – my personal favourite, Biofreeze, got used every single time. Personally I'd tuck away the hiking poles and rely more on hands and feet. Putting on climbing gloves will save your hands from thorns entering the skin when you grab the wrong tree (such as the black spiky one I chose) and will make you feel more secure in terms of the local fauna, too. We did spot a 2m cobra preta, though.

Costura (⊕ *08.00–noon Mon–Fri*) has recently set up shop with French backing; watch women make colourful garments out of African fabrics. There is no phone number, but try to check it's still running before making a special visit. Senhor Fica is the contact there, you can get hold of him in the former offices of the Roça Brigoma, 2km from Santa Catarina.

Reached by the next (fairly hidden) right turn a bit further along, the **Roça Boca Bela** plantation is locked and not open to the public; only a couple of goats balance along the top of the walls. The Cape Verdean guard told us the sad story of robbers killing the last pigs with stones and rowing them away in canoes. A path leads to the grey-sand **beach**, with the Ponte Furada rock hole visible to the left. From here, you get a good view of Cabumbé mountain (1,403m).

Back on the road, turn right after a few hundred metres for **Roça Ponte Furada**, a cluster of houses around a square. Most inhabitants live by extracting palm wine and few tourists travel this way. There is a tiny shop selling *chouriço* sausage alongside the usual biscuits, etc, and you can ask who has bananas to sell. The road past the turn-off to Ponte Furada, and Bindá, the old colonial road, has recently been reopened by the Satocão company. Where the road runs out the landscape is magical; listen to the sound of thunder rumbling, loud birdsong and the rain falling somewhere across the forest, sounding like a river. This is where the **Volta a ilha** starts, a two-day trek to Porto Alegre, through some of the most remote parts of the island. Beautiful beaches and exciting bird sightings are guaranteed. Contact guide José Spencer (m *991 9305, evenings*) at Mucumbli for details.

5

The Interior

Leaving the capital on the road following the Água Grande River leads through the historic town of Trindade into the heart of the island, through coffee and cocoa plantations, unique species of trees supporting a host of endemic forest birds and orchids, and on to the islands' highest summit: the Pico de São Tomé (see *Chapter 4*).

HIGHLIGHTS

Tick off some endemic birds at Bom Sucesso botanic gardens and enjoy an easy walk in the Obô National Park up to the dry crater lake of Lagoa Amélia. Relax at the historic plantation house of Bombaim; learn to tell your arabica from your robusta coffee, and delve into the colonial past at the Monte Café plantation with its new museum and cafeteria; and taste the fragrant and delicious mountain raspberries sold by the roadside.

GETTING AROUND

Taxis go to Trindade, and some on to Monte Café, but very few go to Nova Moca, and none to Bom Sucesso. To visit these places, it usually makes sense to go on an **organised tour**. No shared taxis go to Bombaim, and the extortionate rate demanded for an individual taxi (1,000,000$ round trip) makes it better value to either **hire a car** or visit that plantation as part of an organised driving or hiking tour. Alternatively, get a shared taxi to Trindade and a **mototaxi** from there.

MADRE DE DEUS

This is a friendly neighbourhood, just within walking distance of the capital on the way to Trindade, where you can visit one of the oldest churches on the islands and an easily accessible waterfall, or just pick up a few bits and bobs from the little shops and catch up with the soap operas in a bar.

Continuing on past Madre de Deus, at the **Bobo Forro** fork in the road – where the hopeful inscription on the façade of the primary school reads *Deus quer, o homem sonha, a obra nasce* ('God wants, man dreams, the work is born', a quote from the iconic Modernist Portuguese poet, Fernando Pessoa) – you can drive two ways, right towards Madalena and some little-visited plantations, or continue straight towards Trindade (see pages 155–6). If you carry on to Trindade, Monte Café and Nova Moca, you will pass a cemetery on your right, and the house of the former president, Fradique de Menezes, guarded Quinta da Favorita, on your left.

WHAT TO SEE AND DO The yellow-stone **Nossa Senhora de Madre de Deus** church (⊕ *04.00–10.00 Sun; Mass 08.00 Sun, 07.00 Mon & Tue, 06.00 Sat*), set slightly back from the main road, on the left-hand side, dates from 1562. This is where a

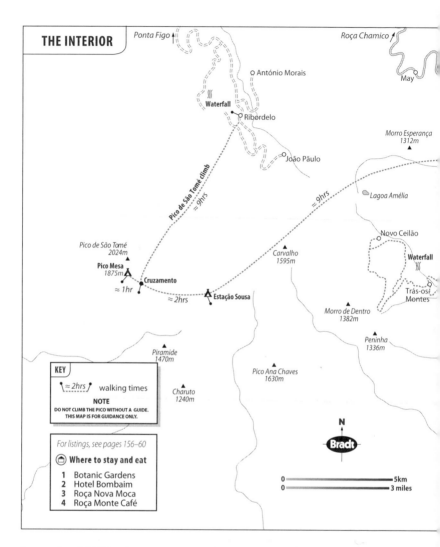

THE INTERIOR

Ponta Figo

Roça Chamico

May

António Morais

Waterfall

Ribórdelo

Morro Esperança
1312m

João Páulo

Pico de São Tomé climb
≈ 9hrs

≈ 9hrs

Lagoa Amélia

Novo Ceilão

Pico de São Tomé
2024m

Carvalho
1595m

Waterfall

Pico Mesa
1875m

Cruzamento

Trás-os-Montes

≈ 1hr

≈ 2hrs

Estação Sousa

Morro de Dentro
1382m

Peninha
1336m

Piramide
1470m

KEY

≈ 2hrs   walking times

NOTE
DO NOT CLIMB THE PICO WITHOUT A GUIDE.
THIS MAP IS FOR GUIDANCE ONLY.

Charuto
1240m

Pico Ana Chaves
1630m

N

Bradt

For listings, see pages 156–60

Where to stay and eat

1 Botanic Gardens
2 Hotel Bombaim
3 Roça Nova Moca
4 Roça Monte Café

0 —————————— 5km
0 —————————— 3 miles

former (until 2008) prime minister, Tomé Vera Cruz, worships and it is also where, traditionally, young mothers bring their seven week old babies to put them under the protection of 'Our Lady'. The key to the church is held by an elderly brother and sister, Senhor Silva and Dona Rosaria; they live down the road (going back towards the capital), on the opposite side from the church, in the house with a small wooden bench in front, next to a house with a large fan palm tree in the garden. Go through the yard, past the first house – you want the house at the back. You cannot visit on your own; Senhor Silva, who has looked after the church for some 40 years, has to come with you. If you can, bring a small present with you such as a candle (*vela*) for the church, some sweets or, if you really want to make Dona Rosaria happy, a perfume miniature. The church's feast day is the second Sunday in September.

Blú Blú waterfall Only a 20-minute walk from here, there is a lovely little *cascata* that is very easy to get to. Take a left off the main road where a dirt track crosses

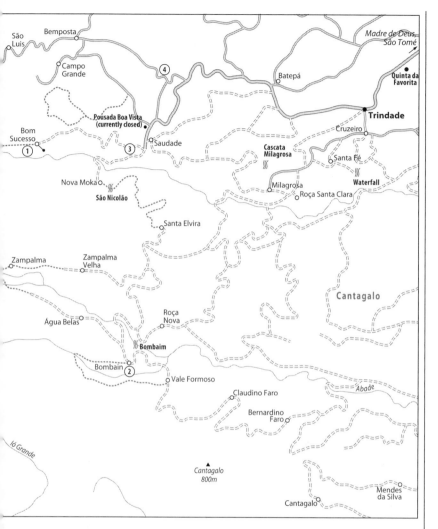

the main roads, just before the football pitch (the track right next to the pitch joins that path after two minutes, too). From there, it is only a five-minute walk to a concrete bridge that crosses the river. Just before the bridge, cut through to the left and follow the river for ten to 15 minutes down to the waterfall. This is easier if you get one of the kids you will meet on the path to show you the way. They were also quite helpful when I visited, as some unpleasant *folha ganhoma* was growing right next to the path (see page 73).

WEST OF MADRE DE DEUS

ROÇA SÃO JOSÉ (m 990 8847; *Agostinho Dória* e *saotomeradical@gmail.com*) What used to be the second-biggest tropical flower plantation in sub-Saharan Africa sadly today lies semi-abandoned. Situated at an altitude of 400m, the plantation, with its large ancient trees and idyllic river, is great for birding, and you are free to wander

5

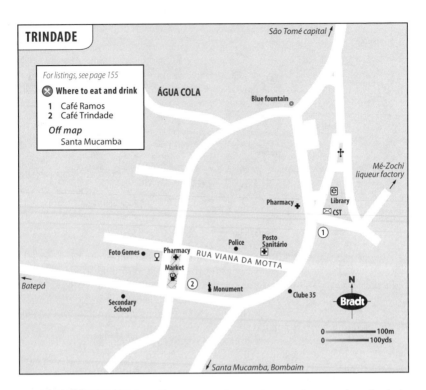

TRINDADE

São Tomé capital ↑

For listings, see page 155

⊗ **Where to eat and drink**
1 Café Ramos
2 Café Trindade
Off map
   Santa Mucamba

ÁGUA COLA

Blue fountain

Mé-Zochi liqueur factory

Pharmacy
Library
CST

Police
Posto Sanitário
Foto Gomes
Pharmacy
RUA VIANA DA MOTTA
Market
①
Batepá
②
Monument
Clube 35
Secondary School

N

Bradt

0 ——— 100m
0 ——— 100yds

↗ Santa Mucamba, Bombaim

around. The manager, Agostinho Dória, who speaks French, Spanish and a little English, is hoping to get adventure tourism off the ground in the Obô Izaquente area, in the shade of huge *cidrela* trees.

Getting there and away On the drive up to São José from the capital, passing through the famous popular **Bobo Forro** neighbourhood, watch out for the **wooden benches** with slogans – they make nice photographs. After 3km, before you reach Madalena, you will see the first sign to the plantation. **Yellow taxis** can drop you at Roça Vista Alegre (30,000$), from where you can walk; for the return, you might be able to catch a lift. At worst – or just for fun – there is a nice walk from nearby **Prado** to **Praia Lagarto** just north of the capital, which should take about 1½ hours, downhill all the way.

VISTA ALEGRE AND SANTA MARGARIDA The nearby plantation of **Vista Alegre**, with sweeping views over the two bays of the capital, is now owned by the brother of the current president, Pinto da Costa; ask the guards whether you can have a look around the beautifully kept *casa grande*. One of the oldest and richest plantations on the island, with a beautiful example of colonial-style architecture, is **Santa Margarida,** a working cocoa plantation. Within hiking distance, there is a campsite. There are plans to have mountain bikes for hire in the future.

ROÇA CHAMIÇO As the crow flies, the atmospheric plantation of Roça Chamiço is only a few kilometres from São José, but situated on a squiggly, difficult, broken-up road and becoming near-inaccessible in the rainy season, so very few tourists come here. I've certainly never managed to get there, but not for lack of trying.

Taxi drivers are also reluctant to travel there; Joaquim Ribeiro (m *990 6491*) will go, but at a price. For more information, also for **hiking trips** up there, contact Nora Rizzo at Casa Amarela (see page 117). To stay at the plantation in very basic conditions (€35 dbl, €25 sgl), contact Laurinda (m *992 49809*), the grand-daughter of the female plantation manager (one of the few); she might be able to organise a monkey or rabbit curry for dinner. Laurinda works at the Ministery of Foreign Affairs, next to the Portuguese Embassy.

TRINDADE

Lying at just above 400m, surrounded by good agricultural land, Trindade, the second-largest town on the island and capital of the Mé-Zochi district, has historically been both a place of refuge from attacks on the capital and a centre of anti-colonial resistance. When pirates came to plunder and burn in the 16th century, priests, nuns and friars would come up the hill to seek refuge in the church; Trindade church was also where 'King' Amador started his bloody slave revolt in 1595. In the 20th century, the town became a focus for the struggle for independence.

One of the most famous Santomean families, the Graça Espírito Santos, hail from here. Members of the family include primary school teacher Maria de Jesus Neves (mother of the late politician and poet Alda Graça de Espirito Santo), whose portrait hangs in the National Museum in São Tomé, and anti-colonial activist Salustino. They all came to prominence in the 1953 rebellion, whilst Julieta da Graça Espírito Santo was the first female medic in the country. Artist and essayist Almada Negreiros (see page 158) and poet Caetano Costa Alegre, as well as classical composer Viana da Motta, were also born in Trindade.

For more on the route from the capital to Trindade, see opposite page.

✗ WHERE TO EAT AND DRINK

✗ **Clube 35** 35 Main road. Currently closed & looking for a new owner for a number of years now, this basement club with upstairs snack restaurant used to attract people all the way from the capital. $$
🖵 **Café Ramos** ⊕ 08.00–21.00 daily. Pastéis, snacks & cake. $
🖵 **Café Trindade** ℻227 1290; m 990 3172,

992 0106; ⊕ 07.30–22.00 Tue–Sun. The place to be in Trindade, selling cakes, local coffee, fresh milk & wine, with outside seating. When I visited, we bought tasty grilled *safús* from a street seller.$
🍷 **Santa Mucamba** Past the Cruzeiro de Trindade area, ask locally. A humble meeting point for drinking palm wine & snacking on hearty salty meat snacks. $

SHOPPING For **clothes**, especially jeans, there are a couple of places in the Rua Viana da Motta/market area.

✚ **Farmácia Irmão Viana** Main road ℻227 1026; ⊕ 08.00–20.00 Mon–Sat, 08.00–13.00 Sun. Well-stocked pharmacy in the centre of town.

Foto Gomes Rua Viana da Motta; m 990 6418; ⊕ 07.00–20.00 Mon–Sat. Photographic supplies.

OTHER PRACTICALITIES

CST ⊕ 07.30–21.00 Mon–Sat, 07.30–19.00 Sun. 4 posts for calling.
✚ **First aid** Posto de Saúde; Rua Viana da Motta; ℻227 1494; ⊕ 24hrs. There is 1 nurse; ask for Nelson, he speaks some English. The ambulance has oxygen.

🌐 **Internet** Ask at the the Câmara Municipal whether you can use their Wi-Fi signal for free, or visit the Library (Biblioteca; next to the yellow Claretian Missionaries' house; ⊕ 14.00–17.00 Mon, 08.00–noon & 14.00–17.00 Tue–Fri, 08.00–14.00 Sat) where there are 9 terminals. Internet

costs 10,000$/hr, printing 2,000$/page. USB sticks will be scanned before you're allowed to use them.
Petrol station Centre of town; ⊕ 06.00–20.00

Police Rua Viana da Motta; ☎227 1333
Post office/CTT Main road

WHAT TO SEE AND DO Dedicated to the Holy Trinity, the current stone **Igreja de Santíssima Trindade** (⊕ *06.00–08.30 daily, novena Mass 18.00 daily, Sun Mass 09.00*) is surrounded by a wide flight of steps and dates from the early 18th century. To get to it, take a sharp left a couple of hundred metres after entering the town, nearly doubling back on yourself, just before the sign pointing the way to the **Mé-Zochi** (m *990 3164; www.mezochi.net;* ⊕ *07.00–14.00 Mon–Sat*) sweet liqueur factory, which can also be visited. There you can watch the production and buy some bottles of liqueur.

This building replaced a wooden church that had suffered various attacks and had been rebuilt twice. Slave 'king' Rei Amador and his fellow armed slaves stormed the church during Mass in 1595. In 1641, sheltering clergy fleeing from the Dutch in the capital, it was given the status of temporary cathedral for a year. The church's popular name is 'Lord God Father', *Senhor Deus Pai*; a festival of the same name, the biggest in Trindade, is celebrated in May, on the Sunday following Whitsun. In the late 19th century, the church was gifted a sculpture of the Eternal Father, carved with a terrifying face. It looked so fearsome that the locals would pray to him to destroy their enemies, so it had to be replaced. Inside, there are the usual three altars. The chapel to the left of the choir displays a statue of its patron saint, in memory of the well-known Portuguese legend of the miracle of Our Lady of Nazaré. A horseman, following a deer at full gallop, was unaware of how close he was to a precipice, when the horse suddenly froze in mid-leap, alerted to the danger by Our Lady of Nazaré. The saint's feast day is celebrated here on the Sunday following 8 September. The last renovation dates from 1962, when the tower was added. If the church is closed, get the key from friendly Padre Domingos next door in the yellow house; the priest has been here a good dozen years.

FROM TRINDADE TO BOMBAIM

To reach Bombaim, take a left in the centre of Trindade, 200m past the (currently closed) Clube 35.

WHERE TO STAY AND EAT At the time of writing, the **Roça Santa Clara** (m *990 3122, 983 4184;* e *santaclaragrupo@gmail.com*) working agricultural plantation near Trindade was in the process of being transformed into an agrotourism venture. One of the three managers, dynamic Nelsy Sousa of STP Tourism, calls their concept *Lugar de Coisas Boas* ('Place of Good Things'). The roça is starting to produce cornmeal and animal feed to reduce imports, and there are plans to create a campsite and to keep horses. Watch this space.

Hotel Bombaim (11 rooms) Distrito de Mé-Zochi, CP 177; ☎222 7788 (office), 222 3439 (house); m 990 3240 (manager Genoveve da Ceita); e hotelbombaim@cstome.net. This historic colonial plantation house has plenty of atmosphere with its beautiful stained-glass windows, & a romantic wraparound balcony with views over the peaks (Formosa Grande, Formosa Pequeno, Carvalho) that's a great place to relax after a day's hiking. The downstairs rooms have their own bathroom, but are fairly dingy & humid, as the bathroom windows never seem to be opened; the upstairs rooms, much lighter & more atmospheric, share a couple of bathrooms on the landing – the price is the same. Showers are cold, but luckily the water supply is not dependent on the generator.

Upstairs is a cosy living room with TV, the dining room & kitchen, as well as a terrace with lovely views, & a good sound system. The downstairs bar in the entrance area is not much used as such, but houses the fridge. The power is usually turned off at around 22.00, but if you pay a surcharge, you can have the light on for longer. In the past, I heard reports of occasional rats in the rooms, so be careful not to keep any food there unless sealed in your luggage, or ask the kitchen staff to put in the fridge. The service can be a bit haphazard when there are few guests. Ask whether they have sap-sap juice for b/fast; this big green spiky fruit grows in the garden. Visit the school a little walk away (ask for *escola*) & the schoolteacher Guilherme can find a globe so you can point out where you're from. The excellent food at Bombaim ranges from grilled fish with vegetables to spaghetti with *chouriço* sausage. **$$**

WHAT TO SEE AND DO

Waterfalls The way to **Cascata Fundo do Morcego** is an easy 1½-hour downhill walk through the abandoned cocoa plantation of **Santa Fé**, past beautiful old trees. (Luckily, I only found out later from an expedition report that the area around Santa Fé is a prime spot for finding tarantulas.) Park the car near the entrance to the plantation. Bring a picnic to have at the river, watching the bats flitting in and out of the basalt rockface. To see the waterfall, you unfortunately have to wade (and swim) across into the opening and climb up on to the rocks. Be careful in the rainy season and if the water turns brown, get out quick. Back on the Bombaim road, the next right turn leads to the Milagrosa plantation. **Cascata Milagrosa** is a beautiful double waterfall symbolising man and woman.

Bombaim Explore the various plants in the garden, starting with the vanilla orchid growing on a nearby wall. Next along, the pillars that used to support the roofs of the cocoa driers now stick out forlornly into the sky. Today, two dozen families rear livestock here but there is quite a forlorn vibe about. Don't leave without tasting the **mangosteen** (*mangostão*). The subtly citrusy-tasting fruit originated in Asia and on São Tomé, Bombaim is the only place where it thrives. Take a walk along the abandoned *roça* buildings opposite the hotel, with the railway tracks all but disappeared under the grass. The big white house alongside the workshop (*oficina*) belonged to the foremen, *capatazes* or *brancos de mato*, literally 'whites of the forest' (referring to their lives adapted to the rough conditions of the island), and there were storage rooms, the book keepers' office, the workers' quarters and the hospital.

There are several **waterfalls** nearby but confusingly all seem to be called Cascata de Bombaim. A 20-minute walk out of the entrance and up the road leads you to two, one after the other, on the left-hand side of the road. There are more, with caves, down to your right, but they are difficult to reach.

For details of staying at Bombain, see opposite page.

Hikes from Bombaim A good stop-off point coming down from the Pico de São Tomé, Bombaim is also a great base for various hikes. The easiest waterfall to get to is the one you pass when you drive in, on the right-hand side of the access road, a 20-minute walk from the plantation. A guide can take you on a two hour morning walk (€10) to the showpiece waterfall: **Cascata Formosa**, a series of three waterfalls more than 100m high. Your guide can also tell you which of the waterfall pools are safe to swim in, depending on the season. According to a friend who did this walk, there are actually three paths you can take to this waterfall: a (slightly unsafe) shortcut, a medium-distance path and a much longer one. A half-day hike around the nearby hills costs €20, a day's hike around the peak of **Formosa Grande** costs €30. One hiking trail leads to São João dos Angolares. It might also be possible to hike the beautiful six-hour 'Bom Sucesso to Bombaim' (see page 160) trail in reverse; see if the Bombaim manager can call ahead to make the booking for the overnight accommodation and transport the following day.

A very pleasant five- to six- hour walk to the **Roça Bernardino Faro** plantation leads through various cultivated areas – a great opportunity to learn about different plants and trees, including avocado, acacia, guava and the tall *capitão* tree. You can have lunch under a big *cajamanga* tree, munching some watercress (*agrião*) picked at the wayside. One thing I remember from arriving at the Bernardo Faro plantation, because it's such a rare sight, was a young man sitting in the shade, reading a book. Passing the primary school at the end of the village at break time, you might have to shake the hand of every single child. When we went through, a delegation followed us for quite a while, asking us to pick some *comida de cobra* (cobra food): small orange berries, hanging too high up for them.

TOWARDS BOM SUCESSO, MONTE CAFÉ AND NOVA MOCA

BATEPÁ AND AROUND The events of 1953 were triggered by a killing in Trindade, while the revolting population that tried to seize the Trindade police station, came from Batepá. However, there is not much to see as the monument to the 'War of Batepá' at Fernão Dias beach (see page 137) is no longer standing. Today, Santomeans come to Batepá for the best, purest **palm wine**. To get there and further inland, you can try to catch a yellow taxi from alongside the market in Trindade. Don't expect them to be that frequent though, as most of the traffic goes in the direction of the capital.

Past Batepá, a short grass track off to the right leads to the **Pousada Boa Vista**. There is, indeed, a beautiful view out to Santana and the coast from the terraced grounds in front of the hotel. The Pousada is currently closed and, despite rumours that it was to be developed and reopened by an Angolan businessman, nothing has happened for years. Nearby is the **Roça Saudade** plantation where **Almada Negreiros** used to live in the early 1900s before moving, at three years of age, to Lisbon where he went on to become one of the major exponents of avant-garde art and literature in Portugal. His Cubist-inspired portrait of writer Fernando Pessoa at the Gulbenkian Museum in Lisbon is amongst his most well-known works. His father José wrote one of the first ethnographic studies of the island.

ROÇA MONTE CAFÉ (☎ 222 3234) At an altitude of 500m, two white stones on the right mark the entrance to the plantation that used to produce most of the island's coffee before independence. Founded by pioneer planter Manuel da Costa Pedreira, Monte Café had ten dependencies and employed thousands of workers. The bell that marked the labourers' work day is still here, along with other photogenic industrial ruins. The inscriptions '1914' and 'Technologia' indicate this plantation's heyday. The wagons on rails and driers are still used for the *roça's* small-scale coffee production, but a big, new hospital building stands empty, only receiving a weekly visit from the Taiwanese medical mission. Charismatic foreman Américo might be available to show you around – and may point you to a house where you can taste the local *ponche* drink, difficult to find in town. Artist **Francisco Júlio** has his atelier on the main road here.

The long-awaited **coffee museum** and **café** (⊕ *08.00–12.30 & 14.00–16.00 Mon–Fri, 09.00–13.00 Sat & Sun; admission €2/50,000$*) finally opened in 2013 in the former administration building, and is a fascinating experience as well as a good example of plantation tourism benefitting the locals. There are displays on the coffee cycle and a documentary about the coffee harvest, featuring interviews with plantation workers (with English, French, Portuguese and Spanish subtitles). You can also usually buy some local coffee at the shop (*loja*); it has an earthy flavour. It is available cheaply (40,000$) in black or transparent bags in the capital's supermarkets, too. At the time of writing, guide Brice Monteiro (m 991 0060) was starting to build a B&B guesthouse, Casa do Brice, with home cooking, guide services, transfers and internet access. A new restaurant has already opened, run by local coffee seller Catoni (m 994 0398/996 0327; *open daily*). At the time of going to press they needed advance notice for their delicious food, but are hoping to change to a more regular service.

ROÇA NOVA MOCA At an altitude of between 800 and 1,000m, in the shade of flame trees, Nova Moca plantation produces most of the country's coffee for export. Some 70 people live here, and there is electricity and water. Nova Moca is becoming the powerhouse for new agricultural initiatives in São Tomé and Príncipe. Park your car next to the football pitch or, if you park a bit lower down you can walk up and see robusta coffee bushes and, over to your right, little stone walls put in place to retain the humidity of the terraced soil. Somebody can probably be found to show you around; or just ask anybody working there.

The owner of Nova Moca, who single-handedly revived coffee culture in São Tomé, is **Claudio Corallo**. Born in 1951 in Florence, the tropical agronomist is passionate about cocoa and coffee, and first gained his expertise cultivating coffee in Zaire (now the Democratic Republic of Congo) in the 1980s. In 1983, Corallo's wife brought back some coffee plants and cocoa pods from a visit to São Tomé and Príncipe. Studying the properties of these ancient varieties, Claudio Corallo found an arabica with the most body he'd ever tasted. The family moved to São Tomé in 1995 and, undeterred in their gourmet quest and despite Claudio's wife, Bettina, nearly dying of malaria, also acquired a cocoa plantation on Príncipe: Terreiro Velho (see page 202). The Corallos now cultivate four varieties of coffee here – three arabica and one robusta – to produce the single-estate blends 'Jambo' and (the more expensive) 'Selecção'. The yield of these varieties is as low as 200kg per hectare for the *café liberica* – modern hybrids can yield up to 4,000kg. To see what these ancient varieties look like, take a right before the tumble-down former administrator's house, walk up a few metres and look to your right; you will see trees marked with different tags – CAT, BB and NM. If you want to experience the difference in taste, Corallo produces a presentation box with coffee beans from the three varieties covered in chocolate made with cocoa from his Príncipe plantation. They offer different taste sensations, with coffee and cocoa hitting the palate in a different sequence, explained in a leaflet that's also available in English. Unfortunately, none of the produce is on sale here yet, but you can buy a presentation box (150,000$ well spent) at the CKADO and Intermar supermarkets in the capital (see page 124; with the leaflet in Portuguese). If you're really organised, buy a box before coming up here and have your own tasting session by picking coffee cherries off the relevant bushes (ask first) – great fun!

Coming down again, on your right, a few steps lead up to a porch where tastings are held for larger groups. The porch overlooks the solar driers for the coffee beans, covered with plastic sheeting when rain threatens. About 250 producers work together at Monte Café in an organic co-operative called CECAFEB, established in 2010.

Basic accommodation ($) and good meals, taken on a platform on stilts, are now available here; contact Luis Mário (m 991 1670; e lumanovamoca@hotmail.com). Vegetarians should request the cabbage (*couve*) to be made without stock, as it is normally chicken stock (*de galinha*).

5

WATERFALL SÃO NICOLÃU At some 30m, this easily accessible *cascata* is possibly the most visited waterfall in the country. The way to it is not signposted, but the dirt track leading there turns off to the left about 200m from the Pousada Boa Vista, just before the sharp right-hand bend up to Bom Sucesso. Leave the car there and walk; there is a wealth of trees and plants to be seen along the short walk to the waterfall above a hazardous-looking broken bridge. It is only a short walk up to the **São Nicolãu plantation**, where people don't see many tourists and are very welcoming. There are a couple of forest paths you can take around the plantation that give you a new perspective on the waterfall, without worrying about getting lost.

BOM SUCESSO
Where to stay

Botanic Gardens (Bom Sucesso) The bungalow here has 3 rooms with en-suite bathrooms (cold shower) & 2 none too comfortable beds for €15pp, payable in advance. There is no electricity. Usually, but not always, a guard can let you in & show you around. If not, try asking a plantation worker on the road how to get hold of somebody. The guard can't take your money though, & it's best to book in advance (through Navetur, see page 112, for instance), as I've heard of people finding the place shut – or occupied, of course. The communal kitchen with crockery & cutlery has a gas stove, but no gas as far as I'm aware. Bring your own supplies, including toilet paper, candles & matches, food, plus maybe a bottle of wine & a corkscrew, & a camping stove if you have one. Put on a warm jumper, open the wine, & sit on the porch overlooking the garden & listen to the owls. The next morning, get up early & enjoy some easy birdwatching at dawn in the botanical garden. **$**

What to see and do

Botanic Gardens (*Jardim Botânico*; *if you speak Portuguese, contact Sr Francisco* m 991 4364) At an altitude of 1,115m, the Jardim Botânico of Bom Sucesso has more than 400 typical plants and 140 orchids. The trees and some of the plants carry a label with basic botanical information, but you really need a guide to explain the native trees' various medicinal qualities, from stomach-calming *canela* to the 'rainforest Viagra', aphrodisiac *pau três*. The main building, used for botany classes, contains some educational material (dried specimens of ferns and other plants, bird posters) and a basic toilet. See above for information about staying overnight.

Hikes from Bom Sucesso Bom Sucesso is a relaxing if basic and not-easy-to-organise base where you can really feel close to nature, as well as an excellent starting point for walks in the Obô National Park: the most popular is an easy walk to the dried-up crater lake of Lagoa Amélia (see below). Organise a guide (€30/40) and explore the excellent five-hour loop known as **Caminho do Fugido** – literally 'Way of the Fugitive', no doubt referring to escaped slaves, some of whom managed to remain hidden for years. Another recommended six-hour hike to **Bombaim** (see page 156) leads past rows of porcelain roses, bamboo, the incredibly atmospheric and photogenic ruins of **Trás-os-Montes**, a *dependência* of Bombaim, past the abandoned *roças* of Nova Ceilão and Zampalma, before following the River Abade. (You can make a detour to Lagoa Amélia.) Another option is a two-day walk up to the **Pico de São Tomé** (see pages 148–9).

Lagoa Amélia A very popular walk of an hour or so leads west through fertile agricultural land where beans, carrots and cabbage grow, to the ancient crater lake of Lagoa Amélia (1,483m) amongst primary rainforest. In theory, you could do this walk on your own if you make sure you take the right-hand path at the fork in the road up from Bom Sucesso and just head up southwest following the middle of the three tracks you see. However, taking a guide not only enhances the experience – learning about the trees, plants and birds you encounter on the way – but also supports the local economy. It is also safer as guides know to look out for the black cobra, just in case. (On one occasion, we saw a juvenile cobra preta right at the entrance to the forest, blending in very well with the leafy soil, and, untypically for the black cobra, not looking very interested in slinking away.)

Early on, to the left of the path, look for a magnificent fallen tree trunk, where the famous strangling fig, *figo estrangulador*, has killed off its host tree completely, leaving a magnificent hollow space amongst the roots that is big enough to step inside. After about half an hour's walk, you enter the **Obô National Park**, marked by a wooden sign. One of the aims in creating the park in 2006 was to stop agricultural land from encroaching further on the important forest habitats around the crater lake. Continuing up, the path is strewn with beautifully coloured leaves and discarded monkey nuts; ask the guide to point out the most distinctive trees, such as the Cubango tree (used to ward off the evil eye), for instance. Note that some trees have wooden identification plaques. Take your time exploring, as the beauty of this walk lies less in the Lagoa itself as in the rich bird- and plantlife encountered on the way; it might be a good idea to make clear early on that you will be stopping frequently. Apart from the common endemics, look out for the maroon pigeon, the São Tomé scops owl, the giant sunbird, the São Tomé oriole and the São Tomé white-eye.

'Amelia Lagoon' is not a lake anymore, but a filled-in crater surrounded by trees and giant begonias. There is a sign asking you not to step on the spongy grass, topping a 3m layer of rainwater, which most visitors ignore, of course. You may see some São Tomé spinetails flitting across, hunting flying insects. There is the possibility of **camping** at the weather station just before you walk down to the crater; there is not much shelter, but it would be a wonderful opportunity for early-morning birding in the middle of the primary rainforest.

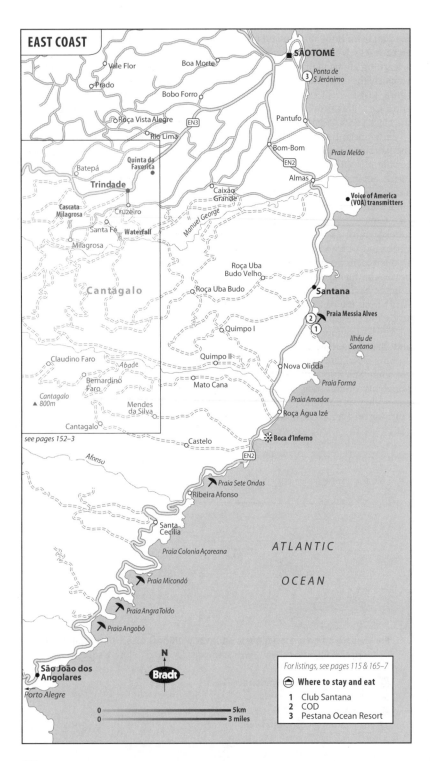

EAST COAST

Vale Flor
Boa Morte
■ SÃO TOMÉ
Prado
③ Ponta de
S Jerónimo
Bobo Forro
Roça Vista Alegre
EN3
Pantufo
Rio Lima
Bom-Bom
EN2
Praia Melão
Quinta da
Favorita
Batepá
Almas
Trindade
Caixão
Grande
Voice of America
(VOA) transmitters
Cascata
Milagrosa
Cruzeiro
Santa Fé
Waterfall
Manuel George
Milagrosa
Roça Uba
Budo Velho
Cantagalo
Roça Uba Budo
● Santana
Praia Messia Alves
Quimpo I
②
①
Ilhéu de
Santana
Quimpo II
Claudino Faro
Abade
Nova Olinda
Bernardino
Faro
Mato Cana
Praia Forma
Cantagalo
▲ 800m
Praia Amador
Mendes
da Silva
Roça Água Izé
Cantagalo
Castelo
Boca d'Inferno
EN2

see pages 152–3

Afonso

Praia Sete Ondas
Ribeira Afonso

Santa
Cecília

ATLANTIC

Praia Colonia Açoreana

OCEAN

Praia Micondó

Praia Angra Toldo

Praia Angobó

N

São João dos
Angolares

Bradt

Porto Alegre

0 _____ 5km
0 _____ 3 miles

For listings, see pages 115 & 165–7

⌂ Where to stay and eat

1 Club Santana
2 COD
3 Pestana Ocean Resort

6

The East and South

The coastal road south from the capital leads past São João dos Angolares, a town at the centre of Angolar culture and the heart of the contemporary arts scene outside the capital, and on to a stretch of fishing villages, alternating with beaches of different-coloured sand. Many visitors agree that the southern beaches are the most beautiful on the island. There are plenty of undiscovered ones, clean and with rich wildlife, kept that way by the advanced state of disrepair of the only access road and lack of development and communications. The further south you go, the poorer generally the people. At the tip of the island, the first ecotourism projects have begun to break the south's isolation and poverty, whilst across the narrow stretch of water a resort next to the Equator mark beckons – a temptation hard to resist. The southwest of the island is still only visited by pioneering travellers.

HIGHLIGHTS

Relax at the Club Santana resort, taste imaginative Santomean food at the atmospheric São João plantation, swim at Praia Piscina, treat yourself to a stay at new Praia Inhame eco-resort and watch turtles at Praia Jalé. Stand on the Equator line on Ilhéu das Rolas, or join the hardcore birders on an expedition up the Xufe-Xufe River.

GETTING AROUND

Yellow taxis ply the coast road from the capital via Santana and São João dos Angolares down to Porto Alegre. A **shared taxi** to Santana, for instance, costs 15,000$, to São João dos Angolares 25,000$ and to Porto Alegre 30,000$. After 15.00 it will probably be tricky to find a taxi to go south; the same goes for the return journey. A **private taxi** to São João dos Angolares would cost around 150,000$, which makes **car hire** a better proposition. **Transport to Ilhéu das Rolas** is usually organised through the resort (see page 179). The friendly Pestana driver picking up passengers coming off the island on the afternoon boat may be able give you a lift back north. An individual taxi from the capital to Porto Alegre will cost you about €60 – even though the road is no longer the car-wrecker it was, it will still take you about two hours.

FROM SÃO TOMÉ TO SÃO JOÃO DOS ANGOLARES

Heading south from the capital on the Marginal, the coast road leads past the parliament on a stretch of straight road to the pleasant fishing village of Pantufo.

PANTUFO If you are self-catering and based in town, Pantufo is a good place to pick up fresh fish for dinner, maybe on your way back from a day at Club Santana. The **yellow church** dedicated to St Peter, patron saint of fishermen, is recent (1939).

On the left-hand side of the coast road, opposite the church, you can't miss the O Império 'boat'; plans to set it up as a bar foundered when the guesthouse and restaurant opposite closed.

✗ Where to eat and drink

✗ O Esconderijo da Ganda Take a right (signposted) just past the viewpoint on the left-hand side; ☏ 222 2058. Pleasant fish restaurant famous for its grilled octopus (*polvo*) & fish – & for the 2 private huts where you can have dinner with somebody you shouldn't officially be seen with (*esconderijo* means 'hideaway'). They can also prepare a *sopa de folha* (*micocó* soup), a local soup made from herbs, but it's probably best to order that the day before. As it's a bit off the beaten track, call ahead to make sure they're open. **$$**

Nightlife

☆ **Oasis** Take a right in front of the church &, some 200m on, take a left; the club is on your left-hand side. The greatest advantage of this *discoteca* is that it's open-air. The locals might still know the club under its former name, 'Argentimoa'. It should have a good atmosphere Sat & Sun, but as with all of these places, don't count on it. Don't get there too early & have a getaway plan, as it's not a place to sit & chat, nothing else will be open in the area at that time & few taxis will be available (though you can always get a mototaxi heading into town). Also, as the club was closed for a while, check locally that it's open before you go.

SOUTH TO SANTANA At weekends, there is a bar service on Praia Pomba on the beach below the transmitters. To visit the Voice of America transmitter station, contact them in advance.

Roça Uba Budo (☏ *226 5117*) This small plantation has a beautiful administrator's house. A kilometre before Santana, a road turns off to the right towards Uba Budo (if you miss that, you can join that road from the centre of Santana; ask for directions as it's easy to get lost). I don't know of any shared taxis going to Uba Budo (check at Taxi Square in São Tomé), and if you can get on one bound for Santana and ask to be dropped off at the turn; you will still have a long walk. Contact José Spencer (**m** *991 9305, evenings*) to organise a **bike trip** from São Tomé to Uba Budo.

Electricity has only recently come to the plantation, through a pilot project managed by Columbia University's **Earth Institute** (see page 29). In the past, only expensive kerosene lamps and candlelight were available; today, a low-cost diesel generator managed by the community provides affordable electricity and, with it, a basis for better education, health and economic growth. There is now a power-saving 7-watt fluorescent bulb in every residence, and a TV for watching cartoons and soap operas, of course. This scheme can give you an insight into successful development work on the islands. If you want to hear more about it (Portuguese only), ask to speak to the president of Uba Budo's community association, Pedro Semedo Tavares.

SANTANA The attractions of the Cantagalo district capital, with some 8,000 inhabitants, are strung out along several kilometres. *Cantagalo* translates as 'the rooster sings', and you will notice that on the islands the roosters start singing very early indeed – at around 03.00! In the home town of the famous *socopé* (traditional dance) group Linda Estrela, you will see many malaria and health education panels; the Red Cross and the National Malaria Control Programme have distributed thousands of impregnated mosquito bed nets here. If you need it, there is an Área de Saúde (first aid) at the entrance of town, on the left-hand side.

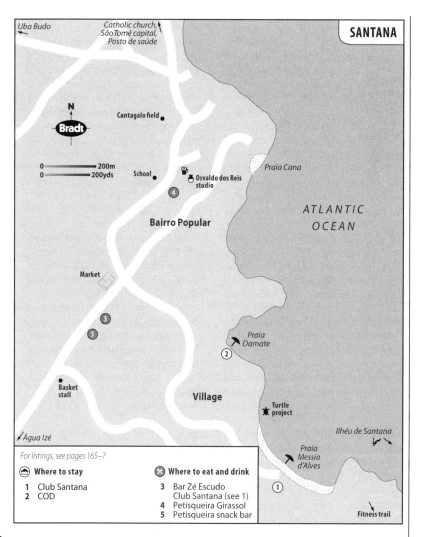

Uba Budo

Catholic church,
São Tomé capital,
Posto de saúde

N

Bradt

Cantagalo field

0 ——— 200m
0 ——— 200yds

School

Osvaldo dos Reis
studio

④

Praia Cana

**ATLANTIC
OCEAN**

Bairro Popular

Market

③

⑤

Praia
Damate

②

Basket
stall

Village

Turtle
project

Ilhéu de Santana

Água Izé

Praia
Messia
d'Alves

①

Fitness trail

For listings, see pages 165–7

⬠ **Where to stay**

1 Club Santana
2 COD

✖ **Where to eat and drink**

3 Bar Zé Escudo
   Club Santana (see 1)
4 Petisqueira Girassol
5 Petisqueira snack bar

Where to stay and eat

🏠 **Club Santana** (31 bungalows) Praia
Messia Alves, CP 144; 🌙 224 2400; e reservas@
clubsantana.com; www.clubsantana.com. The
entrance to the resort is at the top end of the main
Santana road: look for a wooden sign pointing
to the left (palm basketware is often sold here).
From the turn, it's still a 20min walk down to
the resort. A free shuttle service connects the
resort with the city 3 times a day but has to be
confirmed beforehand. The last return shuttle
leaves the capital at 16.00. Club Santana was
refurbished in 2010, & offers individual bungalows
(21 dbl, 10 suites) with AC, frigobar, TV & phone

(UK €2.80/min, US €3.20/min). Rates range from
€135 B&B/€155 HB/€172 FB for a standard sgl
occupancy bungalow to €215/€255/€284 for a
bungalow suite with dbl occupancy. The latter are
suitable for families with children. HB & FB refers
to food only, drinks are not included. HB may
choose between lunch & dinner on a daily basis,
depending on planned activities.Wi-Fi extends to
about 80% of the bungalows (if this is important
to you, specify on booking), the beach, bar &
reception. Residents may use an internet terminal
in the reception area. As in all Western-style hotels,
laundry is expensive (count €7.50 for a skirt, €4.50

for a shirt). If the receptionist seems hesitant, follow your instincts & check back important information such as transfer times for international flights with the management (*gerência*). There are very few mosquitoes here, due to the resort's elevated position & scrupulous cleaning, but there are ants. If you are in the mood for exercise, there is a walking trail starting behind the kitchen, & there is usually a fitness instructor offering stretching exercises at 07.00 on the beach. You can also book a personal fitness session. Bike hire & a swimming pool are planned, & an extension to the beach is underway. Residents can also take advantage of 2 free excursions: a trip to the Cascata de S. Nicolau waterfall & the Monte Café plantation (see pages 158–9), or a half-day visit to the capital. The resort can also arrange a taxi (€40) to take you on a tour of the plantations; good value if there are at least 2 of you. If you're on a budget, walk or hitch a lift up the access path with staff or a guest & flag down a yellow taxi. The post box is not working: hand your mail into reception & they will take care of it. Excellent b/fasts are served in the AC restaurant up top or, if you prefer, at tables outside overlooking the sea, next to a cage with local birds, including lovebirds. Food & drink at the beach snack bar are not cheap, but the resort does not charge a day fee, & hire charges for deckchairs (€3) & towels (€2) for non-residents are reasonable. There is a manned barrier at the entrance; just greet the guard & say '*para o Clube Santana*'. Picnics are not allowed, & min consumption per table is €8. Service is slow, however, & the pizzas are hit-&-miss; order them in advance if you can. French-speaking Santomean head chef, Lurdes Silva, creates amazing French dishes with a local twist, & Santomean specialities using herbs & produce from the garden at the back. Fish is bought fresh from the local fishermen or personally by Lurdes at the market in town. The coffee & chocolate served is Santomean. Every Sat evening, a fantastic if pricey outdoor buffet (€35) on the beach esplanada, with live music (there is a small dance floor), draws the expats. For more on activities at Club Santana, see opposite. **$$$$**

🏠 **COD** (2 suites) Bairro Popular Reboque Santana (GPS LA 0°15'19.04"N LO 6°44'42.88"E); m 990 4382; e pelardeauyves@gmail.com. Casa das Ondas Divinas, aka COD, is a large apartment (160m²) offering sea views from the veranda, a large living room, bathrooms with shower, & a large, fully-equipped kitchen with fridge, washing machine & dishwasher. Beach & surf spot right below the house by private access (surf boards available unless stolen), & gardens. Jeep rental of 7-seater Toyota Prado for €90/day. Contact by email best as Yves spends much of his time in Paris. **$$$$**

What to see and do

The pretty yellow **church** overlooking the rocky bay is a good place to start a walk up the hill through the town, picking up a snack of fruit from roadside vendors to keep you going. The church (⊕ *Sun, ask who has the key*, a chave) is dedicated to Santa Ana, the mother of the Virgin Mary, patron saint of São Tomé and of women in labour. Santa Ana's feast day is 26 July, but the grand procession in her honour takes place in early September. The 1939–40 restoration of the early 16th-century building kept only a few parts of the walls. Inside, under a wooden ceiling, painted blue and decorated with stars, look for a statue of St John the Baptist and a marble statue of Santa Ana, in the traditional representation with the Virgin Mary in her lap.

Carrying on up the hill, past the Cantagalo field, you will come across the studio of one of the island's most popular painters, **Osvaldo dos Reis**, above the large petrol station to the left. Reis has been painting his exuberantly colourful scenes of Santomean daily life, work, leisure, food and traditions for more than a decade. Some of the little kiosks here sell bread rolls and grilled *safú*. There is a bar next to Reis's house (Petisqueira Girassol) which also sells phone top-up cards, and a couple more along the road, such as **Zé Escudo**, with a porch.

The entrance to Santana's **popular quarter** (*bairro popular*) is opposite the market, taking the left of the two dirt tracks; judging by the reaction I got, not many tourists make it here. The houses in the *bairro popular* were built in the early 1950s by a campaign of forced labour, with local men conscripted into this public works effort, building a house every few days and often starting at 02.00 and working for 20 hours at a stretch. This brutal treatment, repeated elsewhere, was one of the contributing factors to the uprising of 1953 (see page 18). If staying at Club Santana, double back on yourself and make an immediate left, walking back down through the fishing village.

Club Santana (see pages 165–6) The beautiful location of this French-owned lodge-style resort on a rocky cliff makes Club Santana very popular with day visitors as well as guests. With its calm waters, the **beach** here is great for snorkelling and is cleaned regularly, so you don't have to worry about stepping on anything. A new **diving centre** started up in 2013, keeping the name of a former operation, Club Maxel, but at the time of writing it was about to be renamed Sete Pedras Diving Center. There is a small turtle project here, too. A few times a year, squid (*lulas*) come ashore to die much to the delight of the locals – a ready-made meal.

Trips out to the tiny **Santana islet** cost €8 for non-residents. The boat will take you right into the islet (the lighthouse on top dates from 1997). Climbing begonias colonise the higher reaches of the basalt rocks, and oysters and yellow and orange corals cling to the waterline. This is a great spot for snorkelling or diving (see page 89); the seaward side of the islet has an 8m cave. There is also a Hobbycat katamaran for hire, and windsurfing boards can be arranged. You can hire a kayak (€3/hr for non-residents) on the spot.

On the other side of Club Santana, there is currently no access to private **Praia Forma** (*www.praiaforma.com*), a beautiful beach of dark-grey sand, *areia mulatta*, but an agritourism project with chalets is planned.

ROÇA ÁGUA IZÉ Back on the coast road, Água Izé, a 30-minute drive from the capital, is one of the biggest (2,600ha) and most-visited plantations. This is where commercial cocoa production first started in the mid 19th century. When the man responsible for introducing cocoa to the islands, João Maria de Sousa e Almeida, was made First Baron of Água Izé in 1868, he was the first *mulatto* nobleman in the Portuguese colonies. In 1884, Água Izé had 50km of internal railway lines running through its 80km² territory and 50 European employees overseeing 2,500 Angolan contract workers. Today, the brown hues of the cocoa beans and hemp sacks in the dusky workshop in the bright yellow repainted buildings make for excellent photo opportunities (the cover photo for our first edition was taken here). If somebody is there, you should be able to taste the cocoa beans. Palm oil is produced here, too, as well as furniture, as part of a Portuguese co-operation project. Walk up through the plantation where kids might be selling fluffy manioc, past the soup kitchen run by a Portuguese charity, keeping to the left. From the top of the hill, you have one of the most photographed views on the island: the beautiful staircase of the crumbling **hospital**, dating from 1928. At the time, this was a state-of-the art hospital, the best in West Africa. To the left, inside the building, sits the rusty hulk of a car. From up here, you have a good view all the way down to the church, the stumps of the pier that in colonial times used to help ferry the beans to the capital, and the beach where a new restaurant/hotel development is being built. From here, it is possible to hike to Bombaim via the plantations of Bernardo and Claudino Faro. The local feast day is 13 May, dedicated to Santa Filomena. If you want to donate some clothing or medicines, ask for the *responsável*, or the Associação dos Moradores, which groups together the inhabitants of the plantation.

BOCA D'INFERNO Probably the oldest tourist attraction on the island, the much-photographed 'Hell's Mouth' is reached by turning off left past Água Izé on to the promontory. Here, the water shoots through rocky basalt channels and gushes high up into the air. Don't be tempted to go too close.

PRAIA SETE ONDAS AND AROUND Next along is the beautiful sweeping beach of the 'Seven Waves' (not signposted); it makes a great picnic spot. You might be joined by youngsters coming down to play with their homemade wooden toys and to practise the Brazilian martial art *capoeira*, quite popular in São Tomé and Príncipe. As with other beaches on this stretch of the coast, a resort is planned, but again, as with others, nothing has really happened yet. It is used as a surfing beach for lessons. Note that this is the only accessible beach on ST where you will easily find the multi-pronged skeletons (*rotulae*) of the rare Gulf of Guinea sea urchins that find their way into craft collars. Allow these *bolachas do mar* (sea cookies) to dry to make them less brittle; they will turn from light blue-green to white.

Just before Santa Cecilia, a path to the right leads in a few minutes to the plantation of **Colónia Açoreana**, passing first by the houses of the workers, painted in light pastel colours. Behind is the main house, still a ruin, but there are plans to renovate the building for tourism. On the left-hand side of the main road, the large abandoned drying facility might be revived again, with a projected plant for the transformation of coconuts, using the whole potential of tree, bark and fruit to produce oil, soap, grated flakes, ropes, cork substitute and isolating material.

PRAIA DE MICONDÓ Past the fishing village of **Ribeira Afonso** (its famous São Isidro saint's day festivities at the end of January draw many Santomeans), the second beach, **Praia de Micondó** (signposted) is a good swimming beach and also one of the best beaches for wildlife watching. As part of a recent ecotourism project (*www.micondo.fr*) you can stay at a lovingly restored plantation up the hill (see below) or in one of the two chalets right on the beach. To the right of the access path to the beach live massive land crabs with blue-grey bodies and fiery red legs. They make great photos, but you have to be quick as they are fairly shy, scurrying back into their holes among the coconut palms fringing the beach if they feel threatened. A trickle of water crossing the path is a favourite haunt for kingfishers, and flocks of smaller birds take off from the bushes as you approach. See how far you can walk up the palm trunk on the beach. There's a changing hut and also a beach bar that is sometimes open, and 5,000$ buys you a fresh coconut *dawa* from the kids playing on the beach.

Where to stay and eat

Praia Micondó m 992 6311; www. micondo.fr. The old plantation house at the foot of Micondó hill has been lovingly restored by a French couple & now provides a welcome addition to the accommodation options along the east coast. Staying at 'Escapade' costs €40 B&B; one of the beach shacks is €35 B&B. It's €10 to pitch your tent. I hear the food is good, but the portions small. The only problem here seems to be with communication & they don't work with agencies. I have heard it's best to go there in person. Sébastien and Cristelle can often be found down at the beach. **$$**

SÃO JOÃO DOS ANGOLARES AND AROUND

The main attraction of this fishing village and centre of the Angolares community (see box, pages 174–5), in the shade of the Pico María Fernandes, is the Roça de São João working plantation, a cultural and gastronomic gem and handy stop-off point on your way south (and/or on the return journey). In the village, as an independent traveller you will probably be quickly surrounded by local kids, it seems that most *brancos*, or *colombas*, only whizz through here in their jeeps. In 2013, the central square was being restored.

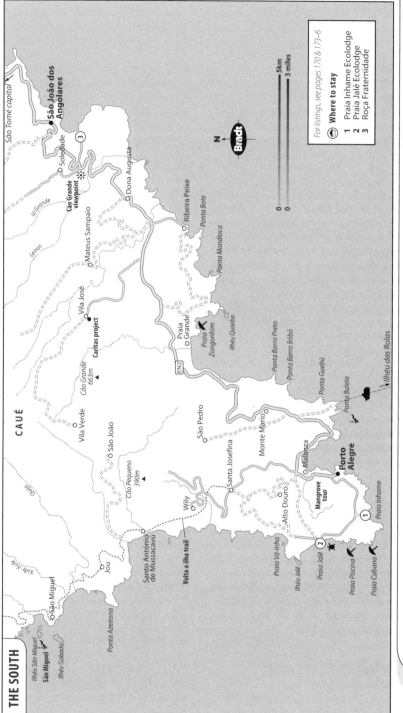

6

169

THE SOUTH

CAUÉ

For listings, see pages 170 & 173–6

Where to stay
1 Praia Inhame Ecolodge
2 Praia Jalé Ecolodge
3 Roça Fraternidade

0 5km
0 3 miles

N

São Tomé capital

São João dos Angolares

Soledade

Cão Grande viewpoint

Dona Augusta

Mateus Sampaio

Vila José

Caritas project

Cão Grande 663m

Vila Verde

São João

Cão Pequeno 390m

São Miguel

Jou

Santo António de Mussacavú

Volta a ilha trail

Wily

São Pedro

São Pedro

Santa Josefina

Monte Mário

Alto Douro

Malanza

Porto Alegre

Mangrove tour

Praia Vd-inha

Ilhéu Jalé

Praia Jalé

Praia Piscina

Praia Cabana

Praia Inhame

Ilhéu das Rolas

Ponta Baleia

Ponta Guebú

Ponta Barro Bóbó

Ponta Barro Preto

Ponta Guebú

Ilhéu Quixibá

Praia Zonganhim

Praia Grande

Ribeira Peixe

Ponta Bote

Ponta Mandioca

EN2

Ponta Azeitona

Ilhéu São Miguel
São Miguel
Ilhéu Gabado

Xufé-Xufé

Quija

Io Grande

Lemos

Ilhéu São Miguel

GETTING THERE AND AWAY A **shared taxi** costs 30,000$ from the capital, but be aware that taxis stop running at around 15.00, and a private run will cost you €50 or more. The same applies for the return journey.

WHERE TO STAY

Roça São João (6 rooms) Signposted to the right as you come into town; 📞 226 1140, 222 5135 (office in the capital); www.rocasjoao.com. This is a successful ecotourism venture in the lovely old administrator's house. The rooms themselves share 4 bathrooms (they vary in facilities, check if you can), & extra beds can be arranged (€9–18). Due to the restaurant's success, diners sometimes use the shared guest bathrooms upstairs, as overflow, which isn't ideal as not all rooms can be locked (in keeping with the open colonial architecture). There is no need for AC as the *roça* lies above the village's humid microclimate. A balcony runs all around the house, with seats where you can put your feet up & look out over the misty forest or past the huge fig tree to the bay, read, or listen to the birds – sometimes white-tailed tropicbirds come in. You may hear a few muffled sounds from the *roça*, maybe workers picking herbs for dinner. There is only cold water, but if you ask nicely, as we did arriving after a day-long forest trek, they can heat a bucket of water for you. You can ask to have your washing done, too. B/fasts include homemade jams & fresh fruit. The only snag is that they are served at a set time of 08.00 & staff only arrive at 07.00. You will definitely see & hear the very vocal sunbird on the ground here & maybe the paradise flycatcher; take a left or a right past the hospital for a longer birdwatching excursion. Power (*luz*) is available from 17.00–22.30. If you're planning to come back late at night, make sure you tell the guard as otherwise you might find yourself locked out. Dinner costs €12, €10 if you're dining 2 nights. For more on the excellent food, see below. **$$**

Mionga (3 rooms) Signposted just outside the village, to the left (no longer on the main road); 📞 226 1141; e nelitopereira81@gmail.com, nelito.mionga.angolares@gmail.com. 2 ground-floor rooms, plus 1 on stilts – the latter is the best option as you can lock the door & it has a mosquito net. With its pretty decoration & friendly welcome,

this is the kind of place I'd love to full-heartedly recommend as an alternative to the Roça de São João but at the time of writing I can't because the dip-in-the-middle mattress made sleep difficult, if not impossible. If owners Nelito & Keta have replaced it, then go for it. Other travellers were kept awake by the local cockerels, but that's a problem all over the islands. The bathroom (cold water) is OK. Good b/fasts, & don't miss lunching in the restaurant (see opposite page). The friendly waiter doubles as a guide. **$**

Prédio (1 apt) Market Sq; m 991 1943. The 1 cheap apt in the building was on a long-term rental to a health project when I last visited. There is a kitchen (you cook with coal or kerosene) & a large dining table, but in the past there were often problems with water pressure; better check first. Ask for Dona Aurea at the bakery next to the church. **$**

Roça Fraternidade (14 rooms) 6km south of São João; 📞 226 1159. A hardy traveller who stayed at this plantation described the experience as 'the loneliest night of my life'. You might want to bring some company then, but the views over the mountains of Trás-os-Montes, Bombaim & María Fernandes are spectacular. To get there, head south on the road lined by the white-flowering wild ginger & turn left up a dirt track when Cão Grande comes into view on your right (the track to the right leads to Roça Soledade). Some 50 families live here; the grounds of the plantation cover 900ha & span 7km. The rooms, in a yellow house built on stilts, have various degrees of comfort, but you should be able to take your pick. Ask for *o cuarto do doutor* (the doctor's room), in the corner at the back, which is nicely furnished. There is drinking water from the spring, but no electricity, so come prepared and bring food. The friendly foreman, João, can advise you but no longer provides meals. At sunset, wander down the path towards the main road again for a good view of Cão Grande. **$**

WHERE TO EAT AND DRINK

Roça de São João Signposted to the right as you come into town; 📞 226 1140, 222 5135 (office in the capital); www.rocasjoao.com. The

roça serves some of the best food in São Tomé & Príncipe, cooked with fresh local ingredients using lots of herbs & spices (if a bit heavy sometimes on

For listings, see pages 170–1

Where to stay

1 Prédio

Off map
   Mionga
   Roça Fraternidade
   Roça São João

Where to eat and drink

2 Bar Pépé
3 Bar Pépé
4 Chez Nezó

Roça São João,
Vale do Carmo
abandoned plantation

Swimming beaches,
São Tomé capital

Police ●

Shop selling petrol

Market ● Shops

CST

Post office/CTT ✉

Main Square

N

Bradt

(SKETCH MAP)
Not to scale

Bakery ●

Catholic church ✝

Irmãs ●
Teresianas

Cão Grande viewpoint,
Roça Fraternidade,
Porto Alegre

Mionga

Beach

Fishery Museum
(under construction)

a single flavour, such as cinnamon or coriander), &
is lovingly presented. Head chef is the local
'Mr Culture', João Carlos Silva, presenter of a
successful TV programme on RTP Africa, *Na Roça
Com Os Tachos* – literally 'On the Plantation with
Cooking Pots' (see page 81, for his *calulú* recipe).
Some travellers have found this place overpriced
but many expats travel here from the capital just
for the food. The cool airy veranda where meals are
taken is great for relaxing, with hammocks, comfy
bamboo furniture, art books, & local produce for
sale such as coffee from the *roça*, fantastic mango
jam, palm oil & pickles. For lunch & dinner, guests
have a choice of fish or meat. For vegetarians, São
João is the best place on the island. Portions are
not huge & if you like 1 dish, make sure you ask
for more before the next course arrives. You are
also welcome just to drop in for a coffee, but while
people are singing on the plantation & life here has
a good vibe, don't expect the service to be as good
when the owners aren't around. $$$

✕ **Bar Pépé** Main road & market; m 996 2254.
The diminutive Pépé seems to have a bit of a
monopoly in town, running a restaurant with disco
next to the market (*calulú* can be ordered in advance),
& a bar at the corner of the main square. $$

✕ **Chez Nezó** Main road; m 991 1474. Good
food at good value, cooked by Kady, the wife
of acclaimed Angolar artist Nezó, served on the
narrow porch. If you visit during the daytime,
Nezó will be happy to show you his work; he is
a very interesting person to talk to, not least to
get a different take on the infamous Agripalma
situation. Currently a large extension, with an
elevated restaurant (where lunch & dinner will
be served, advance order required) & bar is being
built, overlooking the bay. $$

✕ **Mionga** Signposted just outside the village, to
the left; 🕿 226 1141. Simple yet excellent restaurant
attached to accommodation (see opposite page).
Named after the Angolares word for 'ocean' or 'sea'
& run by Nelito & Kela, it has a beautiful view of
the beach from the outdoor balcony. Delicious
soups, fish, breadfruit, etc. A sample menu could be
mokeka de frango, chicken prepared in palm oil with
coconut & vegetables, with ripe banana compote
for afters. Like Nezó's, they are open to suggestions
& prefer diners to book in advance. As there is
stagnant water in front & at the back of Mionga,
mosquitoes unfortunately join the party in the
evening. Your best bet is a fabulous lunch enjoyed
in the colourful & neat interior. $$

The East and South   SÃO JOÃO DOS ANGOLARES AND AROUND

6

OTHER PRACTICALITIES

✚ **Hospital Santa Cruz** Main Sq; ☎ 226 1155, 226 1130 (ambulance); ⏱ 24hrs, to the public 08.00–15.00. The hospital only has limited facilities.

🖥 **Internet** With your own device, you can capture a strong signal sitting on the steps at the side of the Câmara Municipal (09.00–13.00 Mon–Fri, 17.00–22.30 Sat–Sun) – though this can be slightly creepy on your own at night. Inside, there might also be a computer terminal free to use, though it will be popular. With your own device, you could try to access the Wi-Fi from the hospital office, but the *técnico* needs to be there, or ask the

guard to place you below the hub hanging from the ceiling (have a small tip handy). If you speak Portuguese, ask for Senhor Marconi (m 996 0864).

⛽ **Petrol** Diesel is available from a couple of shacks along the main street. Make sure you fill up with the correct fuel.

Police Main road; ☎ 226 1125

✉ **Post** The CTT is open 08.00–noon & 14.00–17.00. Postal services are patchy – on a recent visit, they didn't have stamps & couldn't mail a small parcel.

☎ **Telephone** The CST phone exchange is on the main road. Mobile signal is pretty good.

WHAT TO SEE AND DO While the **Irmãs Teresianas** next to the church sadly no longer have their simple guest room available, one of the friendly Sisters (all from Angola) might be able to show you around. The feast day of Santa Cruz de Angolares is on 13 September. On the other end of the spiritual spectrum, I'm told a well-known faith healer resides in the village. If you would like to experience that part of the local culture, ask around for the *curandeiro*.

Reached by taking a left past Nezó's house, the town **beach** is OK to walk along, but too close to the town, fairly littered, and too popular with pigs and horseflies to swim. If you do want to swim here, make sure you go to the far end. The colourful restored house at the start of the beach, its pier painted a bright red, is the **Panhá Voador** project, a new **fishery museum** connected with the Roça de São João; a seafood snack bar is also planned. You can usually buy a coconut from one of the locals working down at the beach (local price 500$, tourist price 5,000$). If you arrive at the right time, you can also buy a ready-grilled fish for about 30,000$, sold straight out of a couple of *piroga* boats.

The better swimming beaches, **Praia de Micondó** (see page 168), **Praia Angobó** and the dark-sand **Praia Angra Toldo**, are about 4km away to the north. If you don't have a car, hitch a ride with one of the many yellow taxis leaving São João.

Explore the **forest** around the Pico María Fernandes with a guide from the *roça* (see below) who can take you on a walk to the Fraternidade plantation (see page 170), a 15km round trip with spectacular views. You can take a trip over to **Ilhéu das Rolas** (see pages 178–84) to see the Equator mark if you catch the 10.30 boat (☎ *226 1195, phone ahead to check it's running*), returning to the mainland on the afternoon boat.

Roça São João ☎ *226 1140, 222 5135 (office in the capital); www.rocasjoao.com*) Overlooking the bay of Santa Cruz, this rural ecotourism plantation venture has a cosy inviting feel, with paintings and sculptures by local artists everywhere. For the past 20 years, João Carlos Silva has been a man on a mission: to transform the former slave trade hub of São Tomé into a hub for culture, especially for the countries sharing the Portuguese language. This is where the first Bienal (see page 38) was held in 1995, and artistic creation continues in the form of residences and other projects. A bit set back, past the calabash trees and passionfruit hedges, is the former hospital, which has spaces for art and music classes, and workshops where local girls produce woodwork as part of the Agarra a Vida and Roçamundo social projects. This pretty **Hospital da Criação** (creative hospital), also has two simply furnished rooms (one double and one single), used as overflow for tour leaders, for instance. Especially when you're on your own, sensitive minds will feel the heavy history of a plantation hospital.

Cookery classes can be arranged here, and it's educational and enormous fun to pull out manioc by the root, cut some okra shoots, piri-piri and Taiwanese lemons, and then to prepare a *feijoada a modo da terra* (meaty bean stew), salted mangoes, coconut slivers with cinnamon, pineapple rice and maybe a filled breadfruit.

There are various guided **nature trails** on foot, by bike or canoe (reserve at least a day before as there are no bikes on site); picnics cost €8–10, a guide €45 per day. A *bulaué* band also can be organised (€60). Birdwatchers can track down the rare endemic **dwarf olive ibis** with friendly guide Zeca (though he told me when I visited in 2013 that its habitat has now shifted with the encroachment of oil palm plantations). You can spot other fabulous endemic birds, including: the speirops, olho grosso; Newton's yellow-breasted sunbird, tsélélé; the Gulf of Guinea thrush, toldo; and the oriole, papafigo. You may also get tantalisingly close to the elusive emerald cuckoo, ossobó. For most of the time, you are walking on the **old Bombaim road** (a 12-hour walk in total, requiring camping; if you fancy it, one of the guides could probably take you, with advance planning), passing the palm wine seller's place, marked by cut-off plastic bottles upended on sticks, and the abandoned plantation of **Vale do Carmo**. Zeca can also take you on a giant sunbird mission to Dona Augusta and around the peaks of María Fernandes or Cão Grande. The services of the guides for this trip cost €20 for half-a-day, €40 for a whole day There is a waterfall 30 minutes' walk away, but I'm told it's only worth a visit in the rainy season.

FROM SÃO JOÃO DOS ANGOLARES TO PORTO ALEGRE

On your way down south, you will see the destruction inflicted by Agripalma first-hand (see page 15). Ignore any signs to the Emolve palm oil factory as the current set-up is not interested in visitors, being at the centre of one of the biggest controversies on the island. As in other African countries, the rainforest is being threatened through the extensive planting of palm trees. Further along, the bridge fell in a few years ago; the detour is a couple of metres to the right. A 15-minute walk up from **Ribeira Peixe** bridge is the Ribeira Peixe **waterfall**. Get a local guide to show you the way, not least as the area is a favourite haunt of the black cobra. This is also an excellent birding area; a Birdquest group I met camped two nights here and saw practically everything they hoped to see. A 4km **cycling circuit** runs around this area, taking in Vila José, the orange plantation of Mateus Sampaio, and a waterfall, and another cycling circuit is currently being opened around the Malanza Mangrove between Porto Alegre, Praia Jalé and Malanza.

PORTO ALEGRE

To be honest, there's nothing much in this large and very poor fishing village to detain you; consequently, most people just drive through on the way to **Praia Jalé**. If you're headed to the ecolodge, drive through the village, hugging the left, carry on straight and drive across the central square – surrounded by crumbling colonial buildings, such as the old army barracks, with painted figures and 'Jesus Saves' messages – and head for the path to the right at the back.

🏠 **WHERE TO STAY**

🏠 **Praia Inhame Eco Lodge** (12 chalets)
m 990 4312; e lucarvalho70@hotmail.com; www.

hotelpraiainhame.com. Situated within walking distance of Porto Alegre, in the area of the former

SÃO TOMÉ'S 'MAROON' COMMUNITY: THE ANGOLARES

Thanks to Gerhard Seibert and Paulo Alves Pereira

The Angolares, a fishing people populating the coastal stretches of the island, from Santa Catarina in the west down to Ilhéu das Rolas in the south, have fascinated the local imagination and Western researchers for a long time. A distinct socio-cultural group of several thousand people, the Angolares speak their own language, *n'gola*, not intelligible to other Santomeans (see box, pages 34–5). For centuries, mystery surrounded the question of how the Angolares people came to be on the island. The traditional story is that the Angolares are the descendants of a slave ship shipwrecked on the Sete Pedras rocks to the southwest of the island. Some 200 slaves are said to have swum ashore and founded a community. This romantic notion, handed down by oral transmission and promoted by a colonial government embarrassed by the draining of their workforce, has been disproved by recent historical, genetic and linguistic research. The Angolares are, in fact, a 'maroon' society established by runaway slaves, who, in the early 16th century in particular, were fleeing the harsh conditions on the plantations to form communities of fugitives (known as *fugões* since the 19th century). From the impenetrable *obô* forest they would mount raids on plantations, destroy sugar mills and take slave women and provisions back to their *quilombos*. The most successful slave uprising was led in 1595 by Rei Amador, a slave from the town. Whilst the portrait of Amador on dobra banknotes is pure fiction, and the claim that he was 'king' of the Angolares and the date of the feast day commemorating his execution by the colonial government (4 January), have no historical base, he remains very important to the culture of the Angolares, and to Santomean national identity. In any case, it was only in 1693 that the Angolares were defeated by the Portuguese. Apart from the prisoners, who were enslaved, the rest of the community remained fairly autonomous until, in the mid 19th century, Angolares and Portuguese met again during re-colonisation. With new cocoa plantations encroaching on their lands, the Angolares were obliged to provide fish to the plantations in exchange for not being conscripted to work there.

Alto Douro & São Josefina plantations, this is the star in recent Santomean tourism development. The quiet, beautifully appointed wooden chalets on a slope by the beach cost between €50 & €60; solo travellers pay €40. A couple of them have kitchen facilities. Local materials, beautiful wooden floors & pretty African fabrics. Bathrooms are spotless & b/fasts excellent. Open to non-residents, the restaurant is not cheap but has fine food & a fabulous wine selection. While not the best swimming beach in the area (Praia Piscina is a 15min walk away), Praia Inhame is a prime turtle beach. Owners Nazaré & Luisa proudly display a photograph of a huge *ambulância* turtle that took shelter below the restaurant one Christmas, deposited 200 eggs – & couldn't get out. In season, a member of staff patrols the beach at night for

egg-laying activity, & will wake you up if you request it. A short walk up Morro Chapa hill at the back reveals fine views & an interesting historic surprise: a huge rusty Soviet-era radar station, picturesquely entangled in the forest. The lodge hires out bikes (€5/day) & snorkelling equipment, & half- or full-day fishing trips can be organised. The ecoresort supports the local community; for instance, half the fee for hiring a guide (€15/day) or taking a mangrove boat trip (€10) is donated to an old people's home in Porto Alegre. Boat trips on the traditional *barco* cost €40, if you find enough people to join you, a *Volta a ilha* tour can be organised, too. The resort is solar-powered & uses a coconut-waste-burning oven to heat the water. Wi-Fi was being installed at the time of going to print. Note that the owners live primarily in the

Today, the Angolares make up the vast majority of fishermen on the island, following the fish along the coast. Politically, the Angolares are usually affiliated with the MLSTP/PSD party (see page 19). Socially, as they have always refused work on the plantations, they remained outside mainstream *forro* and *contratados* contract worker communities. They continue to live in their typical fishermen's huts, called *vampleglá*, made of wooden planks and covered with interlacing palm fronds, and use the *dongo* dug-out canoe and harpoons for their artisanal fishing. The culture of the Angolares, *angolaridade* – art, music, a strong sense of tradition and of freedom – was celebrated by the late Portuguese author Fernando de Macedo (1923–2006), who claimed to be the descendant of the last Angolar king, Simão Andreza. Poems such as 'Capitango, capitango' and 'Rema, Pescador, Resiste' ('Row, Fisherman, Resist') evoke the imagery of traditional Angolar society and the exaltations and dangers of the sea. The centre of *angolar* culture is around the town of São João dos Angolares in the southeastern Caué district. The most important site for meditation and communication between the living and the dead is the Budo Bachana mountain, whilst the border between the Angolar kingdom, *Anguéné*, and the outside world is still taken to be at Praia do Rei. In the Angolar animist worldview, mountains, rivers and animals such as the owl and the shrew are holy. The *ocá* tree is particularly revered, and, as in the American Indian tradition, before any tree is felled, its spirit is asked for permission.

Linguistic studies reveal the *n'gola* lexicon to consist of 65% Portuguese, 14% Bantu languages, 1% Kwa, with the remaining 20% still unidentified, disproving the cherished hypothesis that the Angolares were the descendants of Angolan slaves or pre-discovery explorers. Whilst there is no written tradition, Angolar culture remains alive in language and rituals, in *bulaué* music and the work of resident painter and musician Nezó and sculptor Nelito, owner of the Mionga hotel/restaurant (see page 170). If you are passing through São João dos Angolares in the second week of September, don't miss their biggest religious celebration in honour of Santa Cruz. On any day of the year, impress the locals you'll meet along the main *monja* (street) with a few words of their language: *Ma vira-ó?*: 'Everything OK?' *N' sabóa!*: 'Everything OK!'

city (Nazaré owns the Padaria Moderna bakery, see page 124), so make sure you have everything you need, & be aware that things might not run as smoothly when they aren't there. I've heard that sometimes email bookings from outside the island can be difficult, so if you don't hear back & are planning to stay in high season, book through an agency. $$$

🏠 **Praia Jalé Ecolodge** (3 en-suite bungalows, 1 suitable for groups & families, tent spaces) m 991 7009 (for reservations); e marapastp@gmail.com. Bed down next to the crashing waves in the southernmost corner of the island. This popular ecolodge reopened in 2014, the former coconut-wood bungalows giving way to new lodgings & an eating area that follow the principles of eco-architecture: using bamboo, local stone, clay & vegetable fibres. Meals are taken at the beach restaurant (can be vegetarian) or you can use the kitchen. The restaurant is open to non-residents, but it might be best to book ahead. You can also wash your clothes here. The ecolodge is powered by renewable energy, & uses river & rain water. There is an educational area explaining the local heritage & ecosystems. Praia Jalé lies in the buffer zone of Obô National Park & is a famous turtle beach; Malanza mangrove (see page 176) is just round the corner. In season, you can see all the island's species of turtle laying eggs, or the release of hatchlings to the sea. Outside the season, at night, you'll have hundreds of crabs for company; bring flip-flops & don't worry if you step on them as they are very resilient. The area is not really suitable for swimming (see pages 177–80) but

A very relaxing and rewarding experience is to be steered through the quiet waters of São Tomé's largest mangrove in a traditional dugout canoe, organised through MARAPA, an NGO, with all profits going directly to community development projects. The two-hour tour costs €10 per person, bookable/payable either at the MARAPA office in the capital (see pages 113–14), in Porto Alegre at the Praia Jalé reception (see page 175), Praia Inhame reception (see page 173; they revert part of the costs to an old-people's home and travellers are encouraged to hand over the donation in person) or directly with Senhor Vitalo in Malanza.

Starting from the bridge just outside Malanza, your guide will paddle you south across the calm waters bordered by red and white mangrove trees. The bark of the red mangrove was traditionally used on the plantations to dye the sacks for cocoa and copra; today the fishermen use it to tint the white fishing nets, to make them less shiny and less likely to scare the fish away. However, taking the bark leaves the tree vulnerable to salt and water damage and the trees can die, destabilising the ecosystem. The white mangrove tree helps stop erosion by its roots extending out of the water; it is also an important food source for the mudskipper (*cucumba*). The mangrove trees' underwater roots can also temporarily immobilise your canoe. Although many fish come here to reproduce, mangroves support only a few specific species of tree and animal. The most common bird species found here are the moorhen (*galinha-d'agua*), the malachite kingfisher (*conóbia*) and the reed cormorant (*pato-de-água*). As part of the tour, the guide moors the boat at a wooden walkway usually frequented by the only primate on the islands, the mona monkey (*macaco*).

The Malanza brochure, in Portuguese and French, is sold in the Ossobô shop in São Tomé (€5; see page 125).

---

ask around for surfing contacts. Bring your own board if you want to be sure of catching equatorial waves. For more on surfing, see page 92. **$–$$**
🏠 **Casa de Vado e Milú** 🔧 991 7602. 1 basic self-catering room with kitchen (€20 for 1 or 2

people, with b/fast) right in Porto Alegre, run by Vado & his wife Milú. A good-value base for those travellers who like to experience the popular fishing-village vibe; good beaches are within walking distance. **$**

🍴 **WHERE TO EAT AND DRINK** The **Praia Inhame** and **Praia Jalé** (reserve in advance) ecolodges serve meals to non-residents.

🍴**Vado e Milú** On the left-hand side as you come into Porto Alegre; m 991 7602. Milú's place sells self-catering staples like biscuits, spaghetti & rice, bottled soft drinks, beer & water. For €5 Vado will bring a

freshly grilled fish lunch to you on the beach. **$**
🍴 **Nei** Next to Vado's place; 🔧 226 1026; m 992 3407. A recommended option for freshly caught fish. **$**

OTHER PRACTICALITIES Up on the hill; the **posto de saúde** (first aid) is housed in the yellow building near the New Apostolic church. The **disco** situation in town shifts; just ask around or listen out for the action.

WHAT TO SEE AND DO A **guide** can be arranged to show you around, but if you just wander about somebody will usually materialise, and I've found people

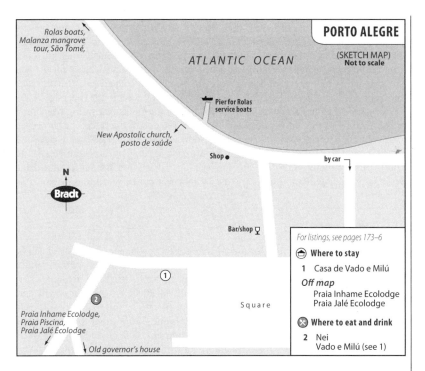

ATLANTIC OCEAN

(SKETCH MAP)
Not to scale

Rolas boats,
Malanza mangrove
tour, São Tomé,

Pier for Rolas
service boats

New Apostolic church,
posto de saúde

Shop ●

by car

N

Bradt

Bar/shop

①

②

Square

Praia Inhame Ecolodge,
Praia Piscina,
Praia Jalé Ecolodge

Old governor's house

For listings, see pages 173–6

🏠 **Where to stay**

1   Casa de Vado e Milú

Off map
    Praia Inhame Ecolodge
    Praia Jalé Ecolodge

❌ **Where to eat and drink**

2   Nei
    Vado e Milú (see 1)

very friendly and appreciative of the interest. Goats hop among the ruins and abandoned farm machinery, while the tall brick chimneys are no longer in use for palm oil production. The most impressive building in Porto Alegre is the big white New Apostolic church up on the hill – most people assume this is the **old governor's house**, which is, in fact, a ruin on a bluff the other side of the bay. It is privately owned and not open to the public, but you can take a pleasant 30 minute walk up to the old governor's house for a good view over the town and the bay. To visit it, leave Porto Alegre on the coast path leading towards Praia Jalé; five minutes after passing the Praia Jalé reception a gentle path leads up to your left. Continuing along the coast track towards good swimming beaches, you're likely to meet a fisherman with his colourful daily catch dangling from his harpoon, or a palm wine tapper working high up in the tree. A local fisherman/diver should be able to offer **snorkelling trips**. The best diver and a good cook is Manel, 'Nei' (✆ 226 1026; m 992 3407), you will find his restaurant next to Vado's (see above). It is also possible to organise **mangrove tours** from here (see box, opposite), and there are a number of activities on offer at Praia Inhame Ecolodge (see above).

Beaches The beaches on this stretch of coast are all **turtle beaches**. In season (November–March) you can watch female turtles laying eggs. The release of hatchlings takes place between September and April. The closest beach to Porto Alegre, **Praia Cabana**, is not signposted. Listen out for the waves when you've walked maybe 15 minutes from Porto Alegre; there are two entrances, with a widely disregarded anti-litter sign. Still within walking distance of Porto Alegre (signposted from the coastal track, the next beach after Praia Cabana), **Praia Piscina** is one of the best beaches on the island, a sweeping expanse of white sand, framed by black basalt rock. There's a shallow pool to the left (the small sea urchins

The East and South   PORTO ALEGRE

6

177

are fine, but mind the big ones: their spines can bring on a fever), and beware as the middle pool receives sudden waves crashing over the rocks at the back. The best swimming is to the right, though there can be some strong currents, too. Litter is encroaching even here, sadly, and the beach's popularity means you should take care of your belongings, too. The beautifully tucked-away turtle beach of **Praia Jalé** is mainly visited on an overnight stop at the ecolodge (see pages 175–6). Because of some treacherous currents, it is not really a swimming beach and nor is **Praia Va inhá**, a 20-minute walk away to the end of the track. It is, however, one of the most secluded on the island, and is completely litter-free as access is on foot only from where you park your car at a bend. This is where you'll find the plantation where the delicious Delicias das Ilhas jams, aromatics and dried fruit are produced. Park the car and ask Senhor Marcolino to mind it for you, just in case.

ILHÉU DAS ROLAS

If you want to just stand on the Equator mark once in your life, Rolas Island can be visited on an organised lunch trip, but for relaxation and to really enjoy the island, a four to five night stay is ideal, longer if you are planning to do a lot of diving.

When the Pestana Equador resort was built in 2000, the Angolares villagers of **São Francisco** had to move, receiving some compensation. Later, the Pestana Group tried to entice the villagers to leave the island entirely, but there was some resistance and criticism of the low level of compensation offered. The state has since moved the school to Porto Alegre. Meanwhile, Pestana has provided energy provision, a community TV, etc. Resort jobs are very sought-after locally, despite a waiter here earning only the minimum wage, about €45 a month. Look out for the little chapel dedicated to St Francis, to the right of the pier, when you arrive.

GETTING THERE AND AWAY There is a boat service (the crossing takes around 20 minutes) connecting the **Ponte Baleia** embarkation point with Ilhéu das Rolas. Ponte Baleia is a good two-hour drive on the road south from the capital, with wonderful views of the Cão Grande. The turn-off to Ponte Baleia is now signposted; once you have passed Monte Mario (where, sometimes, monkeys play in the trees), and are going down the hill again towards Malanza, look out for a wooden sign on the right-hand side of the road pointing to a bumpy track to your left.

If you've booked a Pestana package, your crossing is taken care of, and the boat will usually leave for the island at 10.30 and return at 16.30. A private transfer costs €35 per person. A new boat is expected to start service in 2014; in the past, guests sometimes had to change over to the wooden service boat mid-crossing. For €10 each way, you can leave the Pestana Ocean Resort hotel in São Tomé (see page 115) in the morning at 07.30 and make the return journey at around 17.00, picking up clients from the 16.30 boat from the island. There is a daily service, costing €50 for all transfers by bus and boat from the capital and buffet lunch. If you have your own car, at weekends, a buffet lunch-only package includes both lunch and the crossing.

If you're booked to stay on the island, be sure to confirm in advance which boat you want to take. As the radio at Ponte Baleia is solar-powered it doesn't work at night and staff can't alert reception if you are late. Late arrival is discouraged, but if you do arrive late and don't want to pay €35 a head, try to zoom over to Porto Alegre, a few minutes' drive further south, where a *carioco* wooden service boat with outboard motor might be leaving for Rolas between 17.00 and 18.00. If you are too late for that, then you'll have to find (and pay) a sympathetic canoe owner to get you across, though there are obviously no life jackets or radio contact if things should go wrong.

If you want to leave before the 16.30 boat and explore Porto Alegre or one of the nearby beaches, talk to the head receptionist at the Pestana; you might be able to catch an earlier boat taking staff across. All you need to do then is to make sure you are back at Ponte Baleia at 14.45 to catch the minibus back to the capital; the driver often starts the return trip in Porto Alegre, but don't rely on that.

🏠 WHERE TO STAY

🏠 **Pestana Equador** (70 bungalows) CP 851; 📞226 1195; e pestana.equador@pestana.com; www.pestana.com; São Tomé office: Av 12 de Julho; 📞224 4503; e reservas.stome@pestana.com. This 4-star resort is the only commercial accommodation on the island. All the bungalows are pleasant, with TV, fridge, AC & ceiling fan, & a veranda with comfy chairs, and are set in well-tended landscaped gardens, with hibiscus & pineapple borders. The semi-detached bungalows have fairly thin walls; as the resort is hardly ever fully booked, ask for a bungalow without neighbours. No 401/402 Standard is the best choice, as you get a sea view without paying more for it, but it gets booked up quickly. Otherwise, only the front bungalows with the 300 numbers have a sea view; the 600 numbers at the back are more spacious, with cattle egrets grazing outside. Another easy bird to spot around the compound is the pin-tailed whydah (the male has a conspicuously long tail); these were introduced as pet birds & always live close to humans. Lizards flit across the wooden walkways connecting the different parts of the resort. You have gorgeous views of both Cão Grande & Cão Pequeno, framing golden beaches. A 2,300m² landscaped saltwater pool, the largest on the West African coast, snakes its way around a bar, with an infinity pool feature. Cooling off with a midnight swim in the infinity pool under the stars is a truly fitting finish to a night on the Equator. During the day, you can use the pool table & play a round of ping-pong; there is a beach volleyball net, too. There is also a small jacuzzi (refurbished in 2013) with a massage/acupuncture table between the quay & the pool. A 30min massage costs €20, 1hr €40; a 30min acupuncture (Tue, Fri & Sat)

costs €25. The climate on Rolas is even more hot & humid than on the main island, & early in the afternoon mosquitoes will start coming out; while the bungalows are sprayed regularly, don't invite the mozzies in by leaving the doors open. Always have a bottle of fresh water in your bungalow, as you cannot buy anything after the bars close. With 80% of visitors Portuguese, if now increasingly complemented by Italians, Spanish & Angolans, there have been complaints that reception staff don't have enough English. If there are any problems, ask for the day manager (their names are posted on the counter), or the head receptionist; they can usually sort things out for you. Bring cash for your drinks, just in case there's a problem with the credit card machine at check-out. (Also, the link-up with Portugal for the processing adds €3 to the bill.) Resort guests take meals – b/fast, lunch (if you're on FB, joined by day trippers) & dinner – in the Sete Pedras Restaurant, situated on an elevation on the eastern side of the island overlooking two bays & the open sea with the Sete Pedras rocks in the distance. The restaurant is a 5min walk from the bungalows, past egrets feeding on the lawn. The b/fast buffet (07.30–10.00) serves freshly squeezed fruit juices, rolls, brioches, cereals, fresh fruit, Santomean coffee & a variety of teas. The dinner buffet (19.30–22.00) offers 3–4 main courses, fish & meat, prepared in international & African style. Get there early as any buffet food will suffer from being on hot plates for too long. There are 3 bars on site, see below for details. For business visitors, there are also 2 conference rooms. The website offers a Best Rate guarantee for accommodation prices. Chalets **$$$**, suites **$$$**, superior suites **$$$$**

If you are on a tight budget and have a sleeping bag and/or tent, there is nothing to stop you from asking about informal accommodation in the village.

✖ WHERE TO EAT AND DRINK Pestana understandably discourages eating food in
the village; however, standards of hygiene are unlikely to be better or worse than

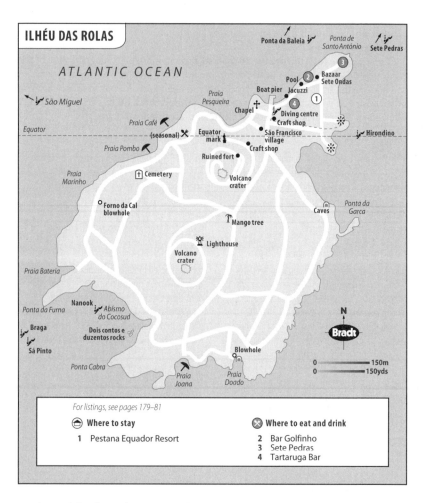

For listings, see pages 179–81

ILHÉU DAS ROLAS

ATLANTIC OCEAN

São Miguel

Equator

Praia Café (seasonal)

Praia Pombo

Praia Pesqueira

Chapel

Equator mark

Ruined fort

Praia Marinho

Cemetery

Forno da Cal blowhole

Volcano crater

Mango tree

Lighthouse

Volcano crater

Praia Bateria

Nanook   Abísmo do Cocosud

Ponta da Furna

Braga

Sá Pinto

Dois contos e duzentos rocks

Ponta Cabra

Praia Joana

Praia Doado

Blowhole

Ponta da Baleia   Ponta de Santo António   Sete Pedras

Pool   Bazaar Sete Ondas

Boat pier   Jacuzzi

Diving centre
Craft shop

São Francisco village

Craft shop

Caves   Ponta da Garca

Hirondino

N

0   150m
0   150yds

Where to stay
1   Pestana Equador Resort

Where to eat and drink
2   Bar Golfinho
3   Sete Pedras
4   Tartaruga Bar

on the mainland, so it's up to you. Youngsters may accost you on your way up to the Equator mark and offer to cook a lunch for €5–10. The Praia Café bar is open in season.

You have to sign a chit for every beverage you consume in the resort bars (a beer costs €2), and pay your collection of chits when you check-out of the resort. This process can be prone to errors, so check your bill. The resort's **swimming pool bar** is open for drinks from 09.30 to 18.00.

✗ Sete Pedras Restaurant Pestana Equador. Resort guests take their meals here, and non-residents are welcome for lunch. The restaurant, with a tasteful terracotta floor & wood carvings, is open on 3 sides, but gets surprisingly hot still; you can escape to the simple wooden tables on the narrow wraparound balcony. Lunch (12.30–14.00) could be pumpkin soup, a matabala stew or beef stroganoff, shrimp curry, Santomean omelette

with herbs, salads & homemade juices. The food is a mix of international & local, & there's always plenty of choice. Vegetarians are well catered for, & the fruit & veg are all organic, grown in the resort's own backyard. At around €15, the Rotas d'Africa house wines are good value. $$$

♀ Bar Golfinho On the way to the restaurant, Pestana Equador; ⊕ 16.00–midnight. A pleasant, airy open space with comfy chairs & tables, the

Golfinho only serves the local Criollo beer &, apart from port, no wines by the glass (consider buying a bottle & taking it through to dinner). There is entertainment here every night from about 21.30, even if there are only a dozen guests. This can range from good-fun *bulaué* & *socopé* dance & *batuque* drum performances to excruciating party games (think passing an apple around without using your hands). There is usually a disco afterwards.

✗ Tartaruga Bar Next to the reception & pier area, Pestana Equador; ⏰ 11.00–19.00. Serves excellent pizzas & salads, desserts & coffees.

SHOPPING Above the Golfinho Bar, on the right-hand side, the (pricey) **Bazaar Sete Ondas** sells clothes (bikinis, shorts, flip-flops), toiletries, including suncream and mosquito repellent, CDs and a range of souvenirs (sand cards, coconut cups, etc). This is also where you book your massages and acupuncture sessions. The shop is open 08.00–noon and 14.00–18.00, but if you need anything, one of the staff can probably get the shop assistant to open up for you.

There is also a crammed little local **craft shop** – selling carvings, bowls and drums made from *cidrela* and *amoreira* wood – around the corner from the diving centre, at the beginning of the path towards the Equator mark. Official opening hours are 06.00–16.30 but if it's closed, somebody should be able to fetch one of the artisans for you. I quite like the friendly *artesanato* shop on your right as you go up to the Equator mark, you might see the youngsters shaping and painting cocoa sculptures and the like outside the shop.

OTHER PRACTICALITIES
Communications There is mobile phone signal, phone lines in all the bungalows, and reception, the Golfinho Bar and the first two rows of bungalows are technically a Wi-Fi zone. At the time of going to press, the entire resort was being set up for Wi-Fi, but here it's best not to rely on these things to work 100%. For guests without laptops, internet access is free for 30 minutes, 07.30–22.00, at a terminal in the little room behind reception; the connection is fairly slow.

Medical facilities The only danger on the island, pointed out by a much-photographed wooden sign, is falling coconuts. A doctor comes over on Fridays, a nurse three times a week, and two members of staff are trained in first aid, as are the Costa Norte diving staff. There is also a first aid post at the entrance of the village. A medic can be brought over from Porto Alegre in case of emergency.

WHAT TO SEE AND DO
Beaches and snorkelling The best beach on the island is **Praia Café**, a ten-minute walk from reception across the staff area and past the Praia Pesqueira fishing beach with a beached, rusty wreck, where you can make friends with the local kids, especially if you're willing to share your snorkelling mask. The Praia Café bar is only open in high season, but there is lovely sand and good shade here. Snorkelling yields sightings of various colourful fish (*asma preto, bolião, caqui, garoupa* – see pages 212–13), with the occasional turtle or moray eel on the little reef to the right. According to the locals, the next beach along, down from the abandoned cemetery, **Praia Pombo**, is also good for snorkelling. Hiring a mask, fins and snorkel costs €7 a day. A *volta a ilha* trip round the island of Rolas, with snorkelling gear included, costs €25.

The beaches at the northern tip, around the restaurant, are great for hiding away with a book or for following the daily dramas in the lives of the hermit crabs played out in the sand, only interrupted by the occasional thud of a falling coconut.

6

Walks There are several walks you can do, and the island is criss-crossed by a number of little trails cutting through the dense forest of coconut palms, but it is quite impossible to get lost. The resort tidies up more than 20km of trails around the island. If in doubt, just plough on straight until you hear the sound of waves. You will hit the path going around the island; following that in either direction will get you back to the resort. **Guided walks** are offered free of charge at 09.30. My guide was very knowledgeable, showing me all kinds of medicinal plants, ferns and trees along the coast trail, leading past blowholes and steep rocky cliffs.

To the Equator mark Some 300m past the village, the road forks: take a right (signposted). A 20-minute gentle uphill stroll leads to the Equator mark, the imaginary line at equal distance from the North and South Poles, dividing the earth. Walking around a colourful mosaic of the world, you can have one foot in the northern hemisphere, the other in the southern. From here, there are good views over the resort and across to the southern tip of São Tomé. The length of the Equator is estimated at around 40,000km, running through 13 countries. One traveller pointed out to me that according to his GPS reading, the Equator now runs right through the village. And true enough, any GPS-enabled device will flash up a point at the very beginning of the track out of the village. If you've brought the family, it's probably best to wait to tell them that when you're on your way down again ...

To the lighthouse If you want a shorter walk, carry on straight at the sign pointing to the Equator mark, turn right at the mango tree with the pile of coconuts beneath, and take the first left at another mango tree: you will wind your way up to the lighthouse. It's nice as a focus for a walk, but the top is fairly overgrown, and there is no view. The lighthouse keeper spends most of his time in the village, so won't usually be available to let you in.

Around the island This 2½- to 3-hour walk around the island is best done in the early morning, or you can take advantage of the free guided walks at 09.30. If you go on your own, you can either start behind the Golfinho Bar or take the track towards the Equator mark. The first route takes you along Praia Santo António and the coastline, and about two-thirds of the way around the island you will come across the blowholes, with the sea swirling beneath and coming up in great whooshing sounds. Return to the resort via Praia Café and the local fishing village. Alternatively, start along the track to the Equator mark but carry on straight towards **Praia Joana**, a good swimming beach. Or just head to Praia Café and continue walking for about 15 minutes. If you start around 05.30 or 06.00, you'll still be back in time for breakfast (take an energy bar or other snack to tide you over). Wear trousers and good shoes and take some water. Most importantly, use a good mosquito repellent. Most of the beautiful beaches you see on your walk unfortunately have no access – plans to build some steps down the steep cliffs don't seem to be materialising just yet. The stunning **Praia Bateria** is used as a secluded beach for honeymooners, but can also form part of a picnic-lunch trip organised by the dive centre.

Diving Diving off the island reveals an undisturbed underwater world of snappers, sweetfish, stingrays, octopus, sea horses, turtles, fan coral, moray eels, sea slugs, etc. There are plenty of surprises for those who haven't got a fixation with the big fish. Sharks are visible, but are not guaranteed on every dive. Whales have passed by occasionally. There are fewer colours than in the Caribbean; visibility is also not perfect, and the open Atlantic brings a strong swell. In 2013, diving operations were

Pestana Equador can organise a three-day extravaganza for those who want to get married on the Equator. This includes a civil or religious ceremony, a gala dinner with live music and a BBQ lunch around the swimming pool.

The **honeymoon package** consists of six nights' full-board for the price of five and an upgrade to a *quarto* or superior suite. Also thrown in is a welcome cocktail, a bottle of bubbly, a guided visit to the Equator with certificate, and a trip to Roça de São João (on São Tomé).

taken over by Portuguese operator Costa Norte for Pestana (*www.costanorte.pt*). If you are organising your diving through the resort, the price comes down if you do ten dives or more. Diving with your own equipment costs €40, with hired equipment €45.

Dive sites

ℐ **Braga** (22m) There's a lot of hard coral here, & it is an excellent place to see red snappers, rays over 1m in diameter & moray eels.

ℐ **Hirondino** (14–17m) The 1st site you will be taken to if you are an inexperienced diver, as it is close by & protected, but you can go down to the rounded top, with the chance of seeing octopus, resident sea horses, soldierfish, sweetlips & parrotfish, as well as blackbar hogfish cleaning the bigger fish between 6 rock formations on an even sandy ground. This is a great site for night dives.

ℐ **Nanook & Sá Pinto** (15–16m) With luck, you can see sand sharks here between the tall rocks.

Fish life is similar to Braga, but at a lesser depth.

ℐ **Ponta da Baleia** (as deep as 26–27m) Good chance of seeing turtles such as the massive leatherback among the impressive blocks of rock near the Rolas boat pier on São Tomé island. You might see red snapper, rock lobster, & a few fan corals. A cave, 1.5–1.8m wide, may hide some big fish surprises.

ℐ **Ponta da Furna** Recommended, but access is dependent on swell conditions.

ℐ **Sete Pedras** (8–30m) Beautiful site with sting rays, small angelfish, corals, etc, on sandy ground. There are more than 'seven rocks', by the way!

Diving courses A Discover Scuba Diving package (with a pool session, a video-supported theory session and time in the open sea) costs €45 and a scuba review is free. If you are familiar with snorkelling (ie: used to putting your head under water), then within the hour you can be gently trundling along the bottom of the pool, controlling your buoyancy by pressing a valve. You will practise taking the mask off under water and putting it back on – not easy, but a vital skill you need to master should your mask become dislocated at 30m. Make sure you don't arrive with a cold, as your ears can't cope with the difference in pressure. In this case, if you're at all flexible, consider postponing your stay at Rolas; management can usually accommodate this. Make sure you drink lots of water and get sufficient sleep. A range of PADI-certified courses are on offer here, including Open Water Diver, Advanced, Rescue, Divemaster and Assistant Instructor. Dives are made from custom-made high-sea fishing boats. There is a boat for night dives. The diving centre is open 07.30–12.30 and 14.00–17.00.

Fishing Depending on how many of you there are, submarine fishing (*pesca submarina*) costs €360 for a four-hour trip (to be divided up between the passengers) to €500 for seven hours. There are three boats available for high-sea sport fishing (*pesca de alto mar*). In the resort restaurant I saw a group of Portuguese visitors happily tucking into the sea bass (*corvina*) they'd harpooned earlier in the day. Line fishing is available at €40 a day.

Excursions As well as swimming, bike rides (€5 per day to hire a bike), kayaking trips (free to hire), walks and maybe even a romantic lunch at the **Miradouro de Amor**, a small picnic shelter only a 5-minute walk away, the resort offers a range of excursions that allow you to make Rolas your base and still see much of what the main island has to offer. These include a half-day (€30) and day trip (€50) by boat around São Tomé island, visiting beaches and dolphin spotting; a day trip to the sights of the capital, including lunch; a trip to the Bombaim plantation; a journey south, including the plantations of Porto Alegre and São João, with lunch at the Roça or Mionga restaurants; and a trip to the central and northern regions of São Tomé, including a visit to the National Museum and the plantations of Monte Café and Agostinho Neto (€80). In season, you can join the nightly **turtle patrol** at 23.00.

THE SOUTHWEST

The remotest area of São Tomé island is currently really only visited by dedicated wildlife enthusiasts, mostly birdwatchers looking to tick off as many of the São Tomé endemics as possible. The area is good for the threatened giant sunbird, the São Tomé sunbird and the São Tomé paradise flycatcher.

The base of the **Xufe-Xufe River** is a four-hour drive by 4x4 vehicle or a three-hour boat trip from São Tomé. Contact Navetur or Luis Mario Almeida (see pages 112 and 159). Alternatively, you can hire a guide and porters at Santo António when you arrive; make sure the arrangements are understood, in particular, if you need the guide to stay the night with you and continue portering luggage up the river. You have to bring everything, and watch out for the horseflies. The recommended campsite for birdwatchers is 3km (two to three hours' walk) upriver, next to the large eastern tributary, home to the giant sunbird.

Hikers will enjoy the two-day **Volta a ilha** trek from Santa Catarina to Porto Alegre (contact José Spencer, see pages 88 and 144), in territory explored by very few tourists, while a **boat trip** (see pages 89 and 112) reveals beautiful coastal scenery.

Part Three

PRÍNCIPE

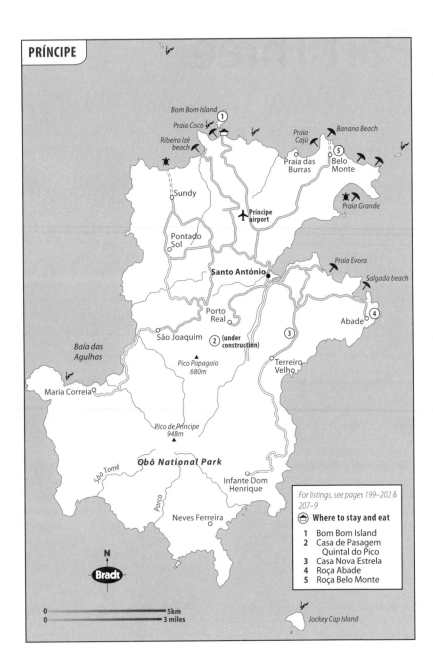

PRÍNCIPE

Bom Bom Island
Praia Coco
Ribeira Izé
beach

Praia
Cajú
Banana Beach

Praia das
Burras
Belo
Monte

Sundy

Praia Grande

Príncipe
airport

Pontado
Sol

Praia Evora

Santo António

Salgada beach

Porto
Real

Abade

São Joaquim

(under
construction)

Baía das
Agulhas

Pico Papagaio
680m

Terreiro
Velho

Maria Correia

Pico de Príncipe
948m

Obô National Park

São Tomé

Infante Dom
Henrique

Porco

N

Neves Ferreira

Bradt

For listings, see pages 199–202 &
207–9

Where to stay and eat

1   Bom Bom Island
2   Casa de Pasagem
    Quintal do Pico
3   Casa Nova Estrela
4   Roça Abade
5   Roça Belo Monte

0 ————————— 5km
0 ————————— 3 miles

Jockey Cap Island

7

Príncipe

If you think São Tomé is beautiful, if a little isolated, just wait till you get to the tiny island of Príncipe …

For the tourist, visiting the Green Island, *a Ilha Verde*, now a UNESCO Biosphere Reserve, has its advantages: an even more authentic travelling experience and sense of discovery, cleaner beaches, a pristine underwater world and great scope for photography. It is the oldest of three oceanic volcanic islands in the Gulf of Guinea. The area includes the entire emerged area of the island of Príncipe, its islets and the Tinhosa Islets. It is home to great biodiversity in terrestrial as well as in marine ecosystems, and is an important place for the reproduction of sea turtles, seabirds and cetaceans. The main economic activities are agriculture, fishing and tourism. It can be considered as a model for promoting integrated ecotourism development in similar islands and may serve as the basis for a larger marine and terrestrial buffer zone.

The risk of malaria is very low – a thorough Taiwanese study a few years ago found few cases, and the island is now officially in the pre-elimination stage, *paludismo*. The remoteness and laid-back atmosphere of this island, with a surface area of only 143km², has real charm; I met travellers who had spent two months on Príncipe without getting bored, and you don't need to stay here that long to be greeted like a long-lost friend. *Leve-leve*? Here, it's called *móli-móli* – it's the same thing, only slower. The flip side of this unspoilt beauty is a very rudimentary tourist infrastructure; if you're on a budget, organising excursions can be hard work, and there's a chance of being ripped-off, with higher prices charged than agreed upon. Also petty theft sometimes occurs. At the moment, many paths leading to abandoned plantations are disused; so few visitors come that they have to be cleared of vegetation by machete again and again. Spectacular basalt phonoliths and lower elevations (called *oques* here) dot the lush rainforest.

On Príncipe, tourists broadly fall into two basic camps: the well-heeled Bom Bom Island resort relaxers and the budget rainforest explorers. For volunteering opportunities, see pages 104–5.

For the people living here, the problems of São Tomé – isolation, poverty and lack of infrastructure and investment – are exacerbated. Levels of education are lower; schooling stops at ninth grade and 20% stay away from school altogether. Unemployment is higher, and alcoholism and mental health problems more visible in this community of some 7,500 people. The power is regularly cut between around midnight and 07.00 (bring a good torch) and between 15.30 and 17.00 on weekdays. At the weekend the power is available from 09.00 until nighttime. All consumer goods, vegetables and construction materials are more expensive than on São Tomé. Between the people of São Tomé and those of Príncipe, inhabitants of one island nation separated by some 160km of sea, prejudices abound. The Santomeans believe their cousins on the smaller island – whom they like to call *moncós* – to be a bit simple, while the inhabitants of Príncipe, mainly *tongas* of Cape Verdean descent, reckon the Santomeans want everything for themselves.

HIGHLIGHTS

Swim at Banana Beach, or relax at the Bom Bom Island resort – for a week, a beach day, a snorkelling session or just one magical dinner depending on your budget. Tick Príncipe's endemic birds off your list, explore the magnificent plantation of Sundy, hike through the rainforest, climb Pico Papagaio, and learn to dance the *kizomba* in Santo António.

HISTORY

Discovered by the Portuguese on 17 January 1471, the island was first called Santo Antão, whose saint's day it was that day. It was granted to the feudal lord António Carneiro in 1502, and made a crown colony in the name of Príncipe in 1753, to pay homage to Prince (later King) Dom João. Similar to São Tomé, the north and the south of the island have distinct climatic zones, which determined the shape of the colonial economy. The north is well suited to the cultivation of the cocoa and coffee crops (that were introduced to Príncipe years before they were established in São Tomé), coconuts, bananas, breadfruit and pineapples, while the south is more mountainous, wilder, and subject to much more precipitation.

The island was temporarily occupied by the Dutch in 1598, and attacked by the French in 1702. In the mid 18th century, the capital of the archipelago was temporarily transferred to Santo António by the colonial government, struggling to maintain order on the main island; the transfer of the capital back to São Tomé 100 years later initiated the archipelago's second colonisation by Portugal. Later, the island was used by the colonial government as a punitive place of exile for troublemakers. In recent memory, in 1981, hunger riots, when no boat with provisions had reached the island for months, were violently put down by the Santomean government, which in turn fuelled secessionist demands. The victims of months of arbitrary imprisonment are still seeking compensation. The island has had autonomy status since 1995, covering the Pagué district. In 2010, this was extended to autonomous region state. Long-serving regional president José Cardoso Cassandra enjoys much popularity.

Currently, the economy on Príncipe runs on diesel (*gasóleo*). Attempts to introduce large-scale oil palm plantations here (see pages 14–15) were accompanied by rumblings of nationalism, whilst the regional government is determined to increase tourism, with the support of a dynamic South African ecotourism venture.

CULTURE AND TRADITION

Due to the island's isolation and poverty, there is little artistic production, but Príncipe has its own distinctive traditions. Like other cultural manifestations on the island, the slow *dexa* dance shows a cultural link with the Minho province of northern Portugal, where many immigrants to São Tomé and Príncipe originated; look out for the **Vijyá Kôtê** group. There is the militant poetry of **Marcelo da Veiga** (1892–1976) and the lyrical expression of **Manuela Margarido** (1925–2007; 'A Ilha te fala'); the murals of **Protásio Dias Xavier Pina** (1960–99); the *musica nacional* of the (now dissolved) **Ilha Verde** band. The late **Camilo Domingos** sang very popular *kizomba* in Cape Verde creole and is remembered in town by a plaque on the square with the Padrão monument. The *puita* dance is being kept alive by a group from the Sundy plantation, the São Joaquim plantation has a *bulaué* percussion group, whilst the contemporary songs of popular singer **Gilberto Gil**

Thanks to Wilfried Günther and Gilberto Gil Umbelina

In 1970, the island's *lung'iye* language (see box, pages 34–5) was prophesied to suffer language death within the next 30 years (especially in the absence of a written tradition), yet it is still clinging on, with a couple of hundred speakers; some even claim a resurgence. Visitors will see manifestations of the language in the names scribbled on the wooden signs of snack bars and shops. Knowing a few common words will astonish and impress the locals. Rejecting the traditional epithet of *moncós*, the inhabitants of Príncipe prefer to call themselves *mínu íye*, 'children of the island', and a long-established dweller of the capital, Santo António is *ibó*. For the first greeting of the day when you meet somebody, 'good morning, good day', *bon-dyá-ó* is used, later, *bwá-tádi-é*, 'good day', and *bwá-nóci-ó*, 'good evening'. Today, a common greeting is *modiê?* ('all OK?'), with the response *malimentê, sá via via* ('all OK'). When you are walking past somebody or taking your leave, you say *pásó*, and the road is called *ulátu*. I am thirsty is *n sa ki sekúra*. How much does it cost? *kwátu kushtá â?* Many thanks is *désu pagá cí* (literally 'may God pay you'). Money is *dyó*, water *áwa*, firewater *deti*, banana *baná*, nice, beautiful *gávi* or *átu*, to sleep *dimí*, and to wash laundry on a stone *dumú upánu*. A white person is *rupéu/a* ('European'). And finally, the local equivalent to the Santomean motto *leve-leve* is *móli-móli*. Informal classes are available; ask around locally.

Umbelina give the island's *lung'íye* language new life. Ask locally whether there are any saint's days (*dias santos*) or popular feasts (*festas populares*) being celebrated: Santo António do Príncipe, 17 January; António de Pádua, 29/30 May; Nossa Senhora da Graça, mid-/end August, when the *dexa* is performed; and Nossa Senhora da Conceiçao on 8 December. If you are on the island over New Year, try to catch the **Vindes Menino** procession on the night of 31 December, which satirises all the little scandals that have happened in the past year. The biggest celebration, however, is around Saint Laurent's in mid August (see box on page 190).

GETTING THERE AND AWAY

BY AIR This is the recommended option: a short hop in a comfortable two-propeller plane with great views of the Tinhosa Islets and the spectacular coastline of Príncipe. Currently, **STP Airways** flies five times a week, using Africa's Connection planes. Buy your ticket from the office in São Tomé (see page 61) and have cash ready as you can't pay by card. Choose a seat on the left-hand side for the best views. A huge new runway is being constructed (due to be completed 2015), but for the time being hens are still pecking around a stranded plane that has been rusting away for years, against the backdrop of rock fingers jutting out of the dense rainforest. The new runway will be nearly 3km long, able to receive larger planes, and will enable holidaymakers to fly direct.

The flights now leave São Tomé from the international airport on the Praia Gamboa road. The journey takes about 40 minutes; however, there is often a delay. Sometimes, the plane can't land because of the mist hanging over the island and a plane chartered by STP Airways is sometimes needed to fight oil spills in the Gulf of Guinea. So, if you need to be back on São Tomé for your flight home,

With thanks to Paulo Alves Pereira

São Tomé has the tchiloli, Príncipe has the Auto de Floripes or *São Lourenço*, after the saint in honour of whom this dramatic piece of street theatre is performed, turning the whole of Santo António into a stage for the biggest party of the year. Introduced to the island in the 18th/19th century (and much akin to a play performed in a village in northern Portugal), the Auto de Floripes is based on an episode in the life of Emperor Charlemagne. At its core lies a battle between the Moors and the Christians. Floripes is a young Moorish princess, who converts to Christianity for the love of a young soldier in Charlemagne's army, Guy of Burgundy (*Gui de Borgonha*).

The show lasts all day, with the main action taking place from around midday. Early in the morning, at 07.00, the inhabitants of Santo António hear the sounds of the first horns, as the two ambassadors, each accompanied by a tambourine player, start gathering their factions. They go on to pay their respects to the ancestors at the town's cemetery and beach. Around midday, the two rival armies meet: the Moors in red, the Christians in elaborate green, blue and white battledress, carrying shields showing their allegiance. Gathering on the main square over the course of the afternoon, they joust, clashing their swords, whilst their leaders hold forth, attempting to convince the adversary to change allegiance. In the same way as in the tchiloli, anachronisms such as telephones or plastic pistols feature alongside crucifixes and mirrors sown into gowns. The battle is commanded from tall wooden structures, decked out in palm fronds: the 'castle' of white-bearded Charlemagne and the Pairs of France in front of the church, defended by Oliveiros, and the Moorish 'castle' of Admiral Balão, next to the pink regional government palace. With the Moors occupying most of the battlefield, Guy of Burgundy wounds the Moor, Ferrabras, son of Admiral Balão, and is taken prisoner. While all this is going on, the fools (*bobos*), cracking whips and wearing frightful masks, hold the public in check and clear the lines of combat, scattering delighted kids.

With Guy of Burgundy facing execution, the young Turkish princess Floripes, sister of Ferrabras and daughter of Admiral Balão, converts to Christianity, turning against her father, and marries Guy in a Christian ceremony, thus saving the life not only of Guy but also the other knights. The drama ends at night, around 20.00, with the Admiral, taken prisoner, refusing to convert to Christianity. The Auto de Floripes is performed by an all-male cast, with hereditary roles, except Floripes, who is played by a young girl who must be a virgin. To catch this colourful spectacle, you have to be on the island on 15 August (the Auto de Floripes is no longer performed on St Laurent's Day, 10 August), or on the following Sunday, when it is performed again in its entirety.

don't cut it too fine; make sure you're back with a couple of days to spare. Tickets (around €200 round trip) can be booked directly through the STP Airways office in the capital (including online, but payments in the office have to be in cash) or through the Navetur or Mistral agencies (see page 112), but seats get booked up quickly, especially for festivities such as São Lourenço in mid-August. If the plane is not full, you can also just turn up and buy your ticket at the airport, but don't rely on this.

Príncipe is now in the pre-elimination stage of malaria, so when you arrive a 'gun' will be held to your head to measure your temperature. If it's high, you'll have to take a quick malaria test, for public health purposes.

There is a good bakery near the airport, in an inconspicuous house marked 035 (ask to be shown), and the Loja do Aeroporto (⊕ *08.00–20.00 or 21.00 Mon–Sat*) behind a small embankment is a useful small shop.

BY SEA Few locals can afford the air fare so most go by cargo boat, on an overnight passage taking about ten hours (fast charter boats can do the trip in 3½ hours). Be aware that boats have gone down on this crossing, with loss of life, and others have lost their way and have had to be rescued. In recent times, one of the vessels mentioned in our first edition of this guide sank, the other exploded. At the time of writing, there was a once- or twice-weekly departure on the *Príncipe* costing about €80 round trip (m *991 5024*). From spring 2014, a new service might be up and running, set up by the Belgian honorary consul, Jean-Philippe Van Nyen (☏ *222 7511;* m *991 3051;* e *jpvnbe@gmail.com*).

Travellers who have travelled by boat reported waking up to dolphins alongside the vessel nearing Príncipe, but a rough return journey due to the wind. Budget travellers could consider taking the boat from São Tomé to Príncipe and flying back. To find out which boats are due in or out, visit the **harbour office** in São Tomé (*Av 12 de Julho;* ☏ *222 1520, 222 2207*) or in Santo António (*Senhor Armando:* ☏ *225 1246;* m *990 9352;* ⊕ *07.00–noon & 13.00–15.30 Mon–Fri*): the Capitánia is the bright-blue building above the pier in front of the hospital.

A regular, reliable and fast boat connection would be one of the best things that could happen to Príncipe, and STP tourism in general, but as long as tourist numbers are low, and air fares to the country high, investors are understandably reluctant.

GETTING AROUND

There are only a few kilometres of paved road: between the airport and Santo António, westwards to Porto Real and south to Santo Cristo. Transport is the biggest issue for budget tourists on the island; part of the difficulty in organising trips lies in the local perception that all white visitors are either staying at the Bom Bom Island resort or can still afford high prices. For backpackers, or travellers, students or researchers on longer stays this can be frustrating. Most visitors will eventually crack, as nobody wants to spend their holiday hunting around for transport. If you're on a budget, your best bet is to bring the price down by sharing with other people. If you hitch a lift, contributing to the cost of *combustível* is good form.

PUBLIC TRANSPORT With the demise of the shared taxis (wrecked by the roads) and the paltry public bus service, the only public transport is by informal **mototaxi** or COMEL's **motorised rickshaw**-type vehicles. The locals get around by lifts.

CAR AND MOTORBIKE HIRE Hired 4x4s come with drivers included, and cost a whopping €90 per day – a month's wages. The Bom Bom Island resort offers driving excursions with English-speaking guides and refreshments, while Pensão Residencial Palhota and the Residencial D&D (also known as Residencial Delmata) guesthouse hire out jeeps, but prices will be steep. Your only chance to get a better deal is to ask around locally. You can also ask for Mario Papagaio, owner of a kiosk at the market; he hires out his Suzuki Vitara for €50 a day.

Oscar Tebus (m *991 5484*) has a 50cc Suzuki to hire out for €10 per day. Otherwise, ask around at **Radio Regional** (see below). At Residencial D&D or Pensão Palhota, a motorbike will probably set you back around €25 per day. See also Residencial D&D in Santo António for car and motorbike hire (see opposite page).

Filling up There is an **ENCO petrol station** [off map, 194 A7] (*bomba de combustível*; ⊕ *07.00–15.30 & 17.00–20.00 Mon–Sat, 08.00–17.00 Sun*), just past the Deus e Amor church on the road west out of town towards Porto Real.

CYCLE HIRE The regular price quoted will be around 100,000$. To get a better deal, drop into the **Radio Regional** [195 E4] (✎ *225 1115*) building; the friendly journalists seem sympathetic to budget travellers and will probably be able to arrange to hire out a motorbike or a bike at better rates. I hired a regular bike for 50,000$ per day from one journalist.

Cycling around Príncipe is no easy job; the road leading north out of Santo António towards the airport and Belo Monte is particularly steep and sweaty, and the one running south is not much better. If you don't mind that though, it is possible to do a day trip cycling to visit Banana Beach, Roça Sundy (uphill all the way, unfortunately) or the beaches along the southeastern rim of the island. The Belo Monte run is beautiful, passing cocoa trees bearing, in the *gravana*, pods in a whole range of colours, but if it's been raining you risk coming off your bike on the rutted track.

BOAT HIRE Ask a guide or contact the head (*responsável*) of a fishing village direct. If you just turn up, expect to pay around 50,000$ for an hour's cruising along the shore in a dug-out (be prepared to scoop water out of the bottom with a plastic bottle). Joaquim 'Gi' Varela, the head of the **Praia dos Burros** fishing community, is a good person to ask as he is keen to encourage tourism rather than make a quick buck. Senhor Varela lives opposite the first aid post, *posto de socorro*. Much closer to town, Ministro, based at **Ponte Mina** beach, can probably help (see page 203). You usually have to pay for the diesel in advance (around 22,000$ per litre; 25 litres is a standard filling). Consider bringing a secret supply of extra diesel in a safe container; I heard more than one report of boat motors nearly packing up at sea for lack of fuel – not a great prospect.

OTHER PRACTICALITIES

COMMUNICATIONS With the isolation of the island, communications aren't helped by constant unscheduled **power cuts** (on top of the regular one every night). **Phone coverage** is now much improved. In any case, many people never seem to have any credit (*saldo*) on their mobile phones.

Internet Internet communication on Príncipe is less concerned with education and more with breaking island isolation. You'll see youngsters in baseball caps chatting via MSN Messenger with family members in Angola – or Brazilian cyber-girls with few clothes on.

MONEY Best bring your own! There is no ATM on the island, though at least Moneygram transfers are now available. Travellers who had spent two months on the island reported speaking to 'many' people printing money; unfortunately, I didn't meet any of them when mine ran out …

SHOPPING Groceries are more expensive than on São Tomé; every single tomato and green bean seems to come over by boat. Try to establish early on that you would like to pay the normal prices, not the double *preços de turista*. While the main biscuits for sale, 'Príncipe' (10,000$, with strawberry, vanilla, chocolate or banana filling) have nothing to do with the island, they make useful energy snacks for hikes. *Folha de chanela* is a stimulating lemon-grass tea, also called *Chá Príncipe*. It is made at Roça Paciencia (a plantation you pass on the way to Belo Monte), and is sometimes sold in the Ossobô shop back in São Tomé. The locals use the fresh or dry leaves for a stimulating diuretic tea. If you ask somebody, they will be happy to pick some for you; either use it fresh or dry it properly in the sun, otherwise it'll go mouldy.

SANTO ANTÓNIO: THE CAPITAL

The capital of Príncipe – the smallest city in the world, according to the *Guinness Book of Records* – is little more than a collection of dilapidated houses and shops in pretty pastel colours along the sluggish Papagaio River, with yawning gaps between them, slowly eroded by the salt air and choked by trees.

WHERE TO STAY

Mid-range

Hotel/Residencial D&D/Delmata (9 rooms, 1 suite) Rua Santo António; 251 296; m 990 6098; e ddclube@cstome.net. With accommodation on the 1st floor (private bathroom, TV, b/fast), a restaurant (various types of food, including Brazilian) & bar, disco (Clube D&D), internet café & shops (mini market, clothes, video hire), this is probably the closest thing to a mall Príncipe will ever have! The 2 brothers are full of enthusiasm to offer a 24hr client-oriented experience. Make a good impression & the price might come down a bit. Guests are offered preferential hire prices for Suzuki motorbikes (€20) & a Galope jeep (€70) with or without driver. Airport transfers. **$$$**

Pensão Residencial Palhota (10 rooms) Av Martíres da Liberdade; 225 1060; m 990 6032; e pensaopalhota@cstome.net. The rooms are spacious, but at between €50 & €70 for a sgl & €80 for a dbl, even with b/fast, Wi-Fi & airport transfer included, they're a bit overpriced. Smoking is allowed. It's probably best to ask to be put up in the new Residencial building nearby (2 rooms, 2 suites). There is a communal living room with a big TV, & a downstairs porch. A swimming pool & a beauty salon are being set up & there's transport & pick-ups to/from Banana Beach, Bom Bom Island resort, Sundy, etc. There is a security guard at night. B/fast is served in the Fakiri restaurant in the garden. HB is available. **$$$**

Budget

Pensão Arca de Noé (6 rooms) Rua UCCLA; 225 1054; m 991 0813. This budget hostel in the middle of town has fans, mirrors & lamps – & there is a nice communal area & pleasant terrace out the back. Recent reports by a long-term resident staying in the best room, at the end of the corridor looking on to the church, suggest this place, if very central, can get quite noisy, with loud & occasionally rude staff. Two rooms have now been fitted with A/C (€35). The public Wi-Fi signal can be picked up from the veranda. **$$**

Pensão Mira-Rio (4 rooms) Rua Martíres da Liberdade, opposite Ponte Papagaio bridge; m 990 6454; e danyneves73@hotmail.com. This new, spacious, bright-white colonial-style building, owned by Daniele Neves from the BISTP bank, is now the 1st choice for most visiting academic & other mission staff, not least for the Wi-Fi signal in the restaurant (986 9003). Rooms are fine & functional. **$$**

Shoestring

Pensão Residencial Osório (4 rooms) Rua dos Trabalhadores; 225 1034; m 990 4056. Just across the river, this hostel (the pink building on the right-hand side of the cobbled road) is popular with budget travellers. The cosy living room has a fridge & a phone, where guests can receive calls or messages can be left with the maid or owner. The shower is cold, but for the price, you can afford to stake your rainforest-trek base camp there;

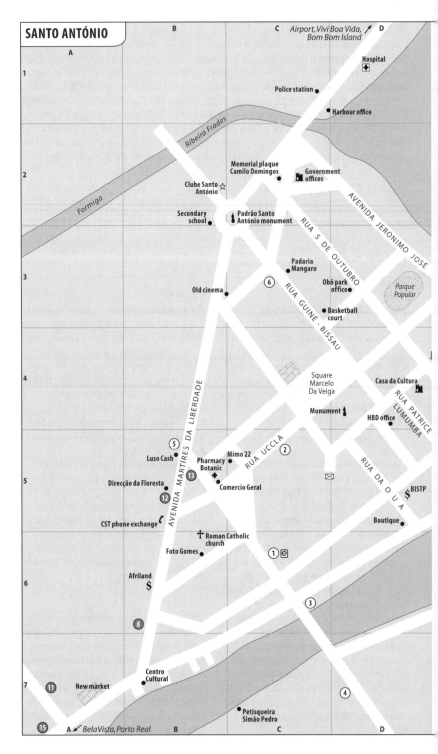

SANTO ANTÓNIO

Airport, Vivi Boa Vida, Bom Bom Island

Hospital

Police station

Harbour office

Ribeira Frades

Memorial plaque Camilo Domingos

Government offices

Clube Santo António

Formiga

AVENIDA JERONIMO JOSÉ

Secondary school

Padrão Santo António monument

RUA 5 DE OUTUBRO

Padaria Mangaro

Obô park office

Parque Popular

Old cinema

⑥

RUA GUINÉ - BISSAU

Basketball court

Square Marcelo Da Veiga

Casa da Cultura

RUA PATRICE LUMUMBA

Monument

HBD office

AVENIDA MARTIRES DA LIBERDADE

⑤ Luso Cash

Mimo 22

RUA UCCLA

②

Pharmacy Botanic

⑬

RUA DA O U A

Direcção da Floresta

Comercio Geral

BISTP

⑫

CST phone exchange

Boutique

✝ Roman Catholic church

① 🖎

Foto Gomes

Afriland

$

③

⑧

④

Centro Cultural

⑪ New market

⑮ A ✈ Bela Vista, Porto Real

Petisqueira Simão Pedro

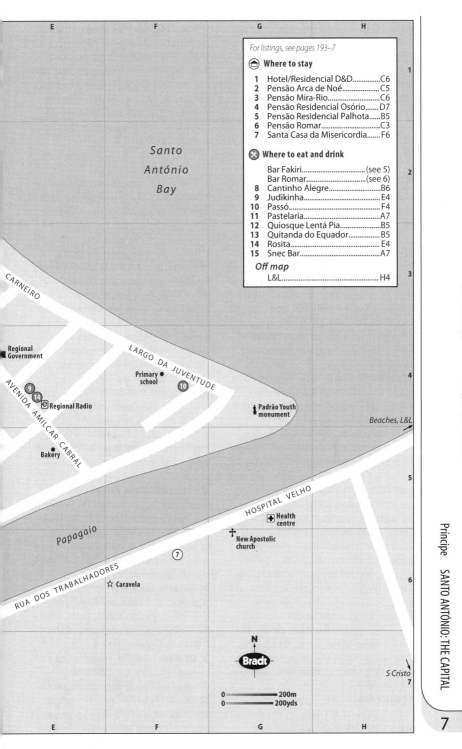

For listings, see pages 193–7

Where to stay

1 Hotel/Residencial D&D..............C6
2 Pensão Arca de Noé....................C5
3 Pensão Mira-Rio.........................C6
4 Pensão Residencial Osório.......D7
5 Pensão Residencial Palhota......B5
6 Pensão Romar...........................C3
7 Santa Casa da Misericordia.......F6

Where to eat and drink

  Bar Fakiri...................................(see 5)
  Bar Romar.................................(see 6)
8 Cantinho Alegre.........................B6
9 Judikinha..................................E4
10 Passó...F4
11 Pastelaria...................................A7
12 Quiosque Lentá Pia....................B5
13 Quitanda do Equador................B5
14 Rosita..E4
15 Snec Bar....................................A7
Off map
  L&L..H4

Santo
António
Bay

CARNEIRO

Regional
Government

LARGO DA JUVENTUDE

AVENIDA AMILCAR CABRAL

Primary ●
school
10

9 14 ℮ Regional Radio

Padrão Youth
monument

Beaches, L&L

Bakery

HOSPITAL VELHO

Health
centre

Papagaio

New Apostolic
church

7

RUA DOS TRABALHADORES

☆ Caravela

N

Bradt

S Cristo
7

0 ━━━ 200m
0 ━━━ 200yds

Príncipe   SANTO ANTÓNIO: THE CAPITAL

7

the friendly owner, Osório Umbelina, is open to flexible arrangements. You are likely to make friends quickly with the children living across the road. There's no food on offer, but airport transfers can be arranged. **$**

🏠 **Pensão Romar** (5 rooms) Rua Guiné-Bissau; m 993 5124 (Zozó). Closed at the time of writing, but with uncertain prospects for reopening. This used to be the best value-for-money option. **$** ·

🏠 **Santa Casa da Misericordia** (4 rooms) Rua dos Trabalhadores; m 992 7808; ✎ 225 1346; m 992 7808. At €15/night for a bed with mosquito net & fan in the old people's home, this is the best budget bet in town, & you are helping a good cause. There are 2 dbls & 2 twin rooms, all very clean. Rooms share 2 bathrooms, with cold showers. Make friends with the locals during afternoon dance classes. **$**

✖ **WHERE TO EAT AND DRINK** Snacks from the kiosks and street food is a good low-cost option; children will sometimes sell delicious ice cream, *sorbete*, for 1,000$. The terrace restaurant of the Pensão Mira-Rio (see page 193) is open daily from 06.00 to 22.00, and has Wi-Fi.

✖ **Bar Fakiri** Pensão Residencial Palhota, Av Martíres da Liberdade; ✎225 1060; ⏲ 07.00–21.00 daily. This restaurant, in a round bamboo hut in the garden of the guesthouse, offers good food & wines, with a lot of variety – but it is a little pricey. If you have booked HB at the Pensão, you will be asked in the morning whether you prefer fish or meat for your main course in the evening. Service varies. **$$$**

✖ **Bar Romar** Pensão Romar, Rua Guiné-Bissau; ✎225 1124; ⏲ 09.00–23.00 Mon–Sat. Bar attached to the Pensão Romar, this too was closed at the time of writing. **$$**

✖ **Cantinho Alegre** Av Martíres da Liberdade; ✎225 1108; ⏲ 07.00–21.30 daily, lunch from noon. Enjoy inexpensive tasty local dishes (such as squid or fish with rice) in a turquoise-coloured house set back slightly from the main road. If you want something specific, let them know the day before. **$$**

✖ **Judikinha** Av Amilcar Cabral; m 991 6310. Owner Judikinha serves traditional island food, with the Príncipe national dish *rancho da terra*, beans & rice with fish & local greens, a speciality. In future, the restaurant may move from a garage-like structure to her new purpose-built house out front. **$$**

✖ **Passó** Marginal, near the Youth monument; m 991 4400. This newish restaurant on the canal promenade run by José Carlos is airy but a few things were missing when I visited, like coffee, for instance. Vegetarians should ask for the aubergine (*beringela*) dish. **$$**

✖ **Pastelaria** António Segundo II; m 991 9539; ⏲ 07.00–12.30 & 14.00–22.00 daily. Most travellers end up eating in the evening at this friendly wood-panelled (& recently refurbished) place, reached by turning right past the Amor e Deus church. Serves excellent b/fasts of earthy local coffee, an omelette with or without cheese, mango juice & bread. Afternoons are nice for pastries, savoury & sweet (such as a cake drizzled with honey). The lovely Minga can cater for vegetarians & in the evenings will make a tasty pasta or rice dish with tomato sauce & vegetables. You can bring in your own veggies from the market, to be cooked in your dinner. Roast chicken with a cream sauce, *feijoada* bean stews, & sometimes there are pizzas too. Minga's husband, Ramos, used to be head chef at the Bom Bom Island resort; on special request, he can make a wonderful black bean vegetarian *feijão pintado*. **$$**

✖ **Petisqueira Simão Pedro** m 9912105. Friendly family-run snack restaurant. Fresh bread in early morning until 08.00–09.00, and always open for lunch & dinner (though better book ahead for the latter). Discover a variety of local dishes (ie not always grilled fish & rice). They are open to requests given enough notice. **$**

✖ **Quitanda do Equador** At the junction of Rua Martíres de Liberdade & Rua UCCLA; ⏲ 07.00–21.00 daily. Cheap & cheerful, serving fish, fried banana & rice with beans, chicken kebab, & *concón* (flying gurnard fish). **$**

✖ **Quiosque Lentá Pia** Rua Martíres da Liberdade. With varying specialities from chargrilled *concón* to the humble *búzio* snails. **$**

✖ **Rosita's** Av Amilcar Cabral. Although she doesn't open regular hours, Rosita's place is a popular ex-pat hang-out serving local food and

reliable cold beer. Impromptu live music on occasion. Ask around town for opening times. **$**
✕ Snec Bar Junction of the road leading west out of town towards Porto Real with the Deus e Amor church; m 999 7926 (Stellito). This new cosy bamboo bar, open daily 6pm to midnight, turns into an occasional dance floor. Their tasty dinners have to be arranged in advance. **$**

ENTERTAINMENT AND NIGHTLIFE Outside the festivities around St Laurent's day in mid-August and other saint's days and public holidays, there is not a lot of entertainment here, but at Príncipe *discotecas* you can often find a good party, mainly at the weekend and mainly playing *kizomba*, *zouk* or *kadance* music. You have to rely on word of mouth to know where the *festa* is. On Saturdays there is sometimes a dance on at the plantations.

☆ **Clube Santo António** [194 B2] Rua Martíres da Liberdade; ⏰ 18.00–02.00 (or longer) Sat & Sun, sometimes Fri. Popular disco that can turn into a bit of a sauna. Cool off with a drink from the bar outside; there is seating, too. Handy & unusual: bar staff can store your bag.

☆ **L&L** [off map, 195 H4] 3km out of town, on the uphill road south towards Terreiro Velho, São Cristo; m 990 4218. This bar/club/restaurant is run by friendly Lélé, who also works at the harbour. Nice set-up, with several little blue palm-bedecked shacks for sitting & chatting, & a friendly atmosphere. The dance floor gets pretty hot. There is snack food, & toilets. Fri nights seem to be best, but ask around before making your way up there. I've walked there & back so it's feasible, if a bit creepy on your own on the dark & fairly pot-holed road.

☆ **Vivi Boa Vida** [off map, 194 D1] Praia Inhame. The name means 'Live your life' in Cape Verdean creole. This is a disco on the airport road. Another option is Azeitona.

SHOPPING

Armazém de Dany Next to Mira-Rio [194 C6]; m 990 6454; ⏰ 08.00–13.00 & 14.00–18.00 Mon–Sat. Grocery selling cosmetics, cheese, soft drinks, biros, etc, wholesale & to individuals.

Clube Santo António [194 B2] Av Martíres da Liberdade. This popular disco (see above) doubles up as a video club & recording studio, *estudio de gravação* (⏰ 07.00–21.00 daily), where you can have assorted CDs recorded for 50,000$ – but try & listen back to them there & then as the set-up isn't as professional as on São Tomé & mine jumped tracks when I got home. Next door, I've sometimes bought fresh vegetables from Antonia, when there weren't any to be found anywhere else. Expect to pay around 40,000$ for a clutch of tomatoes, beans, carrots & onions.

Comercio Geral [194 B5] Rua da UCCLA; ⏰ 08.00–noon & 15.00–17.30 Mon–Fri, 08.00–13.00 Sat. Stocks lots of useful things like toilet rolls, bottled water, UHT milk, olive oil, juices, Lipton tea, tinned food, yoghurts, mayonnaise, fabrics & the odd shoe.

Foto Gomes [194 B6] Behind the church; m 990 6418; ⏰ 07.00–22.00 Mon–Sat. To reach this photo shop-cum-studio turn right just before the new market building & take the second entrance between the stalls. For 5,000$ each, you can have printouts (*postáis*) made from digitals, a wonderful present for local families or kids whose picture you've taken.

Luso Cash [194 B5] Av Martíres da Liberdade; ⏰ 07.00–13.00 & 14.00–18.00 Mon–Fri, 07.00–13.00 & 14.00–21.00 Sat, from 07.00, with changing closing time Sun. This new biggish supermarket, selling cold drinks, cheap mineral water & other staples, is unmarked, but you'll find it between CST & Pensão Residencial Palhota.

Mercado Novo [194 A7] Av Martíres da Liberdade; ⏰ 06.00–16.00 Mon–Sat, 06.00–noon Sun. The handful of vendors in the covered market sell fruit & vegetables, yellow sachets of Evita margarine, clothes, etc. Go in the morning, for fresher produce. One of the vendors, Romana, seems to double up as a traditional healer.

Mimo 22 [194 C5] Rua UCCLA; ⏰ 08.00–noon & 15.00–17.00 Mon–Sat. Bags & shoes, pots & pans, TV/DVD players, perfume, clothes, nappies, rucksacks, etc.

Padaria [195 E5] Rua da OUA; ⏰ 05.00–21.00 daily. The elderly baker, Mario Jaco, might have rolls when the other bakery doesn't. The entrance is set back from the street, down a grassy track.

Padaria Mangaro [194 C3] Rua Guiné-Bissau;

⊕ 05.00–20.00 daily. Follow the aroma of freshly baked bread: rolls (*pão*), loaves (*pão de forma*) & wonderful corn rolls (*broas*, also called *fuba*). Bread is brought out either early in the morning or at 19.00. Bring a plastic bag to carry them away in. Margarine is sold, as are *açucarinhas* (sweet) sometimes. The bakers don't usually mind you coming in & having a look while they're working.

OTHER PRACTICALITIES

Communications Unless the machine is broken, you can make **photocopies** for 1,500$ each in the Casa dos Padres, the yellow house next to the Casa de Cultura.

Telephone The **CST** [194 B5] is on Avenida Martíres da Liberdade (✆ *225 1100, 225 1018;* ⊕ *07.00–noon & 14.00–19.00 Mon–Fri, 07.00–19.00 Sat*), across from the church. It has two telephones but only one can put through international calls. You will hear a beep marking the units; pay after your call at the reception desk. People can ring you back, but double-check beforehand. Recharge cards for 100,000$ and 300,000$ can be bought for your mobile, you can buy a phone and/or SIM card, but you cannot have your phone unblocked.

Postal services The small, friendly post office [194 C5] (CTT; *off Marcelo da Veiga Sq;* ✆ *225 1053;* ⊕ *07.00–noon & 14.00–15.30 Mon–Fri)* offers all postal services, has a fair selection of postcards and sells CST top-ups. With the EMS service, you can send an item weighing up to 500g to Europe within 72 hours (in theory) for around 2,000,000$.

Internet One hour of internet usually costs 20,000$. The central Marcelo da Veiga Square is a **Wi-Fi** area. At weekends, it might be difficult to find an internet café open.

⊡ Centro Cultural [194 B7] Rua Budo-Budo (opposite the market); ✆ 225 1370; ⊕ 08.00–15.30 Mon–Fri. This brand new cultural centre has 10 terminals (20,000$/hr). If you bring in a USB stick, it will have to be checked for viruses first. There is also a library & an archive. At w/ends, events such as films & dance sessions are put on.

There is also an internet café in the Residencial D&D (see page 193).

Hair and beauty The **barber's** selling the *missangas* beads is just a couple of doors down from Salão Margarida. Natural-looking hair extensions are sold at **Foto Gomes** (see above).

Salão de Beleza Rua dos Trabalhadores/Rua Feliz; m 990 3853. Hairdressing, eyebrow-shaping, etc. Ask for Senhora Didi's house.

Laundry The best place in town to get your washing done is the **Pastelaria** [194 A7] (see page 196) on António Segundo II. A big plastic bag of very well-cleaned laundry will only cost around 100,000$, but turnaround depends on drying time (ie: available sunshine).

Medical facilities Santo António has a hospital and a health centre. Possibly the biggest health hazard on the island are the unlit pot-holed streets of Santo António at night. If you sprain something, you might want to try the local *massagista* or *pusha-pé* Jéjé, who lives near the cemetery. A nursing student I met trusted him enough to (successfully) fix her ankle.

✚ **Central Hospital** [194 D1] Chimaló; ☎ 225
1005; ⏰ 24hrs. The hospital, overlooking the bay,
has 3 doctors. Ask for Doutora Ana Silva or José Dos
Prazeres (m 985 9584); he speaks French & a bit of
English. Emergency treatments are free.
✚ **Farmácia Botanic** [194 B5] Rua UCCLA;
⏰ 07.00–19.00 Mon–Fri, sometimes 08.00–
noon Sun. Painkillers, various antibiotics, multi-
vitamins, etc, are usually available. If you find
the pharmacy closed, it could be that the helpful
pharmacist, Senhor Domingos Ramos Menagem

(m 980 1439), is usually up at the hospital.
✚ **Health Centre** [195 G5] Rua dos
Trabalhadores; ☎ 225 1122; ⏰ 07.00–21.00
Mon–Fri, 07.00–14.00 Sat, emergencies only
Sun. Working in conjunction with the hospital,
this *posto sanitário* on the southern side of
Santo António bay has some diagnostic facilities
(malaria test free) & an on-site pharmacy.
However, their 'mosquito bite' cream turned out
to be just a general-purpose ointment.

Money

$ **Afriland** [194 B6] Av Martíres da Liberdade;
☎ 225 1355; ⏰ 08.00–13.00 & 15.00–17.00
Mon–Fri, 08.30–12.30 Sat. The place to go for
Moneygram wire transfers.
$ **BISTP** [194 D5] Rua de OUA; ☎ 225 1140;
⏰ 07.45–11.45 & 14.00–15.15 Mon–Fri,
08.00–noon Sat. The Príncipe branch of the Banco

Internacional de São Tomé & Príncipe is managed
by genial Daniele Neves. He has various business
interests on the island & is the owner of the Mira-
Rio guesthouse. He speaks some English. You can
change money (there are no money-changers
in the streets of Santo António) & arrange cash
advances on credit cards.

Police

Police station [194 C1] Polícia; Airport Rd; ☎ 225
1056. The sky-blue building next to the harbour as
you leave Santo António on the northern road is
the base of 24hr operations for the island's half-a-
dozen police officers. Nobody speaks English here;
the *chefe de serviço* might have a little French or

Spanish. If you need something urgently for your
insurance, bring somebody who speaks Portuguese
& be prepared to insist. It might also be a good
idea to have a short statement in Portuguese or
English already written up to try & get a stamp/
signature on that.

WHAT TO SEE AND DO In the town centre, only the church, the government building
and a handful of other pretty 19th-century colonial buildings found around the
central square have been restored. Pay a visit to the new **Centro Cultural** [194
B7] opposite the market, it has a library and offers a chance to meet ambitious and
educated locals. In the centre of town is the **Nossa Senhora da Conceição church**
[194 B6] (☎ 225 1139; ⏰ 18.00 daily, 06.00 & 09.00 Sun). The church, restored
in 1940, has a light-blue wooden ceiling and yellow-painted walls. Look for the
baptistery font when you come in and the beautiful stone-carved St Anthony to
the left of the altar. On the square outside the church is a little stone pillar with
a tile showing Santo António. St Anthony (feast day 13 June) is the patron saint
of the poor and helps ward off shipwrecks and starvation, and find mislaid items.
Close by, at the cemetery, tamarind shrubs with bright red and orange flowers grow
amongst the graves.

EXPLORING THE REST OF PRÍNCIPE

🏠 **WHERE TO STAY** Accommodation on plantations is gradually developing, but it is
always worth asking the community leader (*responsável*) of a *roça* or fishing village,
whether you can stay/camp somewhere.

🏠 **Roça Belo Monte** (13 suites) São Tome:
Roça Belo Monte, Chalet 6, Av Marginal 12

de Julho; ☎ 222 6983; e sales.stp@africas-
connection.com; International office: Africa´s

Eden, Westervoortsedijk 71k, 6827 AV Arnhem, Netherlands; e marketing@africas-eden.com. The concession holder, Africa's Eden, seems to have succeeded in transforming the complex into a luxury plantation while keeping the original feel of the place. Restoration has been painstaking. The animal stables & hospital were transformed into 10 individually decorated suites. The main house has 3 suites & 2 lounges but can also be booked in full. The restaurant/bar boasts a beautiful terrace overlooking Bom Bom & the bay of Santa Rita. More spectacular views can be enjoyed from the pool deck below the restaurant. At the time of writing, the cocoa drier & worker's accommodation were being transformed into a working museum, research facility & auditorium, providing a space for research on social history & marine ecology. There are several hiking trails around the plantation, making it a good base to explore the island with PhD students & experienced guides – funds permitting, of course. The former owners of Bom Bom have implemented a high-end concept, with prices starting at €250/night FB, including all meals, selected drinks & excursions. Activities will include kayaking, quad & boat trips, as well as diving. The house beaches are Praia Banana & Praia Cajú, the latter is also being developed now, with 3 forest chalets & 5 beach chalets. **$$$$**

🏠 **Roça Abade** (9 rooms, some en suite) Just 7.5km (30mins' drive) from the capital; ☎991 6024; e rocaabade@gmail.com; www.hotelruralrocaabade. You will be given a warm welcome at this satellite of the Porto Real plantation, starting with flowers from the colourful garden on your bed. It is a bit out of the way, but there is a cosy feeling about this place & its remoteness makes it charming, too. At 90m above sea level, there is often a little breeze, which also helps to keep away the mozzies. Of the 3 nearby beaches, pretty Salgada is fairly accessible just down the road, Praia Abade, while nearer, has a fishing village, & to reach Esprainha you really need a guide. Non-motorised travellers can request transport with Carlos or organise a motorbike from town. Meals are taken on the large veranda. B/fasts of fresh fruit, juice, rolls & jams (sometimes local, sometimes imported quince) are good, though you might have to request a couple of things the day before. In the evening, you can request grilled fish with the Príncipe speciality of *molho-no-fogo* (a smoked fish dish), for instance. As a general rule, while Carlos's employee, Ceita, is lovely & gradually picking up some English, you're probably best off staying here when the owner is around. Camping is also planned; at the moment you can bring your own tent & for a small pitching fee also use the bathroom facilities. **$$**

🏠 **Casa de Pasagem Quintal do Pico** (2 rooms) Halfway up the Pico do Papagaio mountain; ☎225 1150 (Pastelaria); m 983 5675. This new accommodation option (planned to open in 2014) is part of a small plantation belonging to Ramos, the owner of the Pastelaria. 2 rooms in a simple wooden house on stilts, 1 twin & 1 sgl. Food can be arranged with the Pastelaria. **$**

🏠 **Casa Nova Estrela (Sea Dragons)** (1 house) South of the capital; m 991 3742; www.principedragons.org. A simple wooden house, run by the Sea Dragons NGO, which also offers hikes & boat trips (see page 204). **$**

PLANTATION HOUSES

Roça Sundy Covering an area of 1,657ha, Sundy is the biggest plantation on the island and gives you a real idea of how self-sufficient some *roças* once were. This was the only coffee-producing plantation on Príncipe. The governors' house is no longer open to visitors, as it will serve as offices for new owners, HBD, who are planning plantation accommodation here too.

Getting there Roça Sundy is some 10km from the capital, and it takes a good while to walk all the way uphill, so start early in the day to take in the beaches as well as look round the plantation.

What to see The **former hospital** is to your left as you come in the entrance, majestically flanked by two towers. Kids will be happy to show you the only thing that is left from the time when this was the most important hospital on the island: an old dentist's chair. (They might also request your empty plastic water bottle.) Next to the hospital, a **marble plaque** in the middle of a field commemorates the experiments conducted here by British astronomer Arthur Eddington in 1919, proving Albert Einstein's relativity theory for the first time. During a total solar eclipse, Sir Arthur demonstrated that gravity would bend the path of light when a massive star passes it and published the results as 'A Determination of the Deflection of Light by the Sun's Gravitational Field'. Behind the governors' house a few panels put up during an astronomers' convention to celebrate the 90th anniversary of the experiment explain the science in simple terms.

The plantation belongs to the state, and the former **owner's house** is kept, waiting for state visits. There are gorgeous views out to sea from the balcony and the colour-co-ordinated bedrooms upstairs. The green one, closest to the bathroom and furthest from possible intruders, was the president's; his bodyguards slept in the red and blue rooms. The whole place, with a large rectangular tree-lined square at its centre, is surrounded by a crenellated wall; over on the other side of the square, the **former stables** have beautiful horseshoe-shaped windows. Railway tracks can still be seen in the soil, with a rusting locomotive. Today, around 400 people live here – of whom about ten have a job in town. The simple **chapel**, dedicated to Our Lady of Lourdes, contains a beautiful crucifix. The church is not open; ask for the key (*chave*) locally. The way down to Sundy **beach** (and the other nearby beaches) starts next to the chapel; get an older kid to show you the way. In the workers' quarters you can also stock up on picnic food for the beach or provisions for the way back in one of the *lojas*. You might see some pet monkeys for sale. The plantation does not have mains electricity, but there are a few generators.

Roça Belo Monte

Getting there To reach Belo Monte from Santo António, head out towards the airport, but take a right at the tarmacked turn-off, going through a village. The tarmac soon turns into a red dirt road, only negotiable by 4x4. At the first fork in the road, take a right (the left-hand track leads to lovely Roça Paciencia).

What to see You enter this plantation through a picturesque fairytale, if slightly askew, crenellated entrance gate, with an old rusty cannon outside. The *casa grande* is a double-storey mansion with arched windows and doors and bare wooden floors, with a large slave bell in one corner. From spring 2014 you can stay overnight on the plantation (see pages 199–200), as it has been turned into a luxury plantation experience, under the supervision of Zimbabwean Henry Cronje, who fell in love with Príncipe. The inhabitants were resettled in two dozen purpose-built houses next door.

A short walk south from the plantation leads to a telecommunications mast with a viewpoint for Praia Macaco. What most visitors do, though, is head north for a sweeping balustrade terrace, the *miradouro*, the best viewpoint for **Banana Beach** (see pages 202–3), also reached after only about ten minutes. A guide once told me of his father relating to him the atrocities of the colonial era that happened here, of men being tied up and thrown over the balustrade. A track leads down to the beach (maybe a 15-minute walk), and from there you can carry on walking along the coast. I've found people here to be very friendly and chatty, and it shouldn't be difficult to arrange a guide. The beach down the other side is the black-sand **Praia Preta**, and the local name for the conical mountain behind is Pico Mae ('mother').

Roça Abade

Getting there Despite being only 7.5km and a 30-minute drive southeast from the capital, Roça Abade feels remote.

What to see The main house of the plantation was resurrected from the ruins, using natural materials by amenable Carlos Pinheiro, of Príncipe Tours. Daily life continues at the small settlement across the green. Various hikes are possible; ask Carlos for the illustrated itinerary sheets he has prepared. The managers sleep in the plantation below. I have wonderful memories of armchair birdspotting from the breakfast table, with monkeys clamouring in the tree behind the house. The cook, Minga, can wash your clothes for you. If you're feeling energetic, Carlos makes available his mountain bike, and if you need to connect to the virtual world, he will bring his Wi-Fi router over. Motocross bikes, and a car with or without driver are available for hire. Information on various guided walks is on offer in English and French. I recommend a longish 5- to 6-hour hike via Azeitona that includes Ribeira Izé with its fine swimming beach, and the site of the first capital of Príncipe. Of the possible boat trips, there is the *volta a ilha* tour around the island, with or without sleepover on Praia Grande Beach. Another very special boat excursion could be organised to the Boné de Joquei islet (305m), for snorkelling and a picnic (note that you have to swim the last bit to get there).

Roça Terreiro Velho
This plantation is **off limits** to visitors, and is situated south of Santo António. Take the steep tarmaced road up past Santo Christo. This is where the Italian **Claudio Corallo** (see page 132) grows the Forastero cocoa for his famous chocolate, and where women workers take the minuscule bitter stem out of each cocoa bean by hand; a job done by machine with industrially produced chocolate. Although Corallo's chocolate is now beginning to become well known abroad, there is not enough work for all the people living here, and the one demand heard again and again here is *emprego* – employment, work. While you may not enter the plantation as such, you can ask for somebody to take you to some **waterfalls** about an hour's walk away, though they're only really flowing in the rainy season. Your guide may also show you inside the humble houses of the *senzalas* (workers' quarters). Most of the people living on the plantation work in the fields, growing basic food crops like matabala and manioc to feed their families.

Roça Porto Real
This abandoned but well-preserved plantation lies on the way west towards São Joaquim. The hospital of this second-biggest *roça* on the island was once more important than the one at Santo António, and vestiges of the railway lines may still be seen. There are plans to develop it into a luxury hotel.

Roça São Joaquim
This plantation is the starting point for hikes down the southwest coast. Bands of half-naked kids push goats and kick makeshift footballs around the central square, overlooked by a friendly shop selling biscuits, soft drinks and *cacharamba* firewater. There are great views of the João Dias Pai and Filho ('father and son') phonolithic peaks and across to Baia das Agulhas. A steepish track to the right of the stark grey façade leads down to the coast. Small **Praia Caixão** is the first beach you come to. Carry on west to **Praia Lapa**, home to a small fishing community of some 60 people, which is served by a couple of shops.

BEACHES
Banana Beach This is the island's most famous beach – perfect for swimming, with white sand curving in a banana shape around turquoise waters. The easiest way to visit is to stay at **Belo Monte** (see pages 199–200). Another way of exploring the beach is on a 25-minute boat trip from Bom Bom. You can also hitch a ride or hike to Belo Monte and walk down from Belo Monte in about 25 minutes, via the

miradouro (viewpoint). A famous ad for Bacardi rum was filmed at this beach. On a recent visit we came across pieces of tortoiseshell, pointing to the fact that for all its UNESCO Biosphere status, turtles are still being hunted here.

Other northern beaches In the north of the island, just before entering **Belo Monte** plantation (see page 201), a path leads down to two good swimming beaches: **Praia Macaco** (with an as-yet abandoned resort project) and **Praia Boi**. Nearby, **Praia Grande** is also a good swimming beach and is home to a turtle project. **Praia dos Burros** is reached by walking west along the coast from Banana Beach. This large fishing village, where you will see plenty of flying fish spread across solar driers, will give you a friendly welcome. Senhor Gi (Joaquim) Varela, the head of the village, is setting up simple tourist accommodation in a typical house on stilts and can also organise somebody to take you fishing.

Western beaches Further along from Praia dos Burros (take a guide), enjoy **Baia das Agulhas**, a wonderful spot for snorkelling, at present unspoilt as the free trading zone is not yet set up. You can camp at the abandoned plantation of **Maria Correia** at the southwestern tip of the island, which is reached either by the (frequently overgrown) coastal path or by skirting Pico Mesa.

Beaches south of Santo António If you take supplies and water, there are several good beach walks that you can do from Santo António without spending a fortune on transport. One possibility is to explore the **beaches to the southeast**, on foot or by bike. Head up the pot-holed road south out of town; coming from the centre of Santo António, cross the bridge and turn left. After a steepish incline, access to **São João** fishermen's beach just beyond town is on foot, by turning off the road past a kiosk and walking down through the houses; you might see kids washing the seeds of the *izaquente* (African breadfruit) by the river. Back on the main road, take the next left-hand turn for a pleasant downhill stroll to the entrance to **Praia Ponta Mina** beach, already better for swimming. Only one family lives here now, headed by the friendly 'Ministro', who speaks French and Spanish, and can organise fishing trips (*saidas de pesca*), with nets (*de rede*), rods (*com canna*), and snorkelling (*submarine, com masca*). This isolation might not last, as if you look up on the hill along the coast, a tourist development is planned in the ruins of the old Portuguese fort. Back on the main road, turn left at the religious monument for **Praia d'Evora**, good for a romantic picture opportunity, sitting on the long trunk of a palm tree slumped across the sand. Unfortunately, being the closest to town, it is now the dirtiest beach on the island, littered with beer bottles and cans at weekends.

Alternatively, if you take the right-hand turn just outside Santo António up the steep tarmacked road south, which continues on as dirt road towards Claudio Corallo's famous cocoa plantation, Terreiro Velho, there are beautiful **views** of the southern mountains, such as the Pico dos Dois Dedos ('peak of the two fingers'), as well as the distinctive Jockey's Cap out to sea. This is the way to the beaches of **Praia Portinho**, **Praia Salgada** and **Praia Abade**; as everywhere on the islands, the swimming beaches are the ones without a big community, as those beaches are often used as toilets. If you haven't got your own transport, try to find a bus going that way and either walk back down or catch a lift down at least part of the way. You get a nice view of Santo António from the **Pincate** plantation (formerly Roça São José) and there are beautiful **waterfalls** on the way to **Monte Alegre**, to the west of Santo António, along the river Frades; you will need a guide.

Generally, booking island tours, boat trips, etc, with the Bom Bom Island resort guarantees you a professional set-up, reflected in prices not geared towards budget travellers. If you're on your own, or travelling as a couple, try to get a group of other travellers together; sharing can bring the price down to very reasonable rates. Also, it is always worth ringing up to see whether you can join an activity. For diving, Bom Bom is really the only possible base, unless you come on an organised diving trip from São Tomé island.

BOAT TRIPS Independent travellers may contact the non-for-profit organisation Sea Dragons, based at Nova Estrela (see page 200; m *999 0323; https: www.facebook. com/principeseadragons*). Currently, the Sea Dragons run snorkelling trips around the northern coast in a small boat, but can organise a larger *embarcação* that could take you on round-the-island trip if there were more people. Profits go towards turtle conservation. A good boat with a good engine is owned by experienced fisherman and supporter of the turtle project Nello (m *992 0859*) and Quebrado (m *991 8737*). Prices start at €30 euros per day, including fuel.

Ilhas Tinhosas These islets, about 22km southwest of Príncipe, are highly recommended for birdwatchers. They look like two islets, but are, in fact, three. The birds nesting there – sooty terns, often encountered in groups, black and brown noddies and brown boobies – are unused to humans, so you can get very close, although you are not advised to land on the islets as it will disturb them, and is fairly dangerous, too. In any case, only the larger islet has conditions for landing. The Tinhosas have the greatest concentration of brown noddies in the Gulf of Guinea, and they often hover above the boats. Look for sandwich and bridled terns, and Wilson's storm petrels skimming the top of the waves searching for food, although in recent years brown boobies have suffered an 80% decline. The most reliable, though expensive, option is to hire a boat from Bom Bom. It takes around 4½ hours to get there, and four hours to get back; the return journey is faster thanks to the Benguela current. A much cheaper, and still reasonably safe, option is Nello's boat (see page 208).

Jockey's Cap The **Boné de Jocquei** (also called Ilhéu de Caroco), a large, rounded volcanic rock, indeed in the shape of a jockey's cap and topped by oil palms, is prized by birdwatchers for the frequent appearance of white-tailed tropicbirds, and Príncipe seedeaters, rare in the north of the island. You can reach it by chartered boat from Bom Bom in about 90 minutes. Natural scientists will be interested to know that this islet is seeing ongoing endemism: the kernels of the oil palm tree are nearly double the size of that on Príncipe, and they seem to have contributed to the emergence of a slightly larger sub-species of the Príncipe seedeater.

Praia Seca This small fishing village has a population that varies in size with the fishing seasons from 5 to 50 people. There's nothing to see or do, but it is the best place to disembark to go hiking in the south of the island. Home to one of the most isolated communities on the island (2½ hours), the sea can be pretty rough and, in this case at least, the 'dry beach' also seemed a bit of a misnomer.

HIKING You could spend weeks exploring the peaks of the island. Be aware that even if you visit in the dry season, you are likely to catch a fair bit of rain; and nothing dries easily on Príncipe, washing or walking boots, no matter how much newspaper you stuff into them. Take plenty of food. **Sea Dragons** (see above) can also organise hikes, for example one leading from Terreiro Velho towards the south, visiting the abandoned Infante plantation and a fishing community, with return by canoe. In the words of the organisers, 'this is not for everybody, as it's rainforest, with mosquitoes, going up and down, and crossing a few not-too-deep rivers.'

Daniel Ramos (m *990 3048; www.obopark.com*), director of the Obô National Park and formerly of the forest ministry, Direcção de Floresta, can advise on hikes and has a motorbike; if he is free, you might be able to book an excursion with him, or else his colleague and guide, Baltazar. As a deputy for the political party (ADI), Daniel is very interesting to talk to about life on the island. For your safety and correct procedure, travellers wanting to hike in the natural park in particular should call in the Park HQ to register their visit and obtain the names of the trained guides.One confusing thing is that the locals, even guides, have different names for the same peak, and are puzzled by visitor's obsession with knowing their 'proper' name.

Pico Papagaio Getting up to the top of the mountain overlooking Santo António is a six-hour, moderately easy (if you don't mind pulling yourself up by roots on steep ground) and very rewarding forest hike, though the peak is often in cloud. There are different trails, and some guides start from the São Joaquim plantation, others from the path starting at António II, going up past the Pastelaria. There are several good birding opportunities.

Follow the red-earth road up past the **Quintal do Pico**, where you should soon be able to overnight (see page 200). There is a fence; you have to attract the guard's attention by ringing a bell and pay a nominal fee (20,000$) to pass. This should be a great base for forest walks, but it's probably best to organise a guide beforehand. Make sure your guide doesn't race you up to the top; a couple of travellers I spoke to ended up doing the Pico Papagaio in a record three hours or so. Tell him *móli-móli*; as long as you're at the summit by around 14.00, it's no problem to get back before dark.

Pico de Príncipe At 924m, the Pico de Príncipe, in the south of the island, is Príncipe's highest point and, although less than half the height of its sister peak on São Tomé, it is trickier to climb. Not many people attempt it; however, the claim that the Pico has only ever been climbed twice, in 1953 and 1999, is not true. Scientists from the California Academy have climbed the Pico in the rainy season, and an Israeli traveller climbing it with the guide Bikigila in the *gravana* a few years ago found it to be entirely feasible. It is definitely on my to-do list for my next visit! You can find a great reportage of a Pico climb in an internet diary written in 1999 by a British zoologist (*www.ggcg.st/jon_principe.htm*), sustained by lots of grilled forest snails. Some sources think that the Pico de Mencorne, further to the east, might really be the real highest point on the island. The hike up to the Pico starts at the **Roça São Joaquim**, and there is at least one night's camping involved. Mind yourself when you are at the top as there is not a lot of space to stand on – and it's a long drop down. If you are looking for a guide, try Balo (m *999 3043*).

Towards Morro Leste An interesting 1½-hour walk up towards the peak of Morro Leste takes you through different habitats, very rich in birds. Head due south out of town along the river, passing through cultivated land and the Roça Bela Vista, then follow the river, mostly on the right-hand bank, until you come to the remains of a hydro-electric plant. When it was inaugurated in 1992, it produced electricity for 30 minutes before breaking down. The lack of maintenance tools and know-how meant that it was never fixed. If you carry on up the stream, there is some climbing over rocks involved, you pass, after a couple of hours, a tiny dam, with crayfish-filled rock pools. Camping upstream from the barrage, you will hear monkeys and parrots in the forest. You can carry on, but you need an experienced guide for this, otherwise you might end up at the top of an unknown waterfall with great views, but with food running out, feeling argumentative and relying on your compass to get you back down to camp. The lesson from that one was: on Príncipe, you can never have enough biscuits!

WILDLIFE WATCHING
Birdwatching The island is heaven for birdwatchers. A walk down any road or track will reveal most of the island's six to nine endemics, such as the Príncipe drongo, Príncipe speirops, Príncipe weaver, Príncipe sunbird, Príncipe glossy starling and Dohrn's thrush-babbler. Príncipe's emblematic grey parrots tend to flit around between the high trees outside the capital, no longer the prey of parrot-trappers. (The redheaded lovebird is already believed to be extinct on the island.) In town at dusk, you are much more likely to see big brown bats (*morcegos*). Even around the airport there is plenty to discover. Ask somebody to show you the bat colony 200m from the airport in two small culverts. An area called Chada, also near the airport, with still water and thick forest, also comes recommended for scientific observation.

Turtle watching Príncipe has two **turtle beaches**: Praia Grande, to the northeast, and Praia Sundy, some 10km out of town, where in season (November–March) you can watch turtles laying eggs and hatchlings being returned to the sea. Book an excursion with Bom Bom, or contact Alexandra Marques (e *xanapica@hotmail.com*), current co-ordinator of all sea-turtle related activities on the island, including **volunteering** with the Portuguese NGO ATM (*www.tartarugasmarinhas.com*). You could probably arrange informal accommodation at the Sundy plantation (see page 200) although it's not yet a plantation hotel.

Whale watching During August to December, humpback whales can be seen along the north coast of the island, especially at low tide around 17.00 or 18.00 and in the early mornings. If you look out from Belo Monte plantation (see page 201) at 07.00, for instance, you should be able to see them passing. Bom Bom can take you out on a motorised *pirogue*.

GUIDES One of the best guides on Príncipe is **Balo** (m *999 3043*), who has experience of the Pico but speaks practically no English. Another recommended guide is **Balthazar**; contact him through the Direcçao das Florestas on Avenida da Liberdade in Santo António. A friendly young guide with a motorbike, who used to work with the now closed Ponta do Sol plantation accommodation, is **Pololo** (m *995 8766*). In the past, some guides charged in dobras but this has changed now and unless you organise an informal guide, you'll be looking at about €30 a day.

For a visit to the beaches, it is easy to find an **informal** guide – one day, struggling on my hire bike up the hill out of town I fell into conversation with a 19-year-old carpenter and ended up being taken on a tour of the northern beaches and having dinner with his family. If you're going down the informal route, be prepared for things to move slowly: guides may arrive late, the boat may turn out to be a wreck or there might be no diesel, or the trip may be postponed by a day. Try to avoid paying for diesel in advance before you have seen the boat, as if the vessel turns out not the be seaworthy you may not get your money back. If you are setting up your own guided walk, take enough **food and water** to share with the guides as unless it's an overnight camping expedition, they will invariably not bring anything with them. Energy bars brought from home are an invaluable top-up food, as is *bobofrito*. If you're interested in learning about the island's fisheries, try MARAPA's Jaconias Semedo (m *995 5921*).

BOM BOM ISLAND RESORT

Bom Bom means 'Good Good' in Portuguese, and this four-star resort in the north of the island, run by HBD – owners of the Omali Lodge hotel in São Tomé (see pages 114–15) and other ventures on the smaller island, such as the Sundy plantation and Praia Macaco – is truly a slice of paradise. A very photogenic wooden walkway connects Bom Bom Island where the restaurant, bar and marina are found, with the bungalows and pool area on mainland Príncipe. If you are coming straight to the resort on a charter flight without passing through São Tomé, visas can be arranged online.

If you're staying at budget accommodation in Santo António, you can still treat yourself to a day or just dinner at the Bom Bom Island resort. The €20 entry fee to the resort, including use of the beach and pool, is usually waived if you buy a meal or similar; the day-rate for entrance, including transfers, lunch and access to a bungalow for the day, is €85. Budget travellers wanting to get to the resort for some early-morning birdwatching or to spend the day there can only visit at management's discretion; costs for a minibus from Abade or other plantations range between €10 and €20.

Around the island there are beautiful rock pools with different ecosystems hosting coral and an array of small tropical fish. Around the pier, yellowtail sardinella/goatfish (grey with yellow) can frequently be seen. At night-time, watch you don't step on the large land crabs, with a span of up to 20cm.

Maybe understandably, some tourists never make it out of Bom Bom but, considering how far out you've come, it would be a shame not to spend a leisurely half-day at least looking around Santo António or the plantations, organised through the resort or by yourselves.

⌂ WHERE TO STAY AND EAT

⌂ **Bom Bom Island resort** (19 bungalows); CP 25; ☎ 225 1114; e reservations@bombomprincipe. com; www.bombomprincipe.com. Accommodation is in spacious individual chalets (currently being refurbished) directly on the beach or built into the rock, with a couple of family bungalows next to the swimming pool. You might be the only person/couple there & have everything to yourself, including the resort's 2 lovely & very clean beaches. The firmer sand of the western beach, Praia de Côco, is great for an early morning run or stroll before b/fast, while the one to the east, the more protected Praia Rita, is best for swimming & snorkelling. The pleasant, medium-sized pool has an artificial waterfall & a pool bar. The price is €150pp/day FB, including all standard activities. As for food & drink, sumptuous b/fasts include cereals, eggs, juices, brioches, croissants, fresh fruit, etc. For lunch, there is usually a choice of 3 dishes & this could include a Santomean *calulú*, or a vegetarian dish. Make sure you work up an appetite for the lavish & often themed dinners. You can also have your meal served on the marina pier, or even on your own private beach, if you've booked a Romance package. For visitors, dinner costs €35 (excl drinks), & you need to make a reservation. From the restaurant, a great western reef-backed heron can often be seen fishing. The shop sells clothes & postcards, as well as local chocolate & coffee, obviously at high prices. There is improved free Wi-Fi for guests, & a babysitting facility. Lights go out at midnight (you are given a wind-up torch at check-in). Credit cards are accepted, though don't rely on them to work, & tips go into a staff kitty. In 2014, the resort won accreditation as a Biosphere resort, & you can join turtle & birdwatching activities. A 'glamping' operation is currently being set up at Praia Sundy (see page 200). $$$$$

WHAT TO SEE AND DO There are a wealth of activities that can be organised through the resort. You can go snorkelling and dolphin watching, take a workshop in nature photography, kayak to a fishing village, go gorge swimming, and enjoy a (seasonal) turtle trip, or rainforest and coastal walks. It's also possible to join an excursion to some of the island's plantations, such as Ribeira Izé with its ruins of a 400-year old church, or a working *roça* tucked-away amongst huge *oká* trees. Check the resort website for details of excursions, which should be booked 12 hours in advance.

Birdwatching The resort is a great birdwatching base. You will quickly meet the resort's tame grey parrot, Chaplin, and both the blue-breasted and white-bellied kingfisher can often be seen flitting around the compound. An early morning walk before breakfast is the easiest way to encounter many of the island's endemics. Joining a 2½ hour walk with a group from the UK, I was able to see golden weavers, Príncipe starlings, bronze mannikins, Príncipe drongos, Dohrn's thrush-babblers (some of the most vocal birds on the island). We also saw swallowtails and beautiful dragonflies. Don't forget to look down, too, for instance for the fascinating Príncipe blue-speckled mudskipper ('walking fish') that might be stretching motionless across a twig in a puddle just alongside the access road.

Boat trips All year round the resort has boats available to visit a beach (the most popular being Banana Beach, 25 minutes away) or for whale or dolphin watching – though sightings are not guaranteed. Depending on the weather, the experience can be very different: during one grey, rainy birdwatching expedition I got soaked to the core peering out over the waves at indistinct moving shapes but the next day, on a three hour excursion, we saw different pods of humpback whales around Jockey Cap Island, as well as plenty of dolphins and birds. Morning boat trips usually leave the jetty around 09.00, afternoon boat trips at 14.30. Be punctual as departures don't run on 'African time'. Flying fish will be your constant companions, propelling themselves out of the boat's path to whir across the waves for up to 300m. Ruffled brown boobies sit on the **Pedra de Galé** offshore rocks, and you might see storm petrels on the way to the **Misterioso** islets – one has a lighthouse, the other is just a small group of rocks popular with nesting noddies and tropicbirds. For a fun photo, strap yourself into the marlin-fighting chair. If you're not staying at the resort but would like to take a trip, it might be worth asking around to find other travellers to share with, to bring the price down.

Diving An average water temperature of 26°C, average visibility of 20–30m and excellent dive sites only a 20-minute boat ride away make the resort a great diving base. Whilst beginners can take advantage of calm waters, experienced divers can go down to a depth of 30m. PADI courses for groups and individuals can be arranged once a decompression chamber is set up on the island – however, at the time of going to press, there were no concrete plans. The water is clearest December to March.

Dive sites
The Arch A great dive for beginners, as you don't have to take a boat; you just walk into the water off Bom Bom Island. Swim through the massive archway at 8m depth to see eels, puffer fish, octopus, snapper & maybe a beginner's luck barracuda.

Baia das Aguinas Listen out for the singing of passing whales whilst diving at 20–25m.

Boné de Jocquei The giant rocks & big vertical walls of Jockey's Cap Island show similar fishlife to the Tinhosa Islets (hammer sharks, sand sharks, red carp, king fish), with the advantage of the site being much closer. You might also spot surgeon fish, trigger fish, snapper, barracuda – & many sea fans. With a depth range of 15–40m, it's suitable for all levels.

Focinho de Cão ('dog's nose') Big rocks on white sandy ground, revealing sand sharks, big manta rays, red snappers, sea bass, barracuda & fan corals at a depth of 15–30m. Suitable for all levels.

Ilhas Tinhosas Known for their seabird colonies, the Tinhosa Islets are a long way off the southwestern tip of the island, but you are rewarded for the 8hr round trip by sand sharks & king fish alongside red carp, beautiful sea slugs & rock lobsters at a depth of 25–30m. If you're lucky, you might even see a hammer shark. A great site for night dives. Pedra de Werner is an amazing rectangular rock with a depth range of 18–50m. Suitable for all levels.

Mosteiros The interlacing rocks of 'the monastery' make for a beautiful & varied site with a depth range of up to 40m. There are plenty of surprises even at 8–20m, including turtles, sand sharks, barracudas hiding in caverns, skates, goatfish, surgeon fish, parrotfish & snapper. Suitable for all levels & also a snorkel spot.

Pedra de Adálio Various fish, eel & octopus can be seen on the reef here formed by 2 rocks at a depth of 15m. Suitable for all levels.

Pedra Galé One of the best sites on Príncipe, with corals, big red carp, various big moray eels, king fish, wahoo & a good chance to see barracuda, nurse sharks & turtles. The depth range is 12–40m but it is recommended for advanced divers only as from the 33m rock plateau there is a drop of a few hundred metres.

Snorkelling Hiring a mask, snorkel and fins is free for guests and included in the day visitor's rate for non-residents. On the Praia Santa Rita beach, check out the reef to the left, where you can see West African butterfly fish and parrotfish. On an ambitious two-hour snorkelling trip around Bom Bom (watch out for currents) you have a good chance of seeing barracuda, sharks, turtles, golden African snapper, the largest of the snapper family the cubera snapper, and the yellow jack, all year round. You will find shoals of small yellowtail sardinella swarming around the pier.

Sport fishing The resort holds seven International Game Fish Association (IGFA) world records from the early 1990s, amongst them a 52kg Atlantic sailfish, locally called *peixe andala*, in the Line Class, and a 27kg barracuda in the Saltwater Fly Rod class. As well as marlins weighing 150–400kg, you can catch yellowfin tuna weighing 20–45kg, wahoo, barracuda, rainbow runner and jacks. True to the Billfish Foundation motto, though – 'No Marlin on the Menu' (*www.billfish.org*) – marlins are always released after being caught. The two 8.5m *True World* marine boats are equipped with 11kg and 23kg Shimano tackle and 36kg Penn International. The dry season, with southern breezes of 10–25 knots, is the best time to come. Chief skipper, Argentino has been with Bom Bom for a quarter of a century.

Appendix 1

WILDLIFE GLOSSARY

This is a – by no means exhaustive – list of the birds, mammals, plants, fruit, vegetables and trees that you might encounter. The English name comes first, followed by the scientific name, then (where known), the local/Portuguese and French names. NB: The Portuguese names are often mere linguistic approximations.

BIRDS With thanks to Patrice Christy, D E Sargeant, Phil Atkinson and Ricardo Lima for the 2014 update

Birds endemic to São Tomé

Dwarf olive ibis	*Bostrychia bocagei*	Galinhola/Ibis	Ibis-de-São-Tomé
São Tomé green pigeon	*Treron sanctithomae*	Cessa/Céssia Pombo-verde de São Tomé	Colombar de São Tomé
Maroon/São Tomé pigeon	*Columba thomensis*	Pombo-do-mato	Pombo marreta Pigeon de São Tomé
São Tomé scops-owl	*Otus hartlaubi*	Kitóli Mocho de São Tomé	Petit-duc de São Tomé
São Tomé fiscal shrike	*Lanius newtoni*	Picanço (de São Tomé)	Pie-grièche de São Tomé
São Tomé oriole	*Oriolus crassirostris*	Papa-figos	Loriot de São Tomé
São Tomé thrush	*Turdus olivaceofuscus*	Tordo	Merle de São Tomé
São Tomé prinia	*Prinia molleri*	Truqui/Tluki Sum Deçu	Prinia de São Tomé
São Tomé short-tail	*Amaurocichla bocagi*	Suim-suim-d'Obô	Nasique de bocage
São Tomé paradise-flycatcher	*Terpiphone atrochalybeia*	Tomé-gagá	Tchitrec de São Tomé
Newton's yellow-breasted sunbird	*Nectarinia newtonii*	Selêlê Beija-flor-de-peito-amarelo	Souimanga de Newton

São Tomé oriole

São Tomé giant sunbird

São Tomé green pigeon

São Tomé giant sunbird	*Dreptes thomensis*	Selêlê-mangotchi Beija flor gigante	Souimanga Géant
São Tomé white-eye	*Zosterops feae*	Neto-de-olho-grosso/Olho branco-de-São-Tomé	Zostérops Becfigue de-São-Tomé
São Tomé speirops	*Zosterops lugubris*	Olho-grosso Olho-branco-sombrio	Speirops de São Tomé
São Tomé grosbeak	*Serinus concolor*	Anjoló Néospize de São Tomé	–
Giant weaver	*Ploceus grandis*	Camussela Tecelão grande	Tisserin Géant
São Tomé weaver	*Ploceus sanctithomae*	Tchim-tchim-tcholó Tecelão-de-São Tomé	Tisserin de São Tomé

Birds species endemic to Príncipe

Dohrn's thrush-babbler	*Horizorhinus dohrni*	Tchibi-fixa Rouxinol-do- Príncipe	Cratérope de Príncipe
Príncipe drongo	*Dicrurus modestus*	Rabotizoura Drongo	Drongo de Príncipe
Príncipe glossy starling	*Lampothornis ornatus*	Estorninho	Choucador de Príncipe
Príncipe sunbird	*Nectarinia hartlaubi*	Beija-flor-do Príncipe	Souimanga de Hartlaub
Príncipe speirops	*Zosterops leucophaeus*	Sorli	Speirops de Príncipe
Príncipe golden weaver	*Ploceus princeps*	Merlo Tecelão do Príncipe	Tisserin de Príncipe
Príncipe thrush	*Turdus xanthorhynchus*	Tordo de Príncipe	Tourd de Príncipe Serin roux
Príncipe white-eye	*Zosterops ficedulinus*	Tchili-tchili	Zosterops de Príncipe

Endemic bird species shared between São Tomé and Príncipe

São Tomé bronze-naped pigeon	*Columba malherbii*	Rola Pombo-de-nuca bronzeada	Pigeon de Malherbe
São Tomé spinetail	*Zoonaven thomensis*	Ferreiro espinhoso	Martinet de São Tomé
Príncipe seedeater	*Serinus rufobrunneus*	Padé/Pardal	Chamariço do Príncipe

Black-winged red bishop

Pin-tailed whydah

Principe seedeater

African grey parrot

Other birds

Black/white-capped noddy	Anous minutus	Caié-preto Garajau-de-cabeça branca	Noddi noir
Black-winged red bishop	Euplecteus hordeaceus	Padé-campo Cardeal coroa-de-fogo	Euplecte monseigneur
Blue waxbill	Uraeginthus angolensis	Suim-suim	Cordon-bleu de l'Angola
Bronze mannikin	Lonchura cucullata	Queblan-cana-preto	Capuchin nonnette Freirinha
Brown/common noddy	Anous stolidus	Padé-do-mal Garajau-pardo	Noddi brun
Brown booby	Sula leucogaster	Matchia-vagé (ST), Pato-marinho (P)	Alcatraz Fou brun
Bridled tern	Onychoprion anathetus	Caié	Sterne bridée
Black kite	Milvus migrans	Falcão Milhafre-preto, Rabo-de-bacalhau	Milan noir
Blue-breasted kingfisher	Halcyon malimbica	Chau-chau pica-peixe-de-peito azul poitrine bleue Martin-Chasseur à	
Cattle egret	Bubulcus ibis	Garça Garça-boeira	Héron Garde-Boeufs
Common sandpiper	Actitis hypoleucos	Maçarico-das-rochas	Chevalier guignette
Common waxbill	Estrilda astrild	Quebra-cana Bico-de-lacre	Astrild ondulé
Emerald cuckoo	Chrysococcyx cupreus	Ossobó, Piongê/pássaro-de-chuva Cuco-esmeraldinho	Coucou foliotocol
Green-backed heron	Butorides striatus	Chuchu/Tchonz Garça-de-cabeça-negra o	Héron Strié
Greenshank	Tringa nebularia	Perna-verde	Chevalier aboyeur
Grey parrot	Psittacus erithacus	Papagaio	Perroquet jaco
Moorhen	Gallinula chloropus	Galinha-de-água	Gallinule poule d'eau
Malachite kingfisher	Alcedo cristata	Conóbia Martin-Pêcheur	Huppé
Palm swift	Cypsiurus parvus Andorinha	Guincho-das-palmeiras	Martinet des palmes
Pin-tailed whydah	Vidua macroura	Viuvinha Viuvinha-cauda-de-fio	Veuve Dominicaine
Reed cormorant	Phalacrocorax africanus	Pato-marinho/Pata-de-água Corvo-marinho-africano	Cormorant Africain
Reef heron/Western reef-egret	Egretta gularis	Garça	Aigrette à Gorge Blanche
Sooty tern	Onychoprion fuscata	Caié-branco/Gaivina fosca	Sterne fuligineuse
Whimbrel	Numenius phaeopus	Meio-maçarico	Courlis corlieu
White-tailed tropicbird	Phaeton lepturus	Coconzuco Rabodejunco	Phaeton à bec jaune

MARINE LIFE

Fish NB: Dashes denote the lack of a common name; often the local name, 'moreia' or 'cobra' covers several different species.

African hind	*Cephalopholis taeniops*	Bobo quema Garoupa-de-pintas	Mérou à points bleus
Atlantic agujon needlefish	*Tylosurus acus rafale*	Agulha quio/Zanve Agulheta-imperial-da-Guiné	Aiguille voyeuse
Atlantic blue marlin	*Makaira nigricans*	Espadim-azul-do-Atlântico Marlim-azul do Atlântico	Makaire bleu
Atlantic flying fish	*Cheilopogon melanurus*	Voador panhã Peixe-voador	Poisson-volant
Atlantic mudskipper	*Periophthalmus papilio*	Cucumba Saltão-da-vasa	Sauteur de vase atlantique
Atlantic sailfish	*Istiophorus albicans*	Peixe andála Bicuda/Espadarte-veleiro/Peixe de vela/Peco	Voilier de l'Atlantique
Balao halfbeak	*Hemiramphus balao*	Maxipombo Agulha	Demi-bec balaou
Ballyhoo	*Hemiramphus brasiliensis*	Agulhinha	Demi-bec du Brésil
Barracuda	*Sphyraena barracuda*	Barracuda	Brochet de mer
Bennett's flyingfish	*Cheilopogon pinnatibarbatus pinnatibarbatus*	Voador rede/anzol Tainhota-voadeira	Exocet de Bennett
Biafra doctorfish	*Prionurus biafrensis*	Peixe-cirurgião	Chirurgien biafra
Biglip grunt	*Plectorhinchus macrolepis*	António-boca Roncador-batata	Diagramme à grosses lèvres
Blackbar hogfish	*Bodianus speciosus*	Bulhão	Pourceau dos noir
Blackbar soldierfish	*Myripristis jacobus*	Mãe de caqui	Marignan mombim
Blue runner	*Caranx crysos*	Bonito Solteira	Carangue coubali
Bluespotted cornetfish	*Fistularia tabacaria*	Agulha buzina	Cornette à taches bleues
Brown chromis	*Chromis multilineata*	Donzela marron	Castagnole grise
Creole fish	*Paranthias furcifer mulato*	Bala bala Pargo-mirim	Badèche créole
Crevalle jack	*Caranx hippos*	Corcovado Xexém	Carangue crevalle
Cubera snapper	*Lutjanus cyanopterus*	Caranho	Vivaneau cubéra
Flaming reef lobster	*Enoplometopus antillensis*	Lagostim das grutas	Homard de récif
Flat needlefish	*Ablennes hians*	Agulha espada	Aiguille voyeuse
Flying fish	*Exocetus volitans*	Peixe-voador	Poisson-volant
Flying gurnard	*Dactylopterus volitans*	Concon Cabrinha-de-leque/Peixe-pássaro	Poule de mer, Poisson volant, Grondin Volant
French butterfly fish	*Prognathodes marcellae*	Tchintchin Peixe-borboleta	Labre
Golden African snapper	*Lutjanus fulgens*	Vermelho Luciano-dourado	Vivaneau doré
Greater amberjack	*Seriola dumerili*	Charuteiro-catarino	Sériole couronnée
Greater soapfish	*Rypticus saponaceus*	peixe sabão Badejo-sabão	Savonnette
Honeycomb moray	*Muraena melanotis*	–	Cobra Murène
Horse-eye jack	*Caranx latus*	Macaco	Cric
Horse mackerel	*Decapterus macarellus*	Carapau cavala Carapau	Carangue maquereau

Large-eye dentex	*Dentex macrophthalmus*	vermelho fundo	Breca Denté à gros yeux
Leopard eel	*Myrichthys pardalis*	cobra do mar Cobra-leopardo	Serpenton léopard
Lesser African threadfin	*Galeoides decadactylus*	barbudo Barbudo-de-dez- barbas	Faux-capitaine
Milk shark	*Rhizoprionodon acutus*	Tubarão-bicud Marracho branco	Requin à nez pointu
Nurse shark	*Ginglymostoma cirratum*	Tubarão-pagem	Requin dormeur
Offshore rockfish	*Pontinus kuhlii*	cangá	Rescasse du large
Parrotfish/Peacock wrasse	*Thalassoma newtonii*	Peixe verde	Girelle-paon
Pistol shrimp	*Alpheus glaber*	Camarão pistola	Crevette-pistolet
Rainbow runner	*Elagatis bipinnulata*	alada Camisa de meia	Comète saumon
Red grouper	*Epinephelus morio*	Garoupa de São Tomé	Nègre
Redfin parrotfish	*Sparisoma rubripinne*	Bulhão congo Boião	Perroquet basto
Red Snapper	*Lutjanus campechanus*	vermelho-de-fundo	Vivaneau rouge
Rockhind	*Epinephelus adscensionis*	Glopim/Garoupa	Mérou oualioula
Round scad	*Decapterus punctatus*	Carapau cavala Carapau	Comète quiaquia
Sand tiger shark	*Carcharias taurus*	Mangona	Requin-taureau
Scalloped hammerhead	*Sphyrna lewini*	Tubarão martelo Peixe-martelo	Requin marteau
Sea bass	*Acanthistius brasilianus*	Corvina Badejo	Serran argentin
Shortfin mako	*Isurus oxyrinchus*	Mako Mako –	
Snakefish/ Bluntnose lizardfish	*Trachinocephalus myops*	Rainha Traíra do alto	Poisson-lézard
Spot-fin porcupinefish	*Diodon hystrix*	Graviola	Porc-épic boubou
Squirrelfish	*Holocentrus ascensionis*	Caqui	Marignan coq
Stout moray	*Muraena robusta*	Moreia congra	Moreia Murène robuste
Swordfish	*Xiphias gladius*	Peixe ferro Peixe-espada/espadarte	Espadon
Three-banded butterflyfish	*Chaetodon robustus*	Tchintchin Peixe-borboleta	Poisson-papillon
Wahoo	*Acanthocybium solandri*	Peixe fumo Cavala-wahoo	Thazard-bâtard
West African angel fish	*Holocanthus africanus*	Tchinchin de fundo	Poisson-ange africain
West African goatfish	*Pseudupeneus prayensis*	salmonete Chalino	Rouget du Sénégal
West African hawkfish	*Cirrhitus atlanticus*	Peixe-falcao	Poisson faucon
West African seahorse	*Hippocampus algiricus*	Cavalo-marinho	Poissons-trompettes
West African Spanish mackerel	*Scomberomorus tritor*	Serra Peixe-serra	Maquereau-bonite
Whale shark	*Rhincodon typus*	Má pinta tubarão-baleia	Requin-baleine
Yellow jack	*Carangoides bartholomaei*	xerelete-amarelo	Carangue grasse
Yellow sea chub	*Kyphosus incisor sopa*	Pirajica	Calicagère jaune
Yellowfin tuna	*Thunnus albacares*	Atum oledê Alvacora	Thon à nageoires jaunes
Yellowtail sardinella	*Sardinella rouxi*	Sardinela-rabo-amarelo	Sardinelle à queue jaune

Crabs and spiders

Cameroon red tarantula	*Hysterocrates gigas*	Samangungú	Tarantula Mygale
Hermit crab	*Pagurus*	Caranguejo ermita	Crabe hermite/pagure
Land crab	*Johngarthia weileri*	–	–
São Tomé giant olive-brown baboon spider	*Hysterocrates scepticus*	Tarantula Samangungú	Mygale

Trap door spider	*Moggridgea occidua*	Simon Aranha alcapão	Araignée de trappe
Whip scorpion	*Amblypigida*	Escorpião sem rabo	Scorpion sans queue de fouet
Whip spider	*Damon tibialis*	Aranha do chicote	Araignée de fouet

Corals and anemones

Fan coral	*Gorgoniacea*	Gorgônia	Gorgone
Collared sand anemone	*Actinostella flosculifera*	anêmona de areia	anémone de sable
Cylinder anemone	*Cerianthus membranaceus*	Anêmona-de-tubo	Anémone de tube
Great star coral	*Montastrea cavernosa*	Cérebro Verde	Grand corail étoilé
Golden cup coral	*Tubastraea aurea*	Coral sol	Aiptasie jaune
Hydro/lace coral	*Stylaster blattea*	Coral-laço	Corail dentelle

MAMMALS

African civet	*Civectittis civetta*	lagaia	Civette
Bent-winged bat	*Miniopterus newtoni*	Morcego de asa grande	Rhinolophe
Black/ship rat	*Rattus rattus*	Rato preto	Rat noir
Brown rat	*Rattus norvegicus*	Ratazans castanha	Rat brun
Common dolphin	*Delphinus delphis*	Golfinho	Dauphin commun
Common weasel	*Mustela nivalis*	Doninha	Belette
House mouse	*Mus musculus*	fingi	Rato Souris
Humpback whale	*Megaptera novaeangliae*	Baleia-de-bossas	Mégaptère/Baleine à bosse
Mona monkey	*Cercopithecus mona*	macaco	Singe Mona
Pantropical spotted dolphin/bridled dolphin	*Stenella attenuata*	golfinho dauphin	tacheté pantropical
São Tomé day-flying bat	*Hipposideros ruber*	Morcego de nariz chato	Rhinolophe
São Tomé free-tailed bat	*Chaerephon tomensis*	Morcego	Molosse de São Tomé
São Tomé little collared fruit bat	*Myonycteris brachycephala*	Pequeno morcego de fruta	Petite roussette
São Tomé white-toothed shrew	*Crocidura thomensis*	Musaranho	Musaraigne
Sperm whale	*Physeter macrocephalus*	–	Cachelot
Straw-coloured fruit-bat	*Eidolon helvum*	Guembú Morcego frugívoro cor-de-palha	Roussette paillée africaine
Wild pig	*Sus scrofa*	porco do mato	Cochon forestier/sauvage

REPTILES AND AMPHIBIANS

Black cobra	*Naja melanoleuca*	cobra preta	Serpent Noir
Beaked snake	*Rhinotyphlops newtoni*	–	Serpent aveugle
Burrowing snake	*Rhinotyphlops feae*	–	Serpent aveugle
Day gecko	*Lygodactylus thomensis osga*	–	Gecko diurne
Gecko	*Hemidactylus greefi osga*	Gecko	–
Green turtle	*Chelonia mydas*	Mão	Grande Tortue verte
Hawksbill turtle	*Eretmochelys imbricata*	Sada	Tortue imbriquee
Leatherback turtle	*Dermochelys coriacea*	Ambulância	Tortue luth
Loggerhead turtle	*Caretta caretta*	Ambo	Tortue carouanne
Many-scaled feylinia	*Feylinia polylepis*	cobra cega	Serpent aveugle
Millipede	*Diplopoda*	Centopeia	Centipède
Moller's gulf frog	*Hyperolius molleri*	Raineta	Grenouille arboricole

Olive ridley turtle	*Lepidochelys olivacea*	Tatô	Tortue olivâtre
Palm forest frog	*Leptopelis palmatus*	Raineta	Grenouille arboricole des forêts de palmiers
Peter's river/ranid frog	*Ptychadena newtoni*	Rã Phrynobatrachus dispar	Grenouille riverine
São Tomé green snake	*Philothamnus thomensis*	Soá-soá	–
São Tomé house snake	*Lamprophis lineatus bedriagae*	Cobra de casa	Serpent de maison de São Tomé
São Tomé tree frog	*Hyperolius thominsis*	Raineta de São Tomé	Grenouille arboricole
Skink	*Panapsis africana*	Mabuya Lagarto	Eumèce
Rat snake	*Boedon lineatus bedriagae*	Gita Cobra-rateira	Serpent rat
West African mud turtle	*Pelusios castaneus*	Benco	Péluse de Schweigger
Yellow-banded blind snake	*Typhlops elegans*	Cobra cego	Serpent aveugle
Yellow caecilian	*Schistometopum thomensis*	cobra bôbô	Cécilie multicolore

GASTROPODS

Forest snail	*Archachatina bicarinata*	Búzio d'Obô/do mato	Escargot terrestre
Sea snail	*Aphlysia*	Búzio do mar	Escargot marin/Aplysie
São Tomé door snail	*Thyrophorella thomensis*	Búzio d'Obô/do mato	Escargot
Millipede	*Lobo centopeia*	–	Millipède
Anemone horseshow worm	*Phoronis autralis*	–	Grand phoronidien

FLOWERS, FRUIT, HERBS AND SPICES, PLANTS AND TREES

Acacia	*Albizzia moluccana*	acácia	Acacie
African breadfruit	*Treculia africana*	Izaquente	Arbre à pain d'Afrique
African corkwood/ Umbrella tree	*Musanga cecropioides*	Gófe	Parasolier
African grape	*Pseudospondias microcarpa/Spondias lutea*	Guêguê	'Raisin d'Afrique'
African oak	*Chlorophora tenuifolia/ Milicia excelsa*	Amoreira	Chêne africain
African oil palm	*Elaecis guineensis andim/déndém*	Palmeira	Palmier à huile
African plum/pear	*Dacryodes edulis*	Safú	Safous
Amaranth	*Amaranthus caudatus*	Jimboa/Gimboa	Amarante queue de renard
Avocado	*Persea americana*	Abacate	Avocat
Bamboo	*Bambusa arundinacea*	Bambú	Bambou
Banana	*Musa paradisiaca*	Banana Quitchibá	Banane
Baobab	*Adansonia digitata*	Micondó Imbondeiro	Baobab africain
Black pepper	*Piper nigrum*	Pimenta do reino	Poivre noir
(Blood tree)	*Harungana madagascariensis*	Pau-sangue	Arbre de sang
Breadfruit	*Artocarpus altilis/ communis*	Fruta-pão	Fruit de pain
Cameroon cardamom	*Afranomum Daniellii*	ossame/ossami	Cardamome cameroonaise
'Cameroonian' tree	*Scytopelatum camerunianum*	Vilo Viro branco	Arbre du Cameroun

Cayenne pepper	*Capsicum annuum*	Pimenta malagueta	Poivre de cayenne
Chilli/Guinea pepper	*Capsicum frutescens*	Piripiri	Poivron
Cinnamon	*Cinnamomum ceylanicum*	Canela	Cannelle
Climbing begonia	*Begonia baccata*	Folha bôba vermelha Begônia	Bégonia grimpante
Cocoa	*Theobroma cacao*	cacaozeiro	Cacaoyer
Coconut palm	*Cocus nucifera*	Côcônja Coqueiro	Palmier de coco
Cocoyam	*Xanthosoma sagittifolium*	Matabala	Inhame Taro
Coffee	*Coffea Arabica*	Cafeeiro	Caféier
Common ginger	*Zingiber officinale*	Gengibre fresco	Gingembre
Croton	*Croton stellulifer*	Cubango	Croton
(Endangered endemic tree, *Flacourtiaceae* family	*Homalium heriquesii*	Quebra machado	Flacourtiacée endémique danger d'extinction
(Endangered endemic *Pandanaceae* tree	*Pandanus thomensis*	Pau esteira	Pandanacée endémique vulnérable
False African currant ('third leg')	*Allophylus africanus*	Pó Tleche Pau-três	Fausse groseille Africaine ('troisième jambe')
Fan palm	*Borassus aethiopium*	Ulua palmeira lêque	Rônier
Fern	*Pterophyta*	Feto	Fougère
Flame tree	*Erythrina poeppigiana/ variegata*	Eritrina	Érythrine
Foxtail	*Setaria megaphylla/ chevalieri*	Uagá-Uagá Capim-de-burro/Pé de Galinha	Queue de renard
Giant begonia	*Begonia crateris*	Fiá bôba d'obô Begônia	Bégonia géant de SãoTomé
Giant lobelia	*Lobelia barnsii*	Lobélia gigante	Lobelia géant
Guava	*Psidium guajava*	Goiaba	Goyave
Kola nut tree	*Cola acuminata*	Cola/Coleira	Noix de kola
Lemongrass	*Cymbopogon citratus*	Chá do Príncipe Chanela/ Capim do Gabão	Citronelle
Jackfruit	*Artocarpus heterophyllus/ interger*	Jaca	Jacquier
Mango	*Mangifera indica*	Manga	Mangue
Mangosteen	*Garcinia mangostona*	Mangostão	Mangoustan
Manioc	*Manihot esculenta*	Mandioca Maioba	Manioc
Millet	*Poaceae*	Milho de sequeiro	Millet/Graminée
Monkey flower	*Costus Gigantus*	Flor de macaco/cana-doce-dos-macacos	'Fleur de singe'
Oil tree	*Santiria trimeira*	Pó Oleo/Bálsamo de São Tomé	Pau óleo Arbre huilier
(Orange-flowering endemic heather)	*Erica thomensis*	Urze de São Tomé florescente cor de laranja	Bruyère endémique aux fleurs oranges
(Orange-flowering endemic Leeaceae)	*Leea tinctoria Cele-alé*	Árvore florescente cor de laranja	Arbre de fleurs rouge-oranges endémique
Oregano basil/Fever bush	*Ocimum viride/ Ocimum gratissimum*	Micocó	Basilic africain
Papaya	*Carica papaya*	Mamão/Mamoeiro (tree)	Papaye
Parrot beak	*Heliconia rostrata*	Hêliconia	Heliconia rostré/Pince de homard
Passionfruit	*Passiflora*	Maracujá	Fruit de la passion
Pepper	*Piper spp.*	Pimenta	Poivre

Pineapple	*Ananas*	Bacatchi Ananás	Ananas
Porcelain rose	*Phoemeria magnifica*	Rosa porcelana	Rose porcelaine
Red mangrove	*Rhizophoraca apiculata/ racemosa Rhizophora*	mangle mangue vermelho	Palétuvier rouge
Saffron	*Curcuma longa*	Saffrom açafrão da India	Safrane
Salad burnet	*Sanguisorba minor/ Sechium*	edule pimpinela	Pimprinelle
Silk cotton tree	*Ceiba pentandra*	Oká	Fromager
Starfruit	*Averrhoa carambola*	Cálambola Carambola	Carambole
Strangler fig	*Ficus aurea*	Figo estranguladora	Figue étrangleur
(São Tomé chestnut)	*Acanthus montanum*	Cundú de muala vé Castanheiro de São Tomé	(Châtaignier de São Tomé)
São Tomé peach tree	*Chytranthus mannii*	Pessegeiro de São Tomé	Pêcher de São Tomé
São Tomé pine	*Afrocarpus/podocarpus mannii*	Ofó Pinheiro de São Tomé	*Pin de São Tomé*
Sap-Sap	*Annona muricata*	Sap-sap Graviola	Corossol
Spanish cedar	*Cedrela odorata*	Cedrela	Acajou amer
Sugarcane	*Saccaharum officinarum*	Cana de açucar	Canne de sucre
Sweet potato	*Ipomaea batatas*	Batata doce	Batate
Tamarind	*Tamarindus indica*	Tamarino	Tamarin
Tomato-fruited eggplant	*Solanum naumannii*	Makêkê	Aubergine amère
Vanilla (orchid)	*Vanila planifolia*	Baunilha	Vanille
Watercress	*Rorippa nasturtium- aquaticum/Lepidium sativum*	Fiá-guinhom Agrião	Cresson
White mangrove	*Avicennia nitida*	mangue de praia	Palétuvier blanc
Wild cinnamon	*Cinnamomum zeylanicum*	Pau canela Caneleira	Canelle sauvage
Wild ginger	*Zingiber officinalis*	Gengimple Gengibre	Gingembre
Wild strawberry	*Rubus pinatus*	Molanga Framboesa brava	Fraise sauvage
(Yellow-flowering endemic tree, *Myristicaceae*	*Staudtia pterocarpa* Myristicacée aux fleurs	Pau vermelho	Arbre endémique/ jaunes
Ylang-Ylang	*Cananga odorata*	Árvore perfume	Ilangue-Ilangue

Appendix 2

LANGUAGE

Portuguese is the official language and is understood by everybody. French is taught in school and is much more likely to be understood than English, though on Príncipe even French is of little use. Visitors who have travelled in Spanish-speaking countries often speak 'Portunhol', a mix that will be understood by most people. However, in everyday situations some 85% of Santomense people use creole, or *forro* (see box, page 34).

Santomeans tend to be polite in their speech, and you will hear few people use swear words. Unlike in continental Portuguese, the informal form of address for young people and friends, *tu*, is less used; it suggests a degree of intimacy. Even children are often addressed as *você* (plural: *vocês* as in Brazilian Portuguese). Any woman above teenage age should be addressed as *Dona*, men as *o Senhor*.

PRONUNCIATION
The alphabet The difficulty in understanding Portuguese lies in the nasalisation, sh sounds, and the fact that words often run into one another.

- Vowels that carry a tilde (~) or that are followed by -m or -n are nasalised: São (saint), quem? (who?)
- Stress usually lies on the penultimate syllable. Exceptions are words ending in -l, -r, -z, nasalised -ã,
- Accents signify stress/emphasis: Tomé, Príncipe, água (water), português (Portuguese)

Português

A2

a = as in c**a**r (*carro*)
a (on its own) = as in **a** (on its own)
ã/an/am = as in **a**ngle
b = as in **b**ig
c = as in **c**at
ch = as in **sh**ame: *chá* (tea)
ç = as in **s**un: *açúcar* (sugar)
d = as in **d**og: *dá-me!* (give me!)
e = as in p**e**t: *esperar* (to wait)
f = as in **f**it: *fogo* (fire)
g = as in **g**od: *grande* (big)
h (at beginning) = dropped
h (after 'l' or 'n') = as in **y**oga: *molho* (sauce)
i = as in t**ea**: *livro* (book)

j = as in Raj: *jantar* (have dinner)
l = as in **l**et: *leve-leve* (easy, relaxed)
m = as in **m**e: *maçâ* (apple)
n = as in **n**o: *noite* (night)
o (stressed) = open, as in olive: *porta* (door) or closed, as in Scottish 'no'
o (unstressed, on its own) = as in root: *carro* (car)
p = as in **p**ig: Portugal
qu = before -a/-o as in **qu**est, before -e/-i as in **k**ettle: *quem*? (who?)
r = articulate strongly: <u>r</u>ua (street)
rr = rolled: *carro* (car)
s (at beginning of word/syllable after consonant, and when spelt 'ss') = as in **s**un: *sábado* (Saturday)
s (between vowels and at end when following word begins with vowel) = as in **z**ealous: *casa* (house), *seis euros* (six euros)
s (at end and before unvoiced consonants: c,[fax],k,p,s,t,x) = as in **sh**ower: *festa* (party)
ss = as in **s**treet: *isso* (this)
t = as in **t**ea: *toma*! (take!)
u = as in **noo**n: *tudo* (all)
v = as in **v**ery: *vamos*! (let's go!)
x = as in **sh**ort: *peixe* (fish) or *táxi* (taxi)
z = at beginning/between vowels: as in **z**en: *azul* (blue); at end: as in Raj: *dez* (ten)

Basic grammar As a sign of respect, often, the third person singular form of the verb is used. For example, if you are a woman somebody might ask you *A Senhora é inglesa?* (literally: 'The lady is English?'). Conversely, if you want to ask (a man) whether he knows where something is, you would ask *O Senhor sabe ónde é?*

Most common verb conjugation: *falar* (to speak) *fal-o*: I speak, *fal-as*: you speak, *fal-a*: he/she/it speaks, *fal-amos*: we speak, *fal-am* (you/plural speak, they speak)

Common compound verbs *ser* (to be – permanently): *sou*: I am, *és*: you are; *é*: he/she/it is, *somos*: we are; *são*: you/plural, they are

Common past forms
fui: I was, *foi*: he/she/it was, *fomos*: we were; *foram*: you/pl, they were
estar: (to be – temporarily/location): *estou, estás, está, estámos, estão*
estive: I was, *esteve*: he/she/it was, *estivemos*: we were, *estiveram*: you/pl., they were
ter: (to have): *tenho, tens, tem, temos, têm*
tive: I had, *teve*: he/she/it had, *tivemos*: we had, *tiveram*: you/pl., they had
ir: (to go): *vou, vais, vai, vamos, vão*
fui: I went, *fomos*: we went, *foram*: they went

Useful verbs

English	Portuguese	Creole
to be	*ser/estar*	*sa*
to speak	*falar*	*fla*
to buy	*comprar*	*kopla*
to get, catch	*apanhar*	*pega/koyê/panha*
to send	*enviar, mandar*	*manda*
to organise	*arranjar*	*luma/lanja/golo*
to give	*dar*	*da/tanda*

OK – thumbs up	OK/fixe
Hello/goodbye – wave hand, palm out, from side to side	olá/adeus
Ask for a lift (hitch-hiking)	boleia

to pick up	pegar	pega/toma
to have	ter	tê/sa ku
to leave, go away	ir-se embora	be dê/lanka xê
to like something/somebody	gostar de algo/alguem	ngosta di kwa
to work	trabalhar	tlaba
to see	ver	pya
to wander around/hang out	passear	paxa
to reach, arrive	chegar	xiga
to rent, hire	alugar	luga

Lungwa Santome sounds

a = as a in 'father'
e = as e in 'yet'
ê = as a in 'place'
i = as ea in 'meat' but shorter
o = as o in 'not'
ô = as oa in 'boat'
u = as oo in 'moon'
tx = as ch in 'chess'
dj = as j in 'joke'
x = as sh in 'shame'

Vocabulary

(Note: *sun* is formal masculine, *san* is formal feminine and *bô* is informal for both masculine and feminine)

Essentials

English	Portuguese	Creole
Good morning	bom dia	bondja ô/abensa ô
Good afternoon	boa tarde	bwas tadji ê
Good evening	boa noite	bwa notxi ê
Hello	olá, oi!	bondja (ô)/abensa ô
Goodbye	adeus	adêsu ê
What is your name?	como é que se chama?	Kê aglasa sun/san/bô ê?
		Kê nomi sun/san/bô ê?
My name is …	o meu nome é …	Aglasa/Nomi mu sa …
Where are you from?	de onde é?	Bô sa ngê d'andji?
		Andji ku tê bô?
I am from … England	sou … Inglês (Inglesa)/	N sa … nglêji
America	Americano (Americana)	amerikanu
France	Francês (Francesa)/	flansêji
Germany	Alemão (Alemã)	alemon
How are you?	Como está?	Sun/San/Bô sa bwa?

	Que ha de nova?	Ki nova ê?/Kuma bô sa?/ Kuma vida sa ê?/ Kuma kwa ska dêsê ê?
How are you? (polite version)	Como vai a saúde?	Ki nova saôdji ê?
All OK (with you)? (very common)	Tudo bem (contigo)?	Sun/san/bô sa bwa?
All OK	Tudo, obrigado/a	N sa bwa/Bwa so
Are you OK?	está bom/boa?	Sun/san/bô sa bwa?
Fine thanks	(estou bem) obrigado/a	N sa bwa/Bwa so
Easy, with calm... (Santomean motto)	lévé-lévé	leve-leve (tan)
OK	Normal	axi-axi
so-so	mais ou menos	mê txibi
Pleased to meet you	Gosto em conhecê-lo/a/prazer	
thank you	Kbrigado(a)	Dêsu ka paga sun/san/bô
Don't mention it	de nada	kwa desu paga ê?
Cheers!	Saúde!	Saôdji!
Yes	sim/pois	Efan/E
No	não	Inô/Nô ô
It's OK/All right then	Kstá bem/está bom	Muntu ben/non sa fladu
I don't understand	não compreendo	N na ska tendê fa
I didn't understand	Kão percebi	N na tendê fa
Please would you speak more slowly	Kor favor pode falar mais devagar	Fla maxi momoli fan
Excuse me?	diga?	Poda mu?
Calm down	(Com) calma	kaluma fan
Do you understand?	está a perceber?	Sun/San/Bô têndê an?
I don't know	Não sei	N na sêbê fa
I would like ...	queria …	N mêsê …

Questions

how?	como?	Kuma?
what?	o quê?	Kê kwa?
where?	onde?	Andji?
what is it?	o que é?	Sa kê kwa?
which?	qual	Kali dinen? (which one?)
when?	quando?	Kê dja?
why?	porquê?	Punda kamanda?/ Punda kê kwa?
who?	quem?	Kê ngê?
how much?	quanto é?	Kantu ku ê sa?

Numbers

1	um	ũa
2	dois	dôsu
3	três	tlêxi
4	quatro	kwatlu
5	cinco	xinku
6	seis	sêxi
7	sete	sete

8	oito	wôtô
9	nove	nove
10	dez	dexi
11	onze	dexi ku ũa
12	doze	dexi ku dôsu
13	treze	dexi ku tlêxi
14	quatorze	dexi ku kwatlu
15	quinze	dexi ku xinku
16	dezasseis	dexi ku sêxi
17	dezassete	dexi ku sete
18	dezoito	dexi ku wôtô
19	dezanove	dexi ku nove
20	vinte	vintxi/dôsu dexi
21	vinte e um/a	vintxi/dôsu dexi ku ũa
30	trinta	tlinta/tlêxi dexi
40	quarenta	kolenta/kwatlu dexi
50	cinquenta	xinkwenta/xinku dexi
60	sessenta	sesenta/sêxi dexi
70	settenta	stenta/sete dexi
80	oitenta	wôtenta/wôtô dexi
90	noventa	noventa/nove dexi
100	cem	sem
101	cent e um/a	sem ku ũa
1,000	mil	mili

Time

What time is it?	Que horas são?	Kê minda d'ola kwa sa ê?
It's … am/pm	São … da manhã/tarde	Sa … plaman/tadji
now	agora	miole/wele
today	hoje	oze
tonight	hoje à noite	oze nôtxi
tomorrow	amanhã	amanha
tomorrow morning	amanhã de manhã	amanha plaman
yesterday	ontem	onten
morning	manhã	plaman
evening	noite	nôtxi

Days

Monday	segunda-feira	segunda fela
Tuesday	terça-feira	tesa fela
Wednesday	quarta-feira	kwata fela
Thursday	quinta-feira	kinta fela
Friday	sexta-feira	sesta fela
Saturday	sábado	sabadu
Sunday	domingo	dja djingu

Months

January	Janeiro	janêlu
February	Fevereiro	fêvêlêlu
March	Março	masu
April	Abril	abli

English	Portuguese	Local
May	*Maio*	*mayu*
June	*Junho*	*junhu*
July	*Julho*	*julhu*
August	*Agosto*	*agôstô*
September	*Setembro*	*setemblu*
October	*Outubro*	*ôtublu*
November	*Novembro*	*novemblu*
December	*Dezembro*	*dezemblu*

Getting around

English	Portuguese	Local
public transport	*transportes públicos*	*karu praça*
a one-way ticket	*um bilhete de ida*	*bilhêtê di be*
a return ticket	*um bilhete de ida e volta*	*bilhêtê di bi*
I want to go to …	*Quero ir para …*	*N mêsê ba …*
How much is it?	*Quanto é que é?*	*Kantu ku ê sa?*
What time does it leave?	*A que horas sai?*	*Kê mind'ola ê ka xê?*
What time is it now?	*Que horas são?*	*Kê mind 'ola kwa sa ê?*
The plane has been …	*O vôo está …*	*avion sa …*
delayed	*atrasado*	*trasadu*
cancelled	*cancelado*	*avion na bila ska bi fa*
first class	*primeira classe*	*primêra klasi*
second class	*segunda classe*	*sêgunda klasi*
ticket office	*bilheteira*	*luge di kopla bilhêtê*
timetable	*horário*	*ola d'avion*
from	*de*	*djina*
to	*para*	*antê*
airport	*aeroporto*	*kampu d'aviason/ kampu d'avion*
port	*porto*	*pôntxi*
plane	*avião*	*avion*
dug out canoe	*canoa*	*kanwa*
boat	*barco*	*vapô*
car	*carro*	*karu*
4x4	*quatro vezes quatro/jeep*	*jipi*
taxi	*taxi*	*karu praça*
minibus	*minibus*	*atukaru txoko*
motorbike/moped	*moto*	*moto*
bicycle	*bicicleta*	*bixketa*
arrival/departure	*chegada/partida*	*ola xiga/ola xê*
here	*aqui*	*nai*
there	*ali*	*nala*
Bon voyage!	*Boa viagem!*	*Be ku Dêsu!* (go with God)

Private transport

English	Portuguese	Local
Is this the road to …?	*Esta é a estrada para …?*	*Stlada se sa stlada di ba …?*
Where is the service station?	*Aonde fica a bomba de combustível?*	*Bomba gasolina sa andji ê*
Please fill it up	*Por favor é para atestar/encher*	*Fen favôlô, xa mutoru*
I'd like … litres	*Queria … litros*	*N mêsê… litlu*

diesel	gasóleo	gasolho
petrol	gasolina	gasolina
lift	boleia	bolêa
I have broken down	Tenho o carro avariado/empanado	Karu mu dana/ karu mundja dê
jack	macaco (lit. 'monkey')	makaku

Road signs

give way	desistir	
danger	perigo	Pligu
entry	entrada	Lentla
detour	desvio	Bila nai
one way	sentido único	Ka be so
no entry	proibida a entrada	Na lentla fa
exit	saída	Xê

Directions

Where is it?	Onde fica?	Andji ku ... sa nê?
Go straight ahead	Sempre em frente	Ka be so
Turn left	Virar à esquerda	Toma mon xkedu
Turn right	Virar à direita	Toma mon glêtu
... at the roundabout	... na rotunda	
north	norte	notxi
south	sul	sulu
east	leste	
west	oeste	
behind	atrás	ni tlaxi
in front of	à frente	ni wê
near	perto	petu/ni bodo/n zuntu
opposite	oposto	biladu wê da

Other useful words and expressions

money	dinheiro	djêlu
nothing	nada	nadaxi
open	aberto	betu
closed	fechado	fisadu
toilets – men/women	casa de banho	ke banhu d'ome/mwala letreti d'ome/letreti mwala
information	informação	informason
Do you speak English/French?	Fala inglês/francês?	Sun/san/bô sêbê fla/ inglêji/flansêji?
He/she went out	Ele/ela saiu	Ê xê
He/she will be back at ...	Ele/ela volta às ...	Ê ka bila bi ... ora

Accommodation

| Where is a cheap/ good hotel? | Onde fica um hotel barato/bom? | Andji ku tê a hotelu/ penson blatu ê? |
| Could you please write the address? | Pode-me escrever a morada por favor? | Sun/San ka pô fe mu favôlô di sklêvê direson? |

English	Portuguese	Crioulo
Do you have any rooms available?	*Tem quartos disponíveis?*	*kwartu sen?*
I'd like …	*Queria …*	*N tava mêsê/N mêsê …*
a single room	*um quarto com uma cama*	*a kwartu k'ũa kama*
a double room	*um quarto de casal*	*a kwartu ku kama kasal/ku kama pla dôsu ngê*
a room with two beds	*um quarto com duas camas*	*a kwartu ku dôsu kama*
a room with a bathroom	*um quarto com casa de banho*	*a kwartu ku ke banhu*
How much is it per night/person?	*Quanto é por cada noite/pessoa?*	*Kantu plô nôtxi?*
Where is the toilet?	*Onde é a casa de banho?*	*Ke banhu sa andji?/ Letreti sa andji?*
Where is the bathroom?	*Onde é a casa de banho?*	*Ke banhu sa andji?*
Is there hot water?	*Tem água quente?*	*Awa kêntxi sen?/ A tê awa kêntxi?*
Is there electricity?	*Tem energia?*	*Kandja/letrisidadi sen?*
There's been a power cut	*Houve um corte de energia*	*Kandja bê dê A kota kandja*
the power will come back at …	*a energia vai voltar…*	*Kandja ka bi … ora*
Is breakfast included?	*O pequeno almoço está incluido?*	*Ku matabisu ô?*
Can you make up a packed lunch?	*Pode preparar uma refeição para levar?*	*A ka pô fe mina kwa k ume pa n be ku ê ô?*
I'd like to speak to the manager, please	*Faz favor, queria falar com o gerente*	*N mêsê fla ku patlon, xefi, jerenti*
I am leaving today	*Vou-me embora hoje*	*N ga be mu oze/n ga xê oze*

Food

English	Portuguese	Crioulo
Do you have a table for … people?	*Tem uma mesa para … pessoas?*	*Meza pla … ngê sen?*
…a children's menu?	*…um menu para crianças?*	*kume pla mina pikina sen?*
I am a vegetarian	*Sou vegetariano/a*	*Na ka kume kani nê pixi fa*
Do you have any vegetarian dishes?	*Tem pratos vegetarianos?*	*Kume fya sen?*
Waiter! (informal)	*Moço/a!/Rapaz!* (but NOT *Rapariga!*)	*Sungê ê!/Sangê ê!*
Please bring me …	*Por favor traga-me …*	*Fe mu favôlô bi ku …*
a fork/knife/spoon/glass/ napkin	*um garfo/faca/colher/copo/ guardanapo*	*galufu/faka/kwiê/kopu gwadanapu*
Can I have the bill please?	*Traga a conta por favor*	*Fe mu favôlô bi ku konta*
meal	*refeição*	*kume*

| packed lunch | refeição para levar | kume di be ku ê |
| Can you heat this up for me, please? | Faz favor, pode-se aquecer? | Sun/san ka pô fe mu favôlô di kenta kwa se da mu? |

Basics

bread	pão	mpon
biscuits/cookies	bolachas	bôlô
butter	manteiga	mantêga
cheese	queijo	kêzu
oil/olive oil/palm oil	óleo/azeite/óleo de palma	olho/zêtê doxi/zêtê (pema)
chilli	piri-piri	magita/
pepper	pimento	pimenton
salt	sal	salu
sugar	açucar	sukli
eggs	ovos	ovu
pasta	esparguete	spalageti

Fruit

papaya	mamão	mamon
bananas	bananas	bôbô, kitxiba, klete, bana (bana ôlô, bana mpon, bana plata, bana plata, bana manson)
pineapple	ananàs	nanaji
mango	manga	manga
orange	laranja	lanza
lime	lima	limon
lemon	limão	limon flansêji
safu (local fruit)	safú	safu
izaquente (local fruit)	izaquente	zêkêntxi
jack fruit	jaca	jaka
breadfruit	frutapão	fluta/flupa mpon
cocoa	cacao	kakaw
fruit from the spondias	cajamanga	kajamanga
coco	coco	kokonja
passion fruit	maracujá	mlakunja
guava	goiaba	ngweva
tomato	tomate	tomatu

Vegetables

yam	inhame	nhami
mandioc	mandioca	mandjoka
spring greens	couve	kôvi
cabbage	repolho	rôpôlhu
(green) beans	feijão (verde)	fezon (vêdê)
carrots	cenoura	sinôra
garlic	alho	ayu
onion	cebola	sabola

| potato/sweet | batata inglesa/doce | batata/batata doxi |
| beans | feijão | fezon |

Fish
fish	peixe	pixi
barracuda	barracuda	bakuda
shark	tubarão	ngandu
flying fish	peixe voador	vadô
mackerel	cavala	kavala
mussels	mexilhão	–
salmon	salmão	salmon
tuna	atum	atun

Meat
beef	carne de vaca	kani bwê
chicken	galinha/frango	nganha
goat	cabra	kabla
monkey	macaco	makaku
bat	morcego	ngembu
pork	porco	plôkô
lamb	borrego	karnêru
sausage	salsicha	salsixa

Drinks
beer	cerveja	sêlêvêja
coffee	café	kafe
tea	chá	xa
fruit juice	sumo de fruta	sumu
fizzy drink (coke, lemonade)	'Sumol' (brand name)	'Sumol'
milk	leite	lêtê
water	água	awa/awa galafa (bottled water)
wine	vinho	vin

Shopping
I'd like to buy …	Queria comprar …	N mêsê kopla …
How much is it?	Quanto é?	Kantu kwa se sa?
Have you got any …?	Tem ...?	Sun/San tê …?
I don't like it	Não gosto	N na ngosta fa
I'm just looking	Estou só a ver	N ska pya so
It's too expensive	É muito caro	Sa djêlu muntu fan
I'll take it	Eu compro	N ga kopla/N ga be ku ê
Please may I have?	Por favor queria?	N mêsê?
There's no more	… Acabou	Ê kaba za/Ê na bila sen fa
Do you accept credit cards?	Aceita-se cartão de crédito?	Sun/san ka toma karton kreditu?
shop	loja	vêndê
change	troco	tloku
small change/coins	moeda	tloku wini-wini

more	mais	maxi
less	menos	menu
smaller	mais pequeno	maxi pikina
bigger	maior	maxi nglandji

Communications

I am looking for …	Estou à procura de …	N ska golo
bank	banco	banku
post office	correios	korêyu
stamps	selos	sêlu
church, cathedral	igreja,catedral	glêza, ase
embassy	embaixada	embaxada
exchange office	câmbio	ke tloka djêlu
public telephone	telefone público	telefoni
mobile/cell phone	telemóvel	telemovel
tourist office	posto de turismo	sentru di turismu

Health

diarrhoea	diarreia	bega kôlê
nausea	náusea	bega uxi
doctor	doutor	dôtôlô
I'd like to make an appointment with …	Queria marcar consulta com …	N mêsê pa dôtôlô kunsuta mu …
prescription	prescrição	papelu mindjan
pharmacy	farmácia	butxika
paracetamol	paracetamol	parasetamol
antibiotics	antibióticos	antibiotiku
antiseptic	anti-sépticos	kwa di vita infeson
tampons	tampões	–
condoms	preservativos	kamisinha
contraceptives	contraceptivos	kumprimidu di na toma bega
sunblock	protector solar	pumada pa solo na kema ngê
It hurts here	Dói-me aquí	Ai ska dwê mu
My head/teeth/ stomach hurts	Dói-me a cabeça/ os dentes/a barriga	Kabesa/ dêntxi/bega ska dwê mu
I am …	Sou …	N sa …
asthmatic	asmático/a	n ga sufli d'asma
epileptic	epilético/a	n ga toma taki
diabetic	diabético/a	n ga sufli diabeti
I'm allergic to …	sou alérgico/a a …	n ga sufli d'alergia
penicillin	penicilina	pinisilina

Travel with children

Is there a … ?	Tem … ?	Ai tê … ?
baby changing room?	quarto para mudar	xitu di muda mina fraldas ao bébé? anzu fralda ô?

a children's menu?	menu para crianças?	kume pla mina pikina ô?
Do you have … ?	Tem … ?	Sun/san tê?
infant milk formula?	leite em pó para bébés?	lêtê en po pla mina anzu ô?
nappies	fraldas	fralda
potty	penico/bacio	baxa/piniku
babysitter	babysitter	ngê toma konta d'anzu
highchair	cadeira para bébé	banku pa mina anzu
How old is he/she?	Quantos anos tem?	Kantu anu ê tê?

Walking

hike	caminhada	skurson/ba matu ba paxa
slippery	escorregadio	Kwa ka kloga
plantation	roça	losa
tree	árvore	po madêra
floresta	floresta	obô/matu
wood	madeira	madela/madêra
tent	tenda	tenda
rain	chuva	suba
How long to get to … ?	Quanto tempo para chegar a … ?	Kantu nda antê ala … ?
How far is it to … ?	A que distancia fica … ?	Ê tê nda montxi … ?

In the club

Are you on your own?	Está sozinho/a?	Sun/san/bô tan ô?
Would you like a drink?	Quer beber alguma coisa?	Bô mêsê bêbê kwakwali kwa?
Would you like to dance?	Quer dançar?	Bô mêsê dansa?/bô mêsê sagudji tumbu?
Where is your husband/wife?	Onde é que está o seu marido/a sua esposa?	Ome/mwala bô s'andji?
Do you have children?	Tem filhos?	Sun/San/Bô tê mina?
How many children do you have?	Quantos filhos?	Kantu mina sun/san/bô tê?
Where are you staying?	Onde mora/está hospedado/a?	Andji sun/san bô ska ta nê?
good-looking	bonito/bonita	glavi
I like you	Gosto de tí	N ngosta bô/N gôgô ku bô
party	festa	fesa
nothing happening	está fraco	kwa sa flakexidu

Other

my/mine/ours/yours	meu(s)/minha(s)/nosso(s)/vosso(s)	dji mu/dji non/dinansê
and/but	e/mas	ku/maji
some	algum(a)	a-a
this/that	isto/aquilo	ise/isala
with	com	ku

IN AN EMERGENCY

Help!	*Socorro!*	*Kidalê!*
Call a doctor!	*Chamem um médico!*	*sama dôtôlô*
There's been an accident	*Houve um acidente*	*a asidenti da*
Careful!	*Cuidado!*	*kwidadu!*
I'm lost	*Estou perdido*	*n plêdê*
Go away!	*Và-se embora!*	*Fô dai*
police	*polícia*	*sode (the corps), polisya* (policeman)
fire	*fogo*	*fôgô*
ambulance	*ambulância*	*ambulansia*
thief	*ladrão*	*ladlon*
They took …	*Roubaram-me …*	*A futa mu …*
hospital	*hospital*	*xipitali*
I am ill	*estou doente*	*n ska dwêntxi*

like that	*assim*	*mo kwa se*
expensive/cheap	*caro/barato*	*karu/blatu*
beautiful/awful	*lindo/horrível*	*glavi/fê*
pretty/ugly	*bonito/feio*	*glavi/fê*
old/new	*velho/novo*	*ve/novu*
good/bad	*bom/mau*	*bwa, bon/ma,mau, bluku*
early/late	*cedo/tarde*	*sedu/tadji*
hot/cold	*quente/frio*	*kentxi/fiô*
difficult/easy	*difícil/fácil*	*kwa tê matxi/kwa na tê matxi fa*
boring/interesting	*chato/interessante*	*sê aglasa/ka da sun vonte*
fast/slow	*rápido/devagar*	*djandjan/momoli*
excellent!	*optimo!*	*fina leke-leke!*
nice	*giro/a*	*glavi*
smart	*esperto/a*	*supetu*
exactly!	*exactamente!*	*efan/axen mé!*
funny	*engraçado/a*	*ka fe sun li*
black	*preto, negro*	*pletu*
white	*branco (colomba* derog.)	*blanku/kolomba*
mixed race	*mulato*	*mulatu*
foreigner	*estrangeiro/a*	*strangêru*
So? What are you up to?	*Então?*	*Kuma?*
Isn't it/isn't that so?	*Não e*	*Na sa axen me fa?*
It's in poor condition/ not fit for use	*Não tem condiçoes na sa buadu fa*	*Ê na ka da fa*
problems, mess	*confusão*	*tlomentu/kunfuson*
Hello (on the telephone)	*Estou* (sim)	*Alô*
Do you see what I mean?	*Ouviu?*	*Sun/san/bô têndê?*
Look!	*Olhe!* (formal)/ *Olha!* (informal)	*Pya!*

There is?	*há?*	*Ê sen?*
What's happened?	*houve?*	*kontêsê?/Tava sen?*
That's enough!	*Já chega!*	*Ê xiga za!*
Damn!	*Bolas!*	*Djanga!*
(Son of a) bitch	*(Filho da) puta*	*Fidaputa!*
Well then, eh! (common exclamation)	*Epá!*	*Êy kompa ê!*
Thingy (filler word)	*coiso*	*kwa*
a lot	*bastante*	*a data/lumadu/muntu/ ku pasa*
Excuse me (eg: pushing through a crowd)	*Com licença*	*Da mu lisensa*

Appendix 3

FURTHER INFORMATION

BOOKS Most books on São Tomé and Príncipe are in Portuguese, but increasingly titles are appearing in English. For reasons of space, this section includes only a selection of the most important titles in Portuguese (P), French (F) and German (G). English is marked as (E) when necessary.

There are no bookshops on the archipelago. On São Tomé island, some publications may be consulted at the **National Archives**, the **National Library** or the **Writers' Union** UNEAS. The **Alliance Française** library is quite well stocked with books on STP, and the Instituto Camões occasionally sells volumes of local poetry. Most of the titles listed here can only be obtained outside the country, most easily online (for instance, on Amazon). Another good source are secondhand booksellers in Portugal; Lisbon has 90 *alfarrabistas* who often stock STP titles. The Lisbon-based **Instituto de Investigação Tropical** (*IICT, Rua da Junqueira, No 86–1, 1300–344 Lisbon;* +351 213 616 340; e *iict@iict.pt; www.iict.pt*) used to publish many STP-related books. The Institute's publications are available from three booksellers, the most central of which is Livraria Portugal (*Rua do Carmo 70–74, 1200–094 Lisbon;* +351 213 474 982; e *direccao@livrariaportugal.pt*). They will mail books abroad and also sell other STP-related titles. The IICT's library, CDI (Centro de Documentação; *Rua Gen. João de Almeida, 15, 1300–266 Lisbon;* +351 213 619 730; e *cdi@iict.pt; www.iict.pt*), is open to the public from 09.00–12.30 and 14.00–17.30 Monday to Friday but you can't take any book away. The **National Library** is at Campo Grande 83, 1749–081 Lisbon (+351 217 982 000; *www.bn.pt*). The British Library Direct service (*www.direct.bl.uk*) offers expensive direct downloads of some 40 catalogue items on São Tomé and Príncipe and the option to order some 250 more.

Fiction

Bragança, Albertino *Rosa do Riboque* Caminho, 1998. Tales from the famous São Tomé neighbourhood (P).

Castro, Manuela and Guedes, Vera (ill) *Missó – Uma Concha em São Tomé* Instituto Camões, 2006. Beautiful moving children's story about a family of those multi-pronged shells you only find on Sete Ondas beach, full of inspiration and messages about equality and tolerance, presented in a fun way (P).

Cohn, Paul D *São Tomé – Journey to the Abyss: Portugal's Stolen Children* Burns-Cole Publications, 2005. Page-turning self-published historical novel following the fate of two Portuguese Jewish children kidnapped and brought to São Tomé.

Espírito Santo, Alda Graça *E Nosso o Solo Sagrado da Terra* Ulmeiro, 1978, and *O Coral das Ilhas* UNEAS, 2006. Poetry by the *grande dame* of Santomean culture and politics.

Guisti, Emilio and Massa, Jean-Michel (eds) *Fablier de São Tomé* Edicef Fleuve et Flamme, 1984. Fourteen Santomense tales, in a P/F bilingual edition.

Marky, Sum *Crónica de Una Guerra Inventada* Vega, 1999. Exploration of the 1953 massacre.

Rosa Mendes, Pedro *Lenin Oil* Dom Quixote, 2006. What happens when oil hits a small island republic on the Equator? Challenging ironic exploration (P) of this issue by a young award-winning Portuguese author – using a first-person narrative of an American oil executive and dramatic elements of the tchiloli. Beautiful illustrations by Alain Corbel.

Sousa Tavares, Miguel *Equador* (see page 43 for an extract) Oficina do Livro, 2003, Bloomsbury, 2008; translation by Peter Bush. Hugely atmospheric novel charting the progress of young dandy Luis Bernardo Valença, sent from Lisbon to be governor of the islands and defeat the impending boycott of Santomean cocoa – only to find himself in hot political waters and a love triangle. The novel has sold over 250,000 copies in Portugal and been translated into a dozen languages and made into a television series for TV1 – filmed, however, in Brazil. The Portuguese publisher also brought out a large format hardback version, beautifully illustrated with period postcards.

Teles, Manuel Neto *Retalhes do Massacre de Batepá* União dos Escritores Angolanos 2008. Historical novel on the 1953 massacre.

Poetry

Lima, Conceição *A Dolorosa Raíz do Micondó* Caminho, 2006. Second collection (P) by acclaimed London-based poet, born and bred in Santana and former BBC World Service producer. In 2012, this was followed by *O País do Akendengue* (Caminho).

Mata, Inocência (ed) *Bendenxa: 25 poemas de São Tomé e Príncipe para os 25 anos de Independência* Caminho, 2000. Inspired selection of past and present Santomean poetry by 11 poets, including some previously unpublished work (P).

Travel guides

Auzias, Dominique and Labourdette, Jean-Paul *Gabon/São Tomé et Príncipe* Le Petit Futé, 2008. Updated 2012/3 in digital format only (around €7) (F).

Gallet, Dominique *São Tomé and Príncipe – Iles du milieu du monde* Karthala, 2001. Lively and detailed cultural guide, though a lot of the travel information is now out of date (F).

Iwainsky, Thomas and Weck, Karl Alexander *Reiseführer São Tomé e Príncipe* Cosmoglobe Communications, 2003. Compact, nicely produced and personal travel guide (G).

Schweinberger, Bernd *São Tomé and Príncipe – Trauminseln auf dem Äquator* 1995. Engaging travel narrative, plus tourism tips (now mostly out of date), by the first non-Portuguese tour operator to offer trips to São Tomé and Príncipe. Available from www.schweinberger.de (G).

Various *São Tomé e Príncipe 2012/3*. Portuguese/English brochure-style guide, with lots of information and colour pictures, however plenty of out-of-date information too; available from the tourist office in São Tomé.

Various *São Tomé e Príncipe – Guia Turístico* Pocket Tropics, 2013. Compact illustrated first Portuguese-language travel guide. Some errors, but plenty of information and fascinating historical illustrations thanks to the authors' work at historical archives.

Travel health

Wilson-Howarth, Dr Jane *Bugs, Bites & Bowels* Cadogan/Globe Pequot, 2006. In-depth and entertaining advice, with case studies.

Wilson-Howarth, Dr Jane and Ellis, Dr Matthew *Your Child Abroad: A Travel Health Guide* Bradt Travel Guides, 2005

General

Alegre, Francisco Costa *A Cidade de São Tomé* UNEAS, 2009. History of the capital city; slightly quirky in places, but full of interesting information.

Espírito Santo, Carlos *Coração ao mar* Cooperação Portuguesa, 1998. Engaging study of forro culture, from birth to death, touching on language, rituals, religion, culture, crafts and medicine, with colour photographs.

Espírito Santo, Carlos *Encyclopédia Fundamental de São Tomé and Príncipe* Cooperação Portuguesa, 2001. Illustrated, extensive if now a bit outdated overview of all aspects of São Tomé and Príncipe life – people, plants, politics, literature, history, local words, customs, etc.

Instituto Marquês de Valle-Flor *São Tomé – Ponto de Partida*, 2008. Coffee-table book by a Portuguese cultural NGO.

Tournadre, Michel *São Tomé and Príncipe* Editions Regards, 2000. Coffee-table book with excellent photography.

Arts and culture

Araújo, Gabriel and Hagemeijer, Tjerk *Dicionário livre do santome-português* São Paulo: Hedra, 2013. Inexpensive compact Santome–Portuguese dictionary.

Barbosa, Maria Christina *Ye, Regnê* BISTP. Study of Príncipe culture, available from Mediateca or Historical Archive (350,000$)

Beja, Olinda *Água Crioula* Pé das Página Editores, 2007. Poetry collection by the author of the children's book *Um grão de café* (2013).

Bragança, Albertino *A música popular santomense* UNEAS, 2005.

Burness, Donald *Ossobó – Essays on the Literature of São Tomé and Príncipe* Africa World Press, 2005. The US-American expert on lusophone African literatures explores the themes of Santomean literature: the mythic Ossobó bird, the massacre of 1953 and Angolar culture. Includes 23 English translations of poetry by ten poets (including Marcelo da Veiga, Francisco José Tenreiro, Fernando de Macedo, Alda Espírito Santo, Carlos Espírito Santo). Also available in Portuguese.

Daio, Olinto Semplu São Tomé: Gesmedia, 2002

Espírito Santo, Carlos *Tipologias do Conto Maravilhoso Africano* Cooperação Portuguesa, 2000. Analysis of African fairytales with focus on São Tomé and Príncipe, reprinting some local examples (P).

Ferraz, Luiz Ivens *The Creole of São Tomé* Witwatersrand University Press, 1979. The first monograph on the local Creole language.

Gründ, Françoise *Tchiloli – Charlemagne à São Tomé sur l'ile du milieu du monde* Magellan & Cie, 2006. Beautifully illustrated study (F) on the islands' unique dramatic cultural expression.

Günther, Wilfried *Das portugiesische Kreolisch der Jlha do Príncipe* author's ed/Marburger Studien zur Afrika- und Asienkunde, Marburg, 1973. Detailed study (G) of the *lung'iye* language spoken on Príncipe, with glossary.

Kalewska, Anna *Baltasar Dias e as metamorfoses do discurso dramatúrgico em Portugal e nas ilhas de São Tomé and Príncipe* Warsaw University, 2005. Study (P) on the sources of the tchiloli.

Laban, Michel *Encontros com Escritores* Funcação António de Almeida, 2002. Interviews with Santomean writers (P).

Lavender, Cristina Brandão *Saber Esperar* Chiado Editora, 2013. First novel by Luso-santomean writer, chronicling the life of Sahira MacDamara, blending the experience of forros, contract workers and colonials forced to abandon the islands after decolonisation – with the story of the author's own long-awaited return to her place of birth.

Loude, Jean-Yves *Coup de théâtre à São Tomé: Carnet d'enquête aux îles du milieu du monde* Actes du Sud, 2007. Engrossing and quirky ethnologist's travelogue (F), with illustrations by Alain Corbel.

Loureiro, João *Postais Antigos de São Tomé e Príncipe* Postais Ultramar, 2005. Over 200 views of São Tomé and Príncipe in the 19th and 20th centuries, some of them used for the illustrated edition of Miguel Sousa Tavares's *Equador* (see above); www.postaisultramar.com.pt (P).

Massa, Françoise and Jean-Michel *Dictionnaire bilingue portugais–français des particularités de la langue portugaise à Saint-Thomas et Prince* CNRS, 1998. Portuguese–French dictionary with emphasis on the islands' linguistic particularities.

Mata, Inocência *A Suave Pátria: Reflexões Político-culturais sobre a Sociedade São-tomense* Edições Colibri, 2004 (P)

Mata, Inocência *Diálogo Com as Ilhas: Sobre Cultura e Literatura de São Tomé e Príncipe* Edições Colibri, 1998. Overview of Santomean culture and literature, by Príncipe-born academic (P).

Mata, Inocência *Francisco José Tenreiro: as Múltiplas Faces de um Intelectual* Edições Colibri, 2010 (P)

Mata, Inocência *Polifonias Insulares: Cultura e Literatura de São Tomé e Príncipe* Edições Colibri, 2010 (P)

Maurer, Philippe *L'angolar. Un créole afro-portugais parlé à São Tomé* Helmut Buske Verlag, 1995. A grammar of Angolar (F).

Maurer, Philippe *Principense: Grammar, texts, and vocabulary of the Afro-Portuguese creole of the Island of Príncipe, Gulf of Guinea* London: Battlebridge, 2009.

Pape, Duarte *As Roças de São Tomé & Príncipe* Lisbon: Tinta da China, 2013 (P)

Pereira, Paulo Alves *Das Tchiloli von São Tomé – Die Wege des karolingischen Universums* IKO Verlag, 2002. Thesis (G) placing the island's unique dramatic expression in its cultural context.

Quintas da Graça, Amadeu *Paga Ngunu* São Tomé: Empresa de Artes Gráficas, 1989 (P)

Reis, Fernando *Pôvô Flogà, O Povo brinca. Folclore de São Tomé e Príncipe* Câmara Municipal de São Tomé, 1969. Seminal exploration of Santomean folklore (P), including the Tchiloli text.

Salvaterra, Jerónimo *Mangungo* São Tomé: Modelo Brindes-Publicitários, Lda, 2009 (P)

Santa-Rita, António José de *A Arquitetura da era colonial de São Tomé e Príncipe, Caracterisações e Identidades – com considerações urbanísticas atuais das Roças (Maria Alice Pires Lobo).* Edições Universitárias Lusófonas, 2013 (P)

Soulié, Tony *São Tomé*, 2005

Soulié, Tony *São Tomé – Le rêve africain* Au Même Titre, 2003. Glossy reproductions of French artist's collage paintings, with an excellent foreword by Bernard Carayon (F).

Tavares, René *A Singularidade do Tchiloli Pela Mão de René Tavares* Lisbon, 2011. Beautiful album of illustrations on the island's unique dramatic tradition by one of the most successful Saotomean artists, with an introduction by Adelaide Ginga (P).

History and society

Caixa Geral de Depósitos/SGE Mediateca *Olhar O Futuro* 2006. Illustrated overview of contemporary São Tomé and Príncipe society, with data on living conditions, health, education (P).

Da Costa, Manuel Pinto *Terra Firme* Edições Afrontamento, 2011. Political autobiography of the country's first (and at the time of writing current) President (P).

Deus Lima, José *História do Massacre de 1953 em São Tomé and Príncipe* 2002. History of the colonial 'massacre' and rallying call for Santomean nationalism (P), including many oral testimonies. Available from the Tourist Information in São Tomé and the National Archives/National Library.

Graça, Carlos *Memórias Políticas de um Nacionalista Santomense* UNEAS 2011 (P)

Henriques, Isabel Castro *São Tomé and Príncipe – A Invenção de uma Sociedade* Vega, 2000. Small but heavily illustrated study by Lisbon-based historian specialised in Africa and decolonialisation (P).

Higgs, Catherine *Chocolate Islands. Cocoa, Slavery and Colonial Africa*. Ohio University Press, 2012

Nascimento, Augusto *História da Ilha do Príncipe* Câmara Municipal de Oeiras, 2010. This sociologist has also written an atlas of lusophony for São Tomé and Príncipe (out of print), explored the Santomean plantation system's heyday (2002), the testimonies of Cape Verdeans returning home from contract labour in STP (2008) and the rôle of sports on the islands in the colonial period (2013). (P).

Satre, Lowell J *Chocolate on Trial: Slavery, Politics, and the Ethics of Business* Ohio University Press, 2005. The story of slavery in West Africa, and São Tomé and Príncipe in particular, and the intervention of William Cadbury, leading to the 1909 boycott of Santomean cocoa.

Seibert, Gerhard *Comrades, Clients and Cousins – Colonialism, Socialism and Democratization in São Tomé and Príncipe* Brill, 2006. The 'bible' of São Tomé and Príncipe: an in-depth (over 600pp) and up-to-date analysis of history, society and party politics by Lisbon-based researcher and authority on São Tomé and Príncipe. The Portuguese translation of the first English edition (1999) was published in 2001.

Shaxson, Nicholas *Poisoned Wells – The Dirty Politics of African Oil* (Palgrave 2007). In this analysis of the volatile African oil sector, this respected journalist devotes a whole chapter to São Tomé and Príncipe.

Valverde, Paulo *Máscara, Mato e Morte em São Tomé* Celta Editora, 2000. Study (P) of Santomean drama, rituals and beliefs.

Natural history Many books may be ordered through the British Natural History Book Service (☏ +44 (0)1803 865913; e customer.services@nhbs.co.uk; www.nhbs.com), who offer an excellent customer service, including a no-quibble refund.

Atkinson, P W, Dutton, J S et al (eds) *A Study of the Birds, Small Mammals, Turtles and Medicinal Plants of São Tomé, with Notes on Príncipe* BirdLife International Study Report No 56, 1992. For a copy of the only available English-language round-up of the islands' flora and fauna, check www.africanbirdclub.org/sales/sales.2.html. At £10 it's worth getting, even if a few things are out of date.

Billes, Alexis *On the tracks of sea turtles in Central Africa* Ecofac, 2005. Useful illustrated booklet describing the different species, their life cycle, identification guide, etc. Available from the MARAPA NGO in São Tomé town (see page 113). Also available in French and Portuguese.

Bordenave, Martine and Fournier, P *Príncipe – Livre Sonore* 2011. A very interesting illustrated sound book on Príncipe life, from fishing to spiritual possession of a group of youngsters, compiled by a French couple. Author's contact: philofournier@wanadoo.fr. For sale (200,000$) at Alliance Française, ST (see page 127).

Borrow, Nik and Demey, Ron *Birds of Western Africa* Princeton Field Guides, 2005. The gold standard, especially if you're combining your trip to São Tomé and Príncipe with Gabon. If you don't want to carry this weighty illustrated tome, just photocopy the back pages with the Gulf of Guinea endemics. Nik Borrow guides with the Birdquest tour operator (see page 50).

Carvalho, I, Brito, C et al *The Waters of São Tomé: a calving ground for West African humpback whales?* Africa Journal of Marine Science, 2011

Christy, Patrice and Clarke, William V *Les oiseaux de São Tomé and Príncipe* Ecofac, 1998. The best bird guide to get, with 32 pages of excellent colour drawings illustrating the French text (introduction in Portuguese, too), and the creole names for many common birds (F/P).

De Naurois, René *Les Oiseaux des Îles du Golfe de Guinée: São Tomé, Prince et Annobon/As Aves das Ilhas Do Golfo da Guinée: São Tomé, Príncipe e Ano Bom* IICT, 1994. This illustrated bird guide (F/P), the fruit of 20 years' ornithological research, is recommended by birders, but at a cover price of around US$100 you're probably better off with the Christy book (see above).

Do Céu, Maria Madureira (ed) *Estudo Etnofarmacológico de Plantas Medicinais de São Tomé e Príncipe* Projecto Pagué, Lisbon, 2012. New edition of seminal 2008 study (P). For an English-language article, see the author's 2010 'Antimalarial Drug Development Research and the Ancient Knowledge of Traditional Medicirnes in São Tomé e Principe Islands' in Tradiciones y transformaciones en Etnobotánica – Traditions and transformations in Ethnobotany, Ed. CYTED (2010), Argentina. Cap. 6.05: 256-264. ISBN: 978-84-96023-95-6.

Exell, A W *Catalogue of the vascular plants of São Tome* British Museum of Natural History, 1944. Still *the* reference work.

Figueiredo, Estrela *Nomes vulgares da flora de São Tomé e Príncipe* IICT, 1998. A list of the common names for many of the local plants and trees (P).

Jones, Peter and Tye, Alan *The Birds of São Tomé and Príncipe with Annobon* British Ornithologists' Union, 2006. A professional checklist with no illustrations and few photographs, this bird book is only for hard-core birders.

Leventis, A P and Olmes, Fábio *The Birds of São Tomé & Príncipe – A Photoguide* São Paulo: Aves & Fotos editora, 2009. Bilingual edition, compact and in colour, the best option for the casual birder.

Loude, Jean-Yves *Les poissons viennent de la forêt – Terres insolites São Tomé*. Lovely illustrated story for children from 11 upwards (F).

Oliveira, Faustino and Stévart, Tariq *As Orchídeas de São Tomé and Príncipe/Guide des Orchidées de São Tomé and Príncipe* Ecofac, 1998 (P/F). Orchid guide, fruit of the work of local botanist, Faustino Oliveira and Belgian colleague Tariq Stévart.

Picanco, C, Carvalho, I et al *Occurrence and distribution of cetaceans in São Tomé and Príncipe tropical archipelago and their relation to environmental variables* Journal of the Marine Biological Association of the United Kingdom, 2009

Roseira, Luís Lopes *Plantas úteis da flora de São Tomé e Príncipe* 2007. Fascinating local study (P) of the medicinal, industrial and ornamental uses of the islands' plants, with some drawings and photos. Available from the capital's Livraria de São Tomé opposite the cathedral.

Sargeant, David E *A Birders' Guide to the Gulf of Guinea Islands of São Tomé and Príncipe* Birders' Guides and Checklists, 1992. Slim A4 checklist by the ornithologist who first sighted São Tomé's rarest bird in recent times, with detailed diaries from his birdwatching trips in 1989 and 1991 and hands-on advice on how to explore the remote southwest.

Various *Guia de Campo 365 Espécies Atlânticas* www.oceanografica.com, 2008. In the absence of a specialised guide, this fish guide, in Portuguese, with other languages, features many of the species you'll find in the waters around the archipelago (P).

Wilme, Lucienne *São Tomé and Príncipe – balade sur deux jeunes îles du plus vieux continent* Ecofac, 2000. Handy illustrated overview of São Tomé and Príncipe's natural beauty, including an extensive Latin, English and French glossary (F).

Cookery

Aguiar, Sandra, Kilcher, Frédéric et al *Receitas com Produtos da Terra* Alisei, 2006. Collection of recipes (P), from coconut cake to banana croquettes and orange wine. Available from the Alisei (see page 104) or Ossobô (see page 125) shops.

Corallo, Claudio and Rovira, Eric *KKO – Esencia de Cacao* (Spanish). A homage to cocoa and chocolate.

Silva, João Carlos *A Roça com os Tachos* Oficina do Livro, 2005. Beautifully produced illustrated cookery book based on an RTP Africa TV programme, featuring traditional recipes and presenting local fruit, herbs and vegetables. Photos by Adriana Freire. Also available as a DVD set, showing the charismatic chef cooking his way around the plantations. The 2006 follow-up, *Façam o Favor de Ser Felices*, contains further recipes and reflections on São Tomé and Príncipe (P).

Valério, Conceição *Cozinha Tradicional de São Tomé e Príncipe* Centro Culturel Português, 2002 (P)

ARTICLES AND NEWSCLIPS

Jary, Emmanuelle and Mallet, Jean-François 'São Tomé et Príncipe – Les îles du milieu du monde' *Saveurs* magazine, Dec 2005/Jan 2006). Reportage and recipes (F).

Various *ABP – Zeitschrift zur portugiesischsprachigen Welt* No. 1, IKO, 1995. Articles (G/P) from a STP symposium at Cologne University.

Various *Revue Internationale de l'Imaginaire* No 14, 1990, Maison des Cultures du Monde. Tchiloli and Santomense culture in general (F).

Various *Biodiversity and conservation in Sao Tomé* Biodiversity and Conservation, Vol 3, No 9, Dec 2004, Springer. Journal articles on birds, medicinal plants, ferns and introduced mammals. Download from www.springerlink.com; US$30.

http://ww1.rtp.pt/noticias/index.php?headline=98&visual=25&article=347735&tema=27. Four-minute newsclip (P) about one of the foremost ornithologists working in STP, Martim de Melo.

MAPS There are few maps of STP available and as they're hard to find outside the country it's probably best to just get whichever one you come across. In São Tomé and Príncipe itself, you will see topographical maps and maritime charts from the 1960s hanging on office walls, but these are not available for sale. A good starting point is the map you can print off the Navetur website (*www.navetur-equatour.st*). The best map for travellers, however, is the one put together by MARAPA's Bastien Loloum, available from the ST tourist office for only €1. The latest São Tomé map to be published was by the Portuguese Pocket Tropics, on the back of their 2013 tourist guide. In a handy format, it is available for sale (€3) at Navetur who co-published it, and at Café Central. You need a magnifying glass for the peak names on Príncipe, but it has a good level of information on the two capital cities, and is very up to date.

The Barcelona-based Caué Association has published a list of maps and related links, which can be accessd here http://atlas.saotomeprincipe.eu/2_atlasstp_geofisica.htm. The Lisbon-based Instituto Geográfico do Exército has STP 1:25,000 topographical maps published by the Portuguese military in the 1930s (São Tomé sheets 1–5, Príncipe 1–2, each sheet €50, €280/£190/US$383 for the set). Available as paper copies and digital files, you need to request advance permission from the STP embassy in Lisbon to obtain them (*Instituto Geográfico do Exército; Av Dr Alfredo Bensaúde, 1849–014 Lisbon;* \ +351 218 505 300; e *igeoe@igeoe.pt; www igeoe.pt*). For an electronic version, check the Gulf of Guinea Biodiversity Network's website www.ggcg.st/maps/mapsintro.html. The first of four geological 1:25.000 maps, Cartas Geológicas (CEAG), with an explanatory booklet, was published in 2006 by Lígia Barros of the Ministry for Natural Resources in Rua Soldado Paulo Ferreira, São Tomé (\ *222 5272*).

Google Maps or Bing show a fair amount of detail, with the former having more contrast. The free-to-download Google Earth aerial survey of the world now covers most of the islands, but just as with Google Maps, the Ilhéu das Rolas is off the radar a bit. Google Earth throws in a bit of 3D relief effect, so you can see the mountain chain around the Pico de São Tomé.

The Centro de Documentação of the IICT (Instituto de Investigação Científica Tropical) in Lisbon sells several large-format maps of late-colonial times: http://www.iict.pt/pgn/pagpgn/vcgr01xx.asp?cod=5

GPS (Global Positioning System) works better in São Tomé than in Príncipe, unless there is too much tree cover or other interference, such as clouds, blocking the satellite signal; the signal quality also depends on the quality of the receiver.

MUSIC In São Tomé and Príncipe, music CDs and DVDs are on sale at *estudios de gravação*, music stores. If you know what you like, you can ask them to make up a mixed CD (80,000$) or simply even a current chart mix. The German-language site www.alewand.de/musik/saotome_music.html is the most-detailed I've seen, and www.kizomba.eu (with English-language option) has over 100 Santomean albums listed for purchase, some with audio clips. Also check www.sonsdafricapt.com. And browse around on Facebook, where you can find groups such as 'Santomean Singers' (*www.Facebook.com/groups/vilasecaguter/*).

Africa Negra *Best of Africa Negra 1 and 2* Sons d'Africa, 2005. Popular traditional São Tomé and Príncipe band.

Batuque da Ilha *Bulaue Belezina*

Domingos, Camilo *The best of Camilo Domingos* Sons d'Africa, 2003. CD/DVD. Available in São Tomé and Príncipe and Lisbon music shops. Other albums: *Maninha my love, Nova Onda, Dor de Mundo*.

Gapa (Álvaro Lima) *Regresso* Sons d'Africa, 2006. Latest solo album by the former frontman of Sangazuza (1983–96) and ambassador of Santomean music.

Juka *Desejo-te Amor* Sons d'Afrique, 2013. Popular Santomean zouk/kizomba singer based in Lisbon.

Mendes, Kalú *Boleia* Sons d'Africa, 2013. Latest album by much-loved singer.

Os MA's *Bligá* Os MA's/Grupo HB 2001. Bligá is a local martial art and the 'Associated Musicians' Oswaldo Santos and Nezó were mixed by Kalú Mendes for a fusion of traditional Santomense styles.

Sangazuza *Conjunto Sangazuza – Na Voz de Helder Camblé – Ana Plata* 2004

Sebastiana *Em nome do pai.* Solos and duets by the islands' most famous female singer.

Trio Tempo *L'île Chocolat ... en chansons!* AEFSTP, 2006. Oswaldo Santos, Nezó and Guillerme Carvalho fuse traditional Santomean styles.

Umbelina, Gilberto Gil *Vôa Papagaio, Vôa!* Mélodie, 1985. Lisbon-based award-winning popular singer from Príncipe, singing in *lung'iye*.

Various *A Viagem dos Sons – Tchiloli São Tomé* Tradisom, 1999. With information in Portuguese and English.

Various *Primeiro Explosão Banda da Ilha, Mualá Tatalugua Sá Cú Beg* 2002. Artists include Príncipe-born singer João Seria, ex-front man of Africa Negra 1977–2003.

Various *Quê Santomé* Sons d'Africa, 2006. CD & DVD. Gapa, Camilo Domingos, Sebastiana, Africa Negra, etc. A good start to your collection; the latest, No 3, dates from 2010. Available from www.lojadamusica.com.

Various; Gomes, Manuel (ed) *São Tomé and Príncipe – Musique de l'Île du Milieu* Paris, Buda Musique, 2005. 17 tracks of traditional Santomean music, with English/French booklet. Available from www.amazon.fr (where you can listen to extracts and purchase a secondhand CD from €8) or www.budamusique.com.

Various; Gomes, Manuel (ed) *São Tomé et Príncipe perdues dans l'océan: São Tomé e Príncipe perdidas no oceano.* 109-page booklet in French/Portuguese, including above CD (E-dite, 2006), €30 from www.amazon.fr.

Various *Socopé – Raiz de noz – Sons de São Tomé e Príncipe.* Compilation including eight songs by the famous Os Úntues.

Vianna Da Motta, José *Piano Concerto In A Major/Fantasia Dramática/Ballada* Hyperion, 1999. A flavour of the São Tomé-born late-romantic composer, with the Gulbenkian Orchestra and pianist Artur Pizarro.

Viegas, Bill Lima P*lôvia miglason – Por Causa da Imigração* 2012. Latest album by young, local kizomba singer, who had great success with *Hirondina* (2007).

FILMS The link http://tomefilm.com redirects to the latest projects by Kris Haamer, an Estonian whizz kid (and one of the TEDx organisers) with a great love for STP, who has made films about Santomean success stories, followed artists around the island and is behind Galo Cantá, a storytelling project. The current film is called *Wê* – which in dialect means to look or see.

Berda, Virginie *São Tomé, cent-pour-cent cacao* Vodeo TV, 2004. Portrait of an island at the crossroads (F). Download from www.vodeo.tv-2-27-1629-sao-tome-cent-pour-cent-cacao.html.

Brödl, Helmut *Frutinho do Equador* 1998. Wacky story of a giant breadfruit's travels around the island of São Tomé, beautifully shot. Not available commercially.

Georges, Paul *The Lost Wave.* Recent surf movie featuring a cool, young, local Santomean surfer. See www.amazon.com.

Torres, Ângelo *Mionga ki ôbo* Lx Filmes, 2005. A 52 minute documentary on the Angolares fishing community.

Vertongen, Derek *Extra Bitter: The Legacy of the Chocolate Islands* 2000.

A 52- minute video (VHS format) telling the story of Santomense slavery through interviews with historians, writers and locals, plus archive material. Available through www.filmakers.com.

Witte, Susanne *São Tomé and Príncipe* SWR, 2005. A 45 minute reportage (G) focusing on the people of the archipelago.

WEBSITES, BLOGS AND WEB LINKS
Culture

www.africultures.com Type in 'Sao Tome' for a list of writers and artists (F).

www.artafrica.gulbenkian.pt has an extensive list of Santomean artists, with visual samples of their work. At the time of writing, the contact list was out of date however.

www.bienal-stp.org Information on the international festival of lusophone culture held every other summer (even years) in São Tomé.

www.biennialfoundation.org English-language information on the design bienal taking place each November in ST.

www.cenalusofona.pt Coimbra-based group of actors involved in living theatre tradition

www.everyculture.com/Sa-Th/S-o-Tom-e-Pr-ncipe.html Excellent overview.

www.foreignaffairs.com/articles/139044/gerhard-seibert/surging-sao-tome A 2013 overview of foreign affairs. Register for free to read.

www.instituto-camoes.pt The website of the Portuguese Cultural Institute, with details of language courses all over the world. Also includes details of their cultural activities in São Tomé and Príncipe.

http://www.rtve.es/alacarta/videos/espanoles-en-el-mundo/espanoles-mundo-santo-tome-principe/1453982/ Spanish programme about Spanish people abroad, featuring the current consul Maite Mendizabal.

www.tchiloli.com Beautifully made page about this uniquely Santomean theatrical tradition, with information on the major groups. In Portuguese, but currently being translated into English.

www.unspoiled-africa.blogspot.pt Beautiful illustrations of island life by award winning illustrator Shadra Strickland, of Maryland Institute College of Art, the result of a 2012 trip with Alain Corbel. The program is ongoing.

Music

www.santolas.net Site run by Santomean students in France, with information and video clips with music you will hear in São Tomé and Príncipe: kizomba, zouk, etc.

www.youtube.com/watch?v=FIbrEpqzIic Mesaro Tela Non song about his home country.

www.youtube.com/watch?v=isgUI8TILsY The Calema Brothers' hymn to their home country.

Development

www.indexmundi.com/sao_tome_and_principe Edited version of CIA World Factbook, with Millennium Development Goals. Always up to date.

www.international-alert.org/our_work/regional/west_africa/sao_tome_principe.php Non-profit mediation agency pilot project on the challenges of oil wealth coming to São Tomé and Príncipe: conflict-resolution workshops, educational/media work.

www.irinnews.org Humanitarian news agency site.

http://moreintelligentlife.co.uk/node/4789 Reportage by *The Economist* on chocolate and slavery in STP.
www.saotomeproject.wordpress.com University of Illinois and São Tomé and Príncipe Partnership site, with blog.
www.unicef.org/saotome/www.unicef.org/infobycountry/stp.html The UN's children's agency.
www.uns.st New site of PNUD, the United Nations's representation in São Tomé and Príncipe.
www.who.int/country/stp São Tomé and Príncipe data from the World Health Organisation.

Media
www.correiodasemana.info Current affairs (P).
www.jornal.st Online news, updated daily, with searchable archive (P).
www.jornaltransparencia.st
www.jornaltropical.st Current affairs (P).
www.macauhub.com.mo Breaking news from the lusophone world (P & E).
www.tedxsatome.com
www.telanon.info
www.vitrina.st
www.voanews.com/engl São Tomé and Príncipe news/archive reports (E) by Voice of America.

Politics and economy
www.afdb.org STP African Economic Outlook, published by the OECD
www.anp-stp.gov.st National Petroleum Agency (P & E)
www.cia.gov/library/publications/the-world-factbook/CIA World Factbook
https://country.eiu.com/sao-tome-and-principe Regular reports on STP by the Economist's Intelligence Unit
www.gov.st Official government site.
www.imf.org/external/country/stp The International Monetary Fund's site has a wealth of up-to-date documents and statistics on São Tomé and Príncipe poverty reduction programmes.
www.parlamento.st National Parliament (P, E & F).
www.worldbank.org/st Country brief.

Tourism
www.africadetodosossonhos.blogspot.com Information/blog on sustainable tourism in São Tomé and Príncipe provided by São Tomé and Príncipe expert Brígida Rocha Brito.
www.banknotes.com/st65.htm Has pictures of all STP notes and sells them too, including older versions.
www.bcstp.st Central Bank site, with daily exchange rate for the dobra.
wwwn.cdc.gov/travel/default.aspx Latest heath and immunisation advice.
www.cstome.net Telecommunications provider site, with links to São Tomé and Príncipe online journals, and much more (P).
http://es.geocities.com/caueass/caue_cat.htm Barcelona-based Caué Association Friends of São Tomé.
www.fotoscaminhadasedescobertastp.blogspot.com Large selection of beautiful photos.
www.mistralvoyages.com Local tour operator, with French connections (see page 112).

www.navetur-equatour.st Local tour operator, best point of contact for English-speakers (see page 112).

www.saotome.st Site run by Swedish internet service provider behind worthy projects training local students to use the net, etc. Good hotel advice and more.

www.sao-tome.com Introduction to the islands, linked to Miramar Hotel (G, P & E).

www.stome.net Detailed information (P).

http://stparquitecturarte.blogspot.pt/2009/12/uba-budo-sede-buenos-aires.html Uba Budo plantation (P).

www.travel.state.gov US Department of State's up-to-date travel information.

www.turismo-stp.org Useful tourist board's official website (P, F & E).

Wildlife

www.aidnature.org A 45 minutes nature documentary on Príncipe, due out in 2014;

www.facebook.com/aidnature.org; https://vimeo.com/77131507#at=1.

www.bigmarinefish.com Pictures and general information on the big species: blue marlin, swordfish, yellowfin tuna.

www.birdlife.org In-depth up-to-date information on the islands' threatened bird species.

www.bird-stamps.org/country/stthom.htm Stamps with São Tomé and Príncipe's bird species for sale.

www.calacademy.org/science_now/sao_tome A 2001 expedition of California Academy of Sciences, hunting trap door spiders, tree frogs, scorpions, algae, etc. Entertaining dispatches, including an ascent report of Pico de Príncipe; excellent pics. For the 2013 update, see ww.calacademy.org.

www.fatbirder.com Detailed information on endemic birds and useful up-to-date links.

www.fco.gov.uk The Foreign Office's official up-to-date travel information for UK citizens.

www.fishbase.org/Photos/ListThumbnails.php?personnel=806&SortBy=genus Fish photos.

www.flickr.com Photo-sharing site with superb close-ups of STP's flora and fauna and other great shots.

www.ggcg.st Excellent site on biodiversity in the Gulf of Guinea. Its first webmaster was the late Angus Gascoigne, a Basque–Scottish naturalist who spent a dozen years living on the islands.

http://islandbiodiversityrace.wildlife.org Blog by veteran US naturalist Bob Drewes, started in 2008 and charting the results of many expeditions.

www.iucn.org World Conservation Union for Nature.

www.medslugs.de/E/Photographers/Peter_Wirtz.htm#photos Images of nudibranch specimens – *vulgo* fluffy sea slugs.

www.montepico.blogspot.com Blog of the Monte Pico guides' association, with useful links and information about ongoing research and conservation projects.

www.obopark.com Grey parrot conservation on Príncipe (2002).

www.seaturtle.org Marine turtle protection.

www.stellarium.org Free high-quality planetarium software showing you constellations anywhere in the world, in real time. Also try the Sky feature in Google Earth, it worked a treat on the remote Abade plantation on Príncipe.

www.stp-parks.org Official site of the two islands' national parks, sadly very out of date.
www.tolweb.org/onlinecontributors/app?page=ContributorImagesPage& service=external&sp=3520 Large (and growing) collection of animal images.
www.surfbirds.com/community-blogs/blog/2014/03/04/government-of-sao-tome-e-principe-unveils-conservation-plans-for-saving-some-of-the-most-threatened-birds-in-africa/

General

www.africa.upenn.edu Run by Pennsylvania University, with links to other sites.
www.cia.gov/library/publications/the-world-factbook/geos/tp.html Regularly updated country profile, which, give or take a couple of inaccuracies, is a good place to start.
www.groups.yahoo.com/group/saotome/messages São Tomé and Príncipe newsgroup, with open access (after registering with your Yahoo ID and password) to members' messages on anything from houses for sale and special offers at restaurants, to the environment and the oil issue. Mainly Portuguese, but postings can be made in English or any Latin language. Becoming a member is the best way to stay abreast of developments on the islands.
www.library.stanford.edu/africa/saotome.html Links to organisations, radio programme transcripts, music labels, etc.
www.mega.ist.utl.pt/~mles/SaoTome/FotografiasAntigas Photos of São Tomé at the turn of the 20th century.
www.odisseiasnosmares.com Site run by Portuguese hardcore traveller and rowing maverick Jorge Trabelo Marques, including an illustrated account of his ascent of Cão Grande, with a couple of Santomeans, in colonial times.
www.principe.st Useful regional government site, with tourism information, a discussion forum, etc.
www.tvciencia.pt/tvcicn/pagicn/tvcicn01.asp?cmb_pesq=loc&txt_pesq=S%E3o+Tom%E9&offset=0 Nearly 300 historical images.
www.youtube.com Hundreds of São Tomé videos of music, sharks, camping tales, carnival, etc.

Index

Page numbers in **bold** indicate major entries; those in *italics* indicate maps.

Abade plantation 200, 201–2
abortion 32
Abuja Joint Declaration 29
acacias 4
accidents 62, 78
accommodation 78–9
   camping 67, 79, 146, 161, 200
   hotel price codes 80
   see also individual locations
activities 88–94
   see also birdwatching; cycling; diving;
   hiking; kayaking; snorkelling; surfing;
   swimming; windsurfing
ADI party 24, 25
African grey parrot 8, 15
Agostinho Neto plantation 18, 19, 35, 102,
   141–2
Agripalma 15, 173
agrotourism 19, 101, 156
Água Grande canal 32
Água Grande district 135
Água Izé plantation 18, 19, 20, 167
aguardente 142
AIDS *see* HIV/AIDS
air travel
   airlines 60–1
   airport 110
   deep vein thrombosis (DVT) 59
   departure tax 60
   luggage 60
   to/from STP 56–61, 189–90
alcoholism 84, 187
Alegre, Caetano Costa 38, 155
Algiers, Treaty of 21
Alliance Française 94, 127
almond trees 4
Alves de Carvalho, Dário Quaresma 37
Amado, Olave 37
Amador, Rei 17, 156, 174
Ana Chaves Bay 6, 91, 109
Ana Chaves peak 149
Anambó 142–3
Angola 17, 22, 25, 30, 58
Angolares 16–17, 34, 174–5

animism 33
Anjos, Frederico Gustavo dos 39
Annobón 6, 35
Anobón 3
ANP (Agência Nacional de Petróleo) 24
antivenom 72
ants 72
apartments 117–18
aphrodisiacs 5, 129, 160
Arch dive site, The 208
area of STP, total 2, 3
art 37–8, 125
arts *see* culture
ATMs 76
Auto de Floripes 47, 94, 190

B&B 79, 116, 117, 165, 168
bacterial conjunctivitis 69–70
Baha'i faith 32
Baía das Aguinas 209
Baía das Agulhas 203
bamboo 4
Banana Beach viii, 201, 202–3
bananas 4, 83
banho practice 25
banks 76
   see also individual locations
baobabs 4
Baptista da Silva, João 17, 20, 133
basalt 3
basketware 165
Batepá 18, 19, 30, 158
bats 114, 146, 157, 206
beaches
   camping 78
   safety 73
   see also Praia ...
beauty salons 128, 193
beer 83, 143
begging 102
begonias 4
Beja, Maria Olinda 39
Bela Vista plantation 205
Belo Monte plantation 199–200, 201

Bernardino Faro plantation 158
Bienal cultural festival 38, 47
bikes *see* cycling
bilharzia 68–9
billfish 10
Bindá 150
biodiversity 7, 14, 15
Bioko 3
birds 6–9, 210–12
birding holidays 50
birdwatching viii, 47, 161, 173, 176, 184,
    204, 206, 208
    endangered species 14–15
black cobra 9, 71–2, 161, 173
black kite 6
Blú Blú waterfall 152–3
blue marlin 10
Boa Entrada plantation 140
Boa Morte 45
board games 123
boat hire 192
boat trips 78, 113–14, 172, 181, 184, 202,
    204, 208
    fishing 183, 209
Bobo Forro 151
bobofrito 83, 86
bobos 30, 43
Boca Bela plantation 149
Boca d'Inferno 167
Bom Bom Island resort viii, 10, 73, 91,
    207–9
Bom Sucesso botanical gardens 6, 8, 147,
    160
Bombaim plantation 19, 149, 157, 160, 167
bone setters 129
Bonfim, Aíto 39
books
    informal libraries 94, 97
    reading lists 233–42
botanical gardens
    Agostinho Neto 142
    Bom Sucesso 6, 8, 147, 160
botany classes 160
Braga dive site 183
Bragança, Albertino 42
braids 87
Branco, Rafael 24, 30, 42
brancos/brancas 30
Brazil 25
breadfruit 4, 82–3
bruma seca 47
budgeting 77
Budo Bachana 175
bulaué music 36, 173, 175, 188
business, doing 100

cabs *see* taxis
CACAU arts centre 94, 134
cacharamba firewater 15, 84, 202
Cadbury, William 20
Caetano, Marcello 19, 20
Caixão Grande 45
calulú 80, 81
Cameroon 32
Caminha, Álvaro de 16, 131
Caminho do Fugido 160
camping 67, 79, 146, 161, 200
Cantagalo 164
Cão Grande 3, 173
Cão Pequeno 3
Cape Verde 17, 25, 30, 35, 59–60
capoeira 94, 168
car rental 78, 111, 191
card games 123
cargo boats 62, 191
Carlos, João 37
Carnation Revolution (Portugal) 20
Carneiro, António 188
Carvalho, Guillerme 37
Carvalho peak 147
Casa Tatô ecomusuem 103, 113, 139
Cascata Água Sampaio 143
Cascata Angolar 146
Cascata Formosa 157
Cascata Fundo do Morcego 157
Cascata Milagrosa 157
cash machines 76
cashback services 130
casino 101, 115
Cassandra, José Cardoso 188
Castro, Adilson 37–8
Castro, Geane 38
cathedral, São Tomé 131–2
cattle egret 7
Caué district 93, 104, 175
cell phones *see* mobile phones
Centro da Lingua Portuguesa 127
Chamiço plantation 154–5
ChevronTexaco 28, 29
children
    child mortality 27, 63
    education 33, 187
    talking with 102
    under-age sex 32
China 25, 30, 31
chocolate vii, 20, 21, 26, 86–7
    factory tour and tastings 132
cholera 27
Christian beliefs 32–3
churches
    cathedral, São Tomé 131–2

Igreja de Santíssima Trindade 156
Nossa Senhora da Guadalupe 140
Nossa Senhora das Neves 144
Nossa Senhora de Madre de Deus 151–2
Santa Ana 166
Claudino Faro plantation 167
Claudio Corallo Chocolate Factory
132
Cláudio, Mário 42
climate 4, 47
climbing 147–9
Pico Papagaio 205
Pico de Príncipe 205
Pico de Sao Tomé 147–9
clothes shopping 123
CLSTP (Comité de Libertaçao de São Tomé
and Príncipe) 19
Club Nautico 92
Club Santana 37, 73, 91, 165–6, 167
clubs 36–7, 122, 197
coat of arms 22
cobra preta see black cobra
cocoa vii, 14–15, 17, 18, 19, 20–1, 26, 167
coconut palms 4
coconut water 84
coffee (drinking) 84
coffee growing 14–15, 17, 18, 19, 20, 147
Coffee Museum 158–9
colomba perjorative 30, 75
Colónia Açoreana plantation 168
colonialism 16–19, 30, 31, 42
communications 95–9, 192
Communidades 146
condoms 32
conjunctivitis 69–70
conservation 7, 12, 13–16
contract workers 17, 20, 36, 167, 175
cookery books 239
cookery classes 173
coral 9–10, 73
Corallo, Claudio 132, 159, 202
corruption 25, 31
Costa, Gabriel 25
Costa Alegre, Caetano 38, 155
courier services 131
CPLP 25
crabs 73, 168, 175, 181
crafts 125, 134, 148–9, 181
crater lake 8, 151, 160, 161
credit cards 76, 130
creole languages 34–5, 174, 189
creoles and creole identity 17, 30,
38, 39
crime 74–5, 140, 187
cruises 49

cultural etiquette 101–2
cultural institutions 127
culture 33, 36–46, 188–9, 235–6, 242
currency 2, 76
cycling 78, 93–4
bike rental 78, 93, 94, 192
Príncipe 192
São Tomé 147, 164, 173

dance 36–7, 94, 188
dancing see clubs
dancing lessons 122
Danço Congo 43, 46, 94, 143
debt, national 26
debt relief 27, 30
decolonisation 19–21
deep vein thrombosis (DVT) 59
deforestation 14, 21
dehydration 63, 66
dengue fever 68
dentists 128
departure tax 60
development aid 25, 27, 30
diarrhoea 66–7
Dias, Haylton 36
Diogo Vaz dive site 90
Diogo Vaz plantation 104
diplomatic relations 30, 53, 54
discos see clubs
diseases 27
dive sites
Príncipe 208–9
Sao Tomé 89, 90–1, 167, 182–3
diving 47, 51, 89–91
courses 89, 90–1, 183
hazards 71, 73
night diving 183
djambi spirit-possession cult 33
dobra 76
doctors 71, 128
dolphin watching 184, 208
domestic violence 31
Domingos, Camilo 36, 188
Dona Augusta 173
drama 43–6, 190
dress code 75
drinking water 66
drinks 83–4
driving 78
car rental 78, 111, 191
petrol stations 112, 192
road accidents 62, 78
dry cleaning and launderettes 128,
198
dwarf olive ibis 7, 8, 14, 173

Earth Institute 29, 164
East Coast and the South (ST) *162*, 162–84, *169*
eating and drinking *see* food and drink
ECCAS (Economic Community of Central African States) 26
ecomuseum 103, 113, 139
economy 2, 22, 26–30
ecotourism 15, 93, 96, 103, 163, 168, 170, 172, 173–6, 187, 188
Eddington, Arthur 201
education 33, 187
electricity 2, 13, 187
email 99
embassies and consulates 54–6
  abroad 54–5
  in São Tomé 55–6
emergencies
  medical 71, 72
  words and phrases 231
Emolve Palm Oil Factory 173
entertainment 43–6, 94
  see also clubs; drama; film screenings; music
entry requirements 53–4
environmental issues 13–16
Environmental Remediation Holding Corporation (ERHC) 28
Equador (novel) 21, 43
Equator vii, 3
Equator mark 182
  marriage and honeymoon package 183
Equatorial Guinea 3, 25, 28, 32, 58
Escadas 6
Escobar, Pedro 16, 133
Espírito Santo, Alda Graça 18, 39
Espírito Santo, Julieta da 155
Estado Novo (Portugal) 19
ethnic mix viii, 30
Evora, Cesária 36
exchange rates 2
Exclusive Economic Zone (EEZ) 28, 29
exports 21, 26
ExxonMobil 28
eye problems 69–70
eye protection 63

fabrics, African 123, 148
Fairtrade 21, 26
faith healer 172
family size 31
Fernando Pô *see* Bioko
Fernão Dias 12, 18, 137, 139
festivals, religious 33, 166, 167, 172, 175, 189

film screenings 94, 122–3
fire worms 72
first aid kit 65
fish 9, 79
  venomous 73–4
fish market 9, 31, 133
Fishery Museum 172
fishing 10, 183, 209
fishing industry 13, 26
flag 2, 22
flame trees 4
Flora Speciosa 153–4
flying fish 10, 79, 208
flying gurnard 10
Focinho de Cão dive site 209
food and drink 79–85
  alcohol 83–4
  coffee and tea 84
  cookery books 239
  cookery classes 173
  drinking water 66
  food hygiene 66
  restaurant price codes 80
  roadside food 80, 83
  self-catering 83
  snack foods 83
  soft drinks 84
  traditional dishes 80–1
  vegetarian food 81–2
forest conservation 13–14
Formosa Grande 157
forros 16, 17, 18, 79
Fort of St Sebastian 109, 133
Fraternidade plantation 170
Free Trading Zone 139
frogs 9
fruit 82–3
fungal infections 69

Gabon 28, 32, 58
GDP 26
geckos 9
geography 3–4
geology 3
gestures 221
giant sunbird 8, 161, 173, 184
Gorgulho, Carlos 18
Graça, Salustino 18
gravana 47, 92
gravanita 47, 147
Greenpeace 143
greetings 189
Guadalupe 140–2, *140*
Guinea-Bissau 25
Gulf of Guinea 3, 9

hair and beauty 87, 128
Harmattan wind 47
hazards
  crime 74–5, 140, 187
  diving 71, 73
  marine dangers 73–4
  rabies 70
  road accidents 62, 78
  toxic plants 73
  wildlife hazards 71–3
healers 5, 33, 129, 172, 197
health 62–74
  bilharzia 68–9
  deep vein thrombosis (DVT) 59
  eye problems 69–70
  faith healer 21
  first aid kit 65
  healers 5, 33, 129, 172, 197
  herbalists 129
  insect bites 67–8, 69
  malaria 63–6
  medical facilities 71
  meningitis 70
  prickly heat 70
  sexually-transmitted diseases 70
  skin infections 69
  sun protection 63
  traditional medicine 5, 129
  travel clinics 63
  travellers' diarrhoea 66–7
  tropical amoeba 70
  vaccinations 62
  see also hazards
hepatitis 62
herbalists 129
higher education 33
highlights 47–8
hiking 47, 88–9
  Caminho do Fugido 160
  guides 88–9, 160, 161
  Príncipe 200, 202, 204–5
  São Tomé 142, 144, 155, 157–8, 160–1,
    173, 184
Hirondino dive site 183
Historical Archive 127
history 16–21, 188, 237
HIV/AIDS 5, 31–2, 70
homestays 79
homosexuality 32
hookworm 67–8
hospitals 71, 128, 172, 199
hotel price codes 80
Human Development Index 27
human rights 26
hunting 7

Igreja de Santíssima Trindade 156
Ilhas Tinhosas 4, 9, 15, 204, 209
Ilhéu das Cabras 3, 10, 139
Ilhéu de Caroco see Jockey's Cap
Ilhéu das Rolas 73, 172, 178–84, 180
immigration authorities (STP) 54
Independence Day 85, 135
independence movement 17–18, 19–21
insect bites 67–8, 69
Instituto Camões 94, 127
Interior, The (ST) 151–61, 152–3
internet 98–9, 192, 198
  websites, blogs and web links 242–5
interpreting services 131
investment opportunities 100
Iô Grande 93
island evolution 4
itineraries 48–9

jackfruit vii, 82
Jehovah's Witnesses 32
jellyfish 74
Jewish heritage 30
jiggers 67
João Dias Pai/Filho peaks 202
Jockey's Cap islet 9, 204, 209
Johnson, Loony 36
judiciary 26
Juka 36

kadançe music 36
katamaran hire 167
kayaking 91, 184
Kia dive site 90
kizomba music, viii 33, 36

Lagoa Amélia 6, 8, 15, 160–1
Lagoa Azul 90, 139–40
land reform 19
land-use pressures 13, 14
languages 34–5
  creole 34–5, 174, 189
  emergency phrases 231
  gestures 221
  greetings 189
  language classes 99
  language guide 219–32
  Portuguese 34, 219–20
  useful words and phrases 102, 221–32
  wildlife glossary 210–18
lemongrass tea 84
leve-leve 30, 100, 101
Levy, Herculano 39
Library, National 127
Liceu Nacional 33

life expectancy 2, 27
lighthouse 182
Lima, Conceição 39, 40–1
liqueurs 84, 156
literacy 33
literature 38–43
litter 15–16
living standards 27
lizards 9
Lobata district 140
logging, illegal 13–14, 15
Lopes, Armindo 37
luggage 60
Lusíadas University 33

Macedo, Fernando de 39, 176
Madre de Deus 151–2
Malanza mangrove tour 15, 176
malaria 24, 30, 63–6, 164, 187, 191
Malé, Eduardo 37
mangoes 82
mangosteens 157
mangrove tour 15, 176
manioc 81
Manuel I 16, 30
Manuel Morais plantation 146
maps iv, 239–40
MARAPA conservation and fishing
    organisation 12, 13, 103, 113–14, 176
Margarido, Maria Manuela 39, 188
Maria Correia plantation 203
María Fernandes peak 173
marine life 9–13, 213–15
markets 85, 95
    fish market 9, 31, 133
    Santo António 197
    São Tomé town 132–3
Marky, Sum 42
marlin 10
marriage age 32
Massacre of Batepá 18, 19, 30
massage 115, 128, 179, 181
Mateus Sampaio plantation 173
MDFM (Movimento Democrático Força de
    Mudança) 24, 25
MDFM/PCD alliance 24
Mé-Zochi 156
media 96–8
Mediateca 127
medical facilities 71, 128–9
medicines 71
Mendes, Dom Manuel António Dos Santos
    132
Mendes, Kalú 37
Mendes, Pedro Rosa 42

Menezes, Fradique de 22, 23, 24, 30
meningitis 70
Mesa Pico Pequeno 6
Milagrosa plantation 157
military coups 22–4
minuiê 30
mist forest 5
Misterioso islets 208
MLSTP (Movimento de Libertaçao de São
    Tome and Príncipe) 19, 20, 21, 22, 23
MLSTP/PSD 22, 23, 24, 25, 30, 31, 175
mobile phones 97–8
moncós (perjorative) 30
money 76–7, 192
    ATMs 76
    banks 76
    budgeting 77
    cashback services 130
    credit cards 76, 130
    currency 2, 76
    everyday groceries, prices of 77
    exchange rates 2
    hotel price codes 80
    money changers 76
    restaurant price codes 80
    transfers 76–7, 130
monoculture cultivation 14, 20
montane forest 5
Monte Café plantation 19, 35, 158–9
Monte Carmo 8
Monteforte plantation 19, 146
moped hire 111
Morro Leste peak 205–6
Morro Peixe 13, 90–1
mosquitoes 63, 67
mosquito nets 63, 79
    see also dengue fever; malaria
Mostelros dive site 209
motorbike hire 111, 191–2
motorbike taxis 110–11
mototaxis 191
Motta, Viana da 155
motto, national 22
Mozambique 17, 25, 30
Mucumbli 10, 144, 146
mudskippers 10, 176, 208
Mulato, Zé 18
mulattos 30, 42
museums
    Casa Tatô ecomusuem 139
    Coffee Museum 158–9
    ecomuseum 103, 113, 139
    Fishery Museum 172
    National Museum 20, 133–4
mushrooms 6

music 33, 36–7, 86, 188, 240–1, 242
Muslim faith 32

Nanook & Sá Pinto dive site 183
national anthem 39
national dish 110
national flag 2, 22
National Library 127
National Museum 20, 133–4
National Oil Agency 29
national park *see* Obô National Park
National Petroleum Council 29
nationalisation 18
nationalism 18
natural history guides 237–9
Negreiros, Almada 38, 155, 158
Negreiros, José 158
Neves 143–4, *143*
Neves, Maria das 31
New Apostolic Church 32
New Year's Day 85
news agency 96
newspapers and magazines 96
Nezó, Joao Carlos 37, 171, 175
NGOs 26, 27, 103, 104–5
Nigeria 24, 25, 28, 29, 31
noites crioulas 36
North and Northwest, The (ST) 137–50,
     138, *145*
Nossa Senhora da Guadalupe 140
Nossa Senhora das Neves 144
Nossa Senhora de Madre de Deus 151–2
Nova Ceilão plantation 160
Nova Moca plantation 8, 19, 159
novelists 39, 42

Obasanjo, Olusugun 24
Obô National Park 3, 5, 14, 161
Oceanarium, Lisbon 89
oil palms 4, 14, 15
oil viii, 24, 25, 28–9
online news 96
opening hours 85
oral tradition 38
orchids 5–6, 47
Organisation of African Unity 19
Os Vibrados 37
ossobó 7, 173

Padrão monument 16, 143, 188
Pagalu *see* Anobón
painting *see* art
Paiva, João de 16, 133
palm oil 26
palm wine 84, 158

PALOPS 25
Pantufo 163–4
Papagaio River 10
parrots 8, 15
parrot-trapping 15
PCD (Partido de Convergência
     Democrática) 24, 25
Pedra da Galé 9, 208, 209
Pedra de Adálio 209
Pedreira, Manuel da Costa 158
Penetcostal churches 32
performance *see* drama; music
personal safety *see* safety
Pestana Equador 178, 179
petrol stations 112, 192
pharmacies 71, 128–9, 199
phonecards 98, 99
phonolitic rockscapes 3
photography 94–5
photography holidays 52
picnics 80, 113, 137, 148, 173, 182, 184, 202
Pico dos Dois Dedos 203
Pico María Fernandes 168, 172, 173
Pico de Mencorne 205
Pico Mesa 147, 203
Pico Papagaio 205
Pico de Príncipe 205
Pico de São Tomé (formerly, Pico Gago
     Coutinho) 3, 6, 147–9, 160
PIDE (Portuguese secret police) 19
Piedade, Orlando 42
Pina, Goretti 42
Pina, Protásio Dias Xavier 37, 188
Pincate plantation 203
Pinto da Costa, Manuel 20, 22, 23, 133
plantations 16, 17, 18–19
     tours 19
     see also individual index entries
plants 4–6, 86
     glossary 216–18
     toxic 73
poetry 38–9, 40–1, 97, 188, 234
police 74, 75, 130, 199
politics and government 22–6, 243
polygyny 32
Ponta da Furna dive site 183
Ponta do Sol plantation 206
Ponta Figo plantation 146, 147
Ponte Baleia 178–9
Ponte da Baleia dive site 183
Ponte Furada 149–50
population 2, 30–2
     Angolares 16–17, 34, 174–5
     ethnic mix viii, 30
     growth 27

life expectancy 2, 27
living standards 27
  women 31
porcelain rose 4
Porto Alegre 93, 173–8, *177*
Porto Real plantation 202
Portugal 16, 17, 19, 20, 25, 30, 42, 52, 54,
  56–7
Portuguese language 34, 219–20
post offices 131, 198
postcards 124, 131
Pousada Boa Vista 158
poverty vii, viii 27
practicalities
  accommodation 78–9
  activities 88–94
  arts and entertainment 94
  business affairs 100
  cultural etiquette 101–2
  eating and drinking 79–85
  embassies and consulates 54–6
  hair and beauty 87
  health 62–74
  highlights 47–8
  itineraries 48–9
  language 99–100
  media and communications 95–8
  money 76–7
  opening hours 85
  photography 94–5
  property deals 100
  public holidays 85
  responsible travel 102–5
  safety 74–5
  shopping and services 85–7
  tour operators 49–53
  tourism 101
  travel around STP 78
  travel to/from STP 56–62
  visas 53–4
  what to take 75–6
  when to visit 47
Prado 154
Praia Abade (P) 203
Praia Angobó (ST) 172
Praia Angra Toldo (ST) 172
Praia Bateria (ST) 182
Praia Boi (P) 203
Praia Brazil (ST) 133, 135
Praia dos Burros (P) 192, 203
Praia Cabana (ST) 177
Praia Café (ST) 181
Praia Caixão (P) 202
Praia das Conchas (ST) 139
Praia dos Tamarindos (ST) 139

Praia d'Evora (P) 203
Praia Forma (ST) 167
Praia Governador (ST) 139
Praia Grande (P) 206
Praia Inhame (ST) 173–5
Praia Jalé (ST) 13, 175–6, 178
Praia Joana (ST) 182
Praia Lapa (P) 202
Praia Macaco (P) 203
Praia Micoló (ST) 10, 13, 137
Praia de Micondó (ST) 168, 172
Praia Monteforte (ST) 146
Praia Morro Peixe (ST) 139
Praia Museu (ST) 134
Praia Piscina (ST) 73, 177–8
Praia Pombo (ST) 181
Praia Ponta Mina (P) 203
Praia Portinho (P) 203
Praia Preta (P) 201
Praia Salgada (P) 203
Praia Santa Rita (P) 209
Praia Seca (P) 204
Praia Sete Ondas(ST) 168
Praia Sundy (P) 206
Praia Va inhá (ST) 178
Praia Zongonhim (ST) 113
Presidential Palace 134
press *see* media
prices
  everyday groceries 77
  hotel price codes 80
  restaurant price codes 80
prickly heat 70
primary forest 5
Príncipe 186–209, *186*
  Bom Bom Island resort viii, 10, 73, 91,
    207–9
  Santo António 17, 193–9, *194–5*
  travel to/from 189–91
Príncipe thrush 7, 8
prinia 7
privatisation 26
property, buying 100–1
prostitution 32
public holidays 2, 85
public phones 98
puita dance 116, 137, 188

Quinta da Favorita 151
Quintal do Pico 205

rabies 70
radio and television 96–7, 123
rainforest 4–5
rainy season 47, 63, 95, 149

Ramos, Maria dos 143
Raposo, Roberto 30
Rei Amador 17, 156, 174
Reis, Fernando 42
Reis, Osvaldo dos 38, 166
religion 2, 32–3
renewable energy 13, 15
rental cars *see* car hire
reptiles and amphibians 9, 215–16
Residencial Avenida 116, 123, 135
responsible travel ii, 102–5
restaurant price codes 80
Ribeira Afonso 33, 93
Ribeira Izé 10, 202
Ribeira Peixe village 8
Ribeira Peixe waterfall 173
Riboque 110
Rio de Ouro plantation *see* Agostinho Neto
rivers 3
road network 78
roadside food 80, 83
roças see plantations
Rolas Island *see* Ilhéu das Rolas
Roman Catholic Church 32
Rosema brewery 143
rum 84
rural tourism 19, 101

sacaia instrument 36
saco azul 26
safe sex 32
safety 74–5
safú fruit 82
sailfish vii, 10, 80
saints' days 33, 166, 167, 172, 175, 189
Salazar, António Oliveira 19, 20
sand art 37, 125
sand sharks viii, 74, 183
Sangazuza 36
Santa Ana church 166
Santa Catarina 148–9
Santa Clara plantation 156
Santa Cruz bay 172
Santa Fé plantation 157
Santa Margarida plantation 154
Santa Sé *see* cathedral
Santana 93, 164–7, *165*
Santana islet 91, 167
Santarém, Joao de 16, 133
Santo António 17, 193–9, *194–5*
    accommodation 193, 196
    bank 199
    communications 198
    entertainment and nightlife 197
    medical facilities 198–9

police 199
shopping 197–8
what to see and do 199
where to eat 196–7
Santo António de Mussacavú 8
Sao Francisco 178
São Joao dos Angolares 16, 157, 163, 168, 170–3, *171*
São Joao plantation 19, 168, 170–1, 172–3
São Joaquim plantation 202
São José plantation 153–4
São Miguel 91
São Nicolau plantation 160
São Nicolau waterfall 160
São Tomé 108–84
    East Coast and the South *162*, 162–84, *169*
    Interior 151–61, *152–3*
    North and Northwest 137–50, *138*, *145*
São Tomé town *108*, 108–35, *109*, *113*
São Tomé Day 85
São Tomé grosbeak 7, 14
São Tomé oriole 7, 147, 161, 173
São Tomé town *108*, 108–35, *109*, *113*
    accommodation 114–18
    airport 110
    banks 129–30
    communications 126
    computer and photocopying services 127
    cultural and research institutions 127
    dry cleaning and launderettes 128
    entertainment and nightlife 121–3
    getting around 110–11
    getting there and away 110
    hair, beauty and massage 128
    internet access 126
    markets 132–3
    medical facilities 128–9
    police 130
    postal and courier services 131
    shopping 123–6
    tourist information 112
    translation and interpreting services 131
    travel agencies 112–14
    walking tour 134–5
    what to see and do 131–5
    where to eat 118–20
sap sap fruit 157
Saudade plantation 158
savannah 4, 7–8, 137
schistosomiasis *see* bilharzia
scops owl 7, 8, 161
scuba diving *see* diving
sculptures 38, 172, 181
sea urchins 73, 86, 168

seabirds 8–9, 15, 204
secondary forest 5
security *see* safety
self-catering 83, 117, 176
    apartments 117–18
Sete Ondas 93
Sete Pedras 8–9, 89, 183
Seventh-Day Adventists 32
sexual activity 31–2
sexually-transmitted diseases 70
    see also HIV/AIDS
shack stores 85
shade forest 4
sharks 74, 182, 183
shells 11, 12, 13, 86, 125, 137, 139
shipwreck legend 16, 174
shopping 85–7
    opening hours 85
    Príncipe 193, 197–8
    São Tomé town 123–6
Silva, Aurélio 38
Silva, Joao Carlos 37, 172
Silva, Lurdes 166
Silva, Otilina 42
SIM cards 97
Simaló plantation 20
single travellers 79
skin infections 69
slavery 16–17, 20, 35, 36, 174
snack foods 83
snails 13, 68, 81
snakes 9, 71–2, 161, 173
    bites 71–2
snorkelling 167, 177, 181, 202, 203, 209
Soares, Mário 19
social networks 96, 98
society 27, 30–46
socopé dance 36, 37, 164, 181
soft drinks 84
Soledade plantation 170
'Somos Todos Primos' 22
Sossô, Mé 38
Soulié, Tony 38
Sousa e Almeida, João Maria de 20, 134,
    167
South, The *169*
    see also East Coast and the South
South Africa 58–9
souvenirs 85–6, 124–6
Spagnol, Bruno 125
spiders 72, 149, 157
sponsoring children/the elderly 104–5
sport fishing 183, 209
Sporting Club 135
squid 167

stamps 131
Stockler, Francisco 38
storytelling 38
STP Digital platform 96
strangling fig 161
street food 80, 83
students 33
subsistence farming 26
sugarcane 4, 16, 17, 82
Sum Canalim 37
sun protection 63
Sundy beach 201
Sundy plantation 200–1
supermarkets 124
surfing 92–3, 94, 168
swearing 219
swimming 92
    beach safety 73
    beaches *see* Praia
swordfish 10

taboos 31, 32
Taiwan 25, 27, 30
Taiwanese Medical Mission 71
tamarinds 4
tarachinha dance 36–7
tarantulas 72, 149, 157
Tavares, Miguel Sousa 21, 42, 43
Tavares, René 37
taxation, local 100
taxis *see* yellow taxis
tchiloli performances 44–5, 94
tea 84
TEDx events 95–6
telephone 97–8, 192, 198
    calls to STP 98
    calls within/from STP 98
    international telephone code 2
    mobile phones 97–8
    SIM cards 97
Tenreiro, Francisco José 39, 40
Terreiro Velho plantation 159, 202
theatre *see* drama
ticks 73
time 2
Tinhosa Islands *see* Ilhas Tinhosas
Tonga Portuguese 35
tongas 17, 30, 187
tortoiseshell 125, 203
tour operators 49–53
tourism 26, 101, 243–4
tourist information 112
toxic plants 73
traditional dishes 80–1
traditional medicine 5, 129

translation services 131
Tras Morro Beach 139
Trás-os-Montes 160
travel around STP 78, 191–2
  see also cycling; driving; moped hire;
  motorbike hire; motorbike taxis; yellow
  taxis
travel clinics 63
travel insurance claims 74
travel to/from STP 56–62
  air travel 56–61, 189–90
  cargo boats 62, 191
  via Africa 57–9
  via Cape Verde 59–60
  via Portugal 56–7
travellers' cheques 129
travellers' diarrhoea 66–7
tree ferns 4
trees 4–5
Trinidade 154, 155–6
tropical amoeba 70
Trovoada, Miguel 20, 22, 23, 25
Trovoada, Patrice 23, 24, 139
tsetse flies 67
tuberculosis 27, 62
tumbu flies 67
tunnel hikes 146
turtles vii–viii, 10–12, 139, 167
  conservation 12, 13
  folklore 11–12
  green turtle 10
  hawksbill turtle 11
  leatherback turtle 11
  loggerhead turtle 11
  nesting 11
  olive ridley turtle 10–11, 12
  threats to 11–13
  trade in eggs, meat and craft artefacts
    12–13
  watching 47, 139, 174, 175, 177, 184, 206
typhoid fever 62

Uba Budo dive site 91
Uba Budo plantation 164
Umbelina, Gilberto Gil 188–9
unemployment 27, 187
UNESCO Biosphere status 15, 187

United Nations 19, 25, 30

vaccinations 62
Vale do Carmo plantation 173
Vaniana, Tubias 37
vanilla 6, 86
vegans 82
vegetarian food 81–2
Veiga, Marcelo da 38–9, 188
Vera Cruz, Tomé 24, 25, 152
Viana de Almeida, João Maria 42
visas 53–4
Vista Alegre plantation 154
volcanic activity 3
Volta a ilha 150, 181, 184, 202
volunteering 102–5

water, sterilisation 66
waterfalls 142, 143, 146, 152–3, 157, 160,
  173, 202, 203
whale watching 47, 139, 206, 208
what to take to STP 75–6
when to visit STP 47
wildlife
  birds 6–9, 210–12
  endemic species 4, 5, 6, 7, 8, 9, 210–11
  glossary 210–18
  hazards 71–3
  marine life 9–13, 213–15
  natural history books 237–9
  reptiles and amphibians 9, 215–16
websites 244
windsurfing 167
wine 83–4
women in STP 31, 37
women travellers 75
World Bank 25, 27, 29
World Monetary Fund 27

Xufe-Xufe River 8, 184

yellow fever 62
yellow taxis 78, 110, 137, 163
Yon Gato 16

Zampalma plantation 160
zouk music 36

INDEX OF ADVERTISERS

SEP 2 2 2014